ASSASSINATION CLASSROOM

YUSEI MATSUI

5

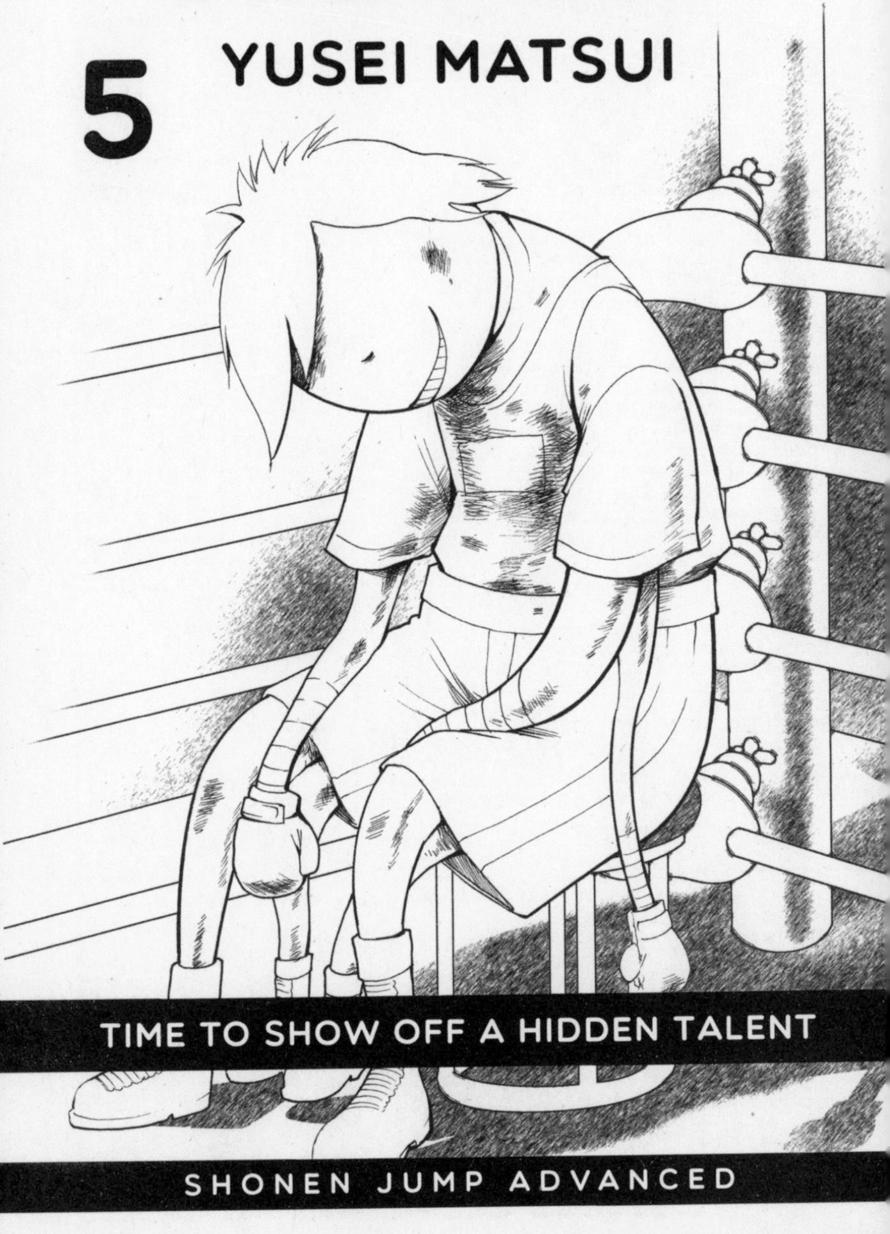

TIME TO SHOW OFF A HIDDEN TALENT

SHONEN JUMP ADVANCED

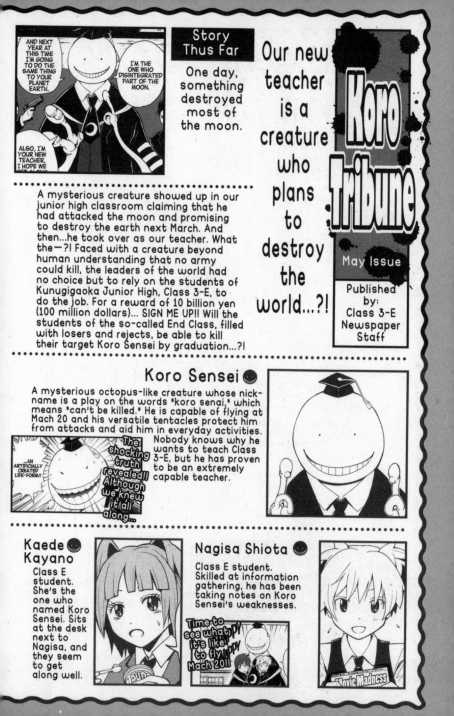

Koro Tribune

May Issue

Published by: Class 3-E Newspaper Staff

Our new teacher is a creature who plans to destroy the world...?!

Story Thus Far

One day, something destroyed most of the moon.

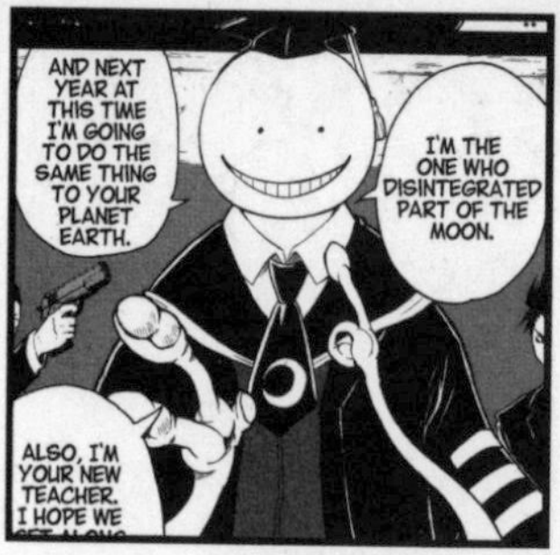
I'M THE ONE WHO DISINTEGRATED PART OF THE MOON.
AND NEXT YEAR AT THIS TIME I'M GOING TO DO THE SAME THING TO YOUR PLANET EARTH.
ALSO, I'M YOUR NEW TEACHER. I HOPE WE

A mysterious creature showed up in our junior high classroom claiming that he had attacked the moon and promising to destroy the earth next March. And then...he took over as our teacher. What the—?! Faced with a creature beyond human understanding that no army could kill, the leaders of the world had no choice but to rely on the students of Kunugigaoka Junior High, Class 3-E, to do the job. For a reward of 10 billion yen (100 million dollars)... SIGN ME UP!! Will the students of the so-called End Class, filled with losers and rejects, be able to kill their target Koro Sensei by graduation...?!

Koro Sensei

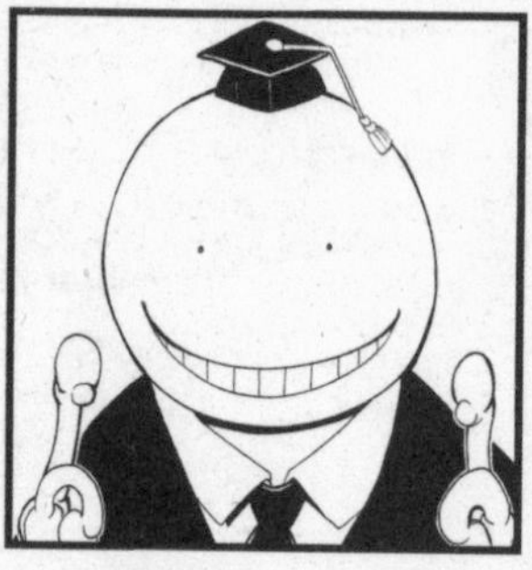

A mysterious octopus-like creature whose nickname is a play on the words "koro senai," which means "can't be killed." He is capable of flying at Mach 20 and his versatile tentacles protect him from attacks and aid him in everyday activities. Nobody knows why he wants to teach Class 3-E, but he has proven to be an extremely capable teacher.

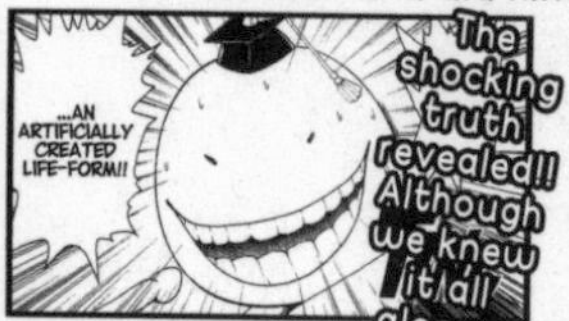
...AN ARTIFICIALLY CREATED LIFE-FORM!!

The shocking truth revealed!! Although we knew it all along...

Kaede Kayano

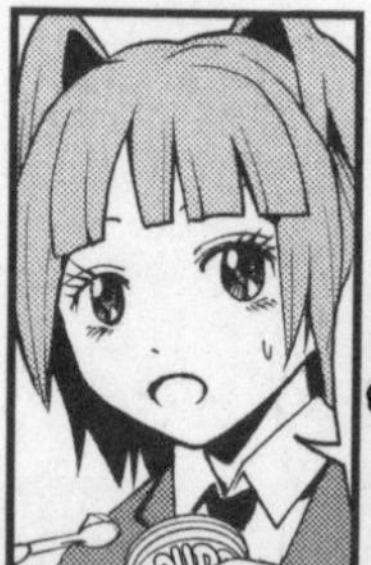

Class E student. She's the one who named Koro Sensei. Sits at the desk next to Nagisa, and they seem to get along well.

Nagisa Shiota

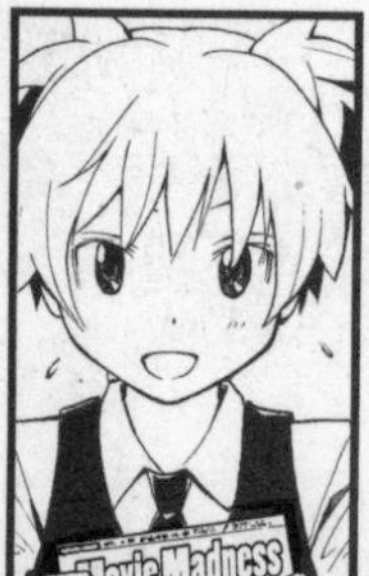
Movie Madness

Class E student. Skilled at information gathering, he has been taking notes on Koro Sensei's weaknesses.

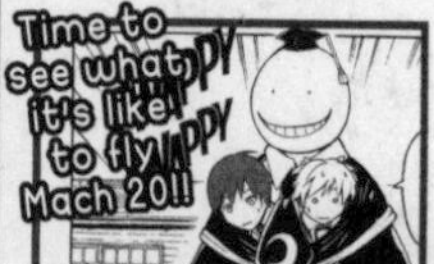

Time to see what it's like to fly Mach 20!!

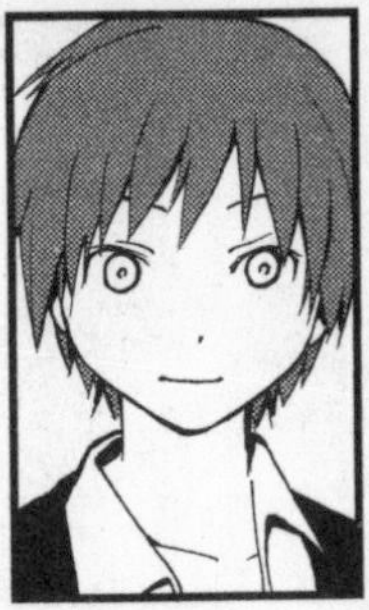

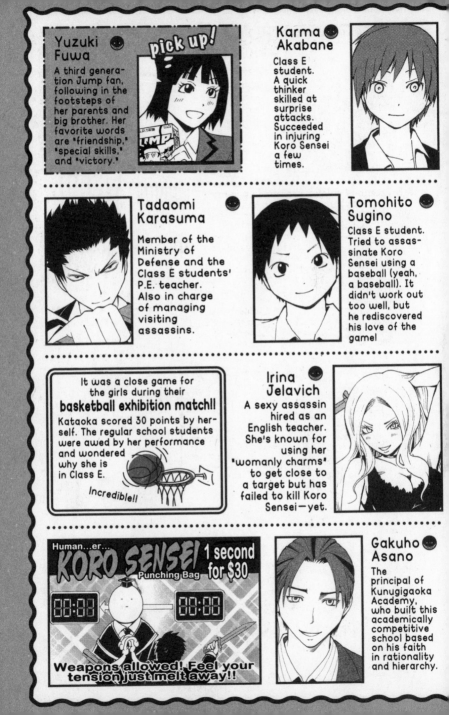

Karma Akabane

Class E student. A quick thinker skilled at surprise attacks. Succeeded in injuring Koro Sensei a few times.

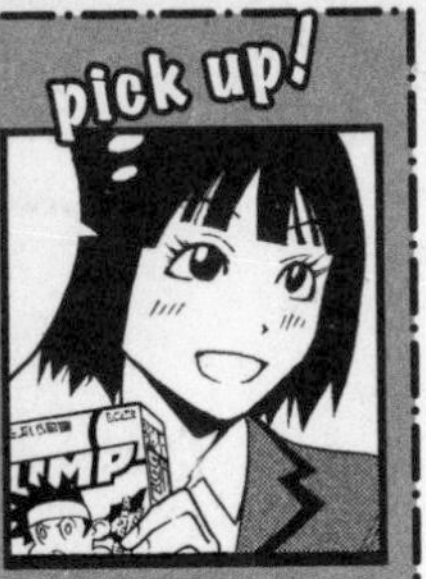
pick up!
JUMP

Yuzuki Fuwa

A third generation Jump fan, following in the footsteps of her parents and big brother. Her favorite words are "friendship," "special skills," and "victory."

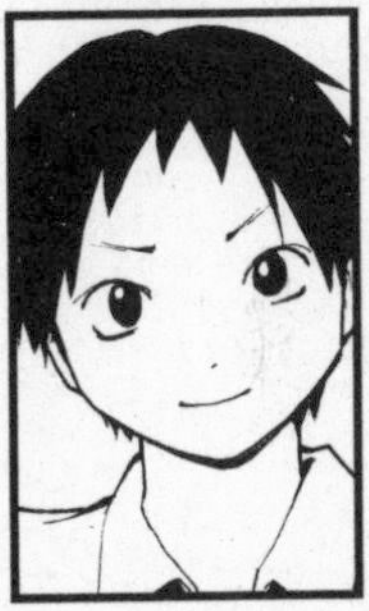

Tomohito Sugino

Class E student. Tried to assassinate Koro Sensei using a baseball (yeah, a baseball). It didn't work out too well, but he rediscovered his love of the game!

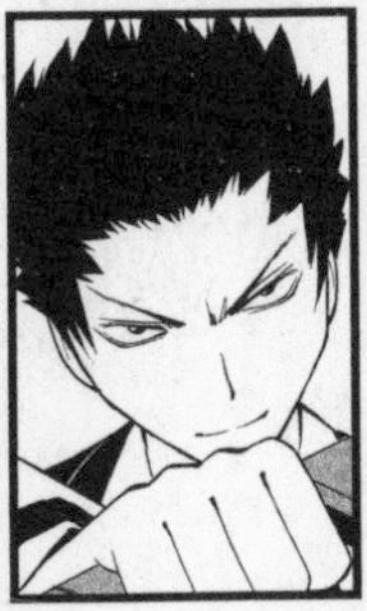

Tadaomi Karasuma

Member of the Ministry of Defense and the Class E students' P.E. teacher. Also in charge of managing visiting assassins.

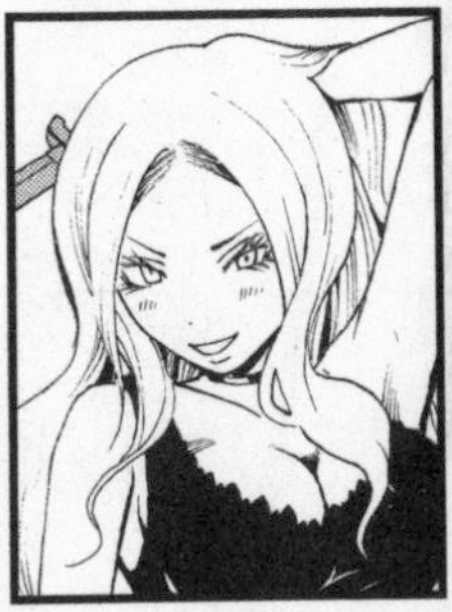

Irina Jelavich

A sexy assassin hired as an English teacher. She's known for using her "womanly charms" to get close to a target but has failed to kill Koro Sensei—yet.

It was a close game for the girls during their

basketball exhibition match!!

Kataoka scored 30 points by herself. The regular school students were awed by her performance and wondered why she is in Class E.

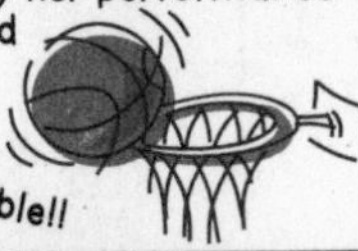

Incredible!!

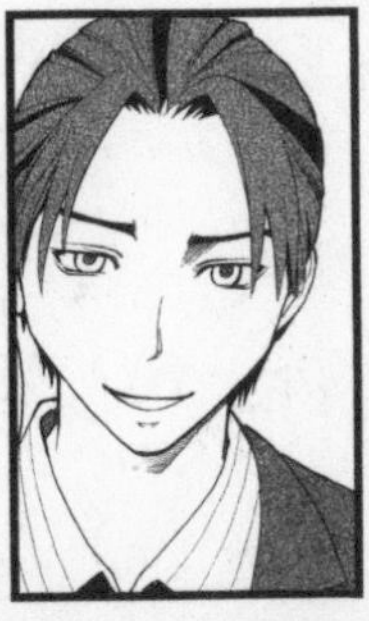

Gakuho Asano

The principal of Kunugigaoka Academy, who built this academically competitive school based on his faith in rationality and hierarchy.

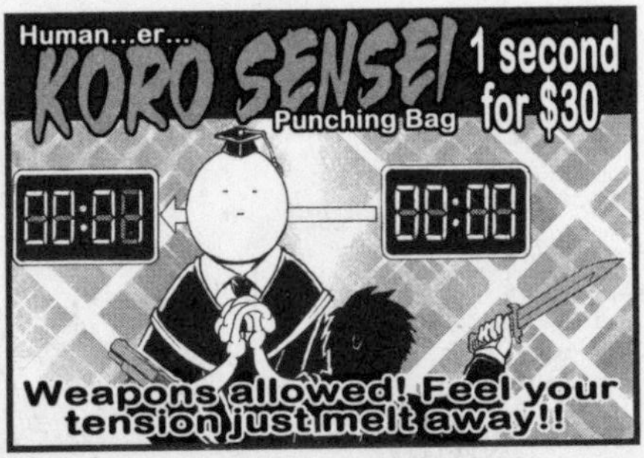
Human...er...
KORO SENSEI
Punching Bag
1 second for $30
00:01
00:00
Weapons allowed! Feel your tension just melt away!!

ASSASSINATION CLASSROOM 5 CONTENTS

(ANSWER SHEET)

| Grade 3 | Class E | Name CONTENTS | Score |

ese History Que

ver the following.

ange. Extreme anir
ecided to create le
financial difficul

ast. Also, the exp
reorganize its fina
ult, the Shogunat
cy. That policy w
orts were increa
port gold and s
eat Tenmei Far
e Council of El
to the hometo
pact of the rev
Edo and Osa
only two yea
the followin
ed Yoshinob

ble out of the following A, B,

B

C

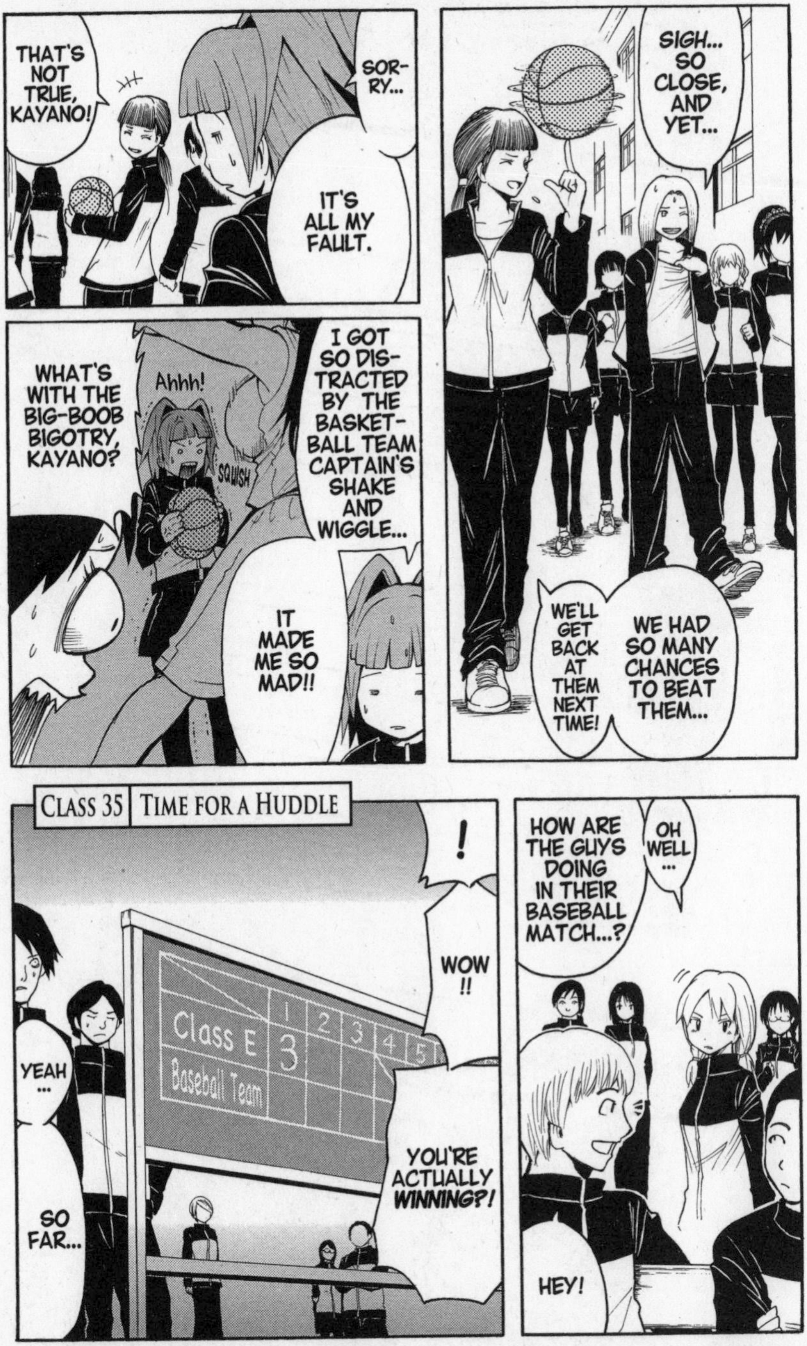
SIGH... SO CLOSE, AND YET...
WE HAD SO MANY CHANCES TO BEAT THEM...
WE'LL GET BACK AT THEM NEXT TIME!
SOR-RY...
IT'S ALL MY FAULT.
THAT'S NOT TRUE, KAYANO!
I GOT SO DIS-TRACTED BY THE BASKET-BALL TEAM CAPTAIN'S SHAKE AND WIGGLE...
IT MADE ME SO MAD!!
WHAT'S WITH THE BIG-BOOB BIGOTRY, KAYANO?
Ahhh!
SQUISH
OH WELL ...
HOW ARE THE GUYS DOING IN THEIR BASEBALL MATCH...?
HEY!
CLASS 35 TIME FOR A HUDDLE
!
WOW !!
YOU'RE ACTUALLY WINNING?!
YEAH ...
SO FAR...
Class E 3
Baseball Team
1 2 3 4 5

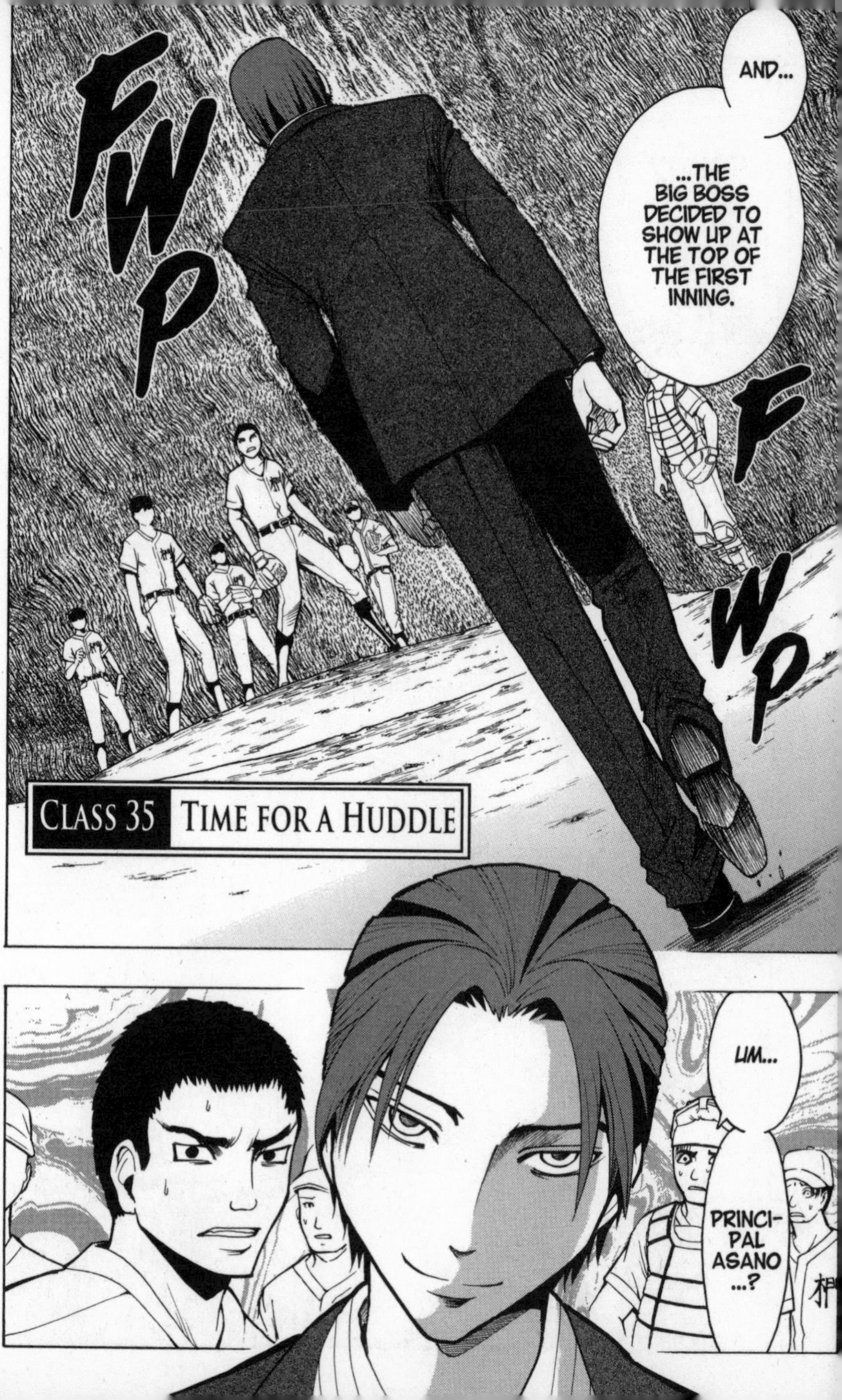
AND...
...THE BIG BOSS DECIDED TO SHOW UP AT THE TOP OF THE FIRST INNING.
FWP
FWP
CLASS 35 TIME FOR A HUDDLE
UM...
PRINCIPAL ASANO...?

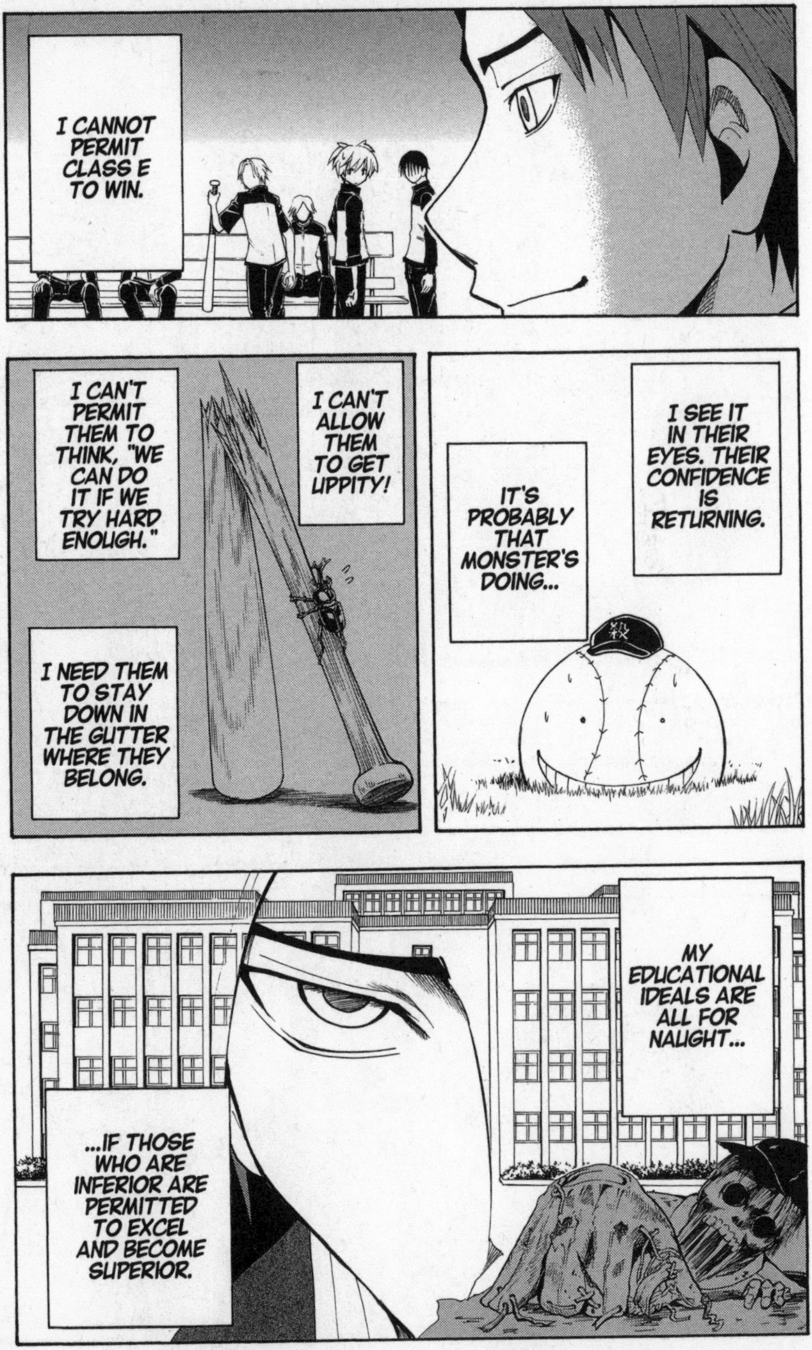
I CANNOT PERMIT CLASS E TO WIN.
I SEE IT IN THEIR EYES. THEIR CONFIDENCE IS RETURNING.
IT'S PROBABLY THAT MONSTER'S DOING...
I CAN'T ALLOW THEM TO GET UPPITY!
I CAN'T PERMIT THEM TO THINK, "WE CAN DO IT IF WE TRY HARD ENOUGH."
I NEED THEM TO STAY DOWN IN THE GUTTER WHERE THEY BELONG.
MY EDUCATIONAL IDEALS ARE ALL FOR NAUGHT...
...IF THOSE WHO ARE INFERIOR ARE PERMITTED TO EXCEL AND BECOME SUPERIOR.

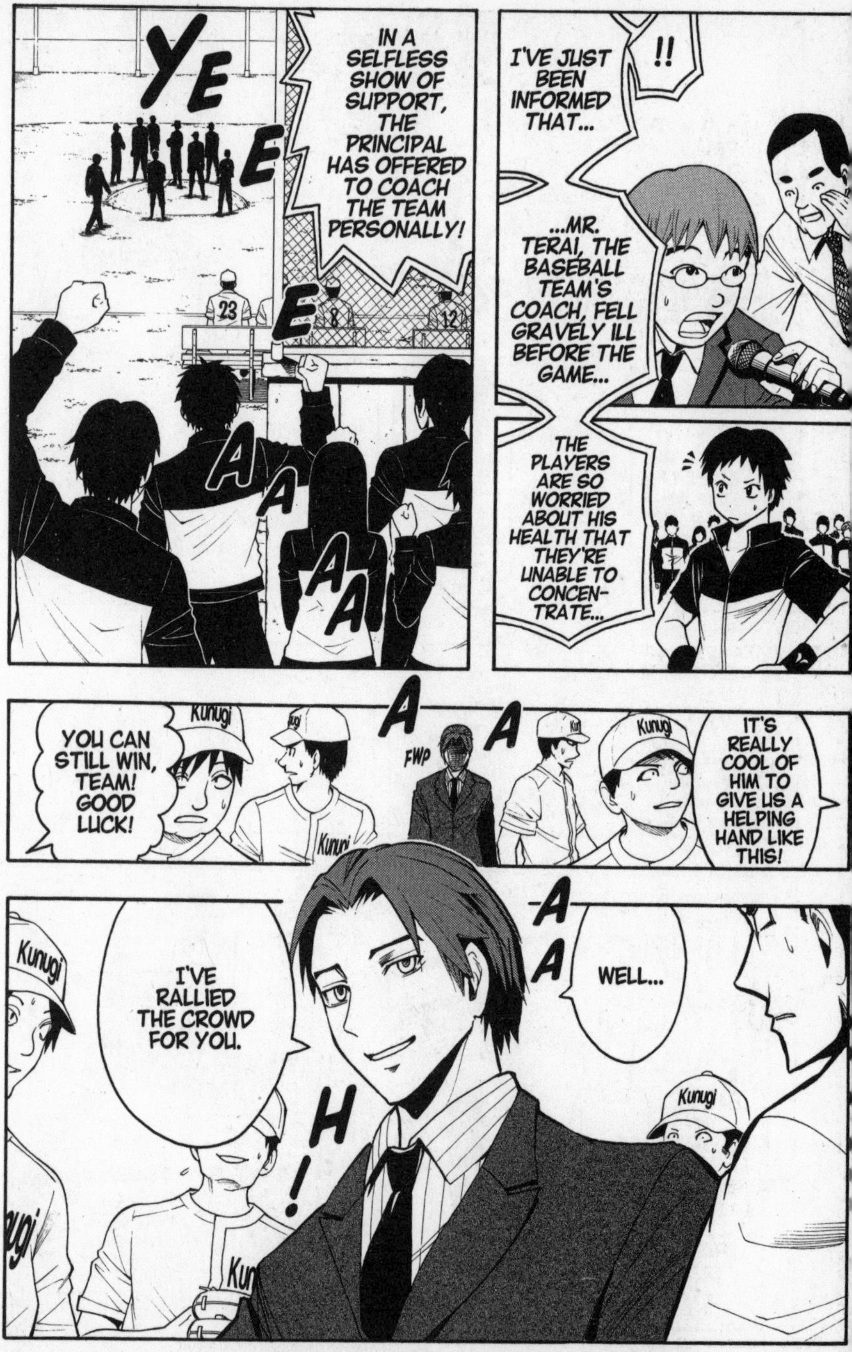
!!
I'VE JUST BEEN INFORMED THAT...
...MR. TERAI, THE BASEBALL TEAM'S COACH, FELL GRAVELY ILL BEFORE THE GAME...
THE PLAYERS ARE SO WORRIED ABOUT HIS HEALTH THAT THEY'RE UNABLE TO CONCENTRATE...
IN A SELFLESS SHOW OF SUPPORT, THE PRINCIPAL HAS OFFERED TO COACH THE TEAM PERSONALLY!
YEEEAAAAA
IT'S REALLY COOL OF HIM TO GIVE US A HELPING HAND LIKE THIS!
AA
FWP
YOU CAN STILL WIN, TEAM! GOOD LUCK!
-AAA
WELL...
I'VE RALLIED THE CROWD FOR YOU.
H!

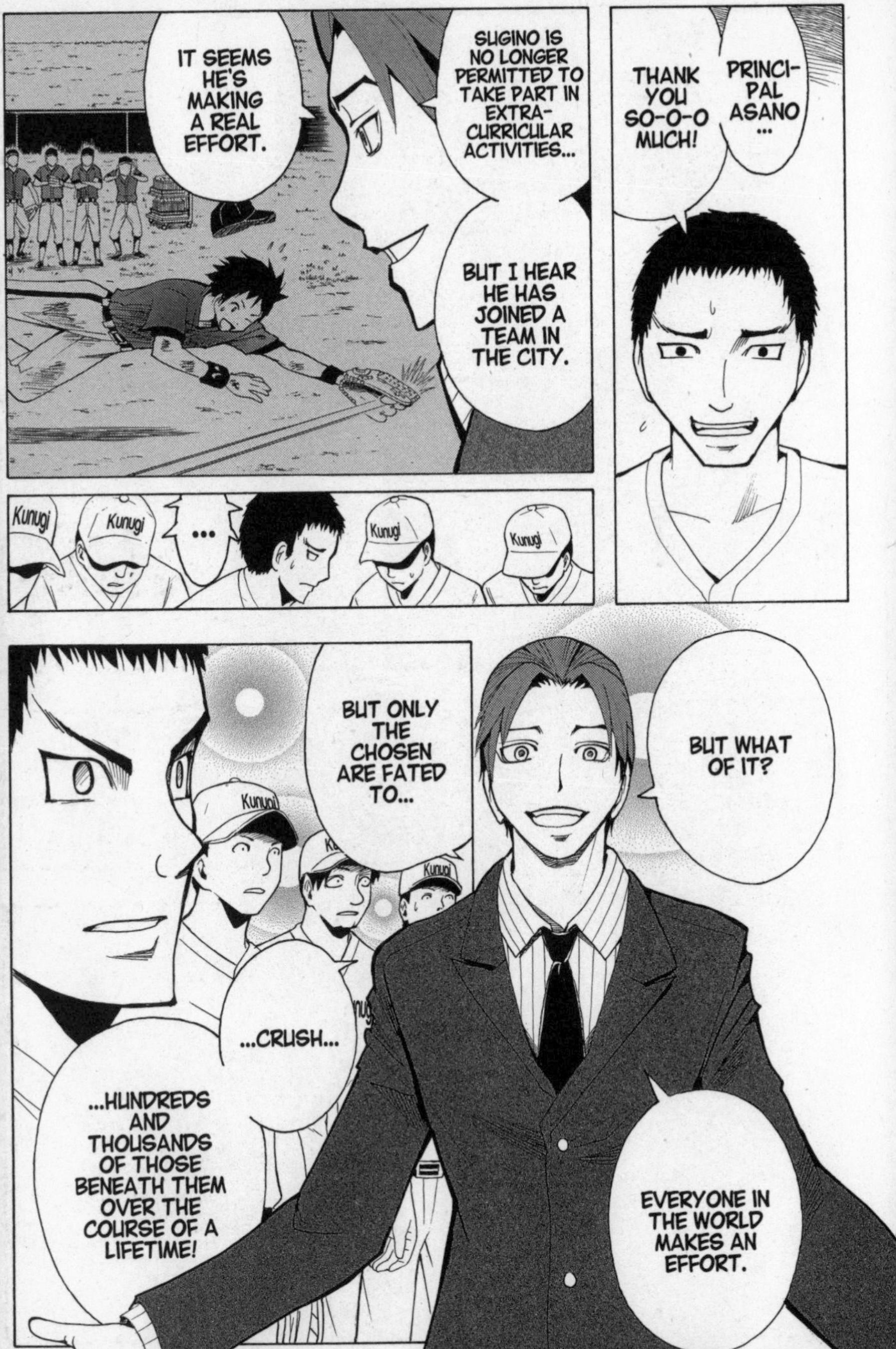
PRINCI-PAL ASANO...
THANK YOU SO-O-O MUCH!
SUGINO IS NO LONGER PERMITTED TO TAKE PART IN EXTRA-CURRICULAR ACTIVITIES...
BUT I HEAR HE HAS JOINED A TEAM IN THE CITY.
IT SEEMS HE'S MAKING A REAL EFFORT.
...
BUT WHAT OF IT?
EVERYONE IN THE WORLD MAKES AN EFFORT.
BUT ONLY THE CHOSEN ARE FATED TO...
...CRUSH...
...HUNDREDS AND THOUSANDS OF THOSE BENEATH THEM OVER THE COURSE OF A LIFETIME!

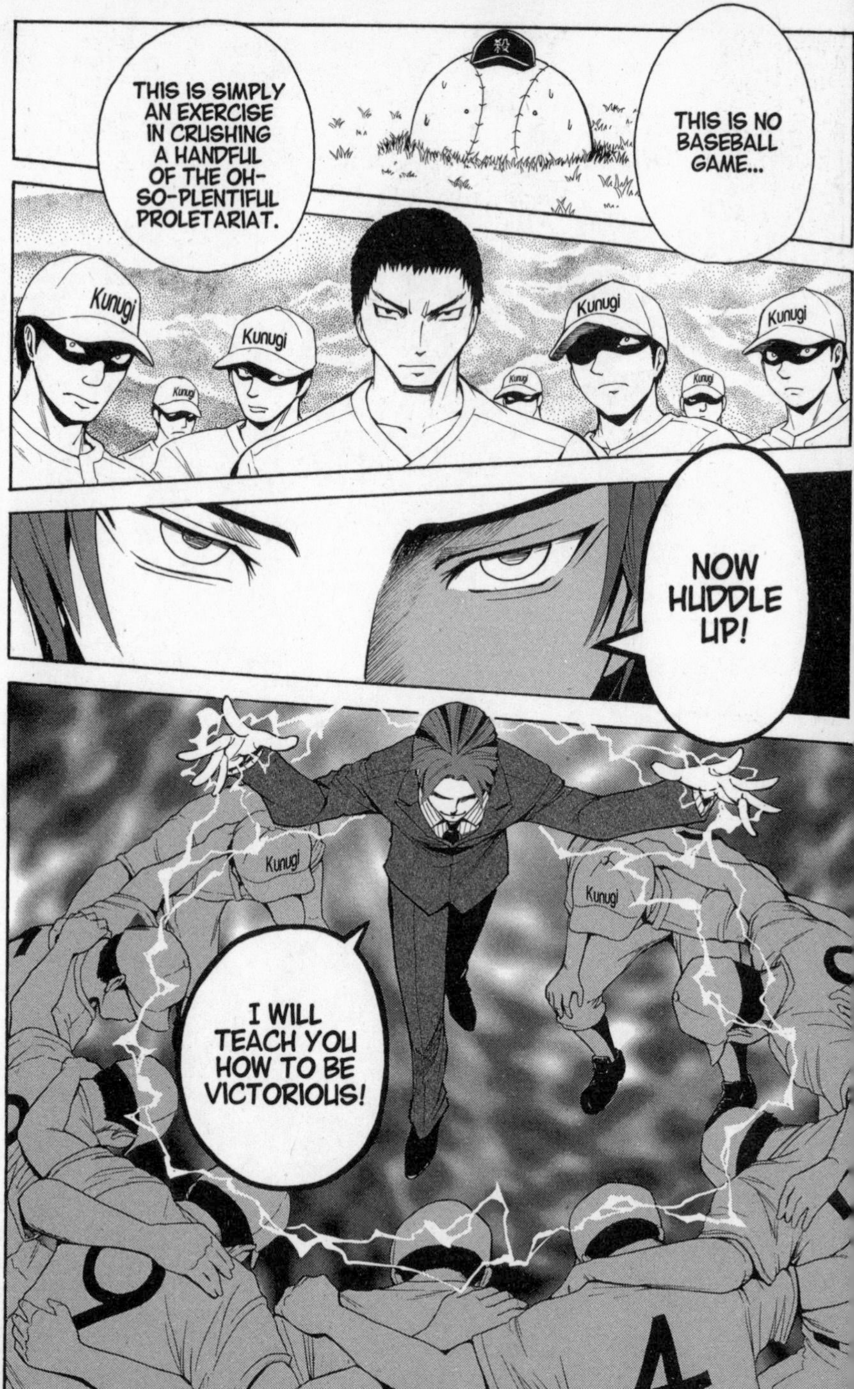
THIS IS NO BASEBALL GAME...
THIS IS SIMPLY AN EXERCISE IN CRUSHING A HANDFUL OF THE OH-SO-PLENTIFUL PROLETARIAT.
NOW HUDDLE UP!
I WILL TEACH YOU HOW TO BE VICTORIOUS!

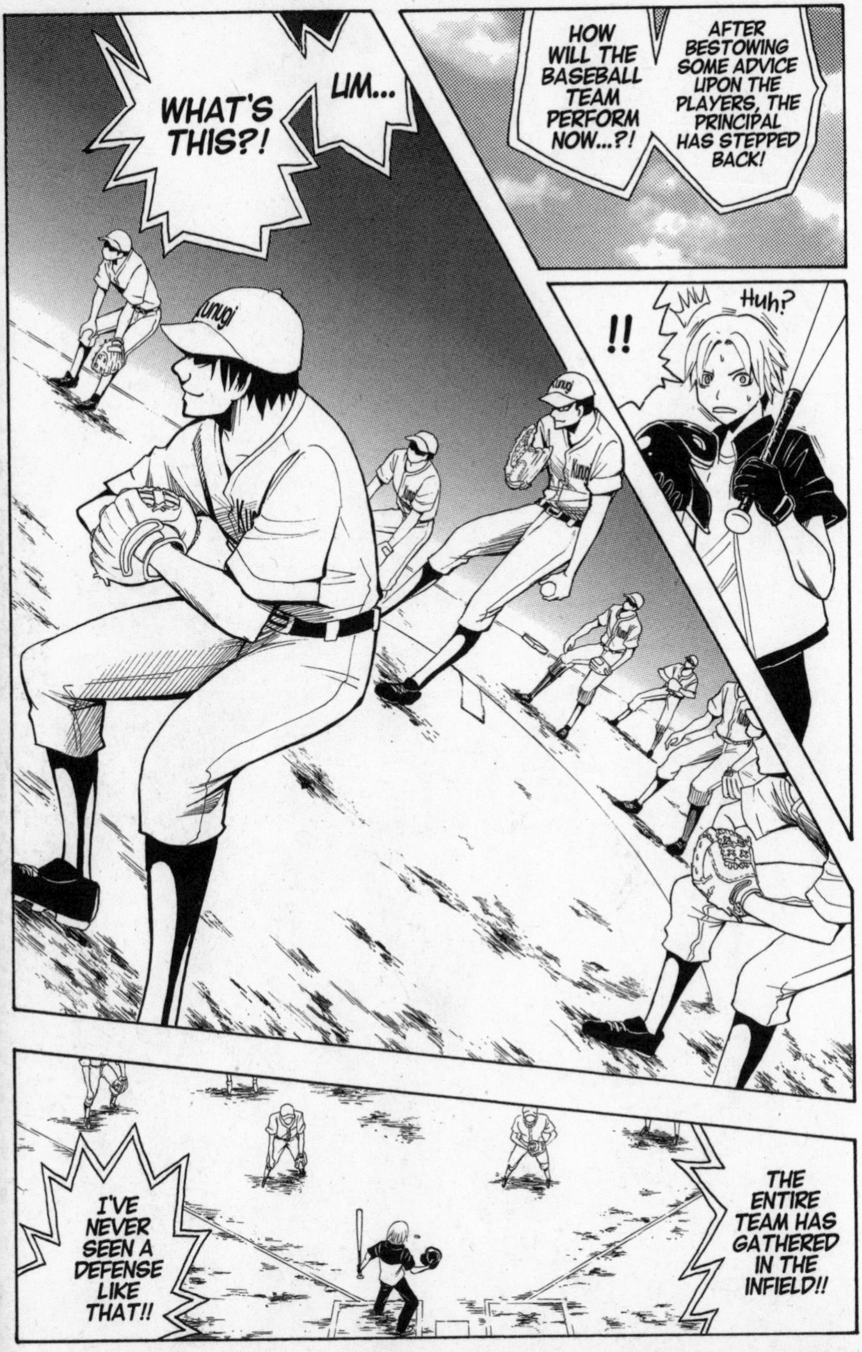
AFTER BESTOWING SOME ADVICE UPON THE PLAYERS, THE PRINCIPAL HAS STEPPED BACK!
HOW WILL THE BASEBALL TEAM PERFORM NOW...?!
Huh?
!!
UM...
WHAT'S THIS?!
THE ENTIRE TEAM HAS GATHERED IN THE INFIELD!!
I'VE NEVER SEEN A DEFENSE LIKE THAT!!

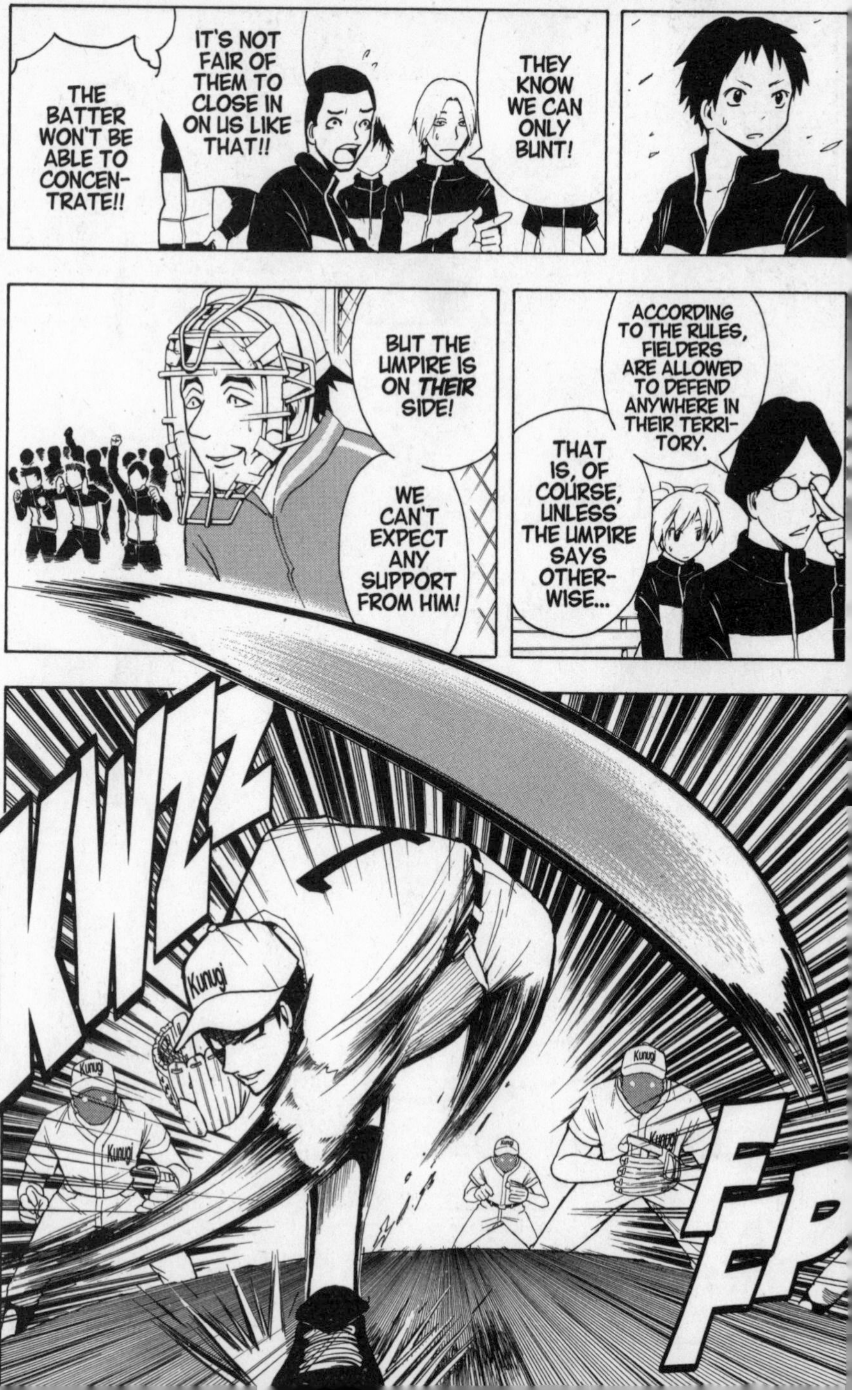
THEY KNOW WE CAN ONLY BUNT!
IT'S NOT FAIR OF THEM TO CLOSE IN ON US LIKE THAT!!
THE BATTER WON'T BE ABLE TO CONCENTRATE!!
ACCORDING TO THE RULES, FIELDERS ARE ALLOWED TO DEFEND ANYWHERE IN THEIR TERRITORY.
THAT IS, OF COURSE, UNLESS THE UMPIRE SAYS OTHERWISE...
BUT THE UMPIRE IS ON *THEIR* SIDE!
WE CAN'T EXPECT ANY SUPPORT FROM HIM!
Kunugi

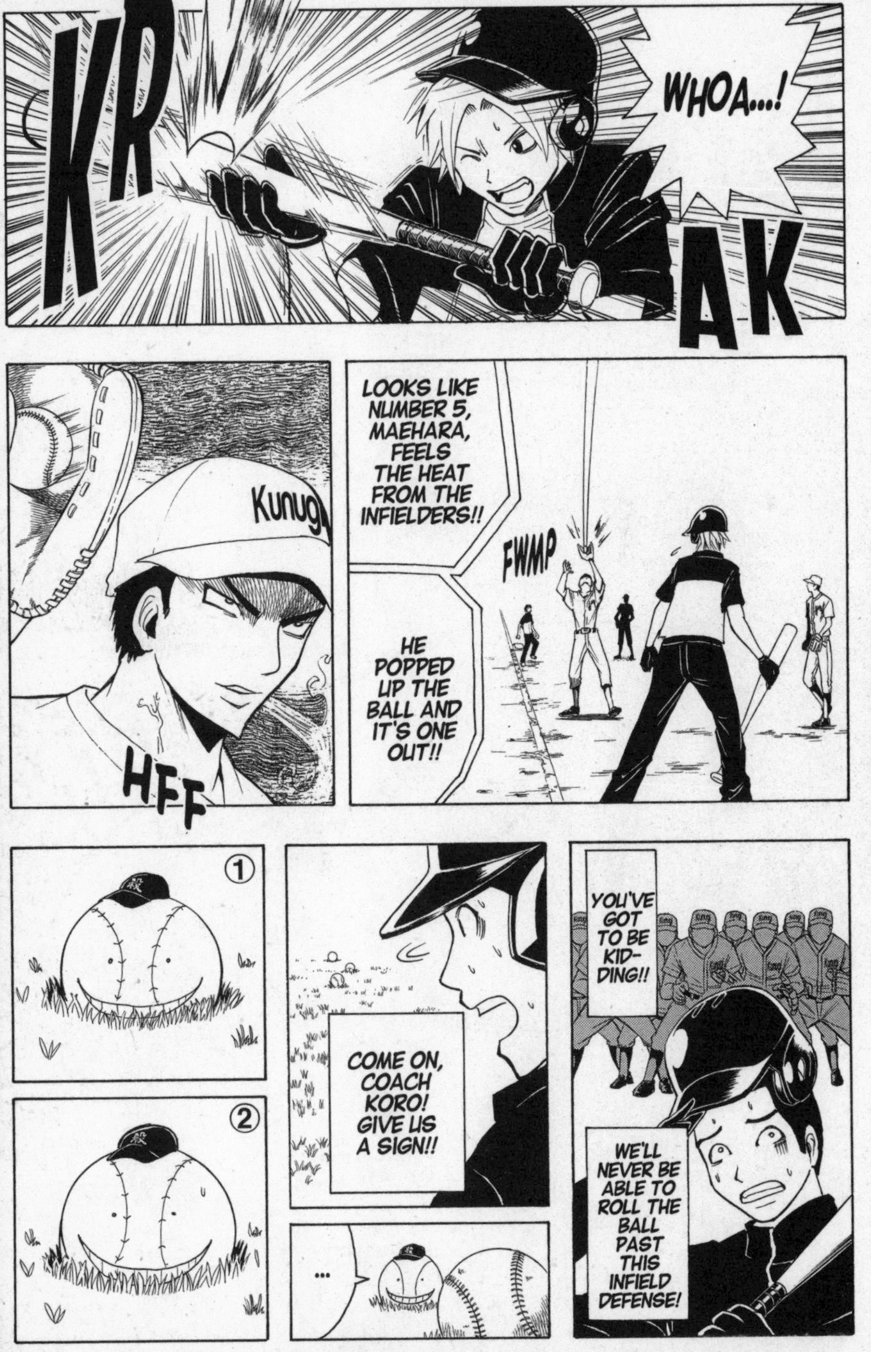
WHOA...!
KR
AK
LOOKS LIKE NUMBER 5, MAEHARA, FEELS THE HEAT FROM THE INFIELDERS!!
HE POPPED UP THE BALL AND IT'S ONE OUT!!
FWMP
Kunug
HFF
YOU'VE GOT TO BE KID-DING!!
WE'LL NEVER BE ABLE TO ROLL THE BALL PAST THIS INFIELD DEFENSE!
COME ON, COACH KORO! GIVE US A SIGN!!
...
①
②

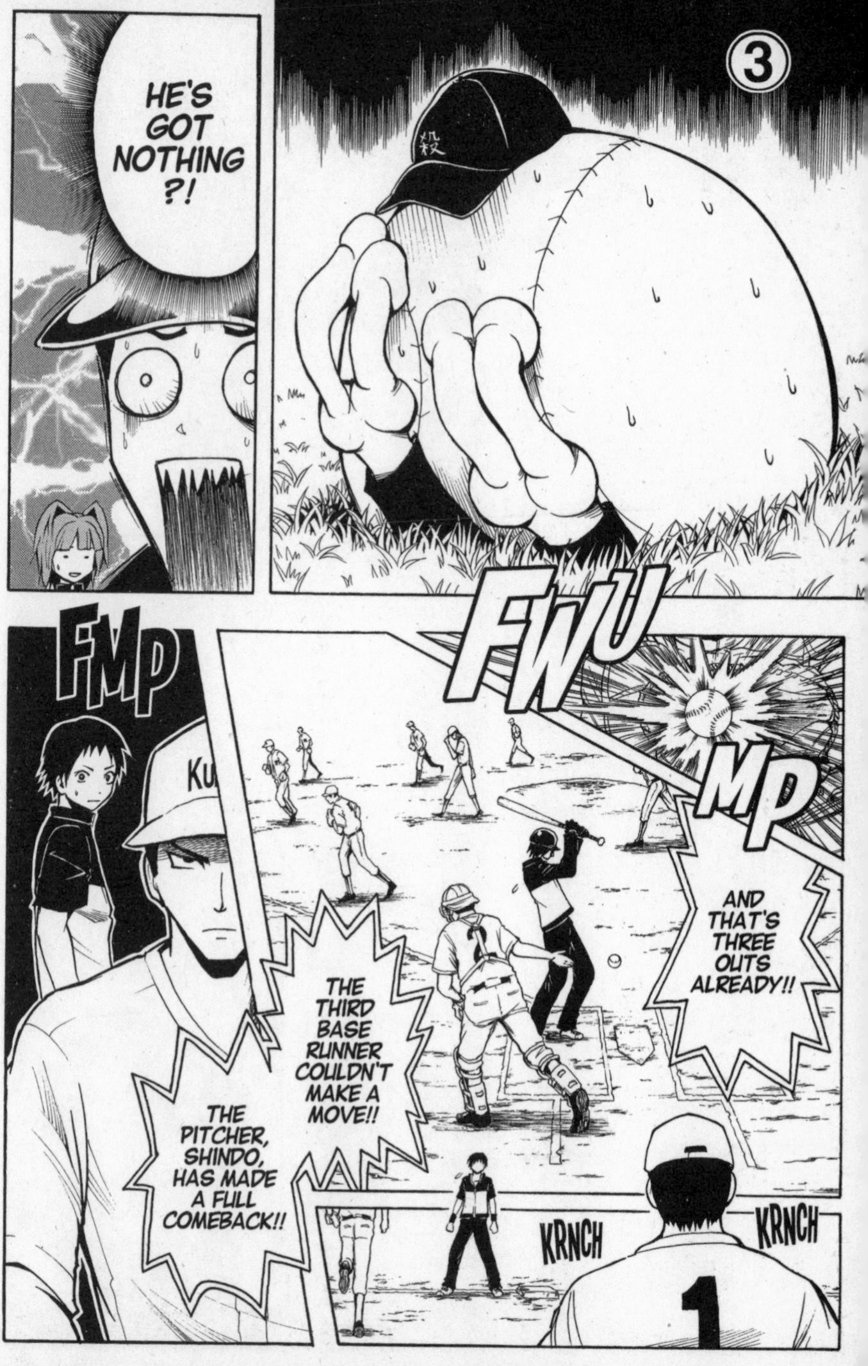
3
HE'S GOT NOTHING?!
FWUMP
AND THAT'S THREE OUTS ALREADY!!
THE THIRD BASE RUNNER COULDN'T MAKE A MOVE!!
FMP
THE PITCHER, SHINDO, HAS MADE A FULL COMEBACK!!
KRNCH
KRNCH

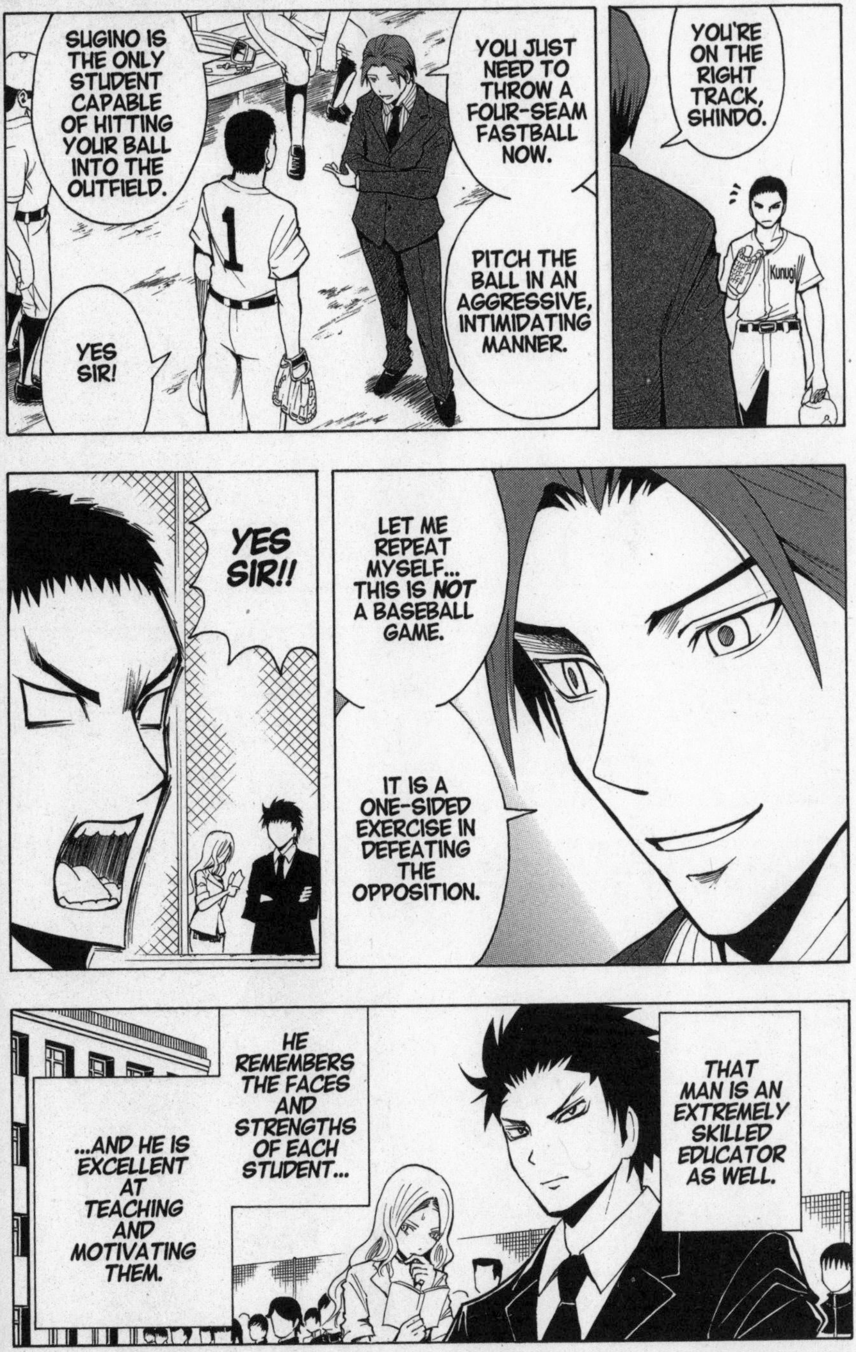
YOU'RE ON THE RIGHT TRACK, SHINDO.
YOU JUST NEED TO THROW A FOUR-SEAM FASTBALL NOW.
SUGINO IS THE ONLY STUDENT CAPABLE OF HITTING YOUR BALL INTO THE OUTFIELD.
PITCH THE BALL IN AN AGGRESSIVE, INTIMIDATING MANNER.
YES SIR!
LET ME REPEAT MYSELF... THIS IS NOT A BASEBALL GAME.
IT IS A ONE-SIDED EXERCISE IN DEFEATING THE OPPOSITION.
YES SIR!!
THAT MAN IS AN EXTREMELY SKILLED EDUCATOR AS WELL.
HE REMEMBERS THE FACES AND STRENGTHS OF EACH STUDENT...
...AND HE IS EXCELLENT AT TEACHING AND MOTIVATING THEM.

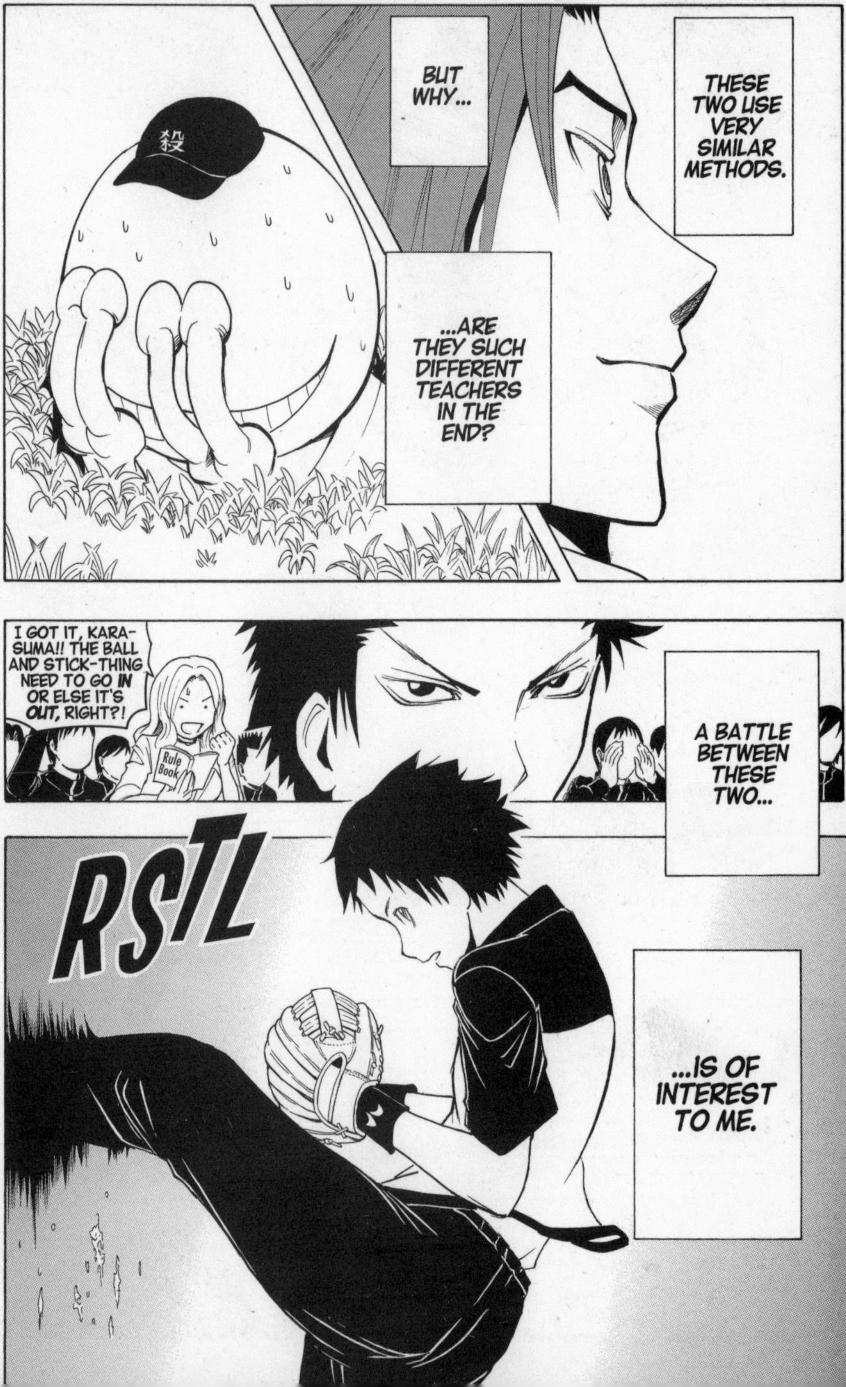
THESE TWO USE VERY SIMILAR METHODS.
BUT WHY...
...ARE THEY SUCH DIFFERENT TEACHERS IN THE END?
A BATTLE BETWEEN THESE TWO...
I GOT IT, KARA-SUMA!! THE BALL AND STICK-THING NEED TO GO IN OR ELSE IT'S OUT, RIGHT?!
Rule Book
RSTL
...IS OF INTEREST TO ME.

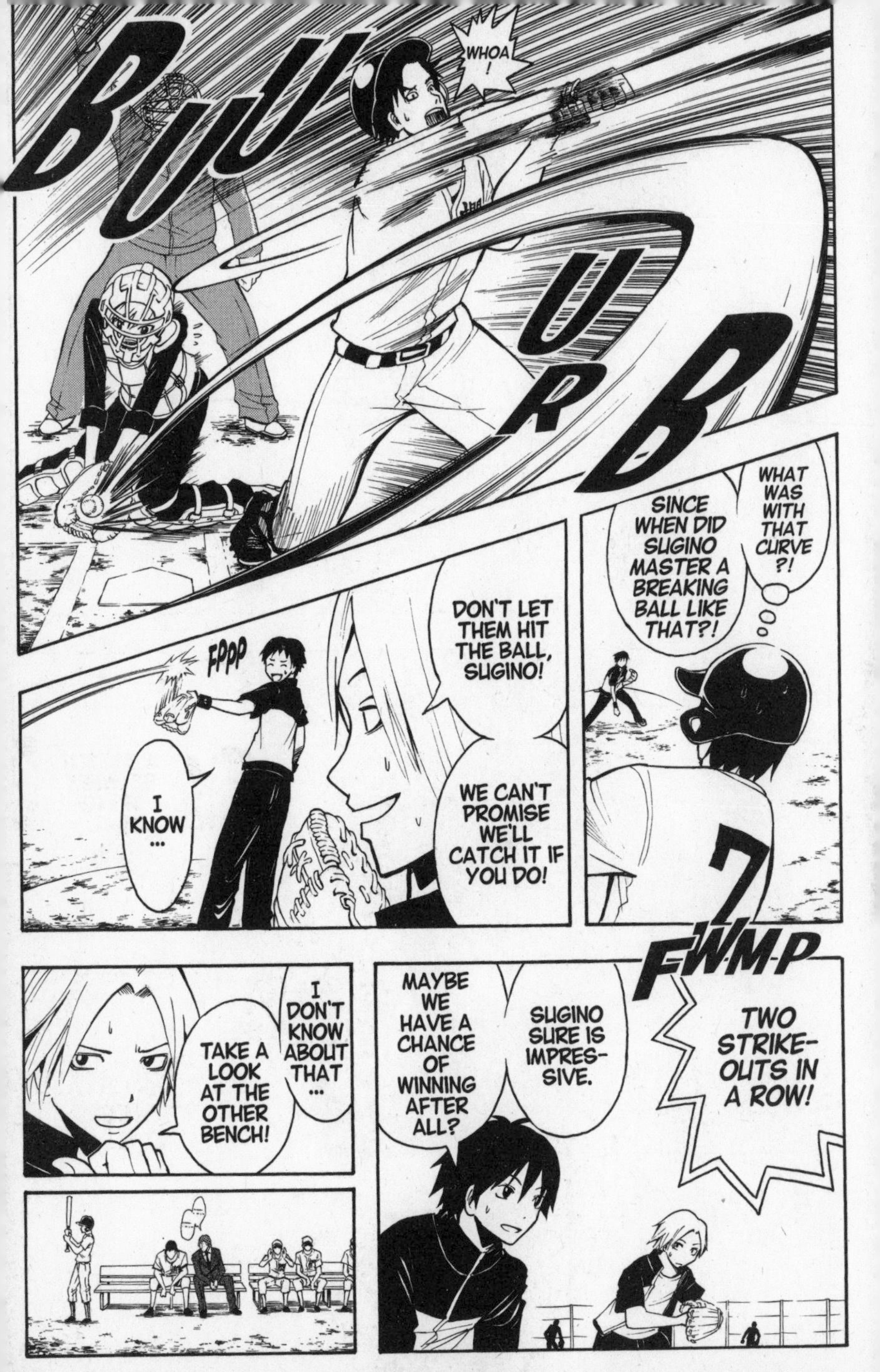
WHOA!
BUUURB
WHAT WAS WITH THAT CURVE?!
SINCE WHEN DID SUGINO MASTER A BREAKING BALL LIKE THAT?!
DON'T LET THEM HIT THE BALL, SUGINO!
FPPP
WE CAN'T PROMISE WE'LL CATCH IT IF YOU DO!
I KNOW ...
FWMP
TWO STRIKE-OUTS IN A ROW!
SUGINO SURE IS IMPRESSIVE.
MAYBE WE HAVE A CHANCE OF WINNING AFTER ALL?
I DON'T KNOW ABOUT THAT ...
TAKE A LOOK AT THE OTHER BENCH!

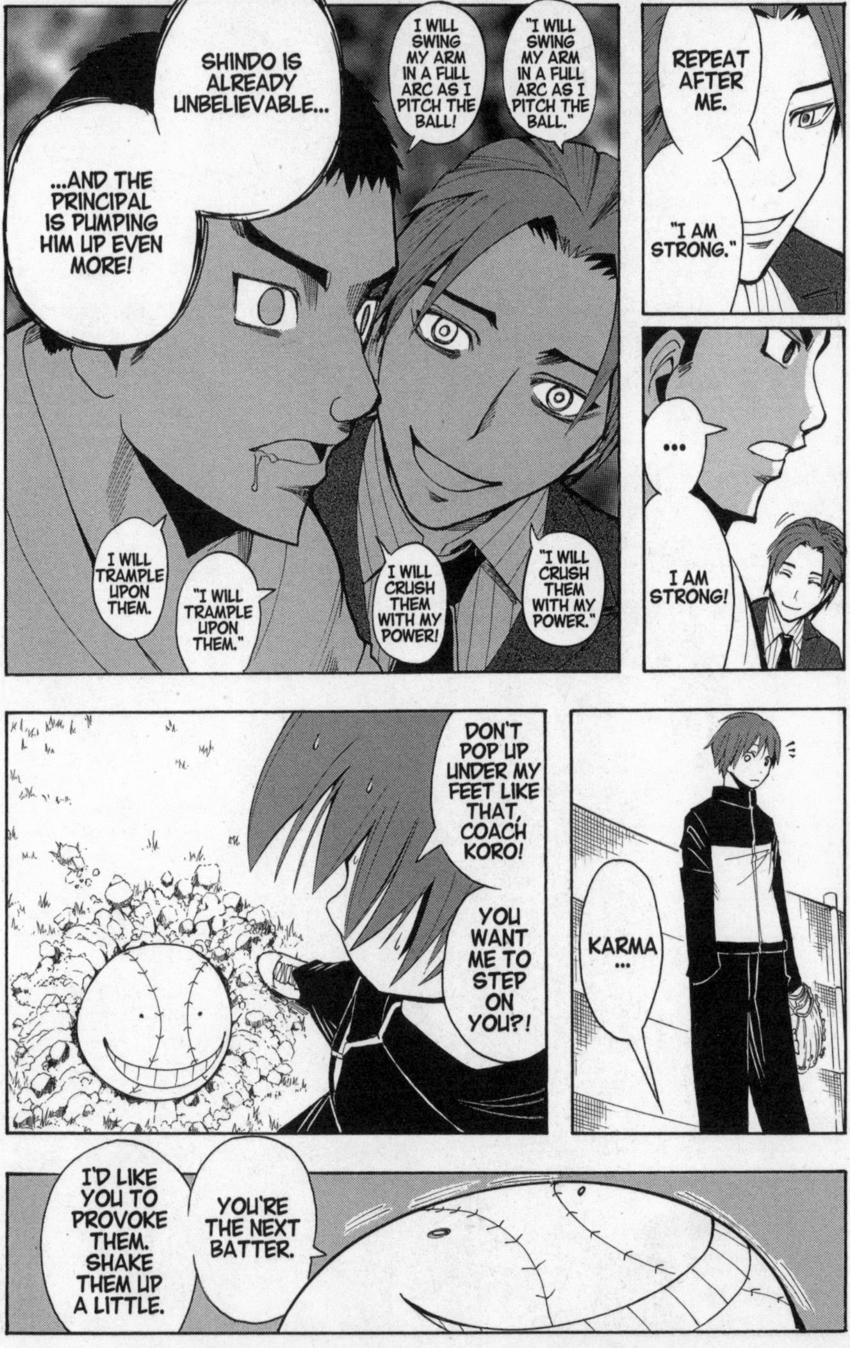
REPEAT AFTER ME.
"I AM STRONG."
...
I AM STRONG!
"I WILL SWING MY ARM IN A FULL ARC AS I PITCH THE BALL."
I WILL SWING MY ARM IN A FULL ARC AS I PITCH THE BALL!
SHINDO IS ALREADY UNBELIEVABLE...
...AND THE PRINCIPAL IS PUMPING HIM UP EVEN MORE!
"I WILL CRUSH THEM WITH MY POWER."
I WILL CRUSH THEM WITH MY POWER!
"I WILL TRAMPLE UPON THEM."
I WILL TRAMPLE UPON THEM.
KARMA...
DON'T POP UP UNDER MY FEET LIKE THAT, COACH KORO!
YOU WANT ME TO STEP ON YOU?!
YOU'RE THE NEXT BATTER.
I'D LIKE YOU TO PROVOKE THEM. SHAKE THEM UP A LITTLE.

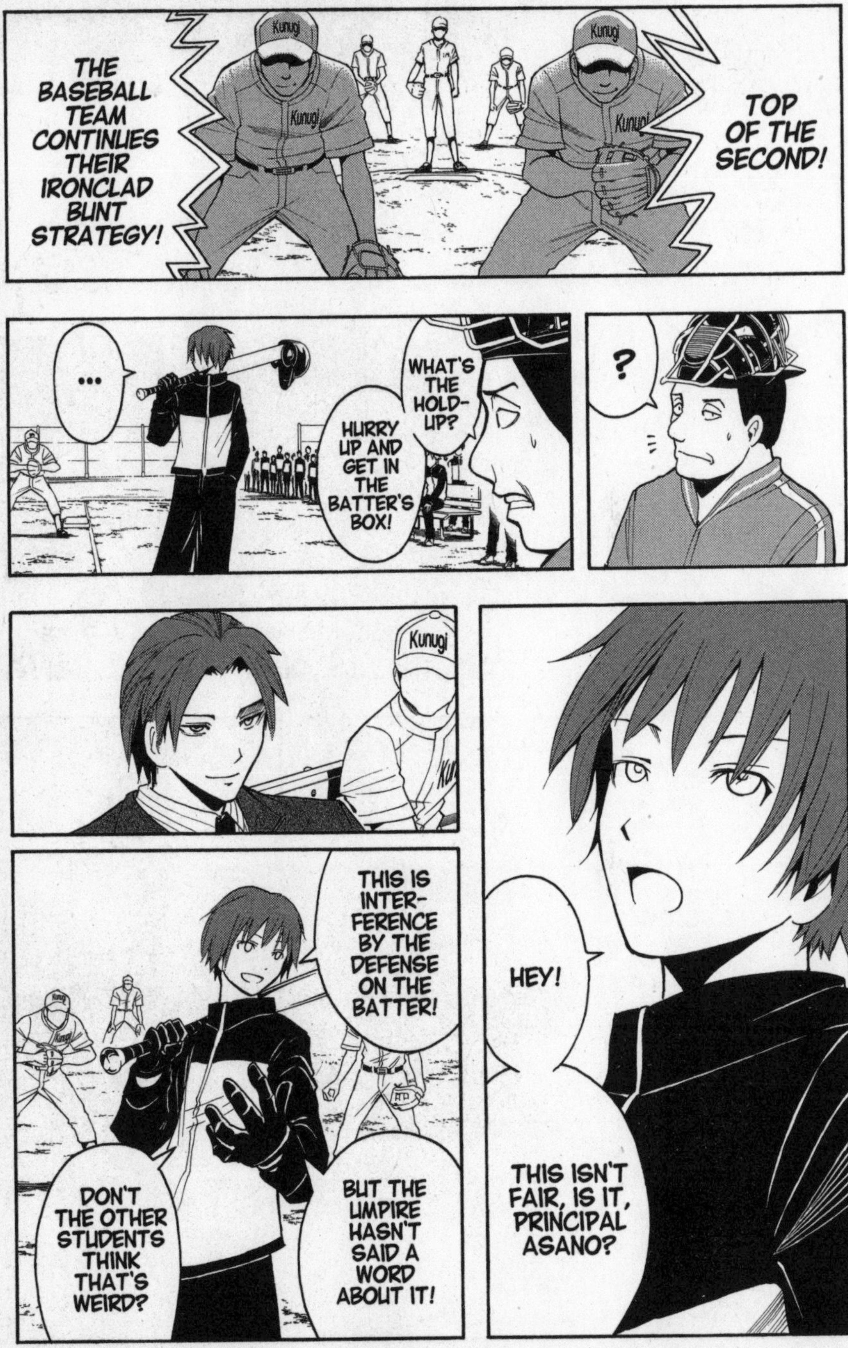
TOP OF THE SECOND!
THE BASEBALL TEAM CONTINUES THEIR IRONCLAD BUNT STRATEGY!
?
WHAT'S THE HOLD-UP?
HURRY UP AND GET IN THE BATTER'S BOX!
...
HEY!
THIS ISN'T FAIR, IS IT, PRINCIPAL ASANO?
THIS IS INTER-FERENCE BY THE DEFENSE ON THE BATTER!
BUT THE UMPIRE HASN'T SAID A WORD ABOUT IT!
DON'T THE OTHER STUDENTS THINK THAT'S WEIRD?

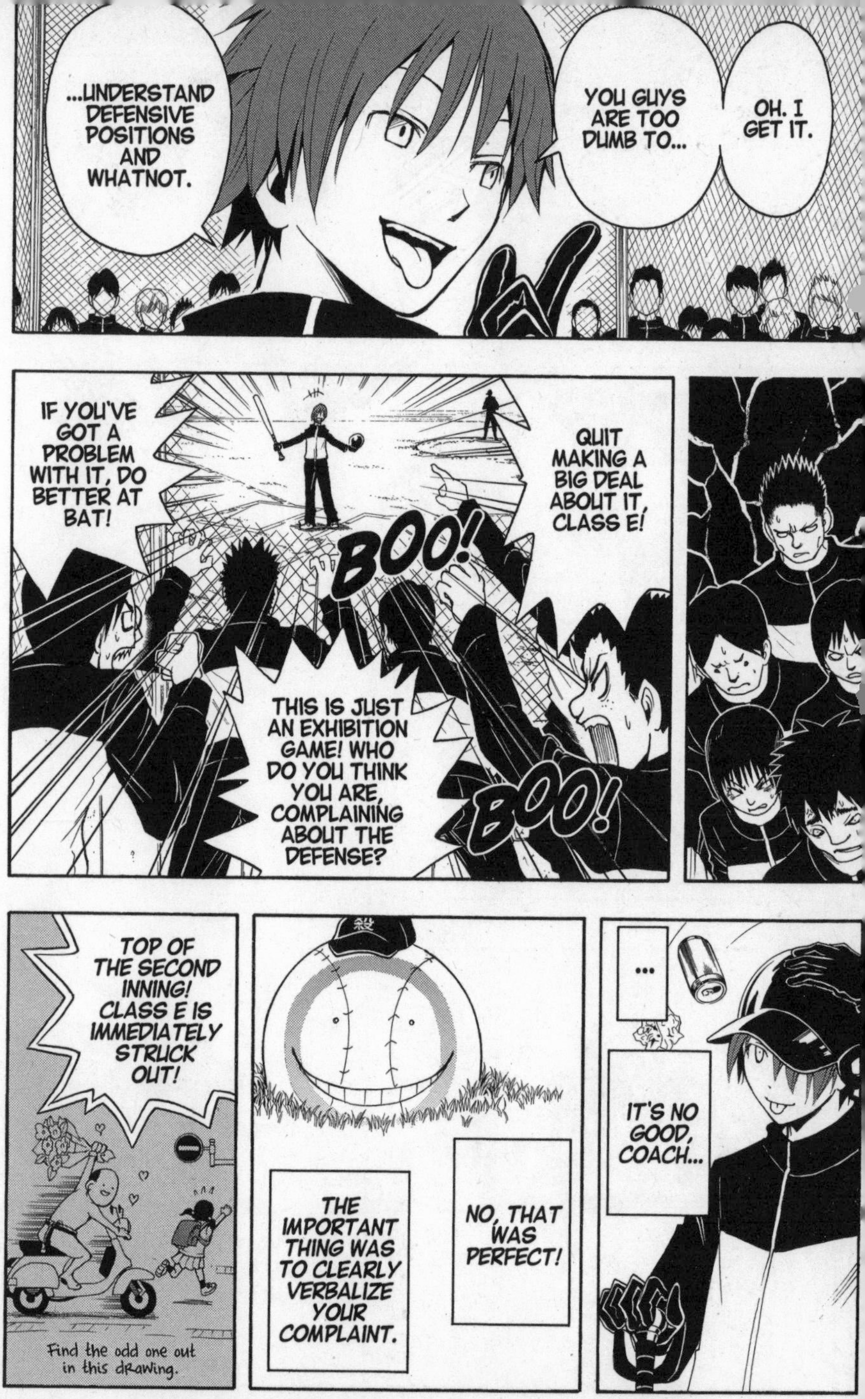
OH. I GET IT.
YOU GUYS ARE TOO DUMB TO...
...UNDERSTAND DEFENSIVE POSITIONS AND WHATNOT.
QUIT MAKING A BIG DEAL ABOUT IT, CLASS E!
IF YOU'VE GOT A PROBLEM WITH IT, DO BETTER AT BAT!
BOO!
THIS IS JUST AN EXHIBITION GAME! WHO DO YOU THINK YOU ARE, COMPLAINING ABOUT THE DEFENSE?
BOO!
...
IT'S NO GOOD, COACH...
殺
NO, THAT WAS PERFECT!
THE IMPORTANT THING WAS TO CLEARLY VERBALIZE YOUR COMPLAINT.
TOP OF THE SECOND INNING! CLASS E IS IMMEDIATELY STRUCK OUT!
Find the odd one out in this drawing.

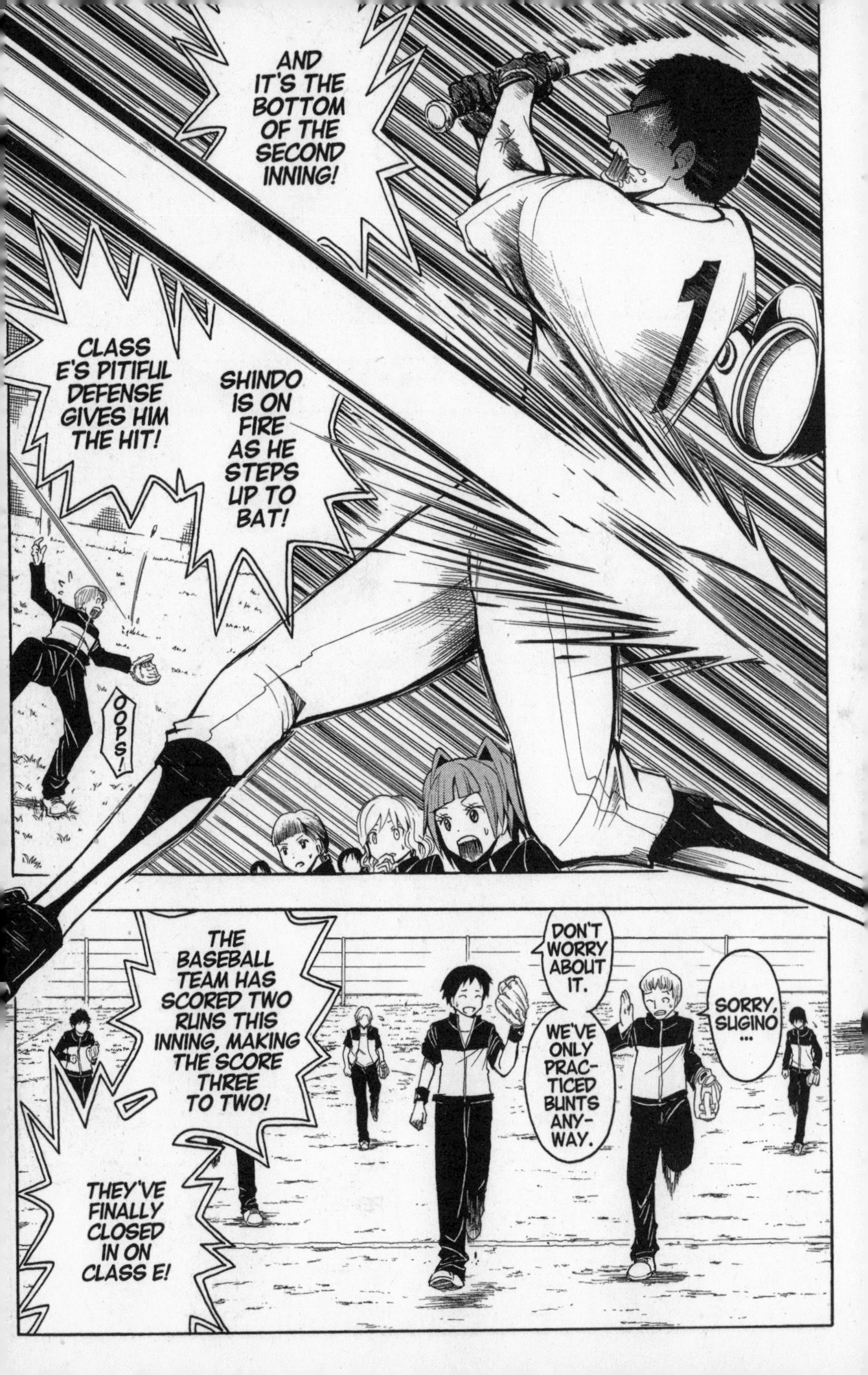
AND IT'S THE BOTTOM OF THE SECOND INNING!
SHINDO IS ON FIRE AS HE STEPS UP TO BAT!
CLASS E'S PITIFUL DEFENSE GIVES HIM THE HIT!
OOPS!
SORRY, SUGINO...
DON'T WORRY ABOUT IT.
WE'VE ONLY PRACTICED BUNTS ANYWAY.
THE BASEBALL TEAM HAS SCORED TWO RUNS THIS INNING, MAKING THE SCORE THREE TO TWO!
THEY'VE FINALLY CLOSED IN ON CLASS E!

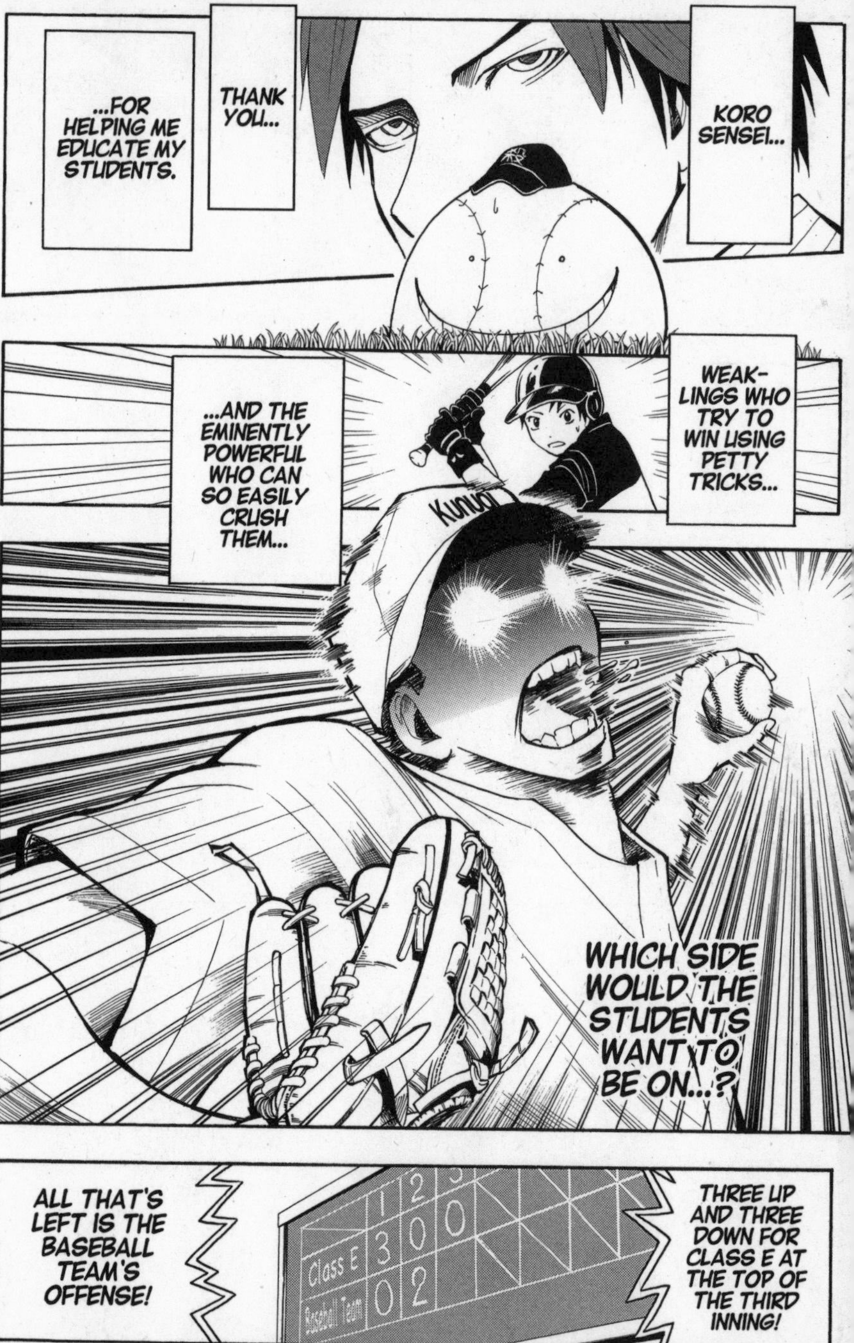
KORO SENSEI...
THANK YOU...
...FOR HELPING ME EDUCATE MY STUDENTS.
WEAK-LINGS WHO TRY TO WIN USING PETTY TRICKS...
...AND THE EMINENTLY POWERFUL WHO CAN SO EASILY CRUSH THEM...
WHICH SIDE WOULD THE STUDENTS WANT TO BE ON...?
THREE UP AND THREE DOWN FOR CLASS E AT THE TOP OF THE THIRD INNING!
1 2
Class E 3 0 0
Baseball Team 0 2
ALL THAT'S LEFT IS THE BASEBALL TEAM'S OFFENSE!

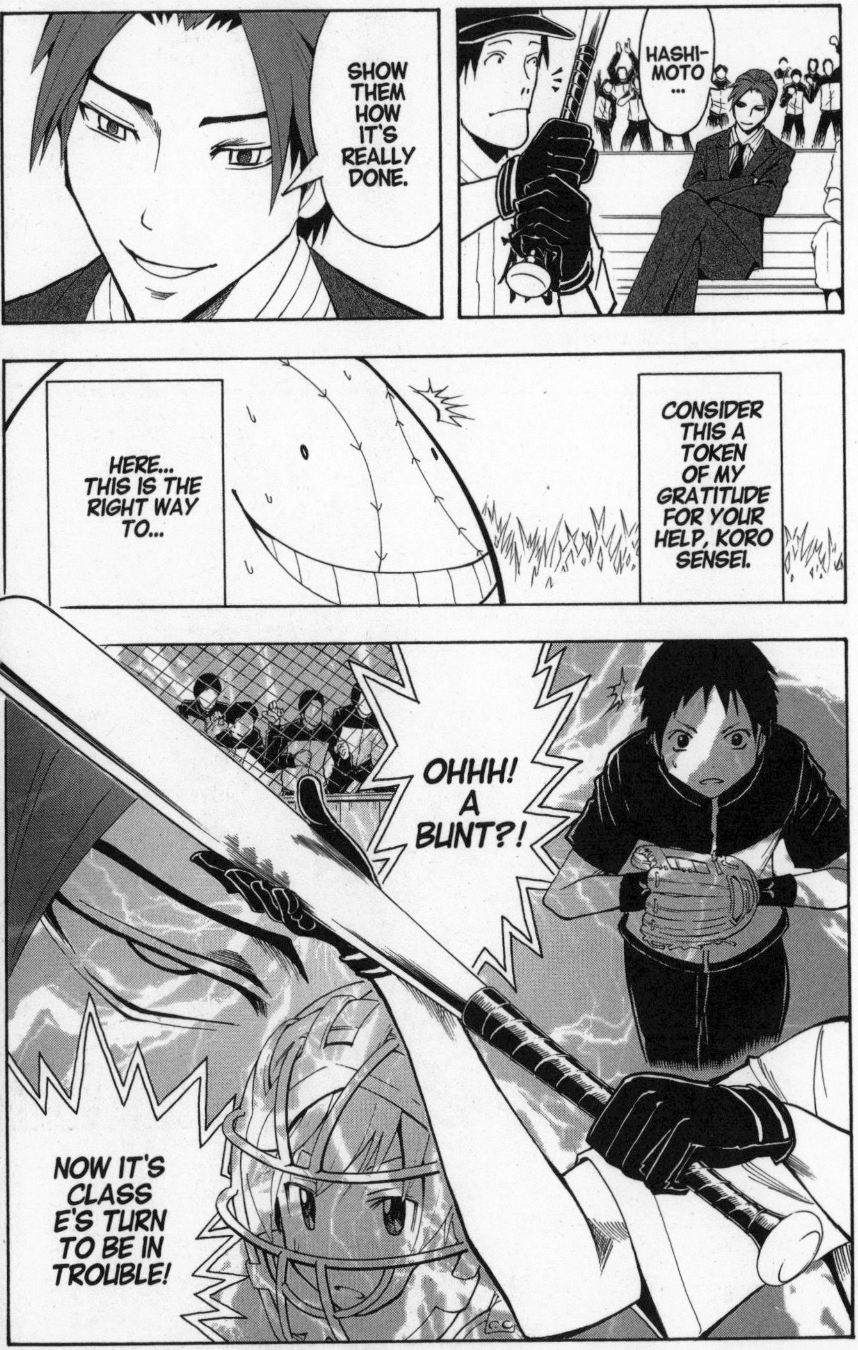
HASHIMOTO...
SHOW THEM HOW IT'S REALLY DONE.
CONSIDER THIS A TOKEN OF MY GRATITUDE FOR YOUR HELP, KORO SENSEI.
HERE... THIS IS THE RIGHT WAY TO...
OHHH! A BUNT?!
NOW IT'S CLASS E'S TURN TO BE IN TROUBLE!

1. No-Entry Sign
2. His Love Interest
3. No Helmet
4. Clothing

4 Outs

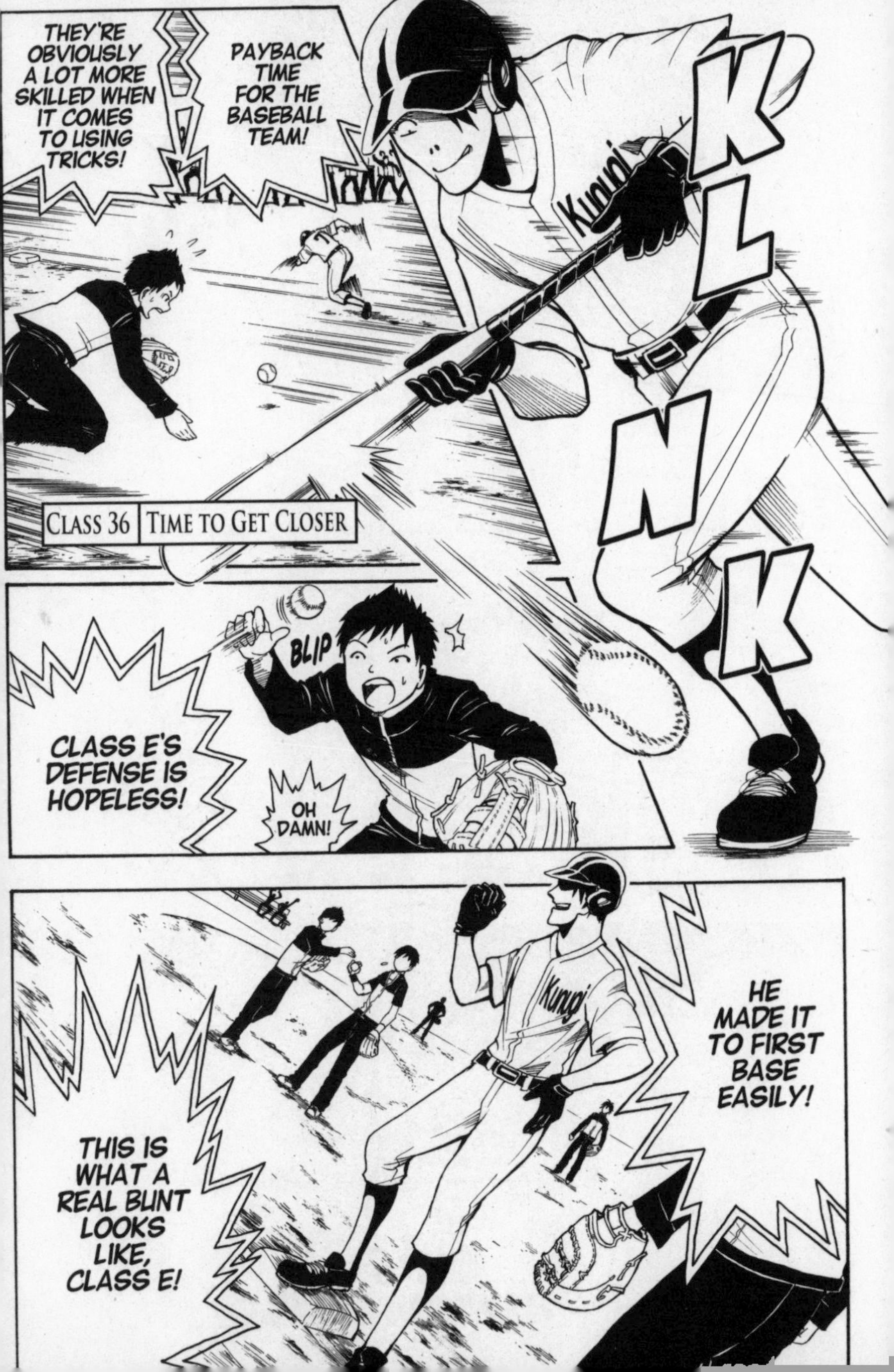
KLNK
PAYBACK TIME FOR THE BASEBALL TEAM!
THEY'RE OBVIOUSLY A LOT MORE SKILLED WHEN IT COMES TO USING TRICKS!
CLASS 36 TIME TO GET CLOSER
BLIP
OH DAMN!
CLASS E'S DEFENSE IS HOPELESS!
HE MADE IT TO FIRST BASE EASILY!
THIS IS WHAT A REAL BUNT LOOKS LIKE, CLASS E!

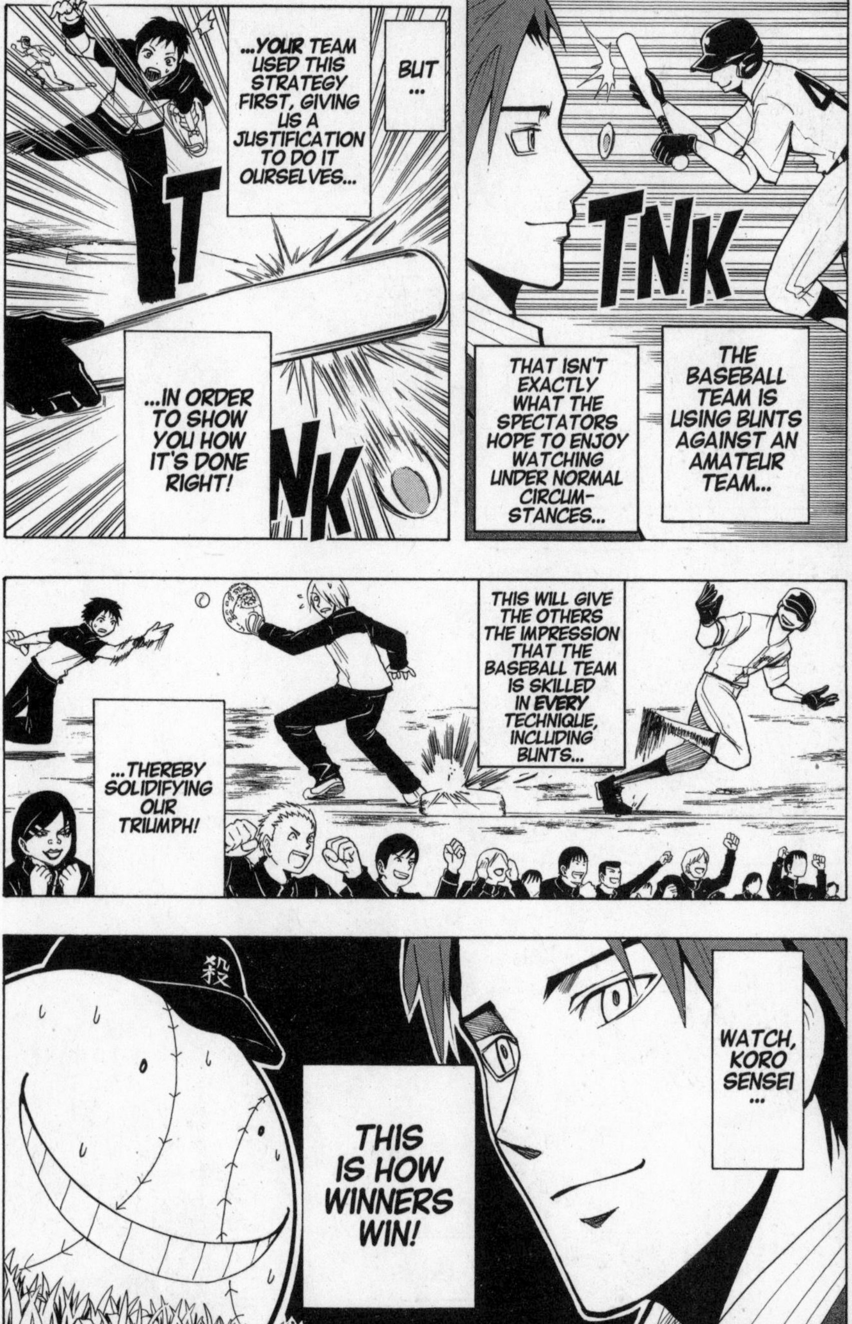
TNK
THE BASEBALL TEAM IS USING BUNTS AGAINST AN AMATEUR TEAM...
THAT ISN'T EXACTLY WHAT THE SPECTATORS HOPE TO ENJOY WATCHING UNDER NORMAL CIRCUM-STANCES...
BUT...
...YOUR TEAM USED THIS STRATEGY FIRST, GIVING US A JUSTIFICATION TO DO IT OURSELVES...
TNK
...IN ORDER TO SHOW YOU HOW IT'S DONE RIGHT!
THIS WILL GIVE THE OTHERS THE IMPRESSION THAT THE BASEBALL TEAM IS SKILLED IN EVERY TECHNIQUE, INCLUDING BUNTS...
...THEREBY SOLIDIFYING OUR TRIUMPH!
WATCH, KORO SENSEI...
殺
THIS IS HOW WINNERS WIN!

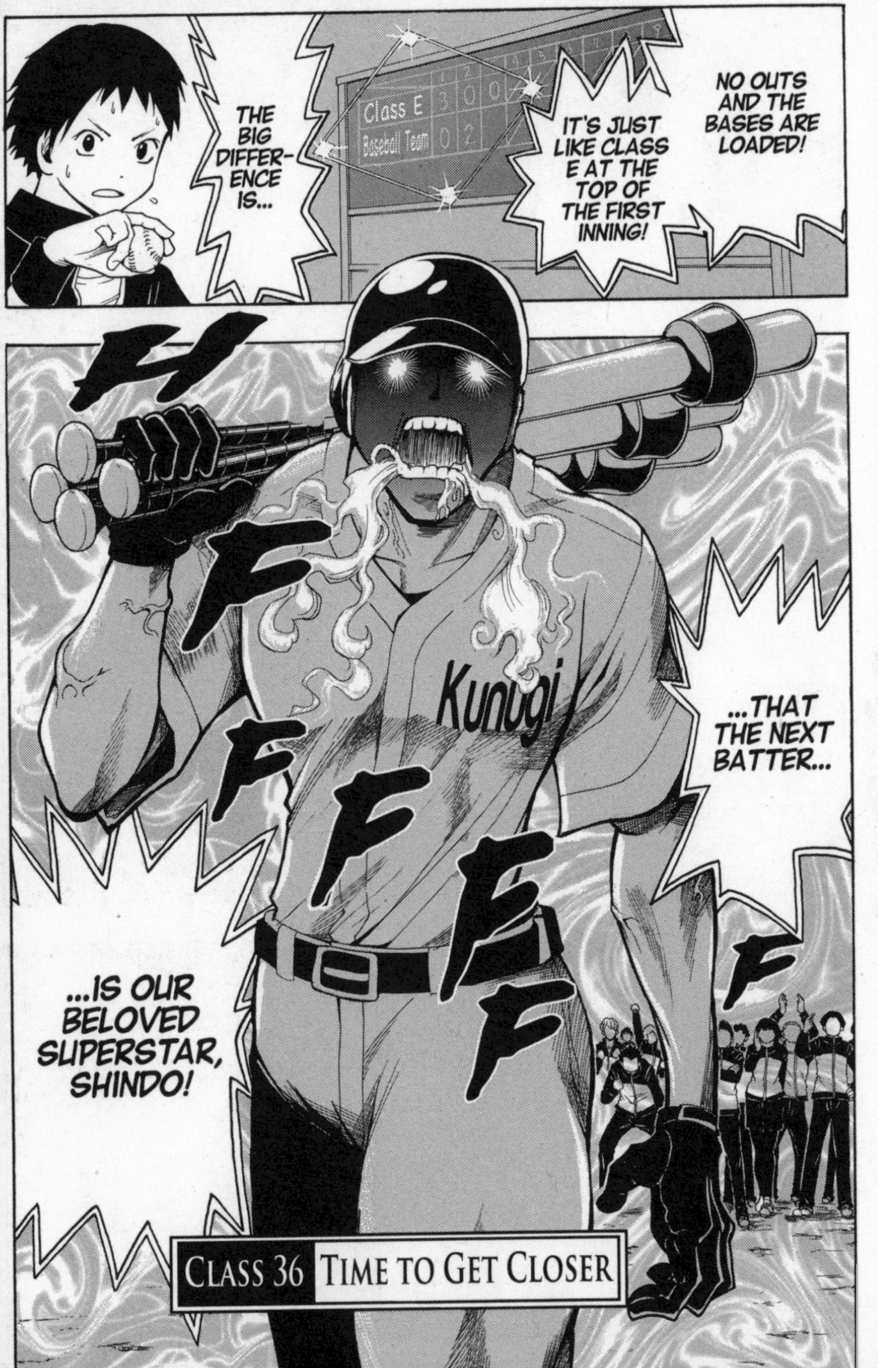
NO OUTS AND THE BASES ARE LOADED!
IT'S JUST LIKE CLASS E AT THE TOP OF THE FIRST INNING!
Class E
Baseball Team
THE BIG DIFFERENCE IS...
...THAT THE NEXT BATTER...
Kunugi
...IS OUR BELOVED SUPERSTAR, SHINDO!

CLASS 36 TIME TO GET CLOSER

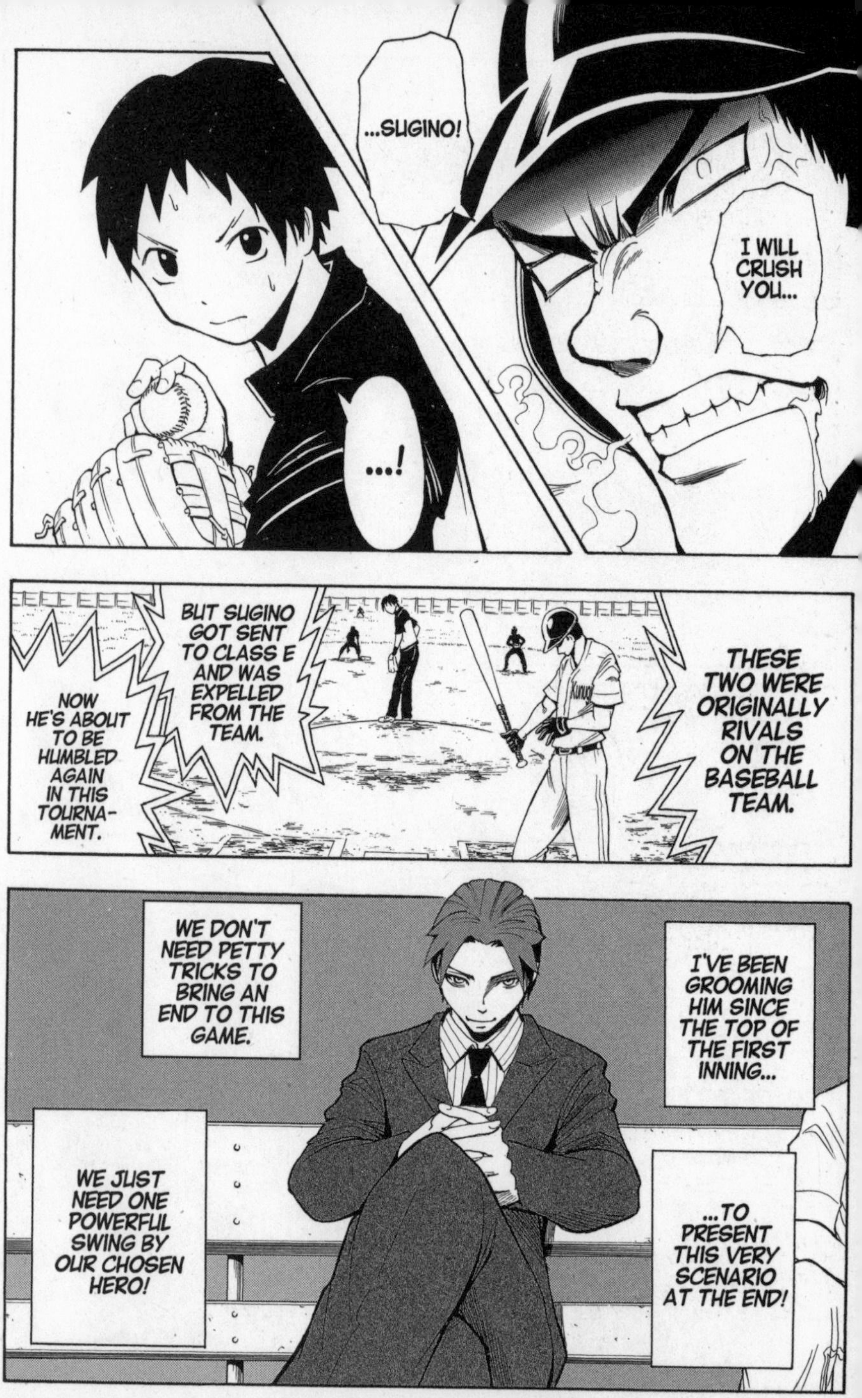
...SUGINO!
I WILL CRUSH YOU...
...!
THESE TWO WERE ORIGINALLY RIVALS ON THE BASEBALL TEAM.
BUT SUGINO GOT SENT TO CLASS E AND WAS EXPELLED FROM THE TEAM.
NOW HE'S ABOUT TO BE HUMBLED AGAIN IN THIS TOURNA-MENT.
I'VE BEEN GROOMING HIM SINCE THE TOP OF THE FIRST INNING...
...TO PRESENT THIS VERY SCENARIO AT THE END!
WE DON'T NEED PETTY TRICKS TO BRING AN END TO THIS GAME.
WE JUST NEED ONE POWERFUL SWING BY OUR CHOSEN HERO!

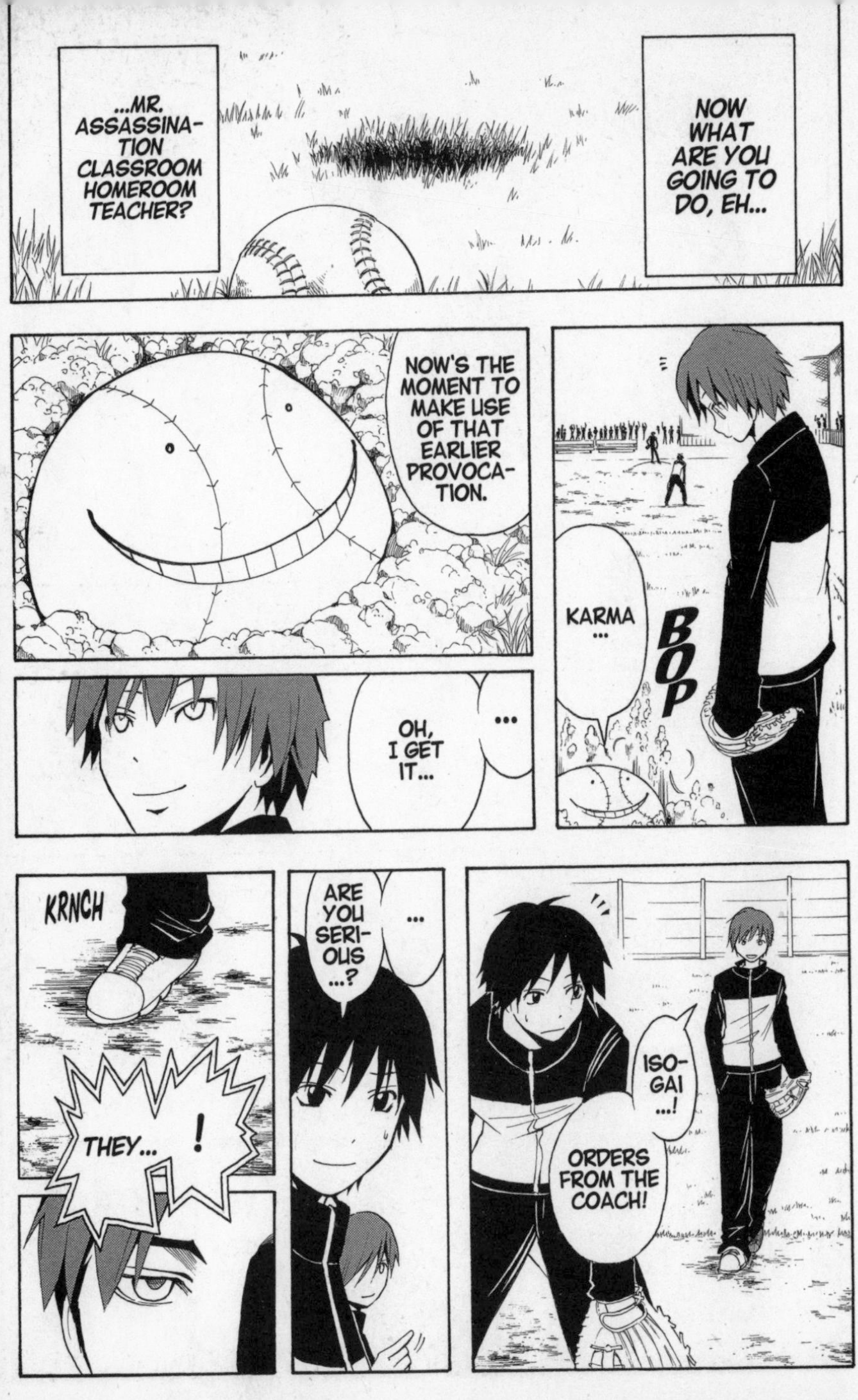
NOW WHAT ARE YOU GOING TO DO, EH...
...MR. ASSASSINATION CLASSROOM HOMEROOM TEACHER?
KARMA ...
BOP
NOW'S THE MOMENT TO MAKE USE OF THAT EARLIER PROVOCATION.
...
OH, I GET IT...
ISOGAI ...!
ORDERS FROM THE COACH!
...
ARE YOU SERIOUS ...?
KRNCH
THEY... !

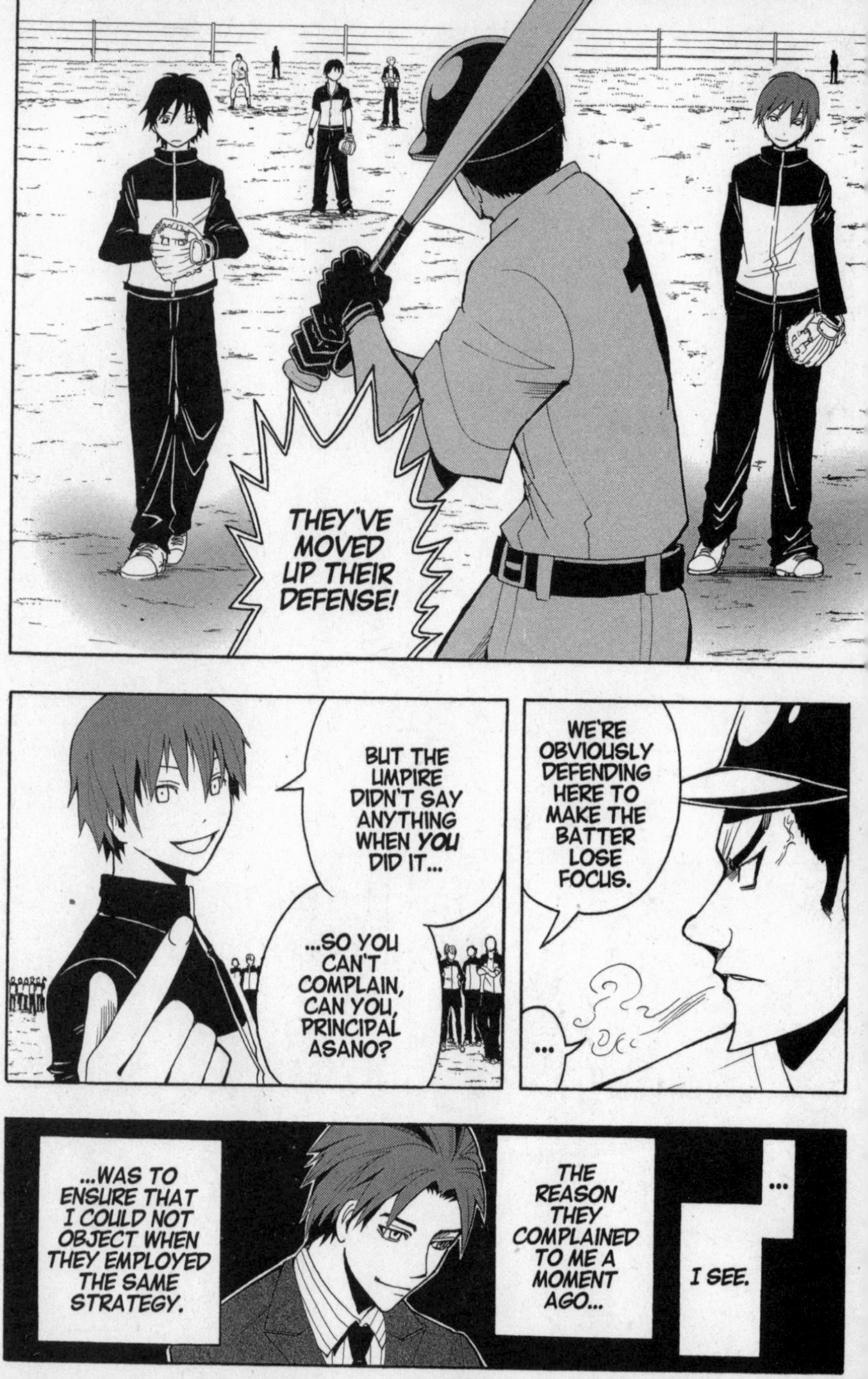
THEY'VE MOVED UP THEIR DEFENSE!
WE'RE OBVIOUSLY DEFENDING HERE TO MAKE THE BATTER LOSE FOCUS.
...
BUT THE UMPIRE DIDN'T SAY ANYTHING WHEN *YOU* DID IT...
...SO YOU CAN'T COMPLAIN, CAN YOU, PRINCIPAL ASANO?
...
I SEE.
THE REASON THEY COMPLAINED TO ME A MOMENT AGO...
...WAS TO ENSURE THAT I COULD NOT OBJECT WHEN THEY EMPLOYED THE SAME STRATEGY.

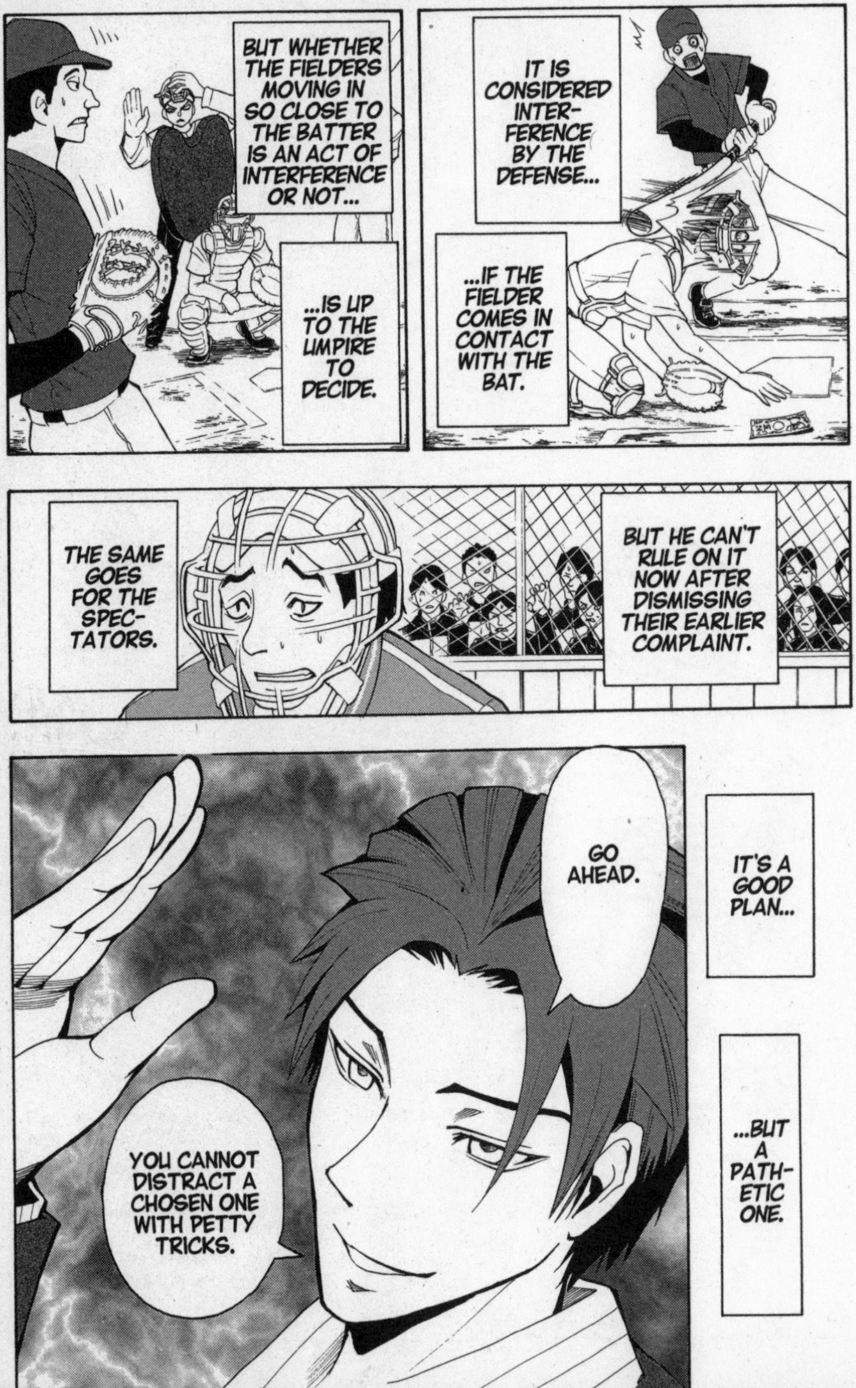
IT IS CONSIDERED INTERFERENCE BY THE DEFENSE...
...IF THE FIELDER COMES IN CONTACT WITH THE BAT.
BUT WHETHER THE FIELDERS MOVING IN SO CLOSE TO THE BATTER IS AN ACT OF INTERFERENCE OR NOT...
...IS UP TO THE UMPIRE TO DECIDE.
BUT HE CAN'T RULE ON IT NOW AFTER DISMISSING THEIR EARLIER COMPLAINT.
THE SAME GOES FOR THE SPECTATORS.
IT'S A GOOD PLAN...
...BUT A PATHETIC ONE.
GO AHEAD.
YOU CANNOT DISTRACT A CHOSEN ONE WITH PETTY TRICKS.

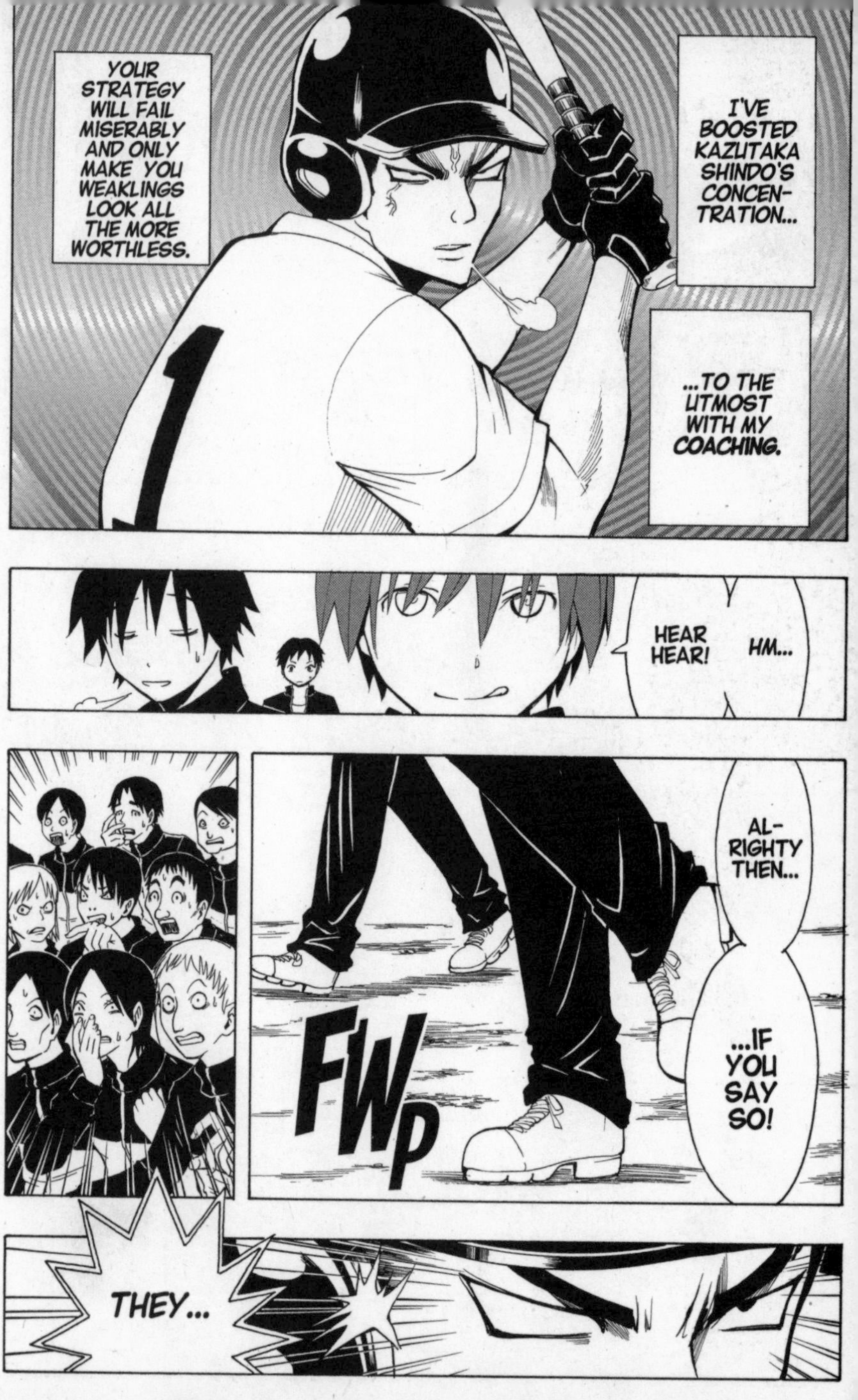
I'VE BOOSTED KAZUTAKA SHINDO'S CONCENTRATION...
...TO THE UTMOST WITH MY COACHING.
YOUR STRATEGY WILL FAIL MISERABLY AND ONLY MAKE YOU WEAKLINGS LOOK ALL THE MORE WORTHLESS.
HM...
HEAR HEAR!
ALRIGHTY THEN...
...IF YOU SAY SO!
FWP
THEY...

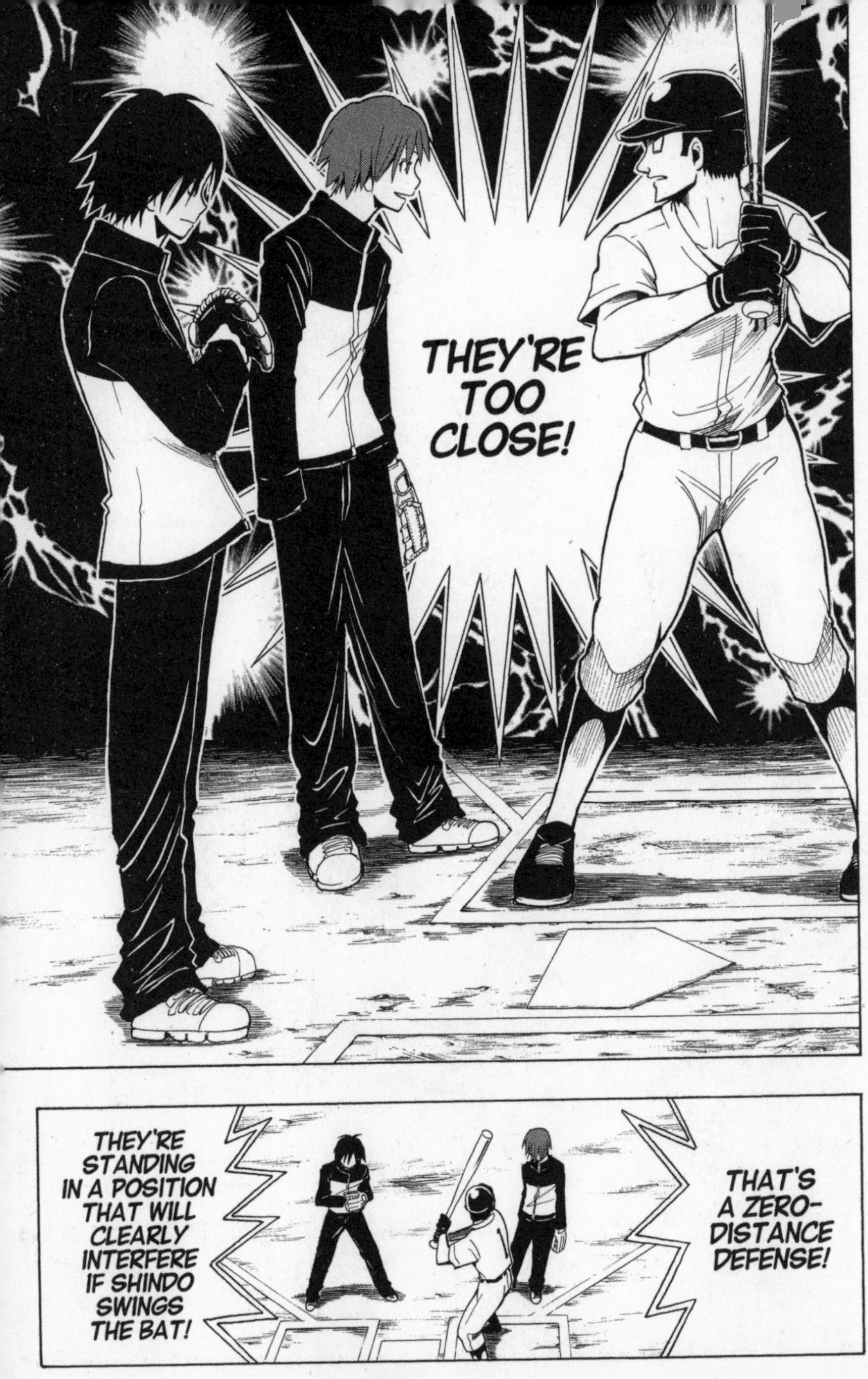
THEY'RE TOO CLOSE!
THAT'S A ZERO-DISTANCE DEFENSE!
THEY'RE STANDING IN A POSITION THAT WILL CLEARLY INTERFERE IF SHINDO SWINGS THE BAT!

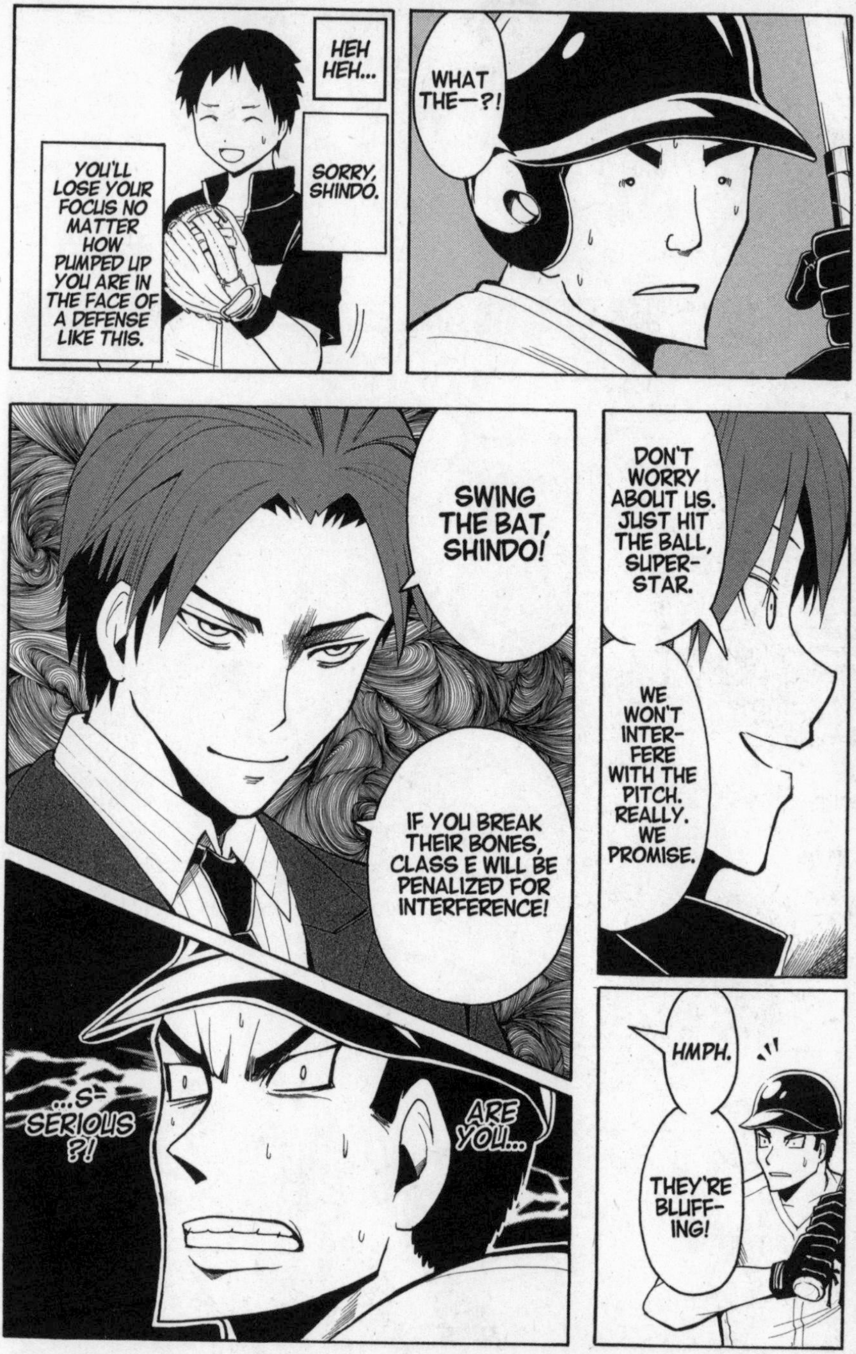
WHAT THE—?!
HEH HEH...
SORRY, SHINDO.
YOU'LL LOSE YOUR FOCUS NO MATTER HOW PUMPED UP YOU ARE IN THE FACE OF A DEFENSE LIKE THIS.
DON'T WORRY ABOUT US. JUST HIT THE BALL, SUPER-STAR.
WE WON'T INTER-FERE WITH THE PITCH. REALLY. WE PROMISE.
HMPH.
THEY'RE BLUFF-ING!
SWING THE BAT, SHINDO!
IF YOU BREAK THEIR BONES, CLASS E WILL BE PENALIZED FOR INTERFERENCE!
ARE YOU...
...S-SERIOUS?!

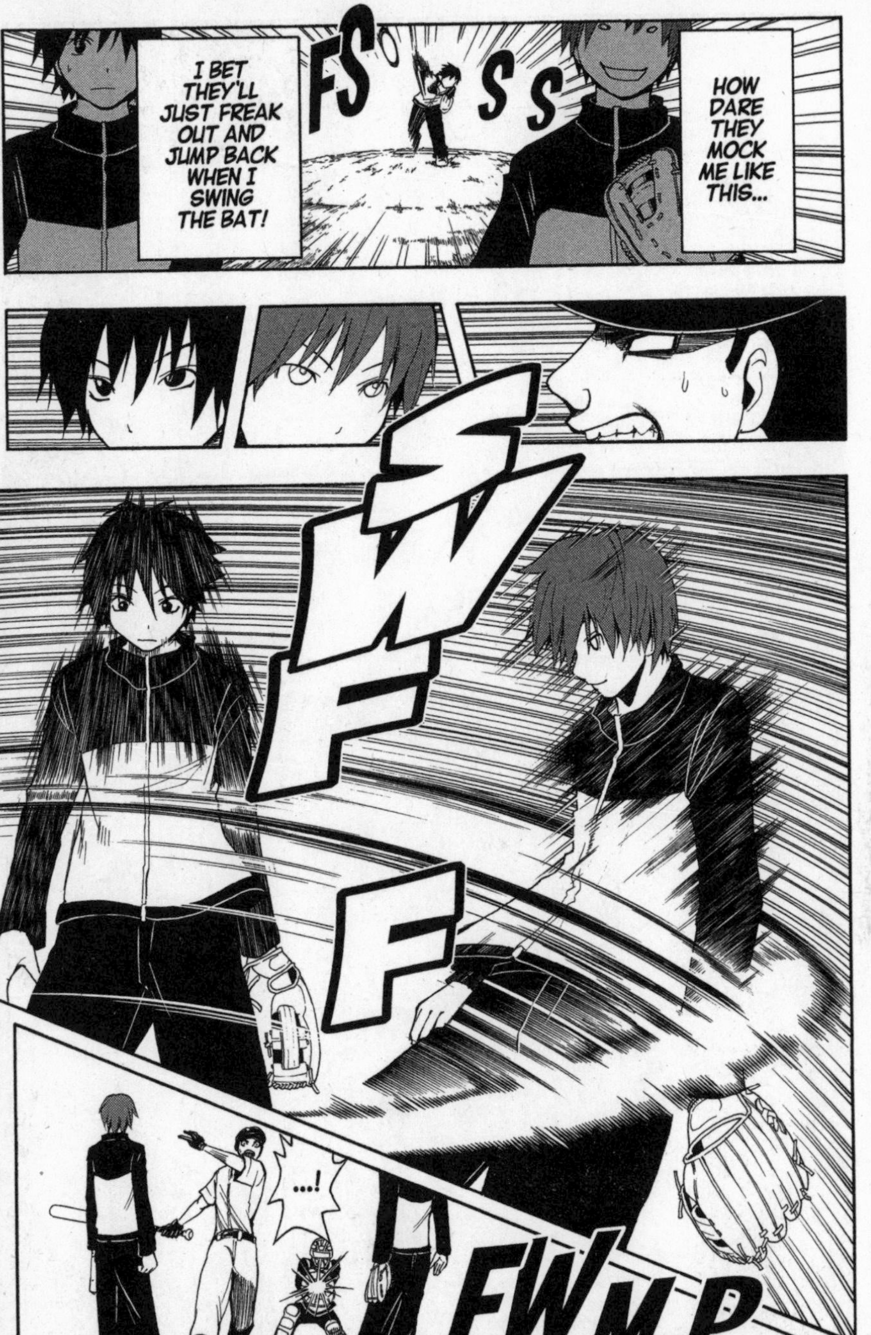
HOW DARE THEY MOCK ME LIKE THIS...
FS S S
I BET THEY'LL JUST FREAK OUT AND JUMP BACK WHEN I SWING THE BAT!
SWFF
...!
FWMP

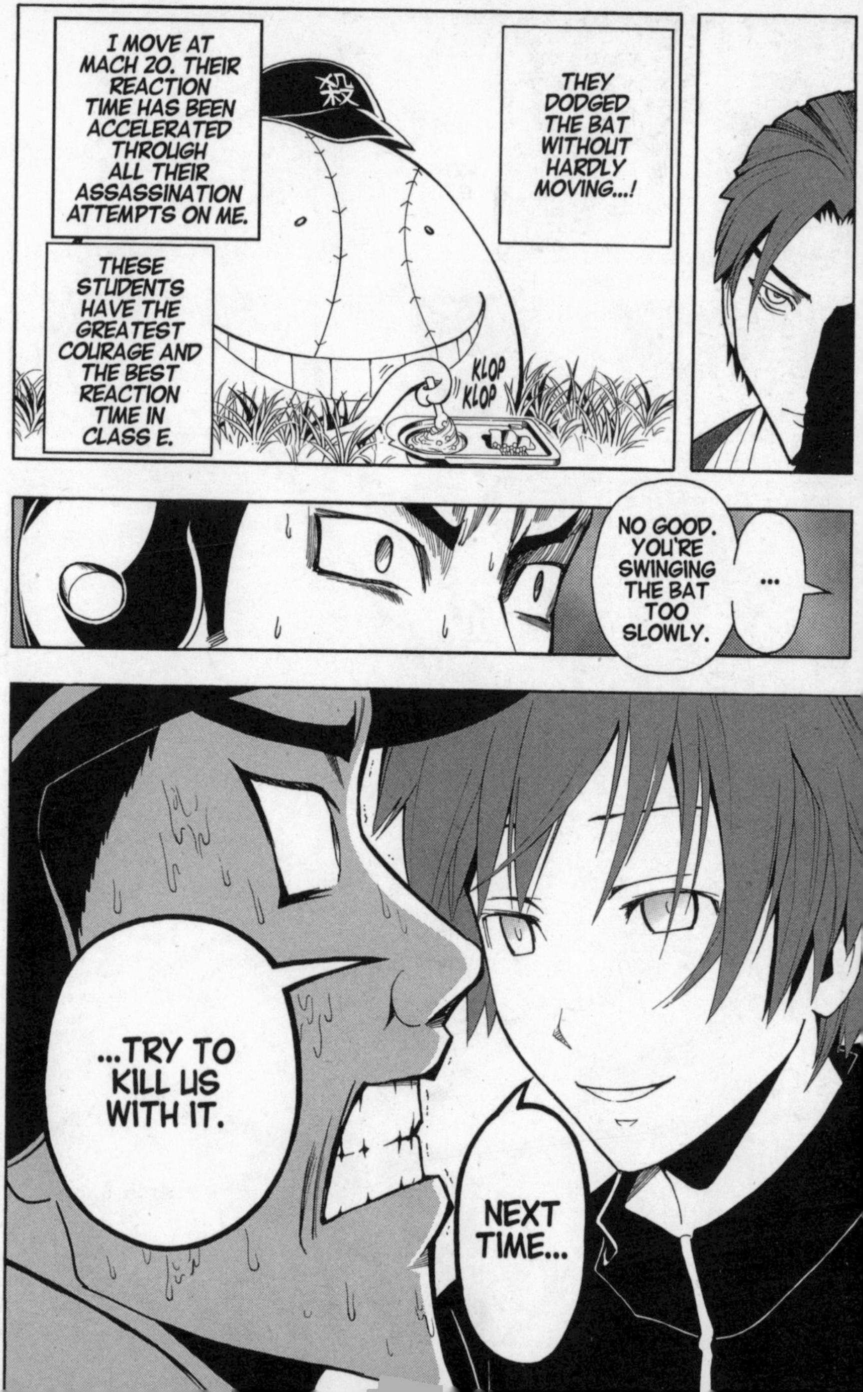
THEY DODGED THE BAT WITHOUT HARDLY MOVING...!
I MOVE AT MACH 20. THEIR REACTION TIME HAS BEEN ACCELERATED THROUGH ALL THEIR ASSASSINATION ATTEMPTS ON ME.
THESE STUDENTS HAVE THE GREATEST COURAGE AND THE BEST REACTION TIME IN CLASS E.
KLOP KLOP
...
NO GOOD. YOU'RE SWINGING THE BAT TOO SLOWLY.
NEXT TIME...
...TRY TO KILL US WITH IT.

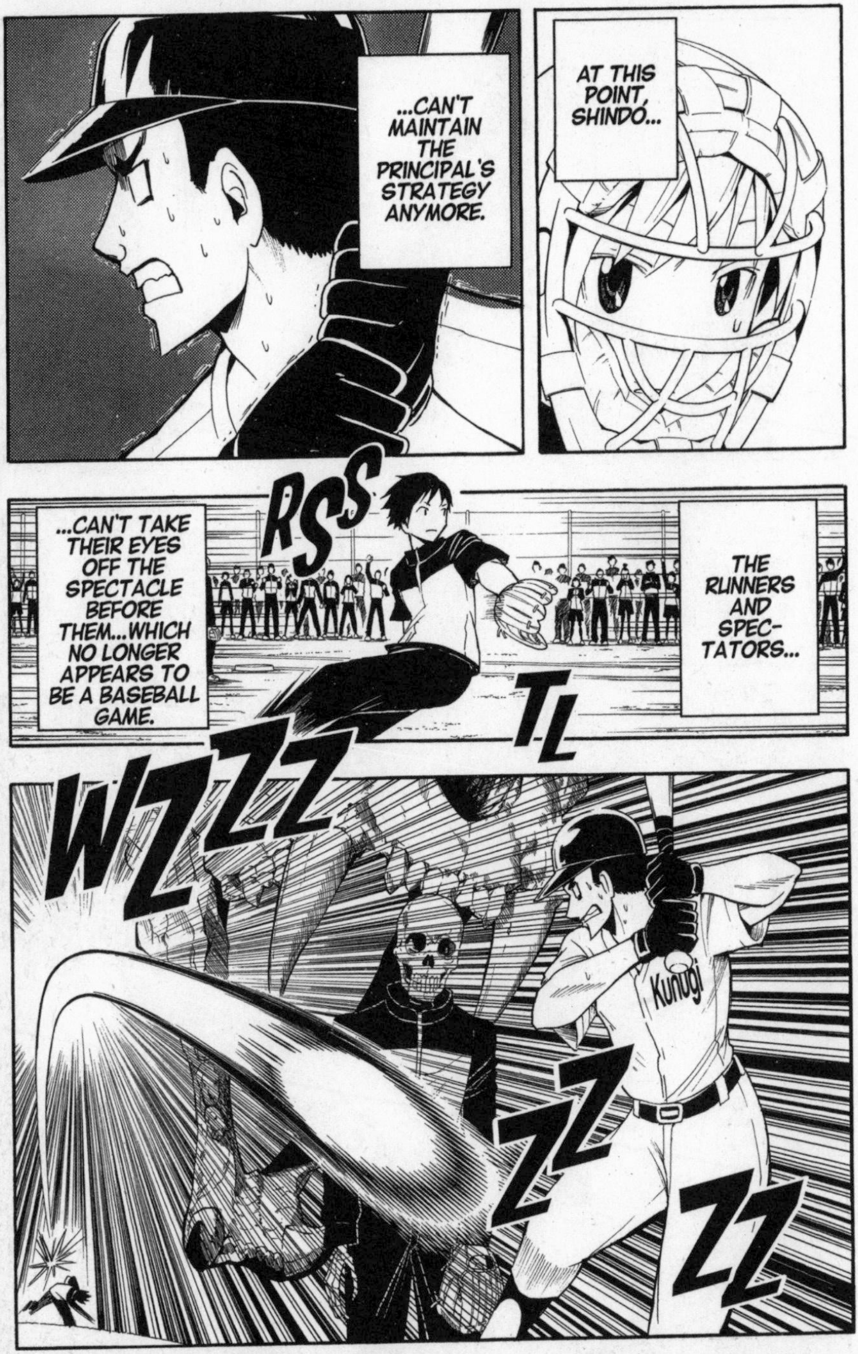
AT THIS POINT, SHINDŌ...
...CAN'T MAINTAIN THE PRINCIPAL'S STRATEGY ANYMORE.
THE RUNNERS AND SPEC-TATORS...
RSS
...CAN'T TAKE THEIR EYES OFF THE SPECTACLE BEFORE THEM...WHICH NO LONGER APPEARS TO BE A BASEBALL GAME.
TL
WZZZ
Kunugi
ZZ
ZZ

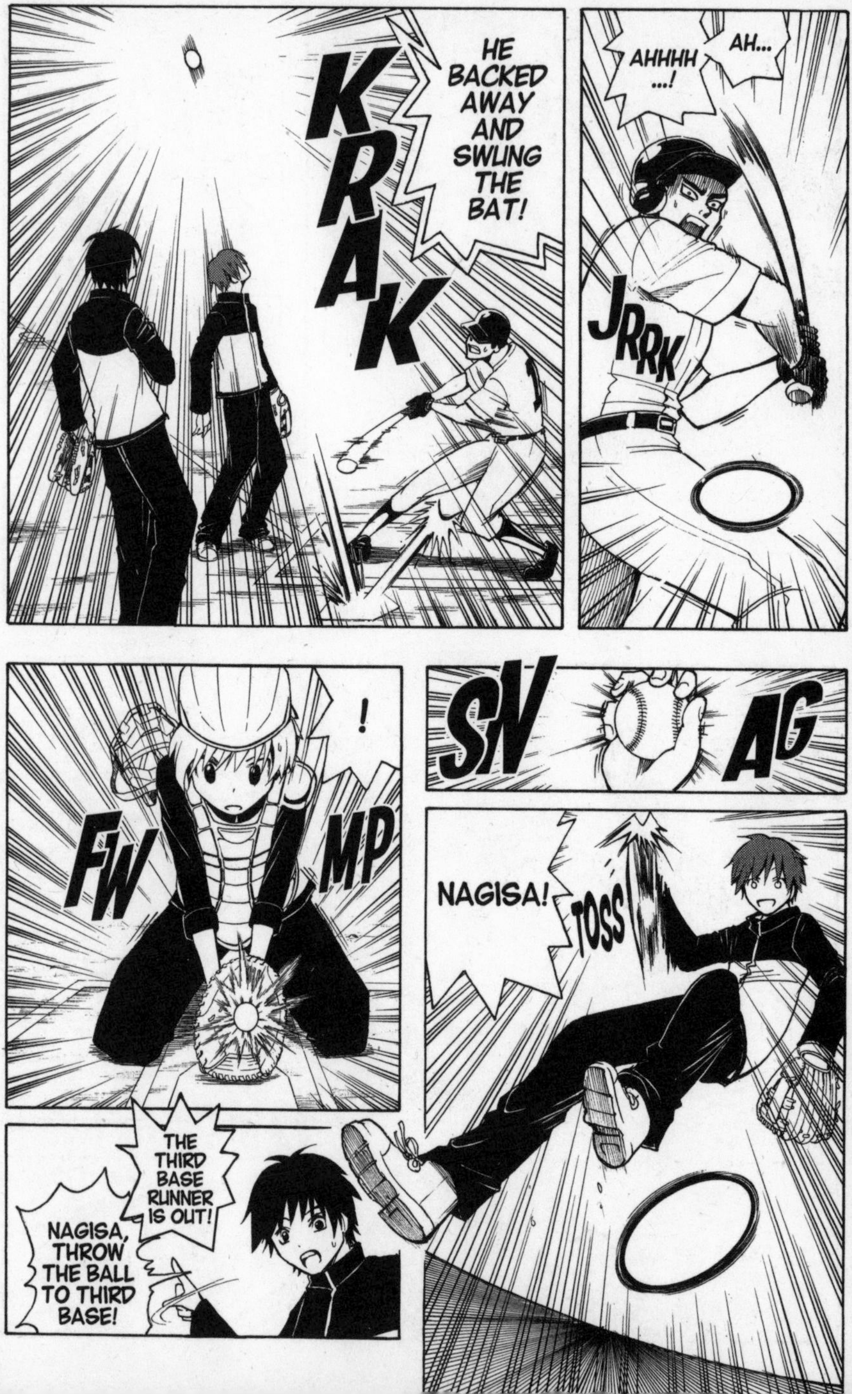
AH...
AHHHH...!
JRRK
HE BACKED AWAY AND SWUNG THE BAT!
KRAK
SNAG
NAGISA!
TOSS
!
FWMP
THE THIRD BASE RUNNER IS OUT!
NAGISA, THROW THE BALL TO THIRD BASE!

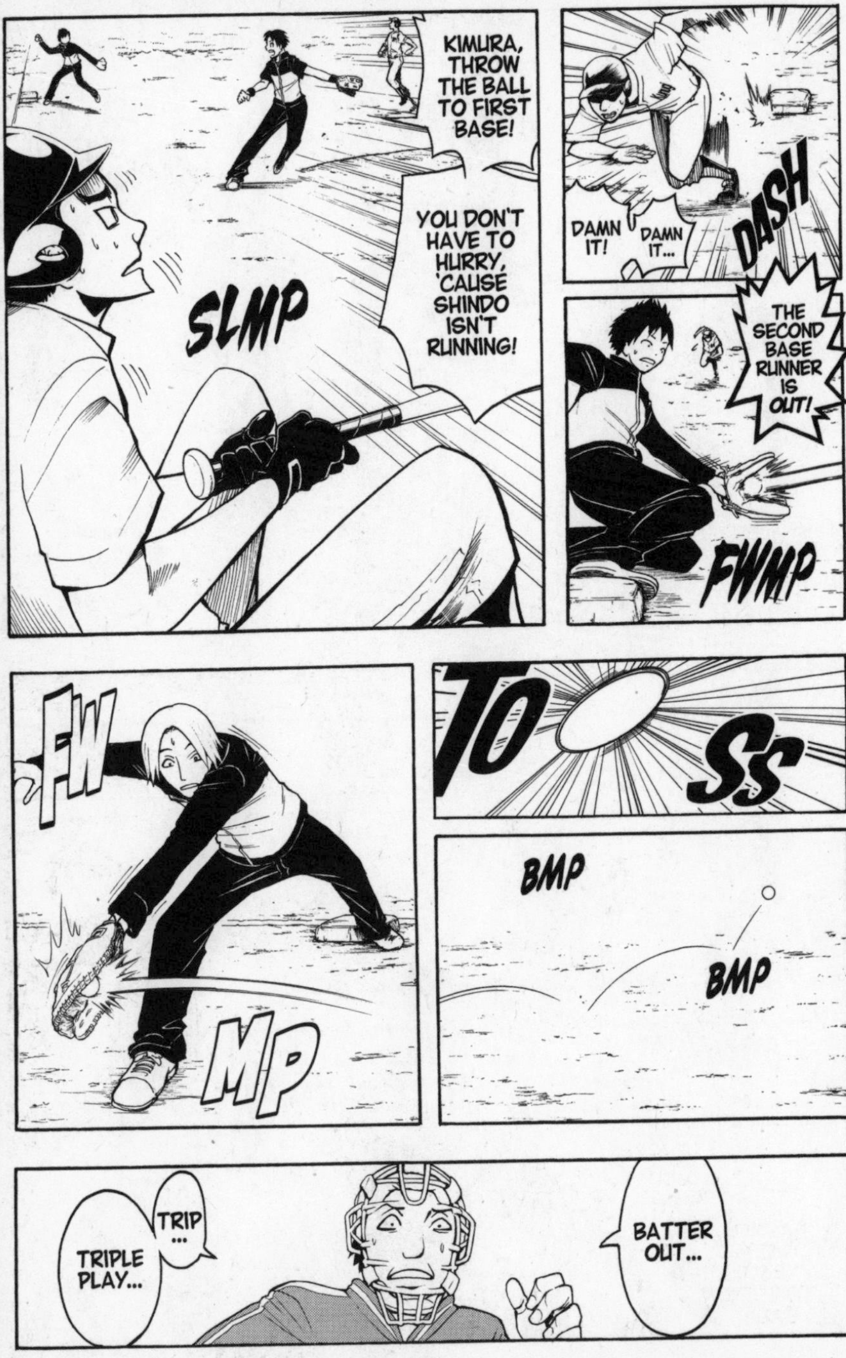
DAMN IT...
DAMN IT!
DASH
THE SECOND BASE RUNNER IS OUT!
FWMP
KIMURA, THROW THE BALL TO FIRST BASE!
YOU DON'T HAVE TO HURRY, 'CAUSE SHINDO ISN'T RUNNING!
SLMP
TOSS
BMP
BMP
FW
MP
BATTER OUT...
TRIP...
TRIPLE PLAY...

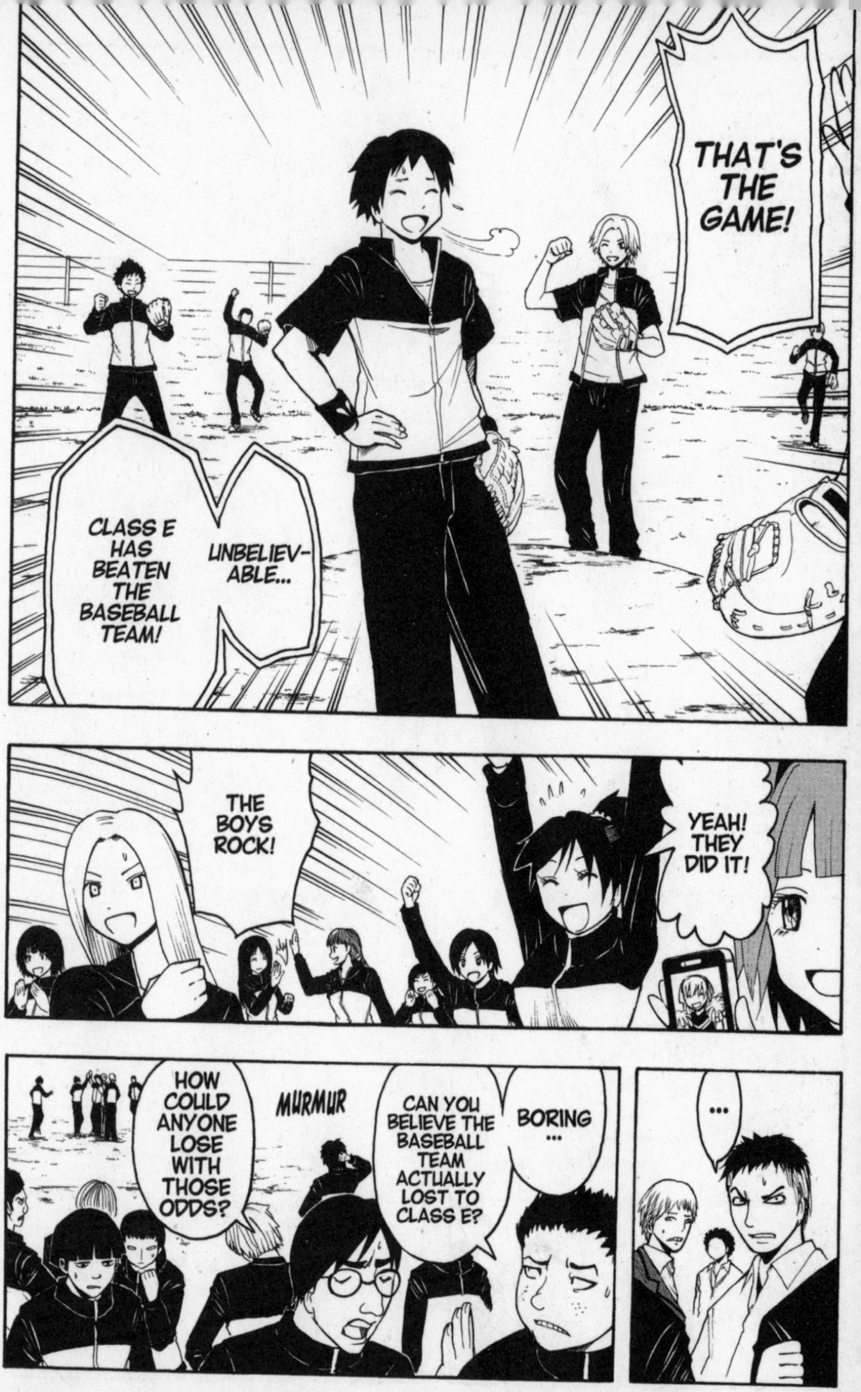
THAT'S THE GAME!
UNBELIEV-ABLE...
CLASS E HAS BEATEN THE BASEBALL TEAM!
YEAH! THEY DID IT!
THE BOYS ROCK!
...
BORING ...
CAN YOU BELIEVE THE BASEBALL TEAM ACTUALLY LOST TO CLASS E?
MURMUR
HOW COULD ANYONE LOSE WITH THOSE ODDS?

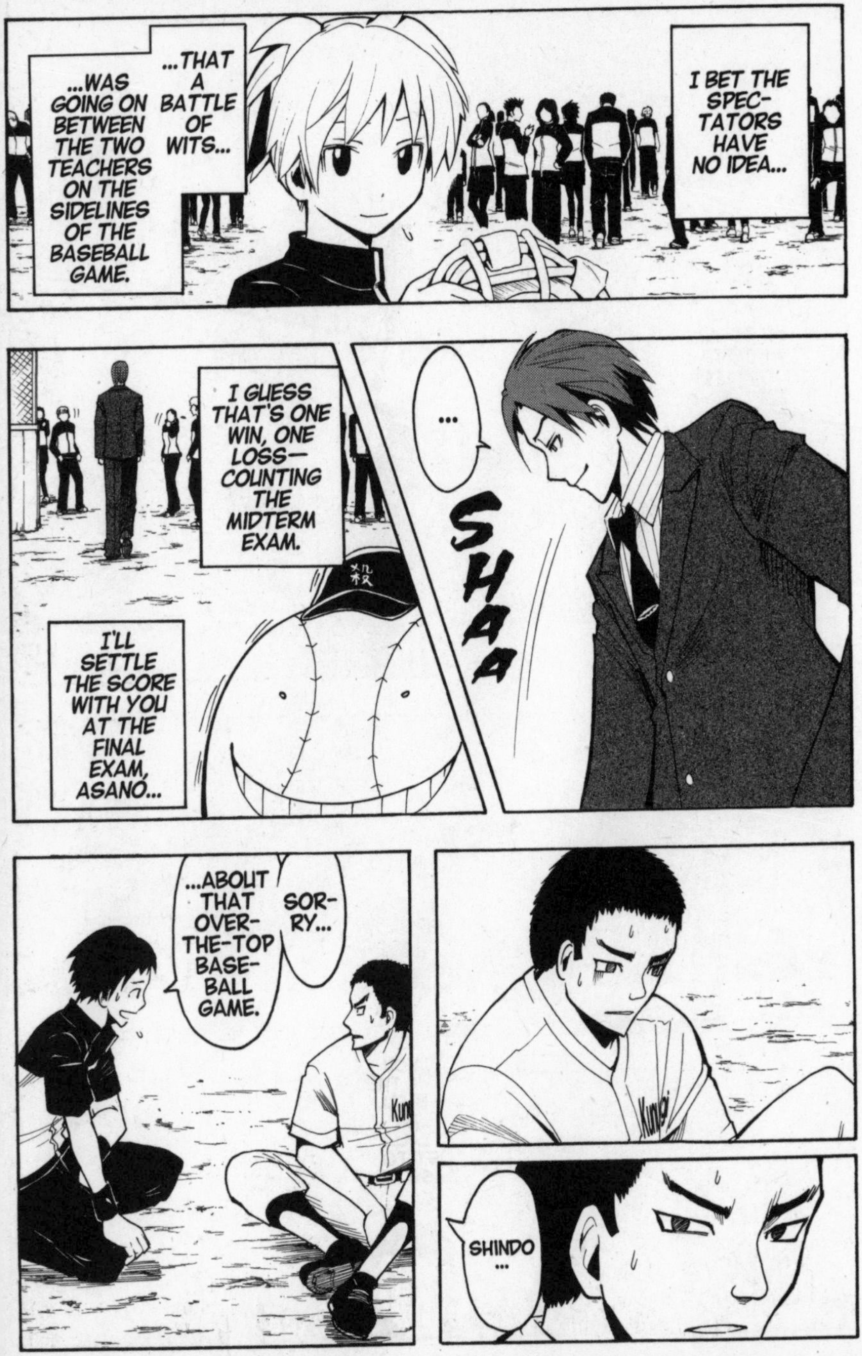
I BET THE SPEC-TATORS HAVE NO IDEA...
...THAT A BATTLE OF WITS...
...WAS GOING ON BETWEEN THE TWO TEACHERS ON THE SIDELINES OF THE BASEBALL GAME.
...
SHAA
I GUESS THAT'S ONE WIN, ONE LOSS—COUNTING THE MIDTERM EXAM.
I'LL SETTLE THE SCORE WITH YOU AT THE FINAL EXAM, ASANO...
SHINDO ...
SOR-RY...
...ABOUT THAT OVER-THE-TOP BASE-BALL GAME.

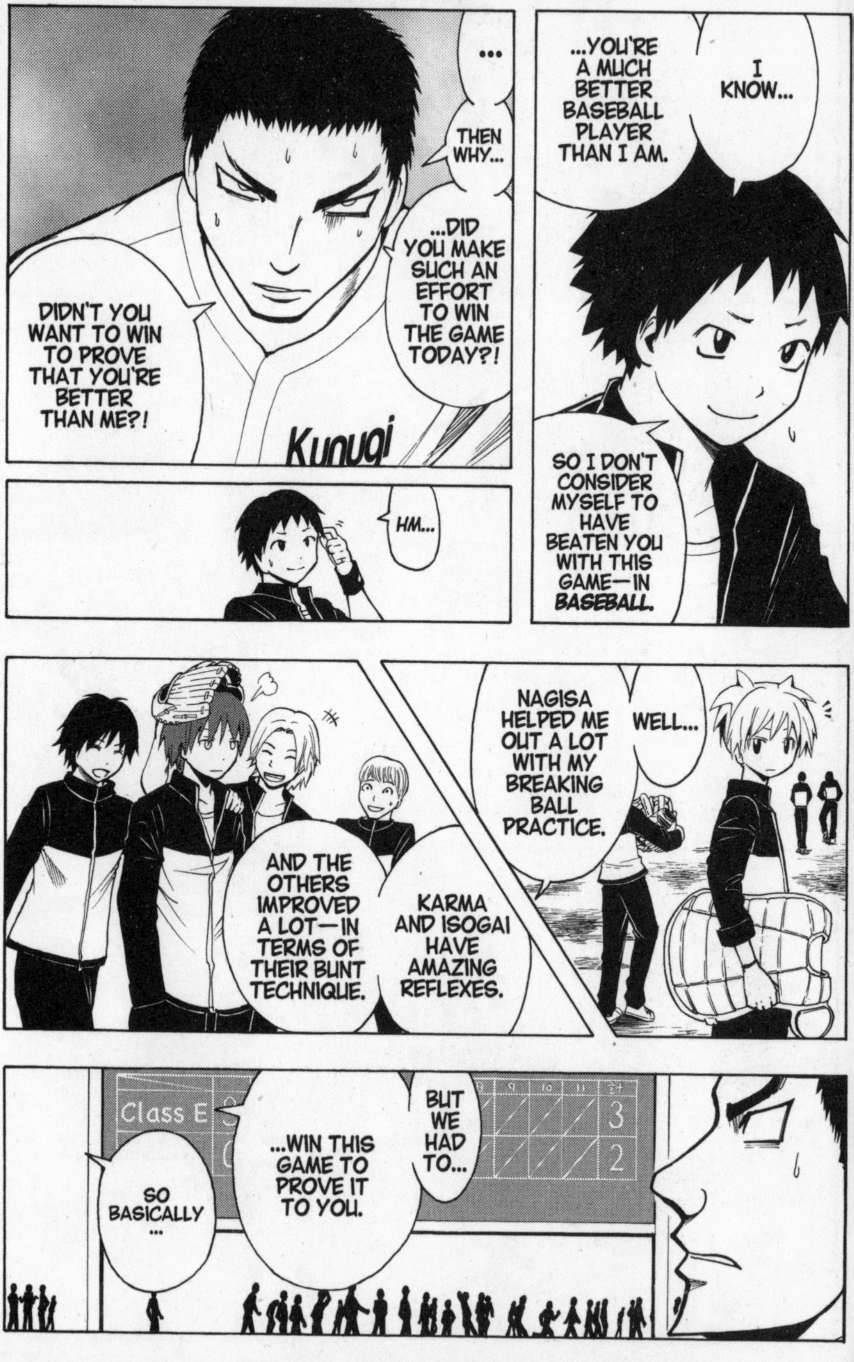
I KNOW...
...YOU'RE A MUCH BETTER BASEBALL PLAYER THAN I AM.
SO I DON'T CONSIDER MYSELF TO HAVE BEATEN YOU WITH THIS GAME—IN BASEBALL.
...
THEN WHY...
...DID YOU MAKE SUCH AN EFFORT TO WIN THE GAME TODAY?!
DIDN'T YOU WANT TO WIN TO PROVE THAT YOU'RE BETTER THAN ME?!
Kunugi
HM...
WELL...
NAGISA HELPED ME OUT A LOT WITH MY BREAKING BALL PRACTICE.
KARMA AND ISOGAI HAVE AMAZING REFLEXES.
AND THE OTHERS IMPROVED A LOT—IN TERMS OF THEIR BUNT TECHNIQUE.
Class E
BUT WE HAD TO...
...WIN THIS GAME TO PROVE IT TO YOU.
SO BASICALLY ...

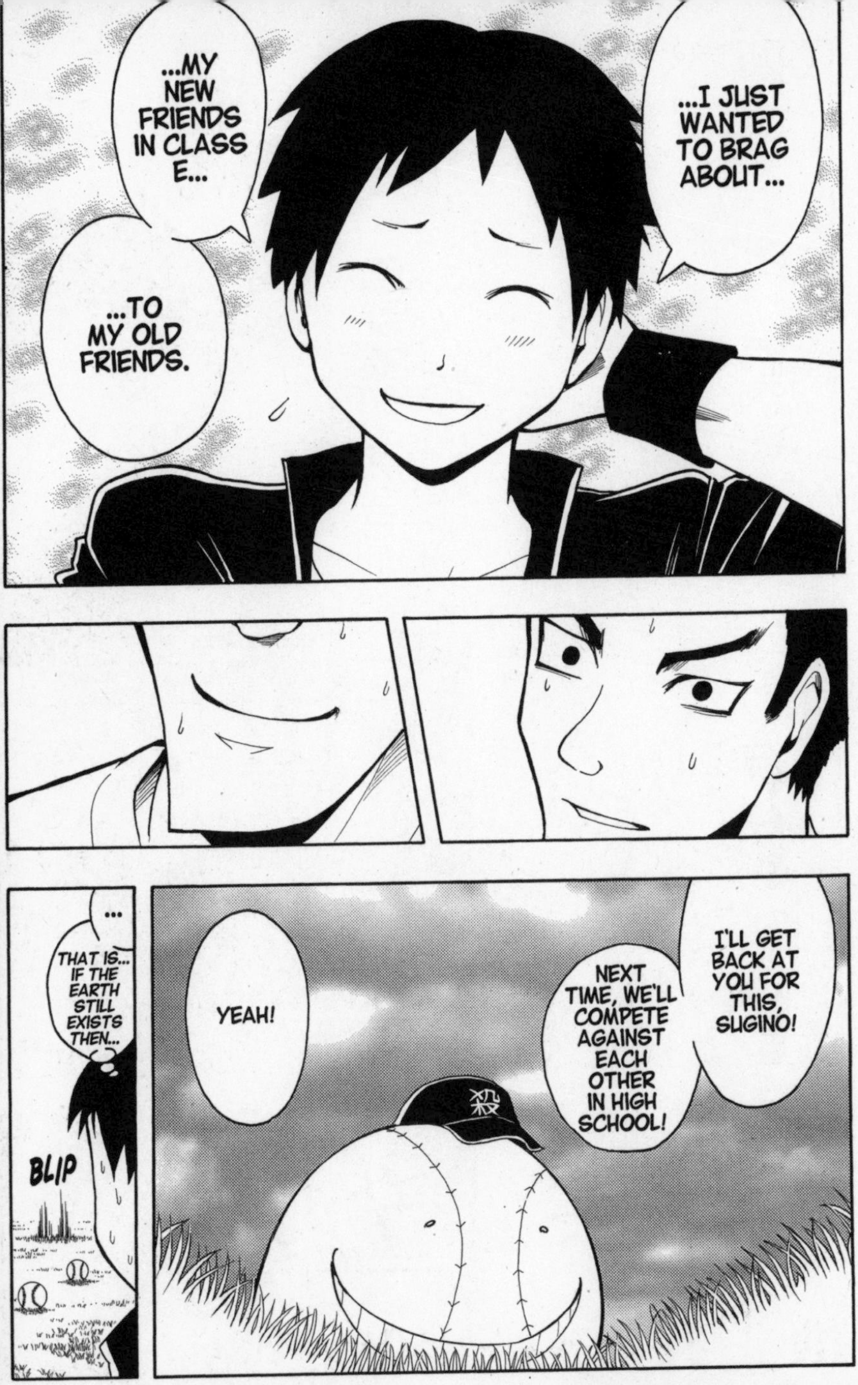
...I JUST WANTED TO BRAG ABOUT...
...MY NEW FRIENDS IN CLASS E...
...TO MY OLD FRIENDS.
I'LL GET BACK AT YOU FOR THIS, SUGINO!
NEXT TIME, WE'LL COMPETE AGAINST EACH OTHER IN HIGH SCHOOL!
YEAH!
...
THAT IS... IF THE EARTH STILL EXISTS THEN...
BLIP

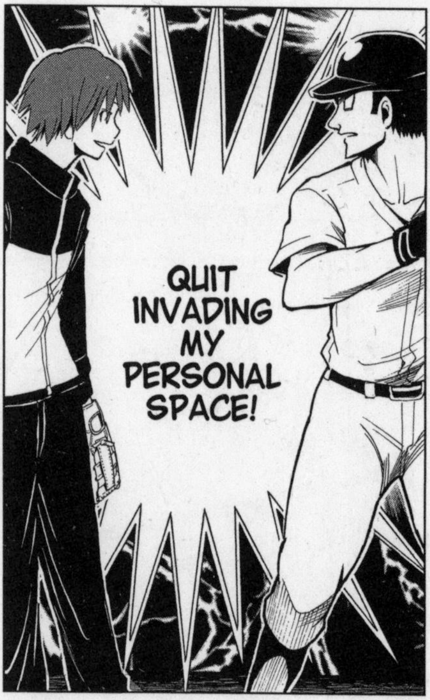
QUIT INVADING MY PERSONAL SPACE!

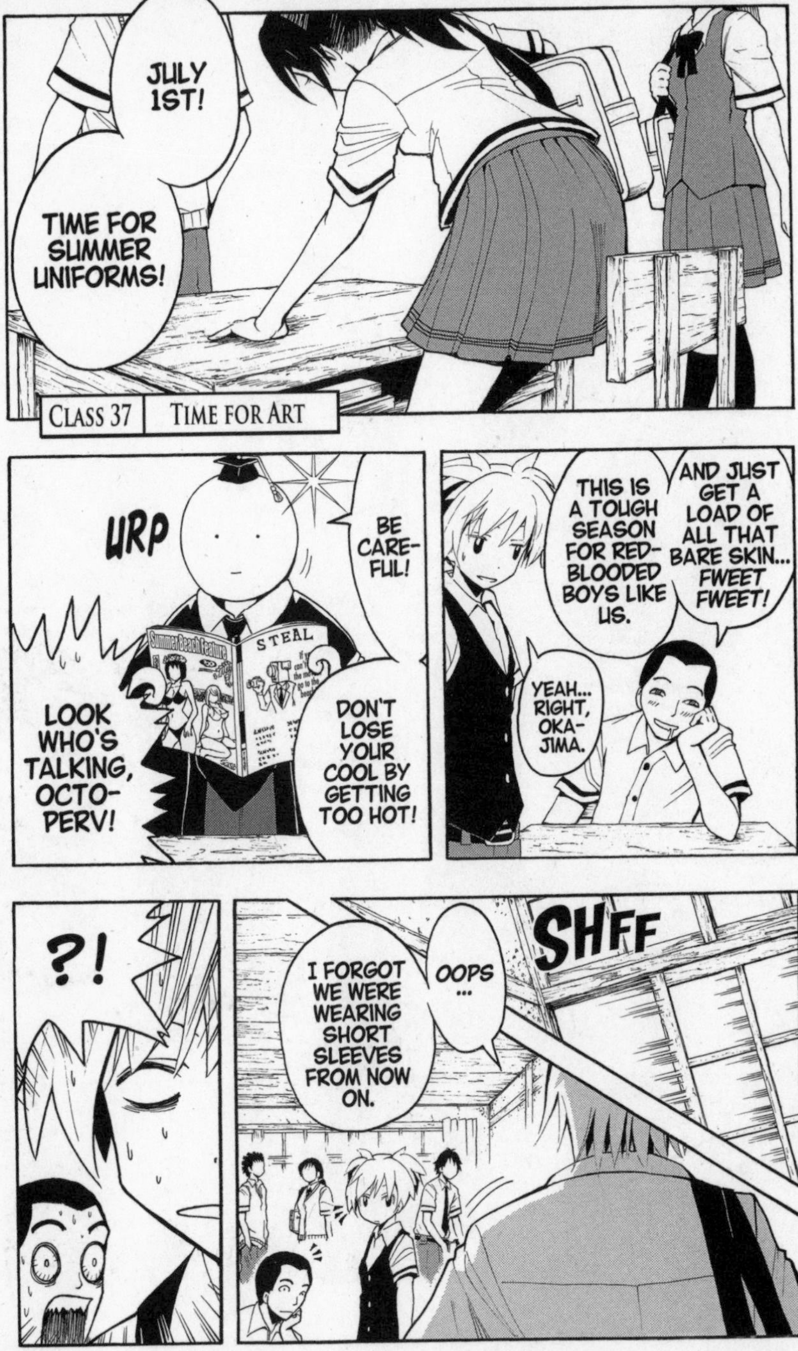
JULY 1ST!
TIME FOR SUMMER UNIFORMS!
CLASS 37 TIME FOR ART
THIS IS A TOUGH SEASON FOR RED-BLOODED BOYS LIKE US.
AND JUST GET A LOAD OF ALL THAT BARE SKIN... FWEET FWEET!
YEAH... RIGHT, OKAJIMA.
BE CAREFUL!
DON'T LOSE YOUR COOL BY GETTING TOO HOT!
Summer Beach Feature
STEAL
URP
LOOK WHO'S TALKING, OCTO-PERV!
SHFF
OOPS...
I FORGOT WE WERE WEARING SHORT SLEEVES FROM NOW ON.
?!

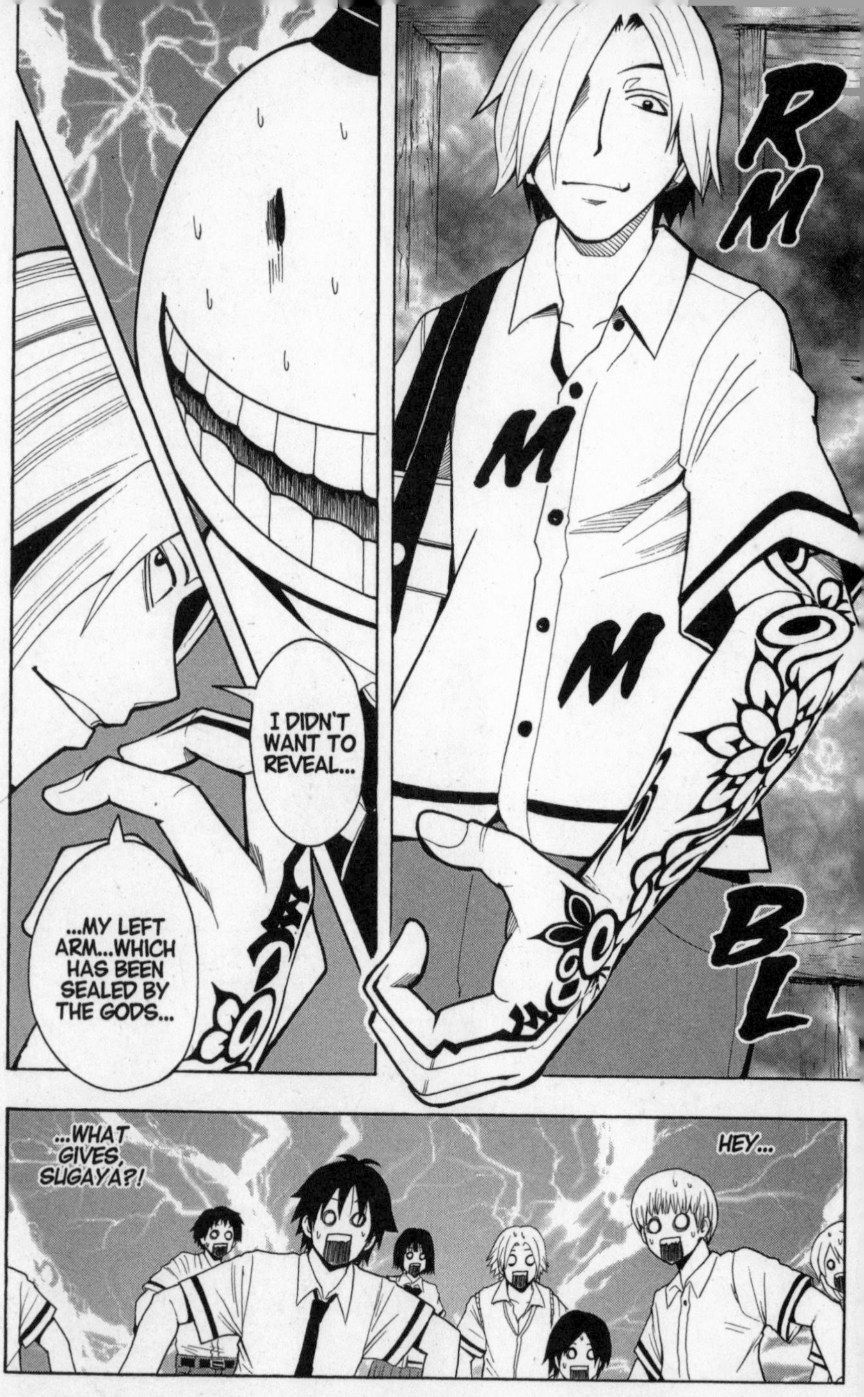
RMMMBL
I DIDN'T WANT TO REVEAL...
...MY LEFT ARM...WHICH HAS BEEN SEALED BY THE GODS...
HEY...
...WHAT GIVES, SUGAYA?!

CLASS 37 TIME FOR ART

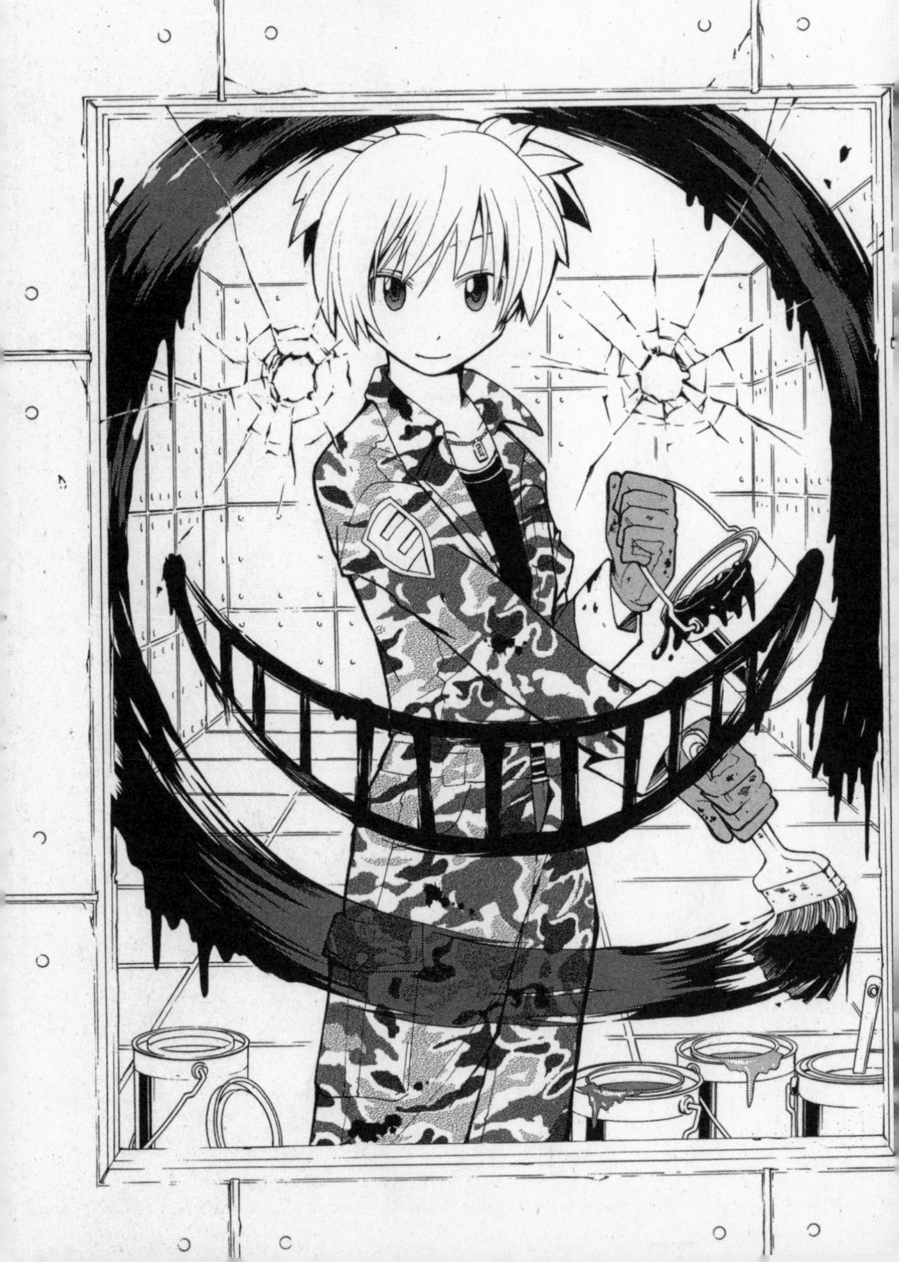

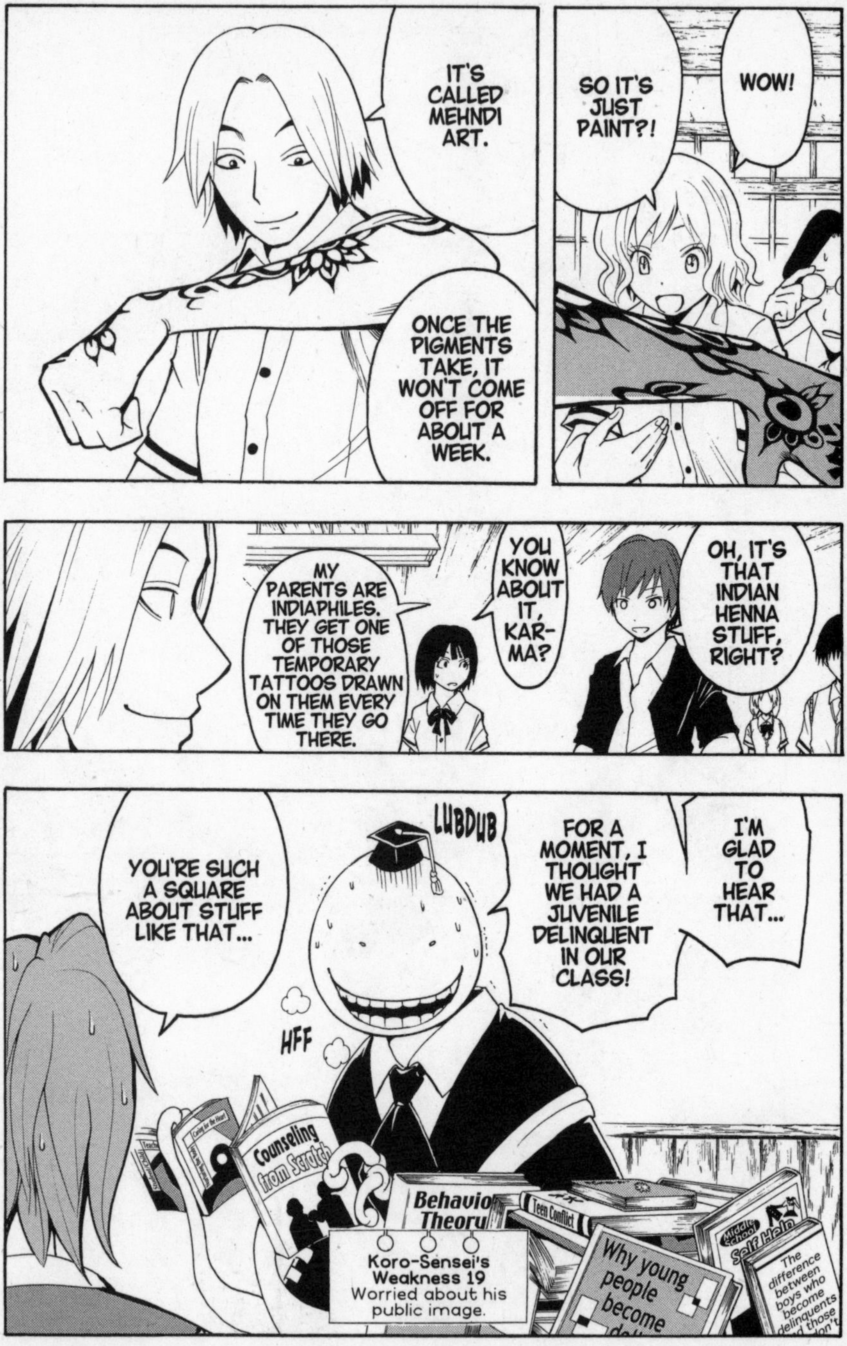
WOW!
SO IT'S JUST PAINT?!
IT'S CALLED MEHNDI ART.
ONCE THE PIGMENTS TAKE, IT WON'T COME OFF FOR ABOUT A WEEK.
OH, IT'S THAT INDIAN HENNA STUFF, RIGHT?
YOU KNOW ABOUT IT, KARMA?
MY PARENTS ARE INDIAPHILES. THEY GET ONE OF THOSE TEMPORARY TATTOOS DRAWN ON THEM EVERY TIME THEY GO THERE.
I'M GLAD TO HEAR THAT...
FOR A MOMENT, I THOUGHT WE HAD A JUVENILE DELINQUENT IN OUR CLASS!
LUBDUB
YOU'RE SUCH A SQUARE ABOUT STUFF LIKE THAT...
HFF
Counseling from Scratch
Teen Conflict
Middle School Self Help
Koro-Sensei's Weakness 19
Worried about his public image.

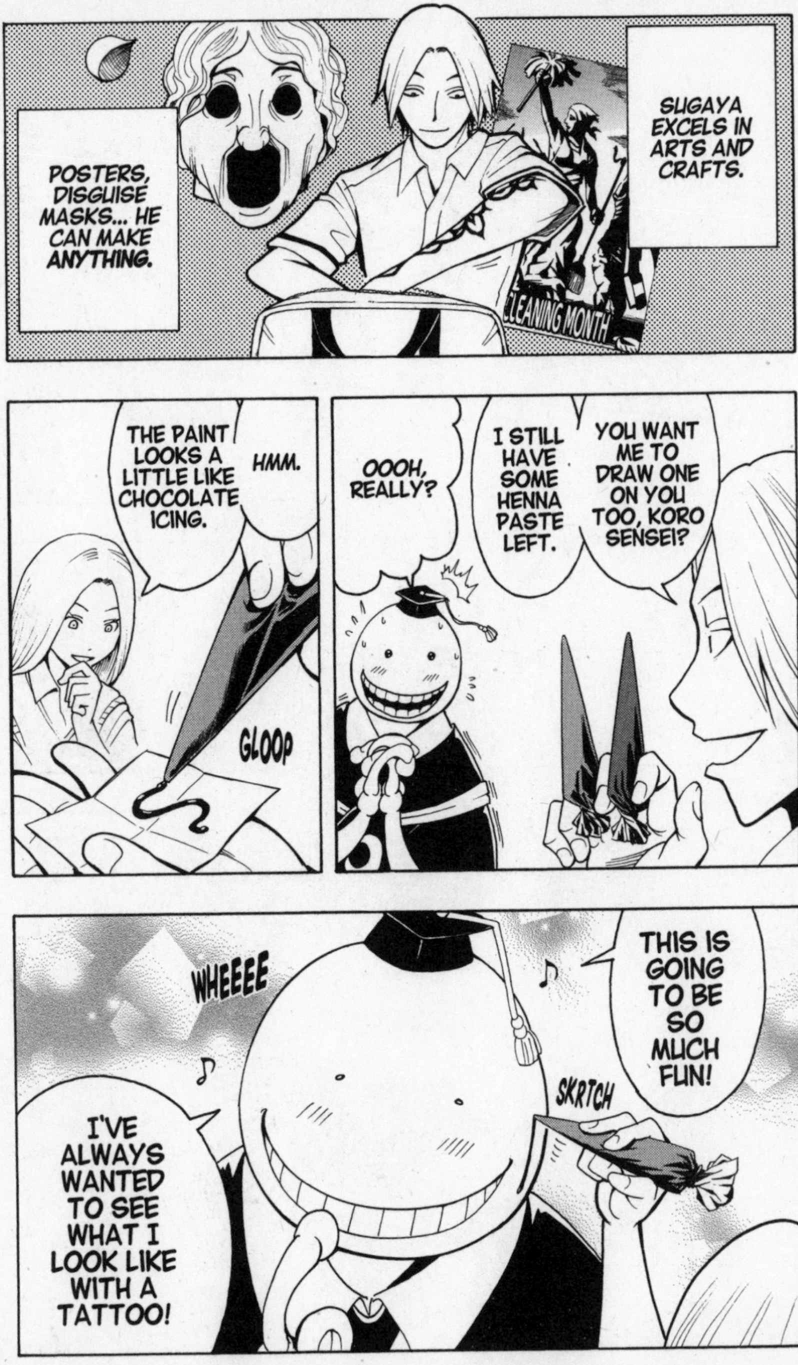
SUGAYA EXCELS IN ARTS AND CRAFTS.
CLEANING MONTH
POSTERS, DISGUISE MASKS... HE CAN MAKE ANYTHING.
YOU WANT ME TO DRAW ONE ON YOU TOO, KORO SENSEI?
I STILL HAVE SOME HENNA PASTE LEFT.
OOOH, REALLY?
HMM.
THE PAINT LOOKS A LITTLE LIKE CHOCOLATE ICING.
GLOOP
THIS IS GOING TO BE SO MUCH FUN!
WHEEEE
SKRTCH
I'VE ALWAYS WANTED TO SEE WHAT I LOOK LIKE WITH A TATTOO!

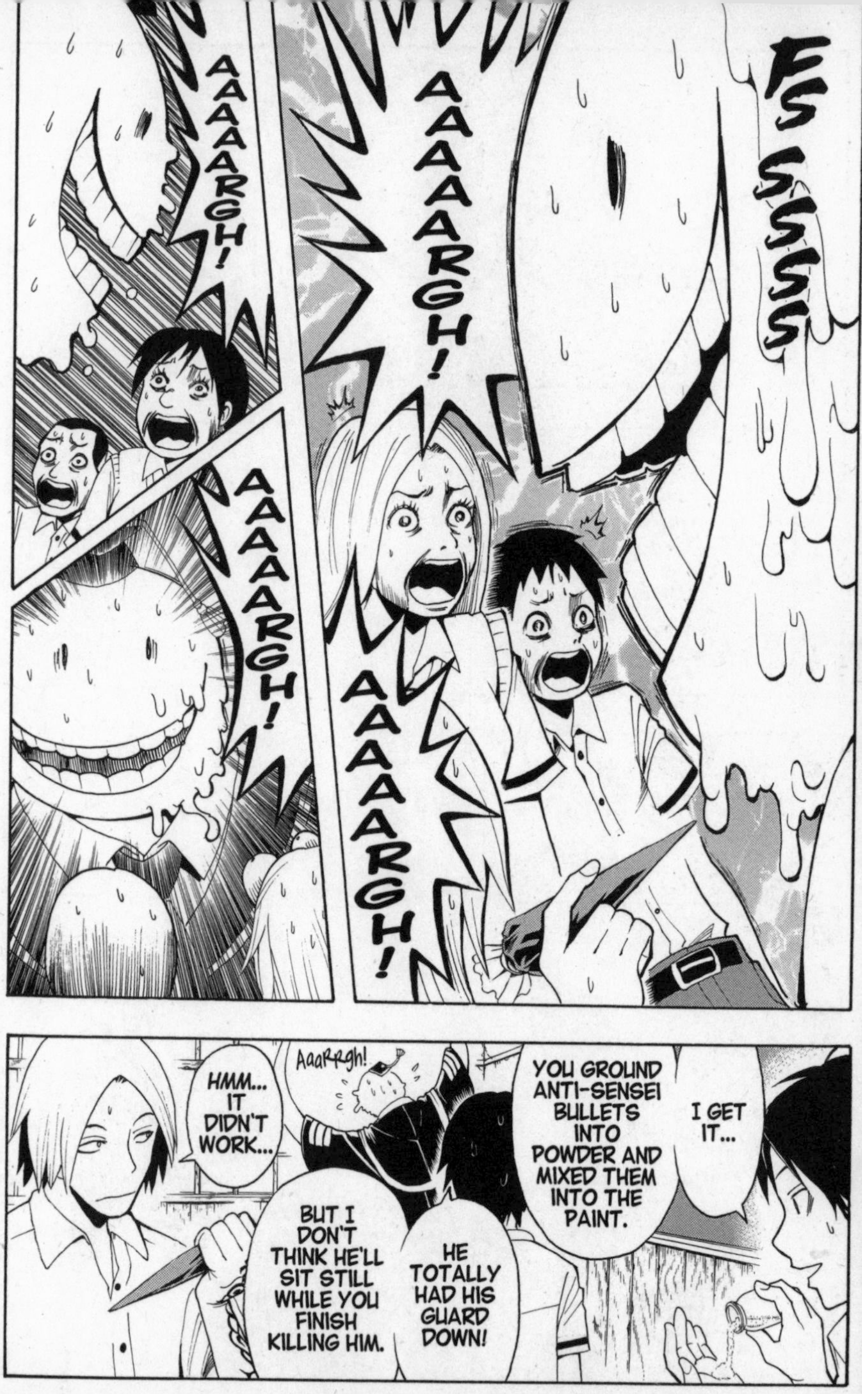
FSSSSSS
AAAAARGH!
AAAAAARGH!
AAAAARGH!
AAAAAARGH!
I GET IT...
YOU GROUND ANTI-SENSEI BULLETS INTO POWDER AND MIXED THEM INTO THE PAINT.
HE TOTALLY HAD HIS GUARD DOWN!
Aaarrgh!
HMM... IT DIDN'T WORK...
BUT I DON'T THINK HE'LL SIT STILL WHILE YOU FINISH KILLING HIM.

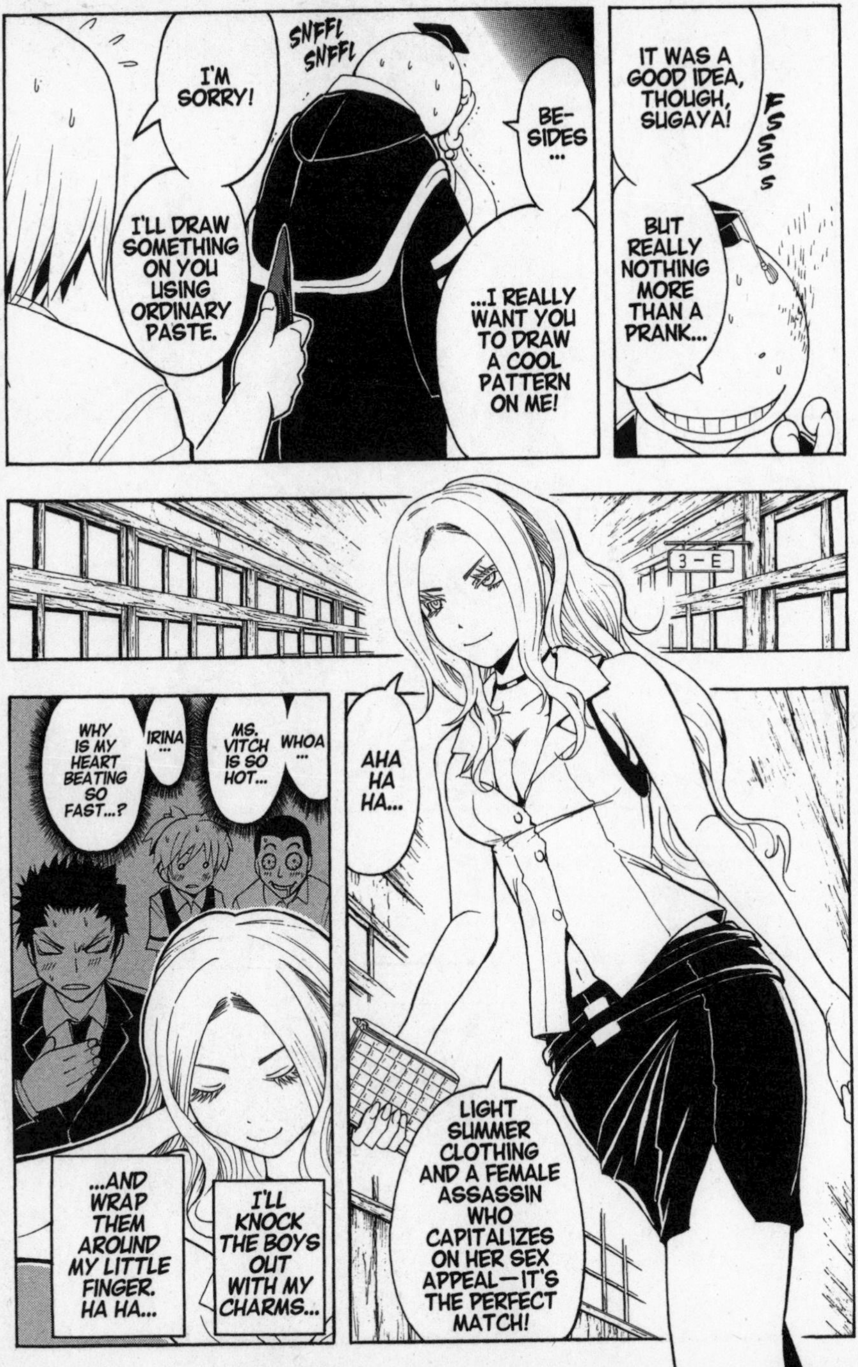
IT WAS A GOOD IDEA, THOUGH, SUGAYA!
FSSSS
BUT REALLY NOTHING MORE THAN A PRANK...
BE-SIDES...
...I REALLY WANT YOU TO DRAW A COOL PATTERN ON ME!
SNFFL SNFFL
I'M SORRY!
I'LL DRAW SOMETHING ON YOU USING ORDINARY PASTE.
3-E
AHA HA HA...
LIGHT SUMMER CLOTHING AND A FEMALE ASSASSIN WHO CAPITALIZES ON HER SEX APPEAL—IT'S THE PERFECT MATCH!
WHOA...
MS. VITCH IS SO HOT...
IRINA...
WHY IS MY HEART BEATING SO FAST...?
I'LL KNOCK THE BOYS OUT WITH MY CHARMS...
...AND WRAP THEM AROUND MY LITTLE FINGER. HA HA...

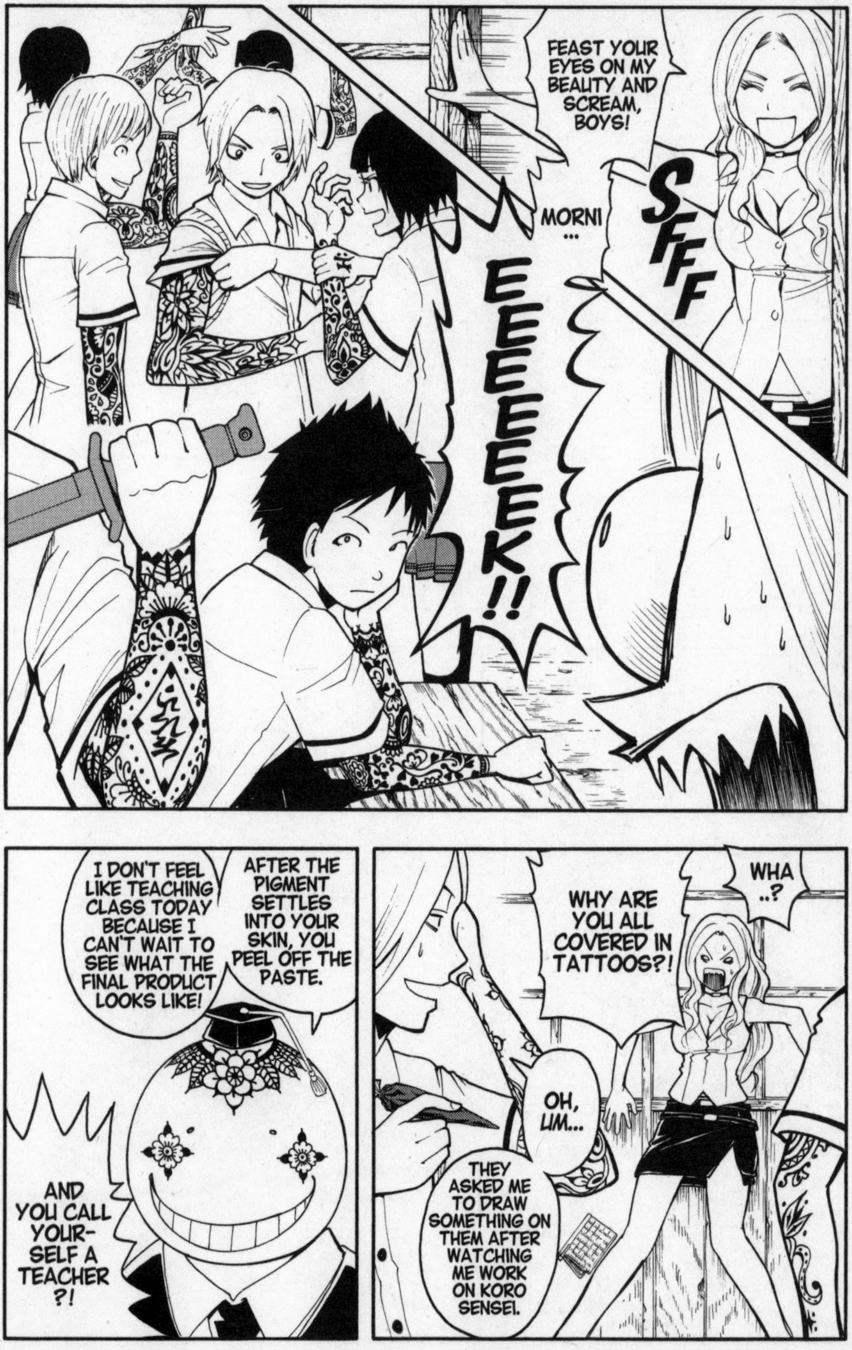
FEAST YOUR EYES ON MY BEAUTY AND SCREAM, BOYS!
SFFF
MORNI ...
EEEEEEEK!!
WHA ..?
WHY ARE YOU ALL COVERED IN TATTOOS?!
OH, UM...
THEY ASKED ME TO DRAW SOMETHING ON THEM AFTER WATCHING ME WORK ON KORO SENSEI.
AFTER THE PIGMENT SETTLES INTO YOUR SKIN, YOU PEEL OFF THE PASTE.
I DON'T FEEL LIKE TEACHING CLASS TODAY BECAUSE I CAN'T WAIT TO SEE WHAT THE FINAL PRODUCT LOOKS LIKE!
AND YOU CALL YOUR-SELF A TEACHER?!

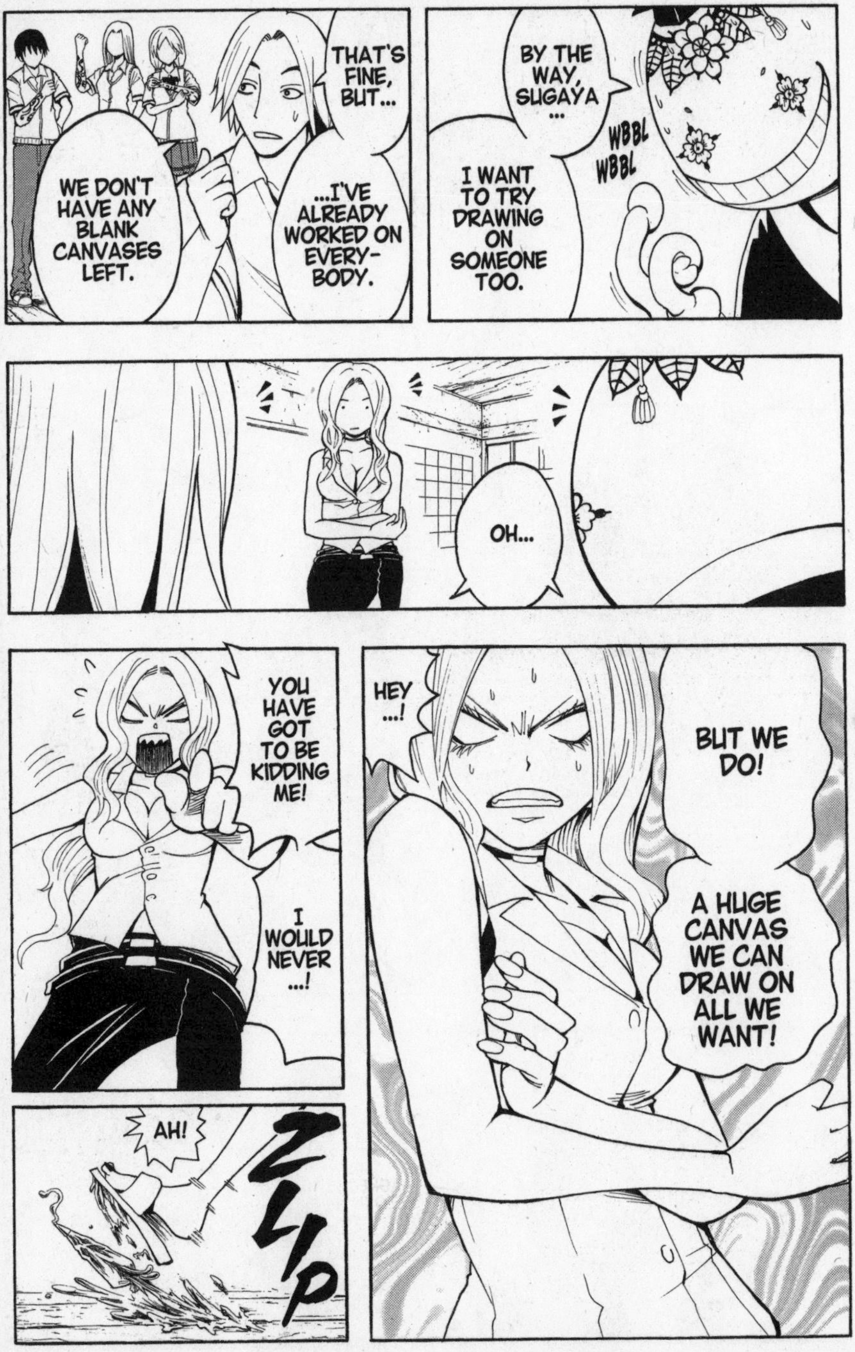
BY THE WAY, SUGAYA ...
WBBL WBBL
I WANT TO TRY DRAWING ON SOMEONE TOO.
THAT'S FINE, BUT...
...I'VE ALREADY WORKED ON EVERY-BODY.
WE DON'T HAVE ANY BLANK CANVASES LEFT.
OH...
BUT WE DO!
A HUGE CANVAS WE CAN DRAW ON ALL WE WANT!
HEY ...!
YOU HAVE GOT TO BE KIDDING ME!
I WOULD NEVER ...!
AH!
ZIP

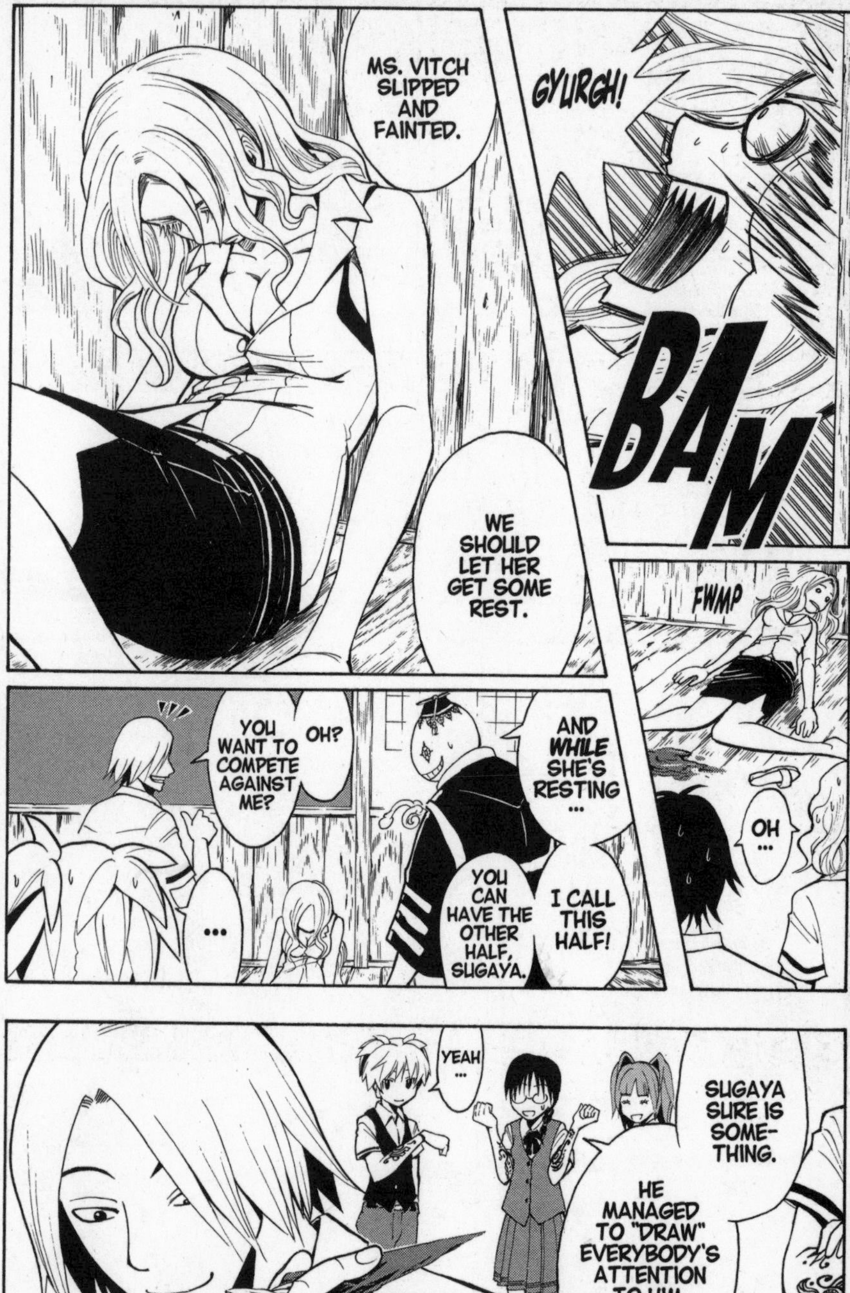
GYURGH!
BAM
FWMP
OH ...
MS. VITCH SLIPPED AND FAINTED.
WE SHOULD LET HER GET SOME REST.
AND WHILE SHE'S RESTING ...
I CALL THIS HALF!
YOU CAN HAVE THE OTHER HALF, SUGAYA.
OH?
YOU WANT TO COMPETE AGAINST ME?
...
SUGAYA SURE IS SOME-THING.
HE MANAGED TO "DRAW" EVERYBODY'S ATTENTION TO HIM.
YEAH ...

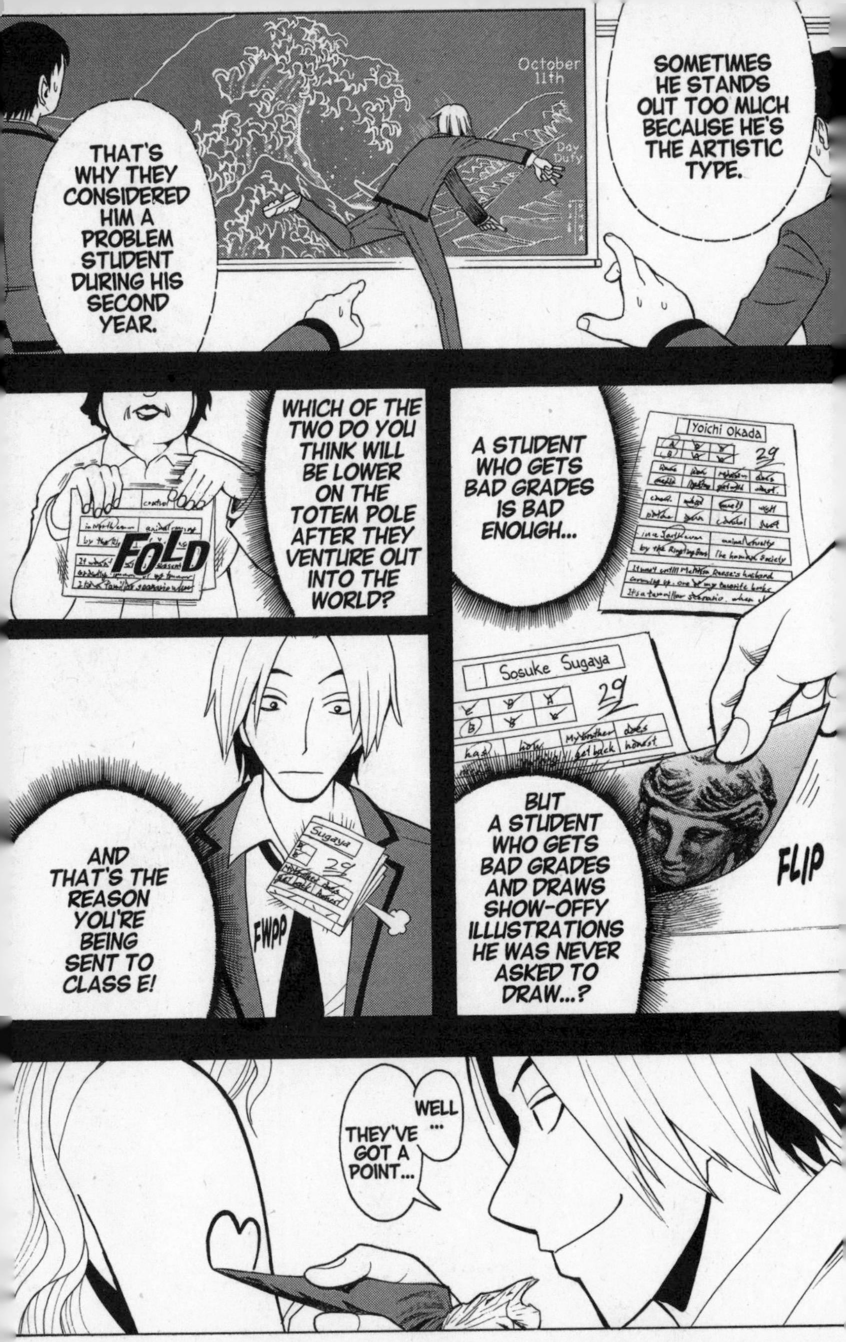
October 11th
Day Duty
SOMETIMES HE STANDS OUT TOO MUCH BECAUSE HE'S THE ARTISTIC TYPE.
THAT'S WHY THEY CONSIDERED HIM A PROBLEM STUDENT DURING HIS SECOND YEAR.
Yoichi Okada
29
A STUDENT WHO GETS BAD GRADES IS BAD ENOUGH...
WHICH OF THE TWO DO YOU THINK WILL BE LOWER ON THE TOTEM POLE AFTER THEY VENTURE OUT INTO THE WORLD?
FOLD
Sosuke Sugaya
29
BUT A STUDENT WHO GETS BAD GRADES AND DRAWS SHOW-OFFY ILLUSTRATIONS HE WAS NEVER ASKED TO DRAW...?
FLIP
Sugaya
29
AND THAT'S THE REASON YOU'RE BEING SENT TO CLASS E!
FWPP
WELL...
THEY'VE GOT A POINT...

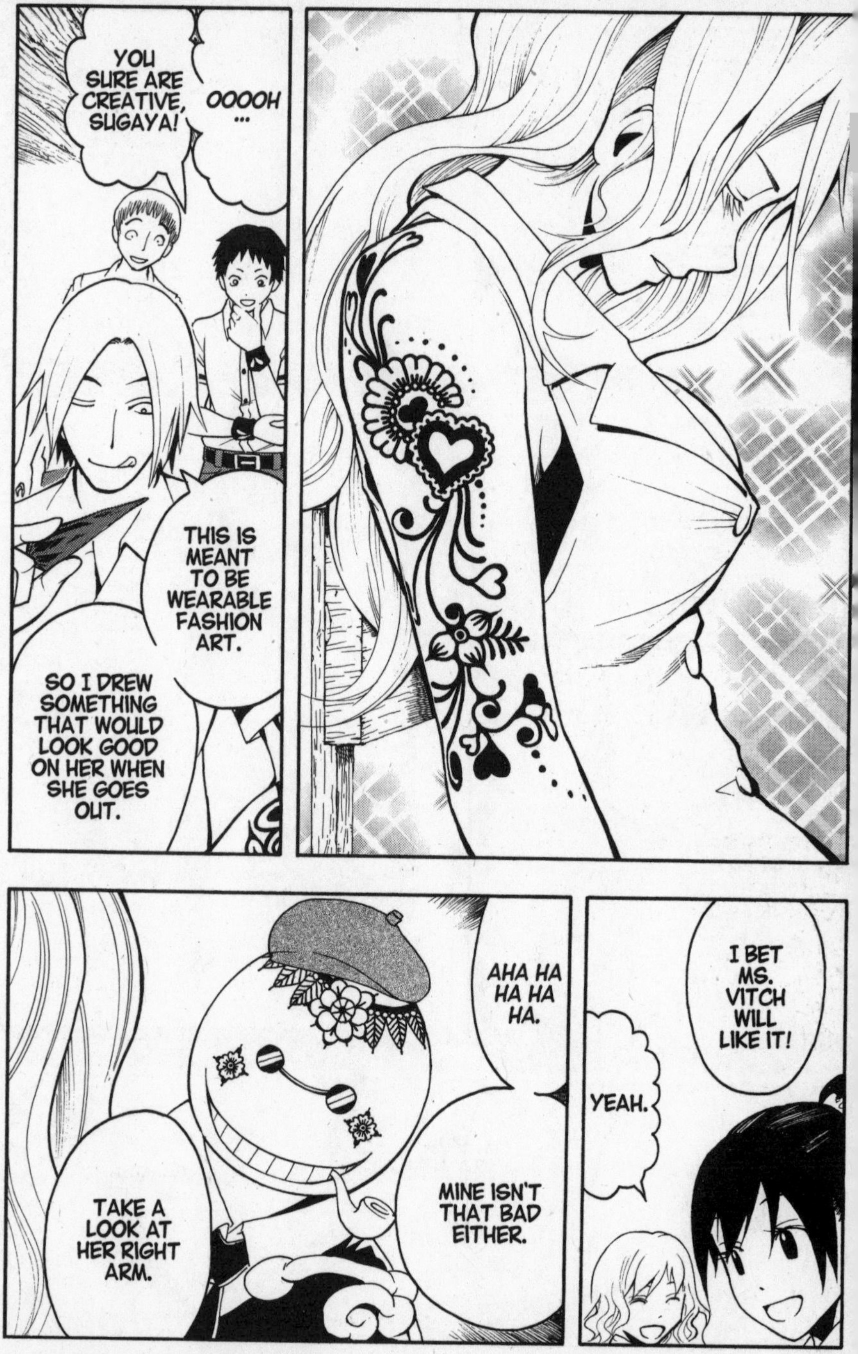
OOOOH ...
YOU SURE ARE CREATIVE, SUGAYA!
THIS IS MEANT TO BE WEARABLE FASHION ART.
SO I DREW SOMETHING THAT WOULD LOOK GOOD ON HER WHEN SHE GOES OUT.
I BET MS. VITCH WILL LIKE IT!
YEAH.
AHA HA HA HA HA.
MINE ISN'T THAT BAD EITHER.
TAKE A LOOK AT HER RIGHT ARM.

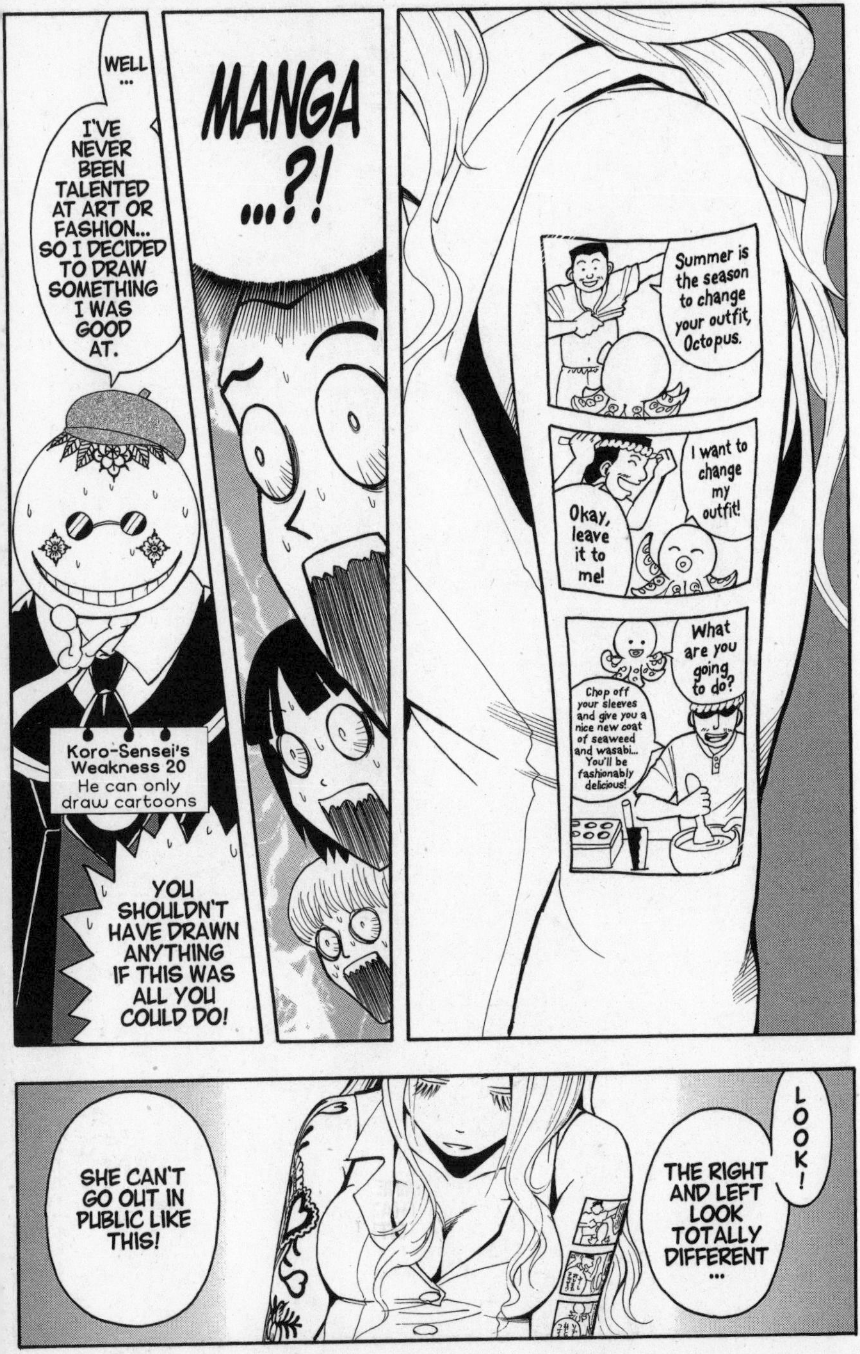
Summer is the season to change your outfit, Octopus.
I want to change my outfit!
Okay, leave it to me!
What are you going to do?
Chop off your sleeves and give you a nice new coat of seaweed and wasabi... You'll be fashionably delicious!
MANGA ...?!
WELL ...
I'VE NEVER BEEN TALENTED AT ART OR FASHION... SO I DECIDED TO DRAW SOMETHING I WAS GOOD AT.
Koro-Sensei's Weakness 20
He can only draw cartoons
YOU SHOULDN'T HAVE DRAWN ANYTHING IF THIS WAS ALL YOU COULD DO!
LOOK!
THE RIGHT AND LEFT LOOK TOTALLY DIFFERENT ...
SHE CAN'T GO OUT IN PUBLIC LIKE THIS!

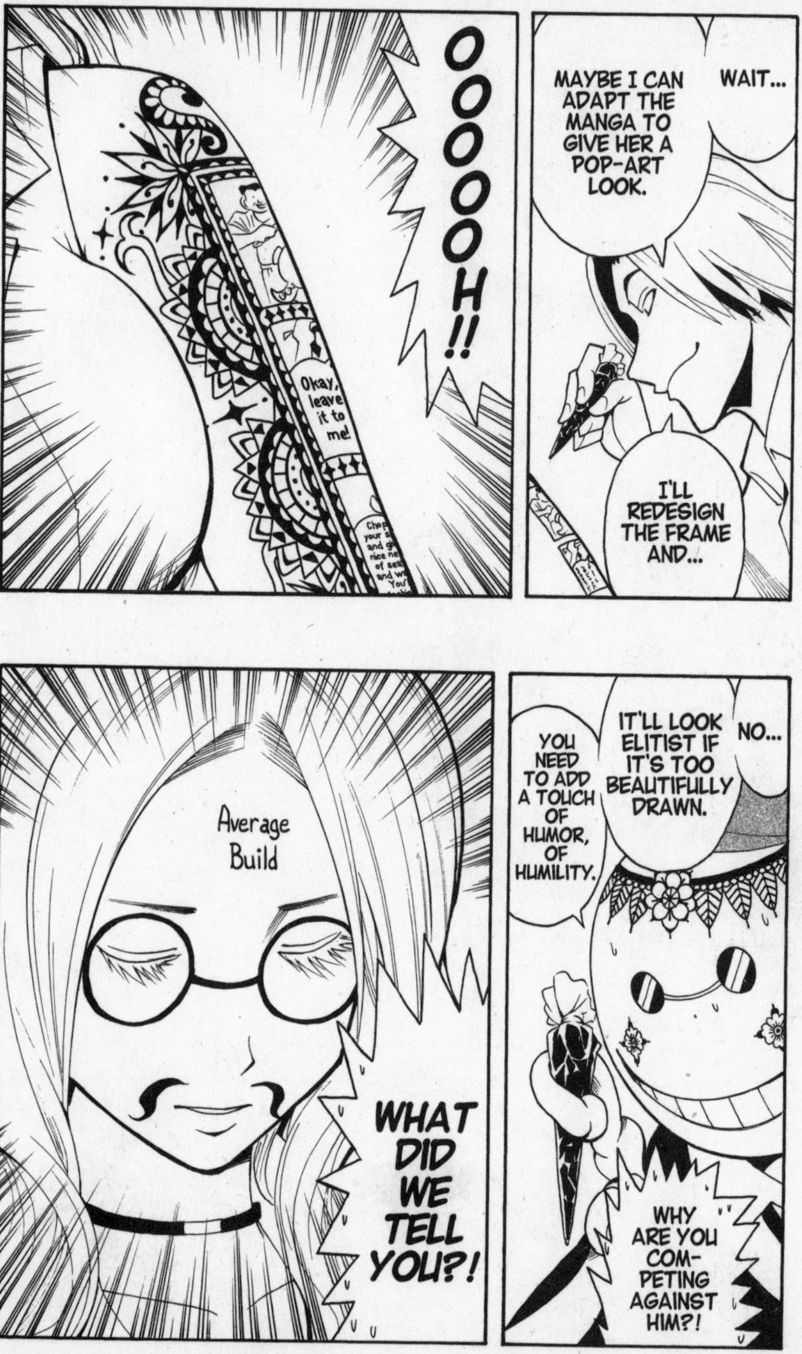
WAIT...
MAYBE I CAN ADAPT THE MANGA TO GIVE HER A POP-ART LOOK.
I'LL REDESIGN THE FRAME AND...
OOOOOH!!
Okay, leave it to me!
NO...
IT'LL LOOK ELITIST IF IT'S TOO BEAUTIFULLY DRAWN.
YOU NEED TO ADD A TOUCH OF HUMOR, OF HUMILITY.
WHY ARE YOU COM-PETING AGAINST HIM?!
Average Build
WHAT DID WE TELL YOU?!

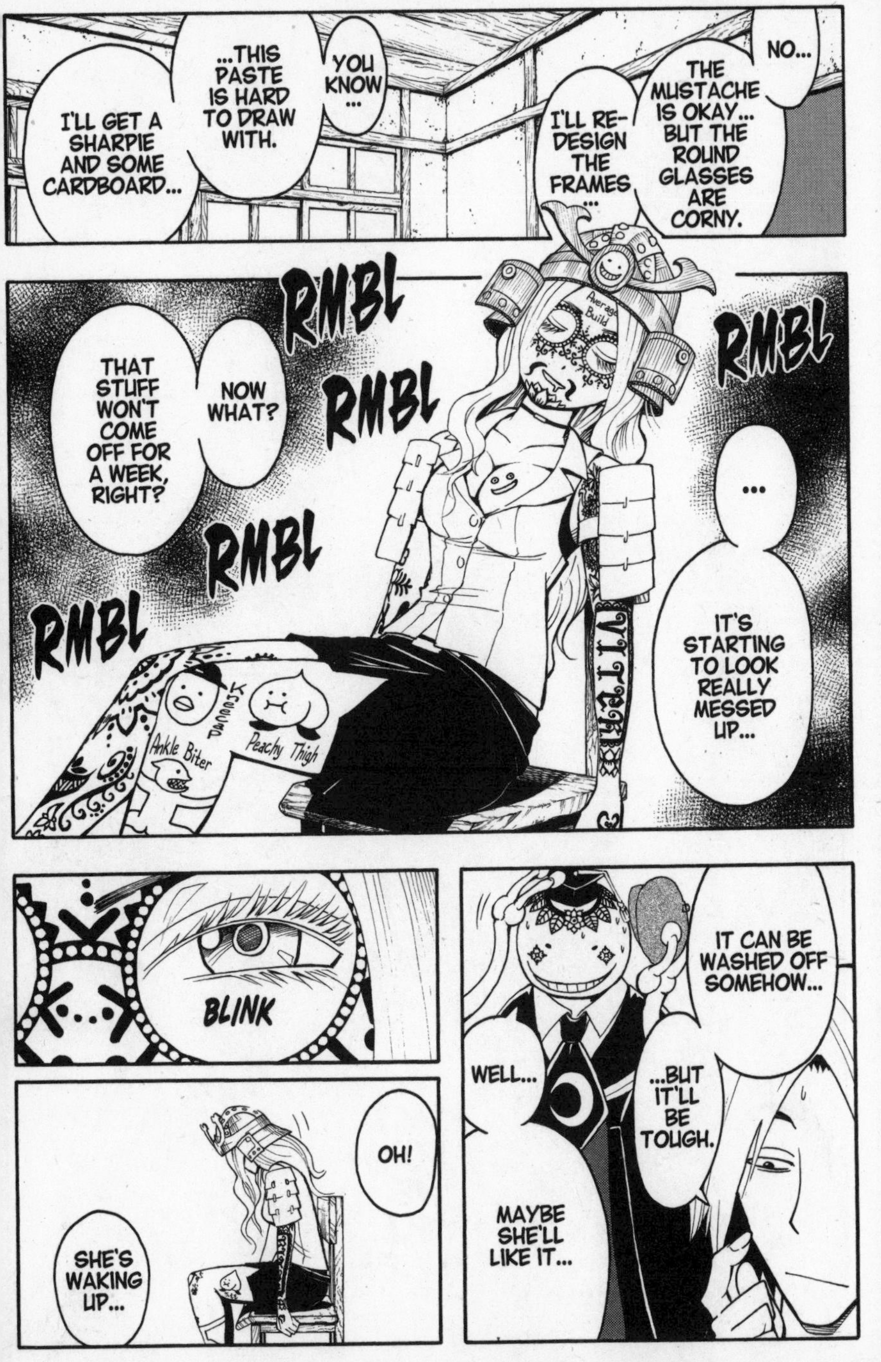
NO...
THE MUSTACHE IS OKAY... BUT THE ROUND GLASSES ARE CORNY.
I'LL RE-DESIGN THE FRAMES ...
YOU KNOW ...
...THIS PASTE IS HARD TO DRAW WITH.
I'LL GET A SHARPIE AND SOME CARDBOARD...
RMBL
...
IT'S STARTING TO LOOK REALLY MESSED UP...
Average Build
RMBL
RMBL
NOW WHAT?
THAT STUFF WON'T COME OFF FOR A WEEK, RIGHT?
RMBL
RMBL
Kneecap
Peachy Thigh
Ankle Biter
IT CAN BE WASHED OFF SOMEHOW...
...BUT IT'LL BE TOUGH.
WELL...
MAYBE SHE'LL LIKE IT...
BLINK
OH!
SHE'S WAKING UP...

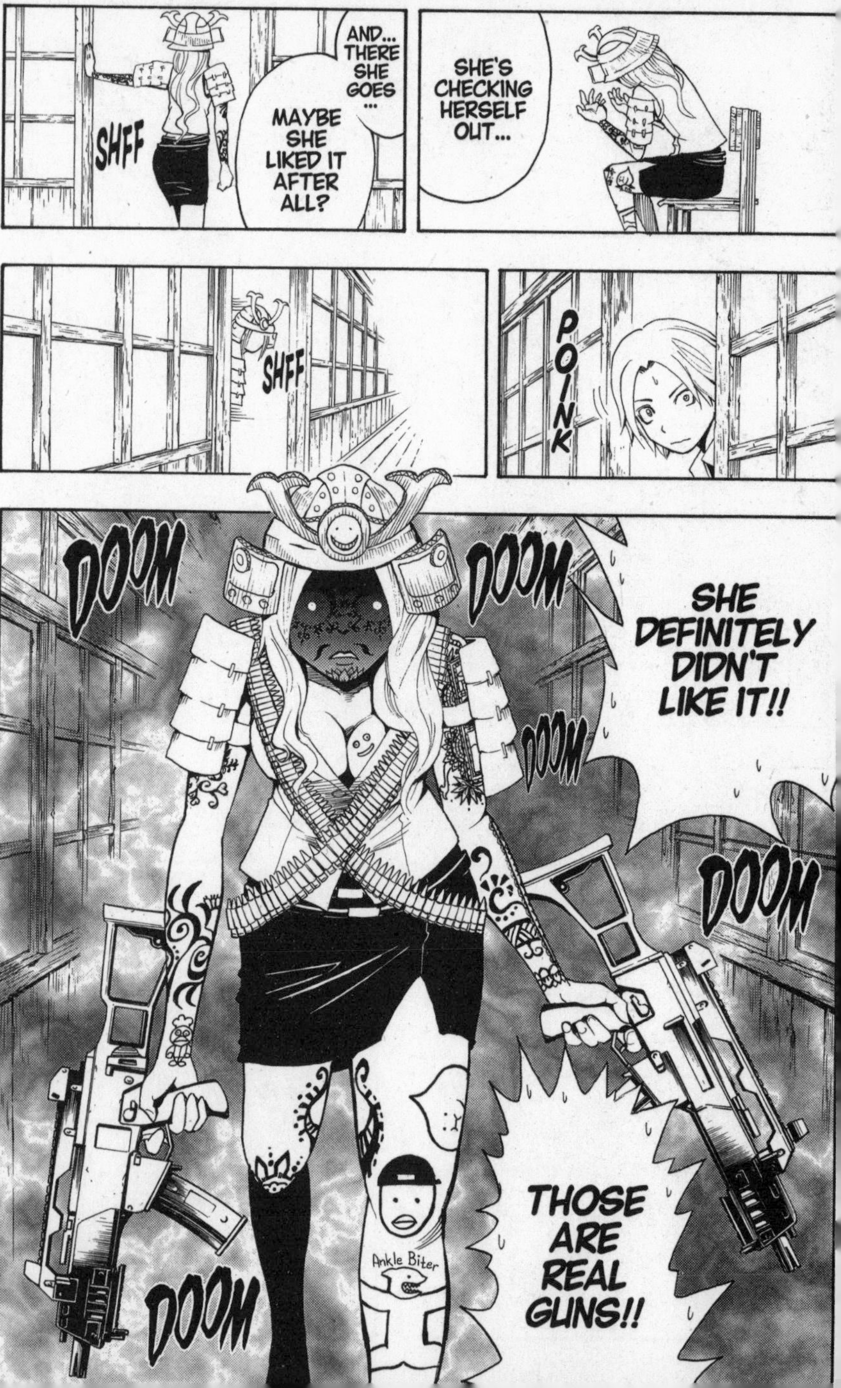
SHE'S CHECKING HERSELF OUT...
AND... THERE SHE GOES ...
MAYBE SHE LIKED IT AFTER ALL?
SHFF
POINK
SHFF
SHE DEFINITELY DIDN'T LIKE IT!!
DOOM
DOOM
DOOM
DOOM
THOSE ARE REAL GUNS!!
Ankle Biter
DOOM

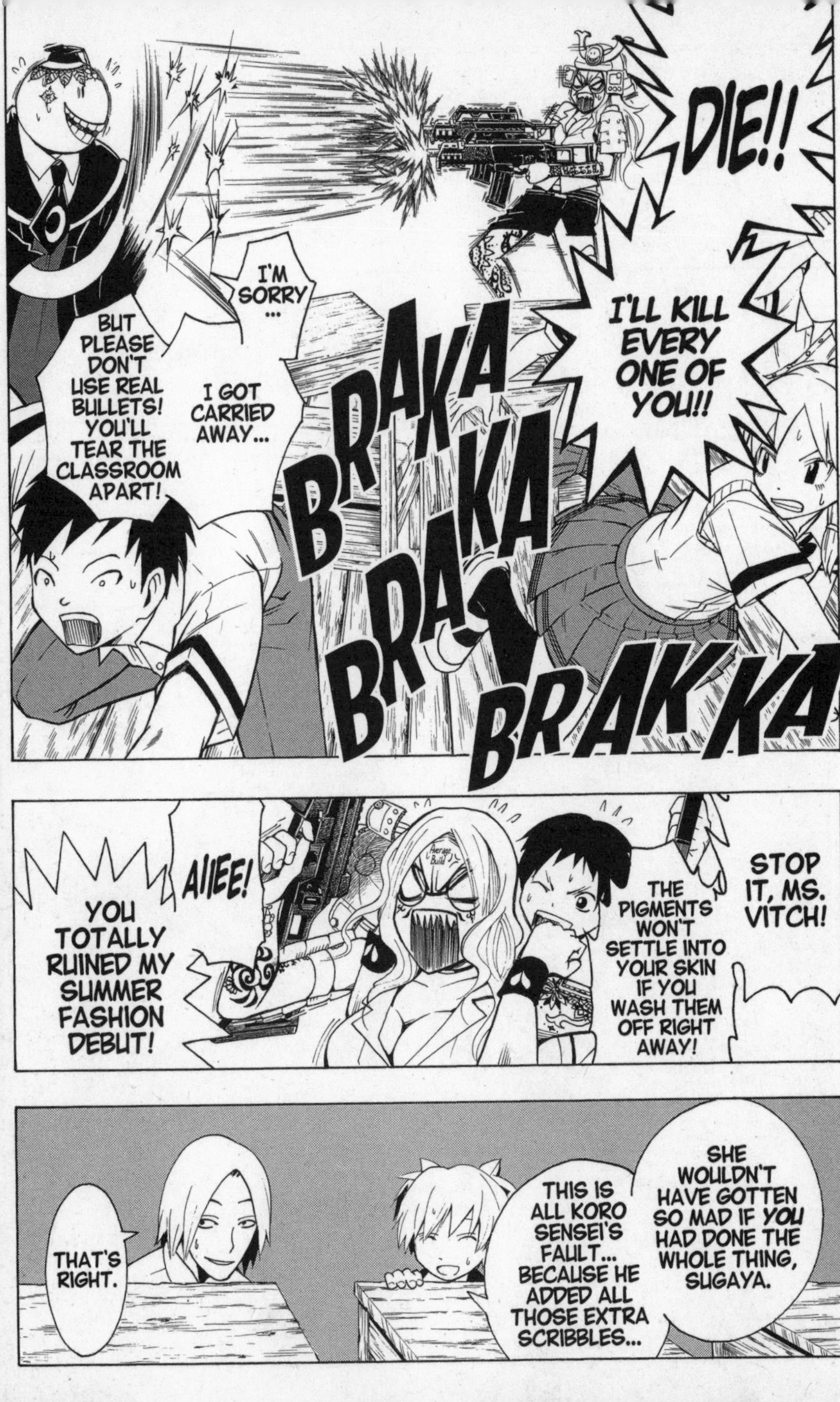
DIE!!
I'LL KILL EVERY ONE OF YOU!!
BRAKA BRAKA BRAKKA
I'M SORRY...
I GOT CARRIED AWAY...
BUT PLEASE DON'T USE REAL BULLETS! YOU'LL TEAR THE CLASSROOM APART!
STOP IT, MS. VITCH!
THE PIGMENTS WON'T SETTLE INTO YOUR SKIN IF YOU WASH THEM OFF RIGHT AWAY!
Average Build
AIIEE!
YOU TOTALLY RUINED MY SUMMER FASHION DEBUT!
SHE WOULDN'T HAVE GOTTEN SO MAD IF YOU HAD DONE THE WHOLE THING, SUGAYA.
THIS IS ALL KORO SENSEI'S FAULT... BECAUSE HE ADDED ALL THOSE EXTRA SCRIBBLES...
THAT'S RIGHT.

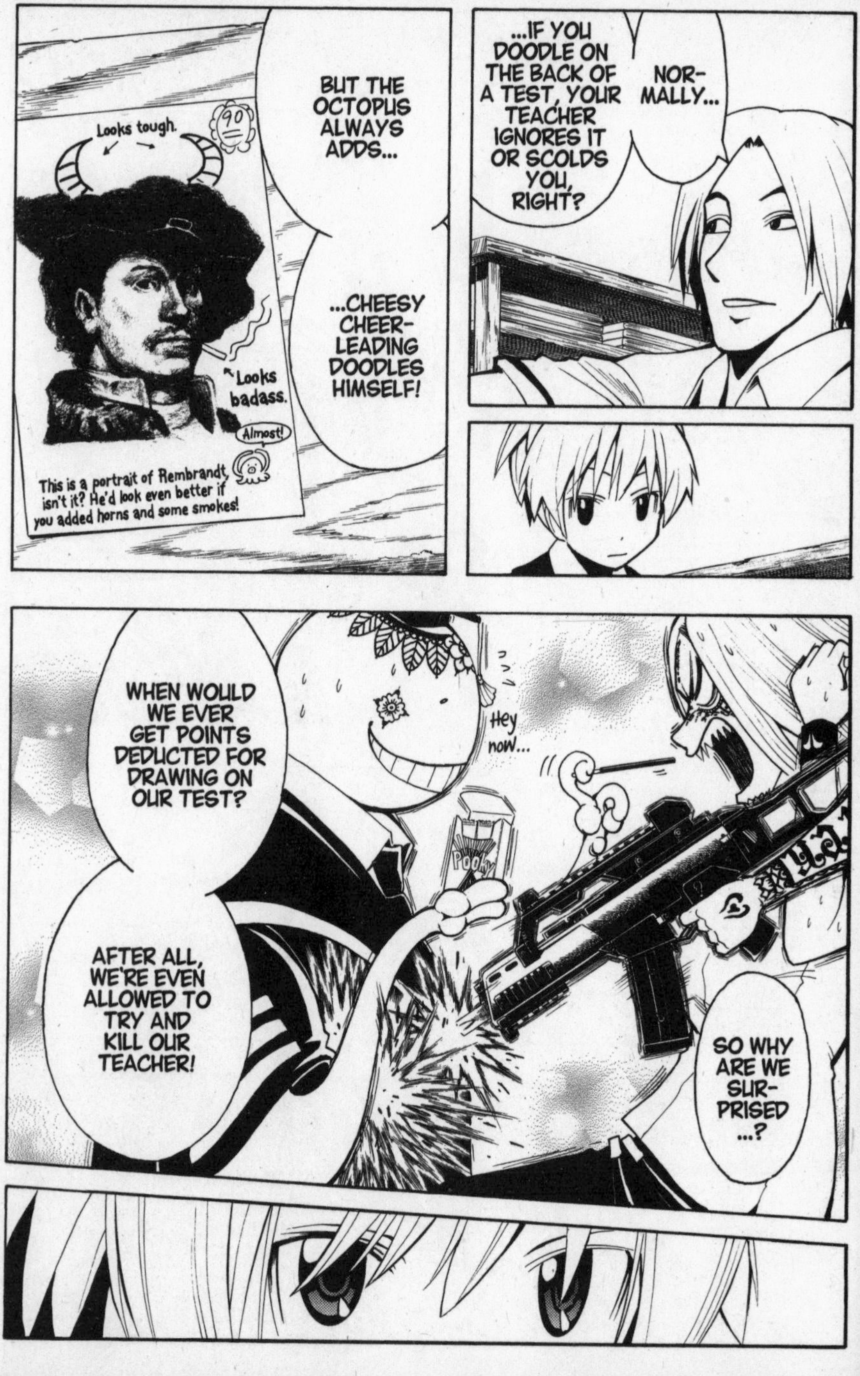
NOR-MALLY...
...IF YOU DOODLE ON THE BACK OF A TEST, YOUR TEACHER IGNORES IT OR SCOLDS YOU, RIGHT?
BUT THE OCTOPUS ALWAYS ADDS...
...CHEESY CHEER-LEADING DOODLES HIMSELF!
90
Looks tough.
Looks badass.
Almost!
This is a portrait of Rembrandt, isn't it? He'd look even better if you added horns and some smokes!
Hey now...
SO WHY ARE WE SUR-PRISED ...?
WHEN WOULD WE EVER GET POINTS DEDUCTED FOR DRAWING ON OUR TEST?
AFTER ALL, WE'RE EVEN ALLOWED TO TRY AND KILL OUR TEACHER!
POCKY

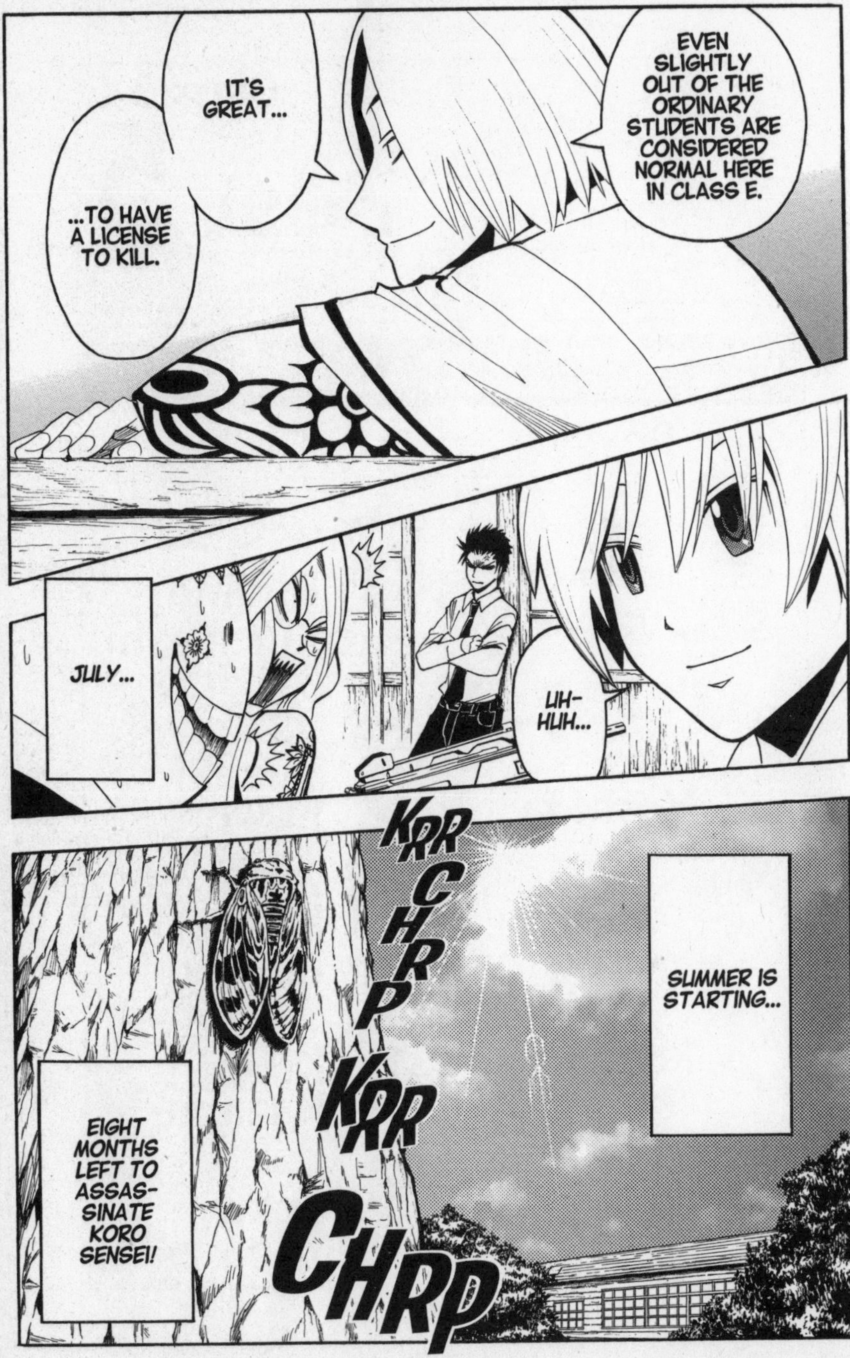
EVEN SLIGHTLY OUT OF THE ORDINARY STUDENTS ARE CONSIDERED NORMAL HERE IN CLASS E.
IT'S GREAT...
...TO HAVE A LICENSE TO KILL.
UH-HUH...
JULY...
SUMMER IS STARTING...
KRR CHRP
KRR CHRP
EIGHT MONTHS LEFT TO ASSAS-SINATE KORO SENSEI!

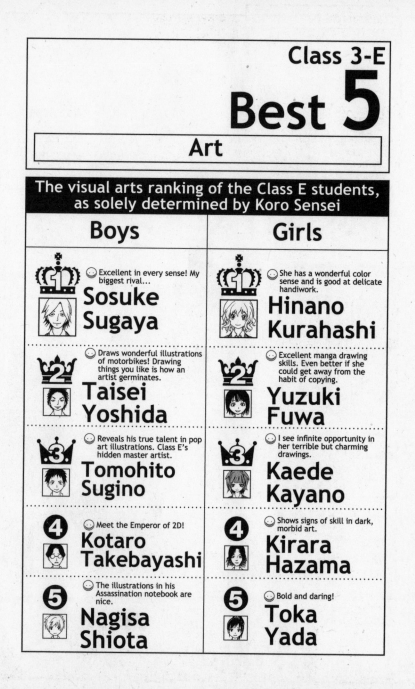

Class 3-E Best 5

Art

The visual arts ranking of the Class E students, as solely determined by Koro Sensei

Boys

1

Excellent in every sense! My biggest rival...
Sosuke Sugaya

2

Draws wonderful illustrations of motorbikes! Drawing things you like is how an artist germinates.
Taisei Yoshida

3

Reveals his true talent in pop art illustrations. Class E's hidden master artist.
Tomohito Sugino

4

Meet the Emperor of 2D!
Kotaro Takebayashi

5

The illustrations in his Assassination notebook are nice.
Nagisa Shiota

Girls

1

She has a wonderful color sense and is good at delicate handiwork.
Hinano Kurahashi

2

Excellent manga drawing skills. Even better if she could get away from the habit of copying.
Yuzuki Fuwa

3

I see infinite opportunity in her terrible but charming drawings.
Kaede Kayano

4

Shows signs of skill in dark, morbid art.
Kirara Hazama

5

Bold and daring!
Toka Yada

Class 38 Time for Training

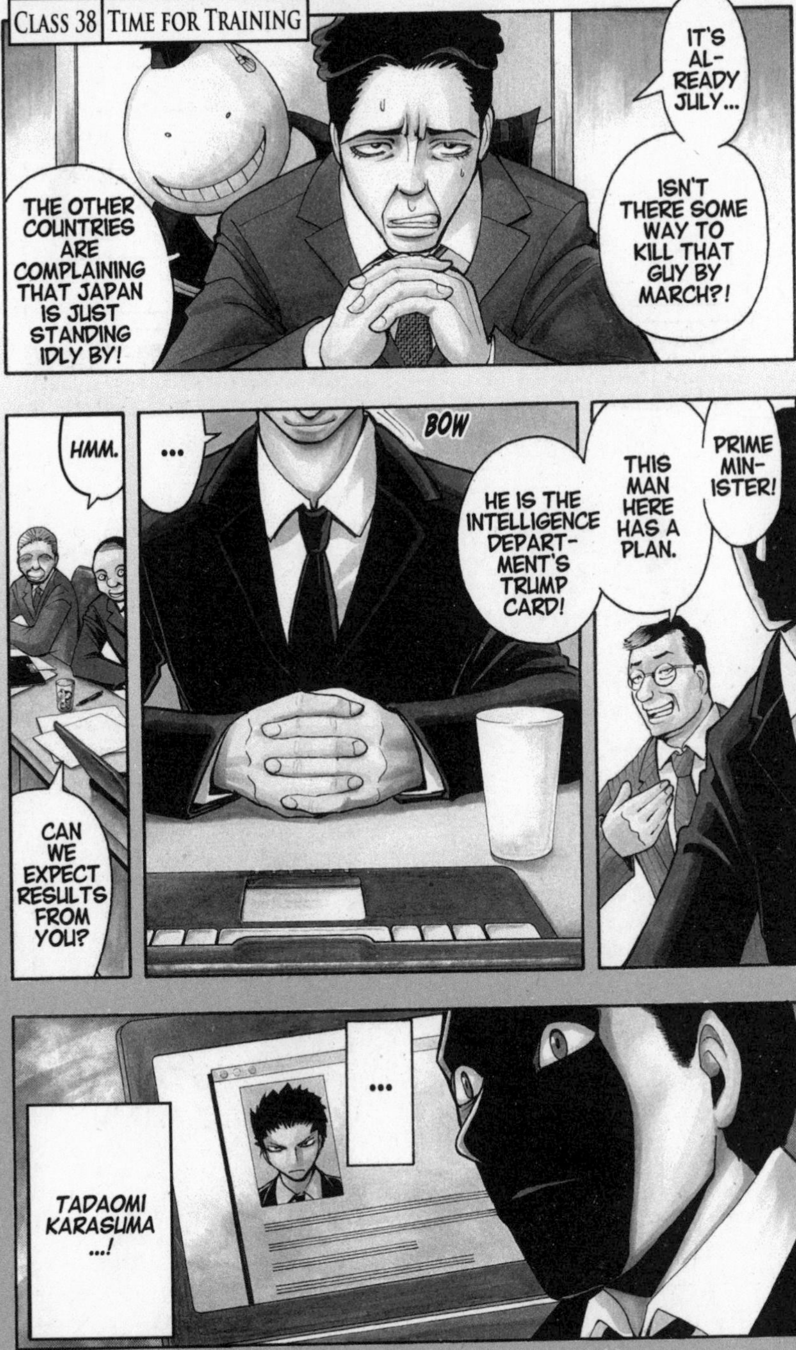
IT'S ALREADY JULY...
ISN'T THERE SOME WAY TO KILL THAT GUY BY MARCH?!
THE OTHER COUNTRIES ARE COMPLAINING THAT JAPAN IS JUST STANDING IDLY BY!
PRIME MINISTER!
THIS MAN HERE HAS A PLAN.
HE IS THE INTELLIGENCE DEPARTMENT'S TRUMP CARD!
BOW
...
HMM.
CAN WE EXPECT RESULTS FROM YOU?
...
TADAOMI KARASUMA ...!

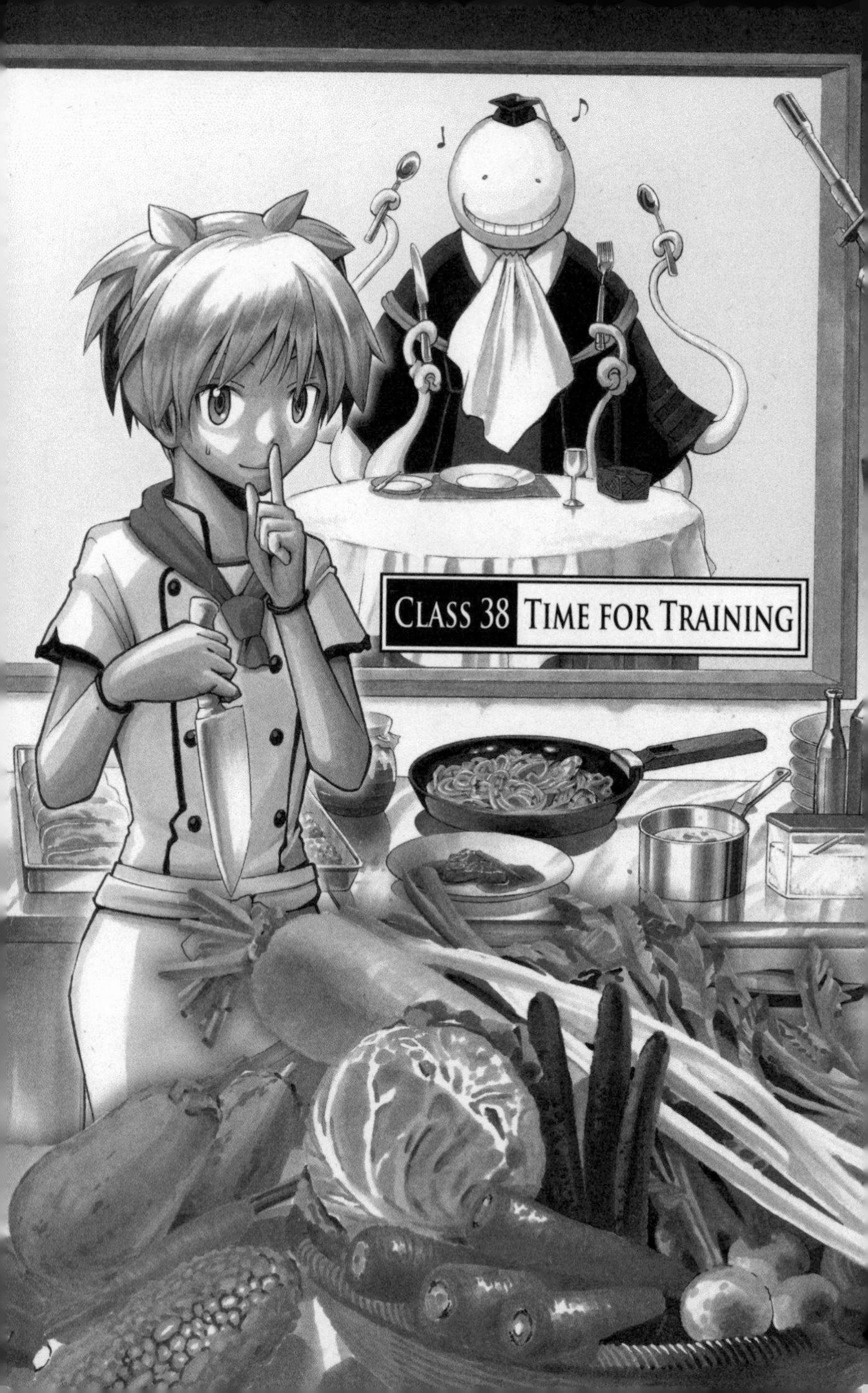
CLASS 38 TIME FOR TRAINING

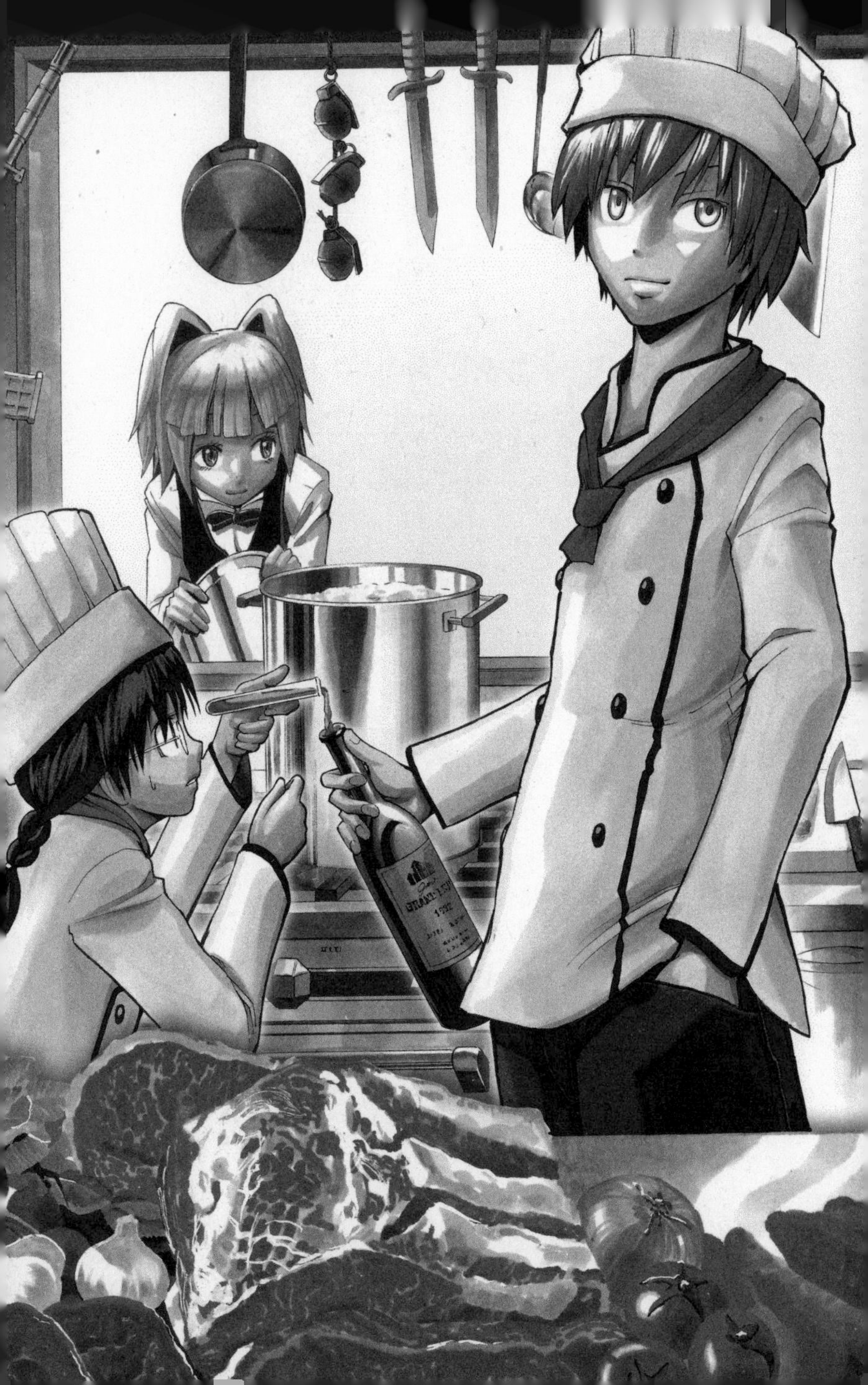

An unexpected spin-off.

From Chapter 82 of
NEURO: Supernatural Detective

I feel a sort of parental love towards the man who became the model for this character, since he's made a comeback after facing a lot of hardship.

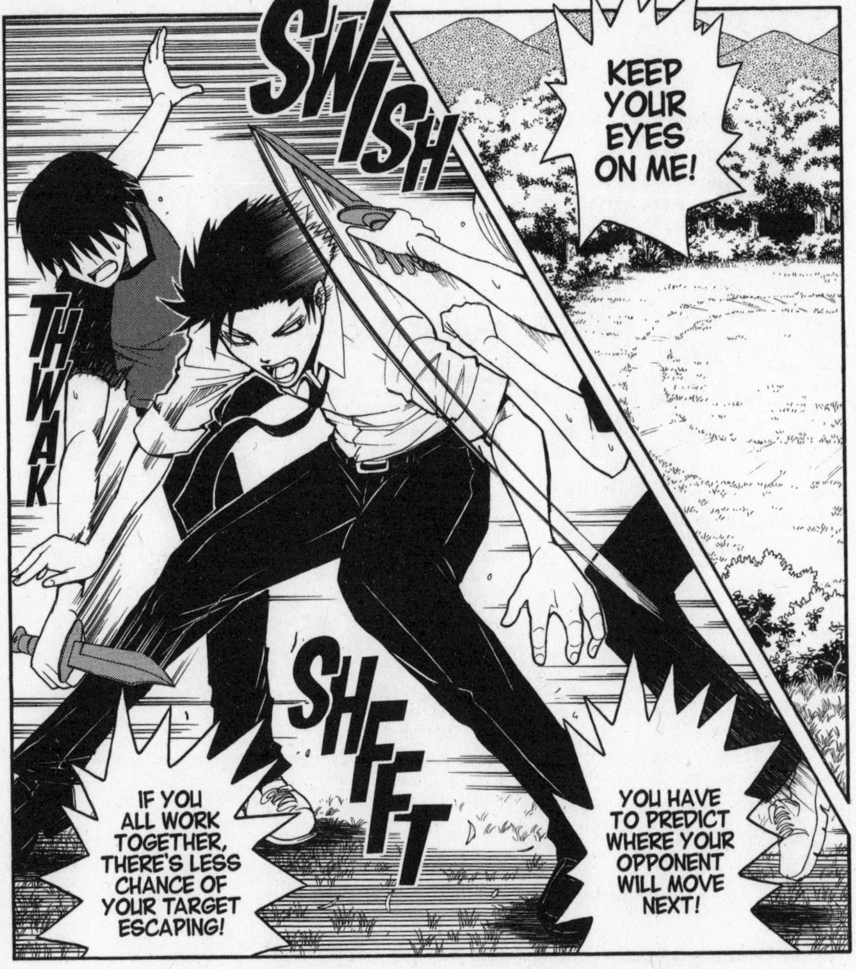
KEEP YOUR EYES ON ME!
SWISH
THWAK
YOU HAVE TO PREDICT WHERE YOUR OPPONENT WILL MOVE NEXT!
SHFFFT
IF YOU ALL WORK TOGETHER, THERE'S LESS CHANCE OF YOUR TARGET ESCAPING!

Assassination Training Interim Report

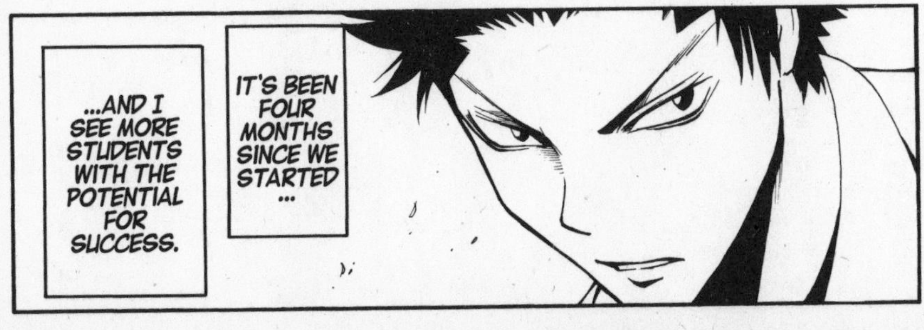
IT'S BEEN FOUR MONTHS SINCE WE STARTED...
...AND I SEE MORE STUDENTS WITH THE POTENTIAL FOR SUCCESS.

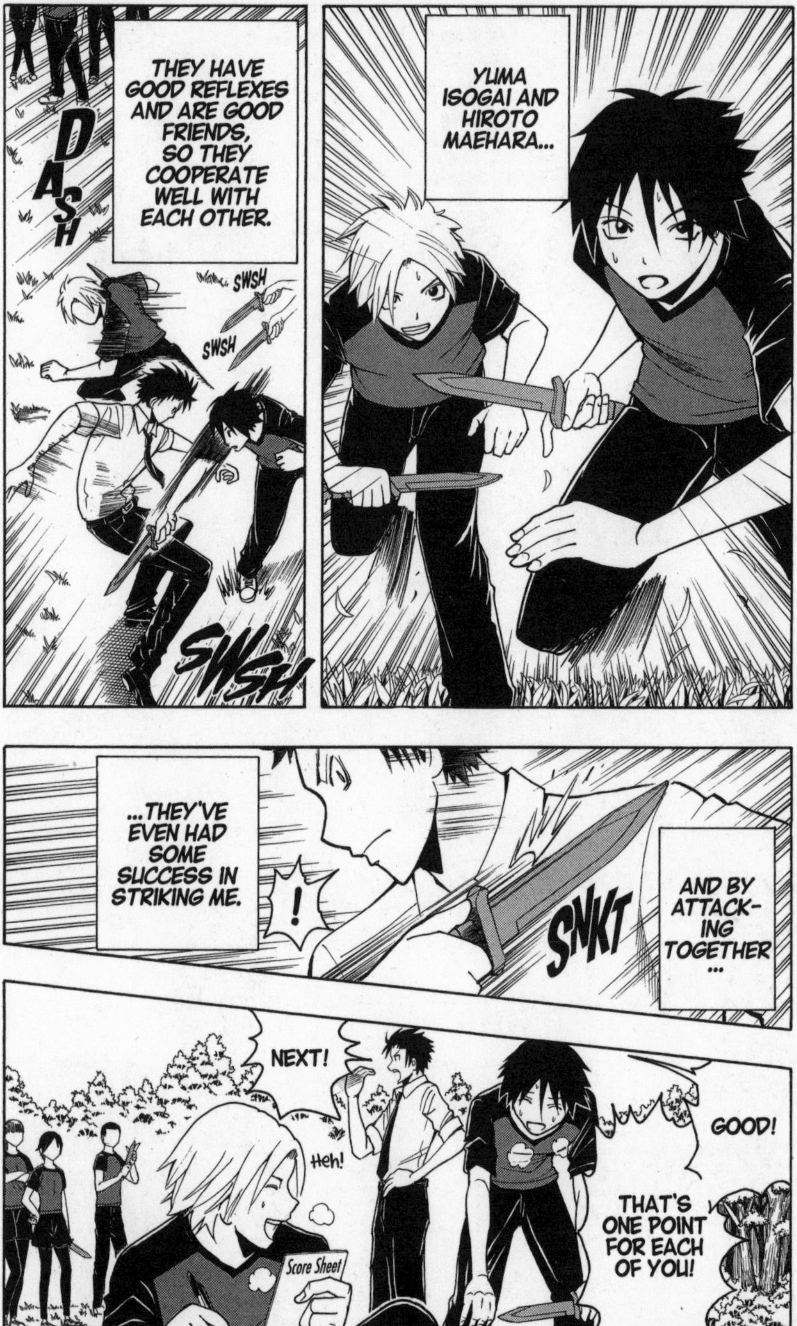
YUMA ISOGAI AND HIROTO MAEHARA...
THEY HAVE GOOD REFLEXES AND ARE GOOD FRIENDS, SO THEY COOPERATE WELL WITH EACH OTHER.
DASH
SWSH
SWSH
SWSH
AND BY ATTACK-ING TOGETHER...
SNKT
!
...THEY'VE EVEN HAD SOME SUCCESS IN STRIKING ME.
GOOD!
THAT'S ONE POINT FOR EACH OF YOU!
NEXT!
Heh!
Score Sheet

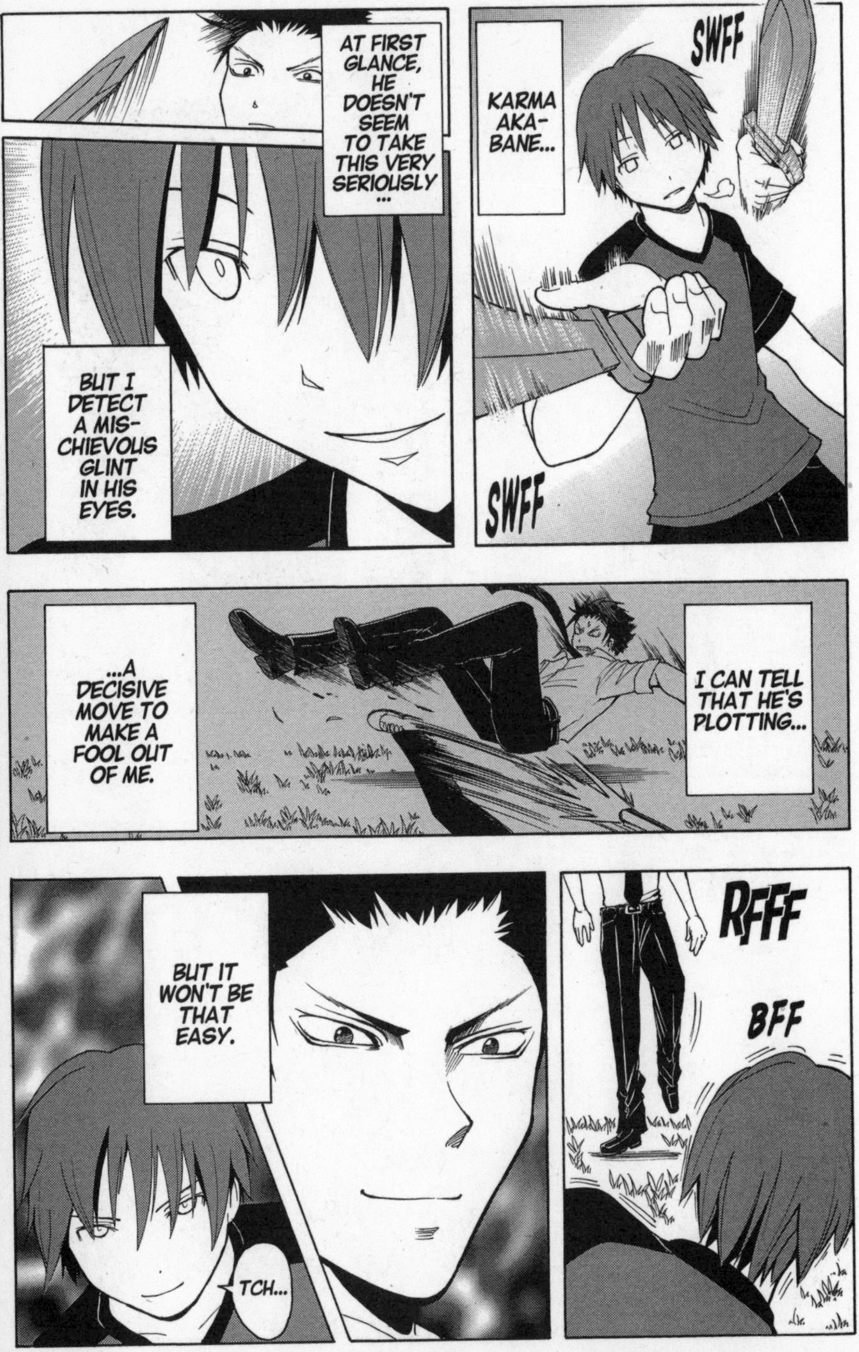
SWFF
KARMA AKA-BANE...
SWFF
AT FIRST GLANCE, HE DOESN'T SEEM TO TAKE THIS VERY SERIOUSLY...
BUT I DETECT A MIS-CHIEVOUS GLINT IN HIS EYES.
I CAN TELL THAT HE'S PLOTTING...
...A DECISIVE MOVE TO MAKE A FOOL OUT OF ME.
RFFF
BFF
BUT IT WON'T BE THAT EASY.
TCH...

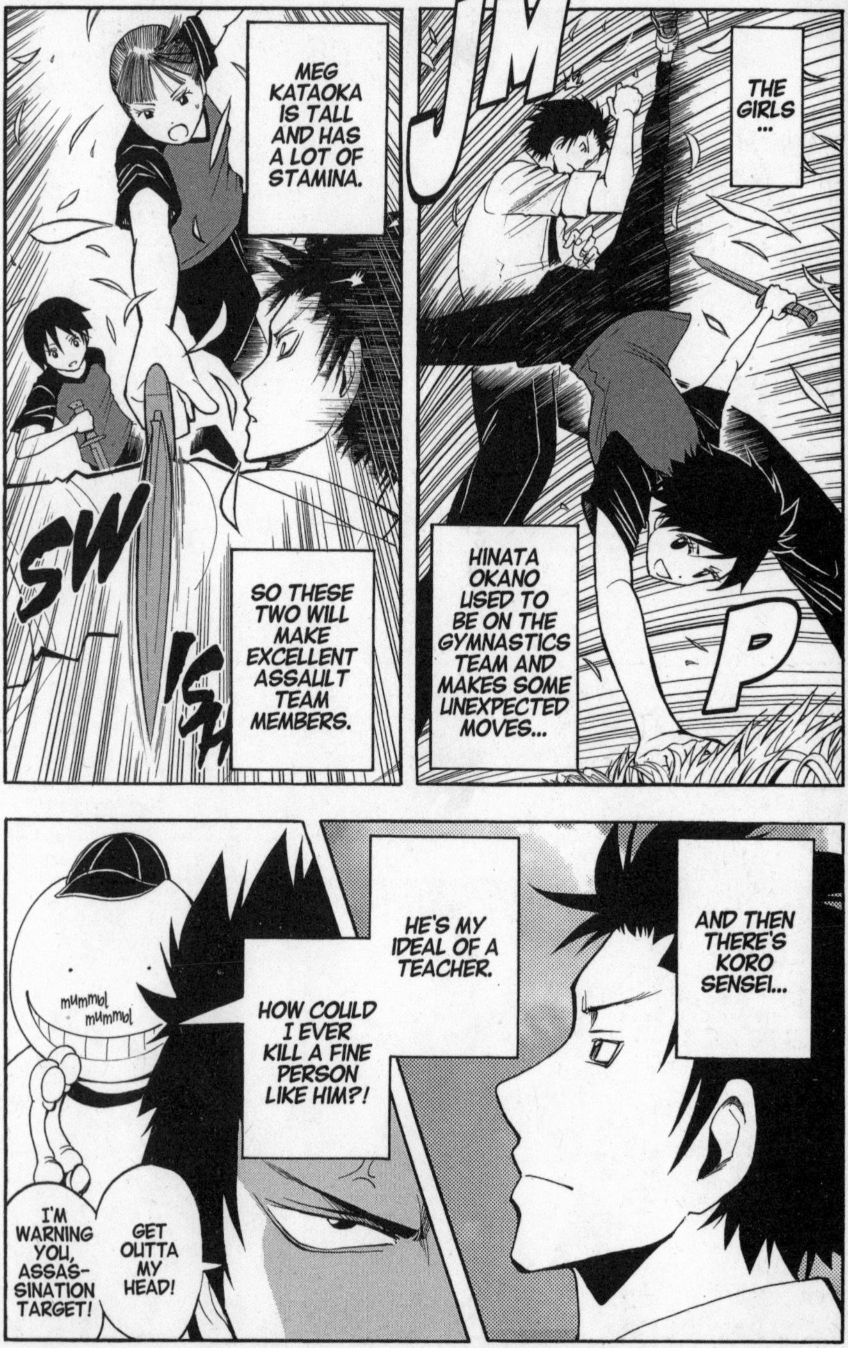
JM
THE GIRLS...
HINATA OKANO USED TO BE ON THE GYMNASTICS TEAM AND MAKES SOME UNEXPECTED MOVES...
P
MEG KATAOKA IS TALL AND HAS A LOT OF STAMINA.
SW
SO THESE TWO WILL MAKE EXCELLENT ASSAULT TEAM MEMBERS.
AND THEN THERE'S KORO SENSEI...
HE'S MY IDEAL OF A TEACHER.
HOW COULD I EVER KILL A FINE PERSON LIKE HIM?!
mumble mumble
GET OUTTA MY HEAD!
I'M WARNING YOU, ASSAS-SINATION TARGET!

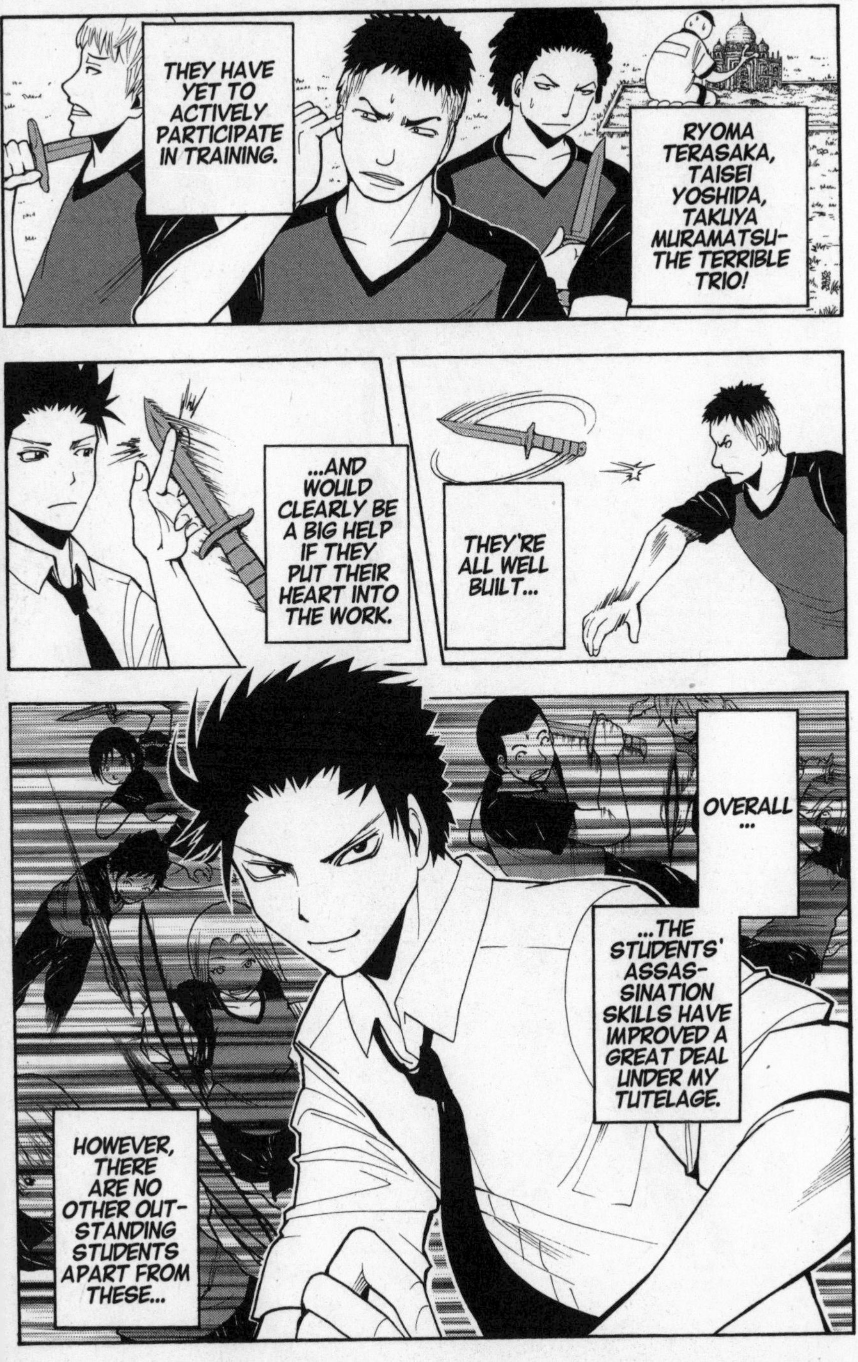

RYOMA TERASAKA, TAISEI YOSHIDA, TAKUYA MURAMATSU-THE TERRIBLE TRIO!
THEY HAVE YET TO ACTIVELY PARTICIPATE IN TRAINING.
THEY'RE ALL WELL BUILT...
...AND WOULD CLEARLY BE A BIG HELP IF THEY PUT THEIR HEART INTO THE WORK.
OVERALL...
...THE STUDENTS' ASSAS-SINATION SKILLS HAVE IMPROVED A GREAT DEAL UNDER MY TUTELAGE.
HOWEVER, THERE ARE NO OTHER OUT-STANDING STUDENTS APART FROM THESE...

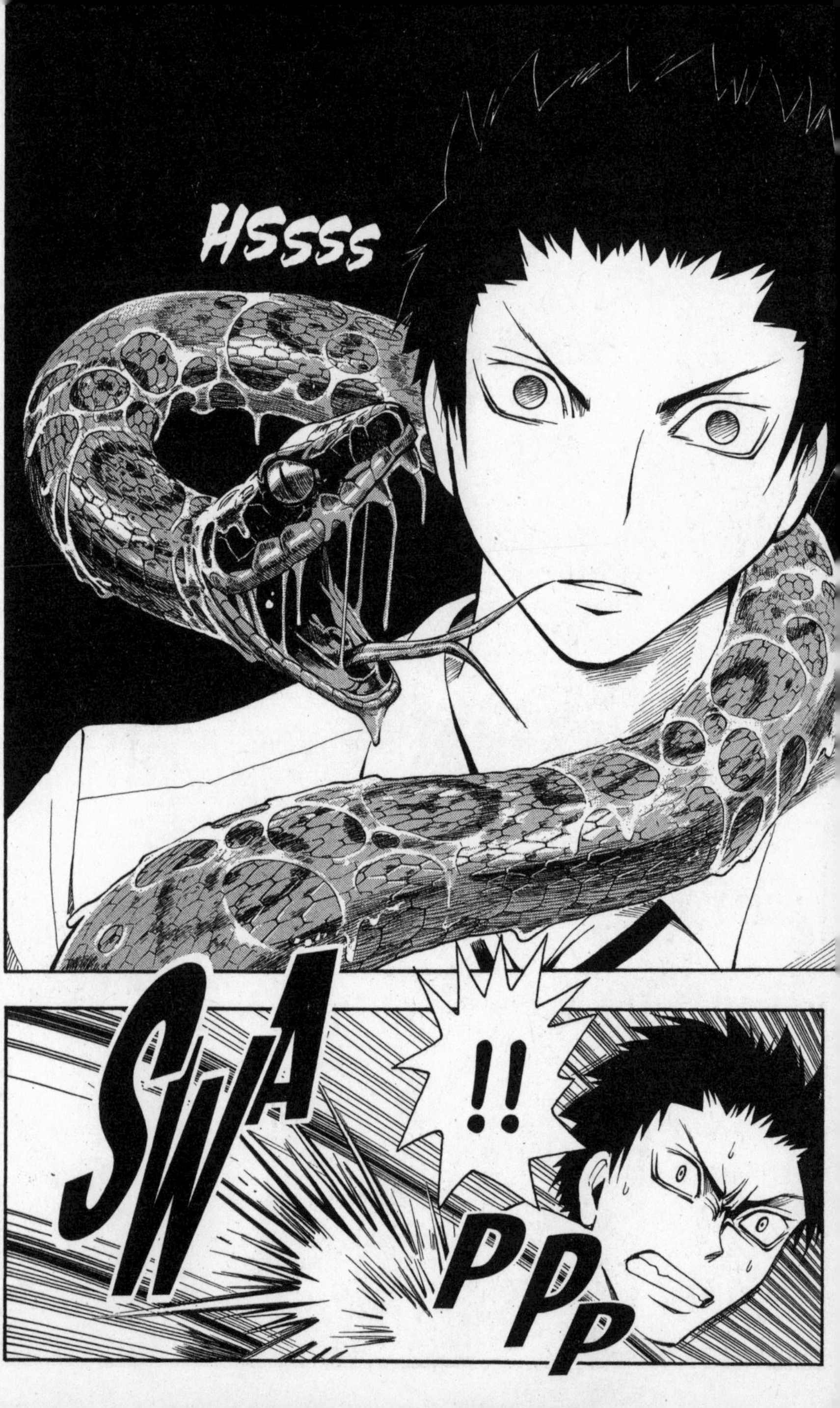
HSSSS
!!
SNAPPP

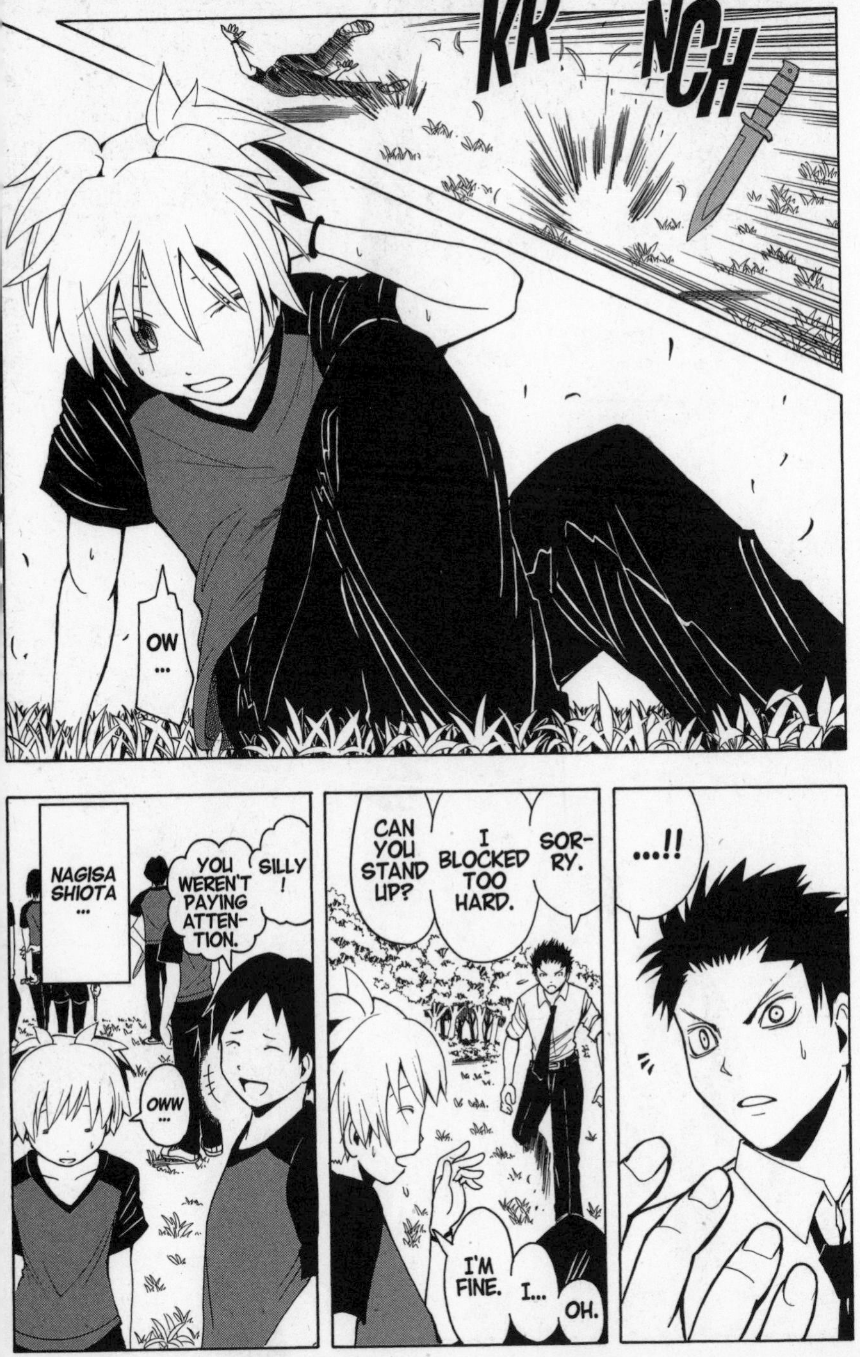
KR NCH
OW...
...!!
SORRY.
I BLOCKED TOO HARD.
CAN YOU STAND UP?
I'M FINE.
I...
OH.
SILLY!
YOU WEREN'T PAYING ATTENTION.
NAGISA SHIOTA...
OWW...

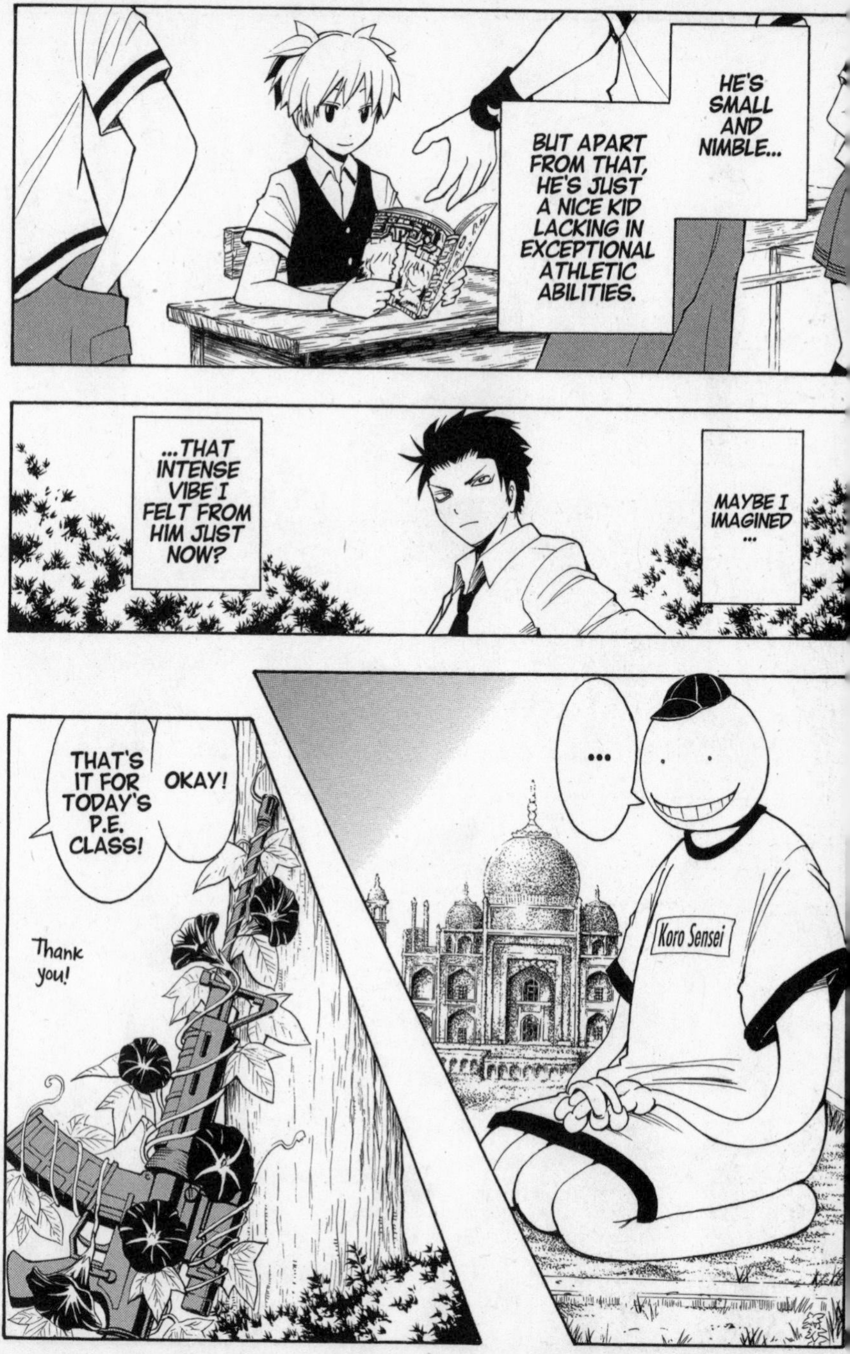
HE'S SMALL AND NIMBLE...
BUT APART FROM THAT, HE'S JUST A NICE KID LACKING IN EXCEPTIONAL ATHLETIC ABILITIES.
MAYBE I IMAGINED...
...THAT INTENSE VIBE I FELT FROM HIM JUST NOW?
...
Koro Sensei
THAT'S IT FOR TODAY'S P.E. CLASS!
OKAY!
Thank you!

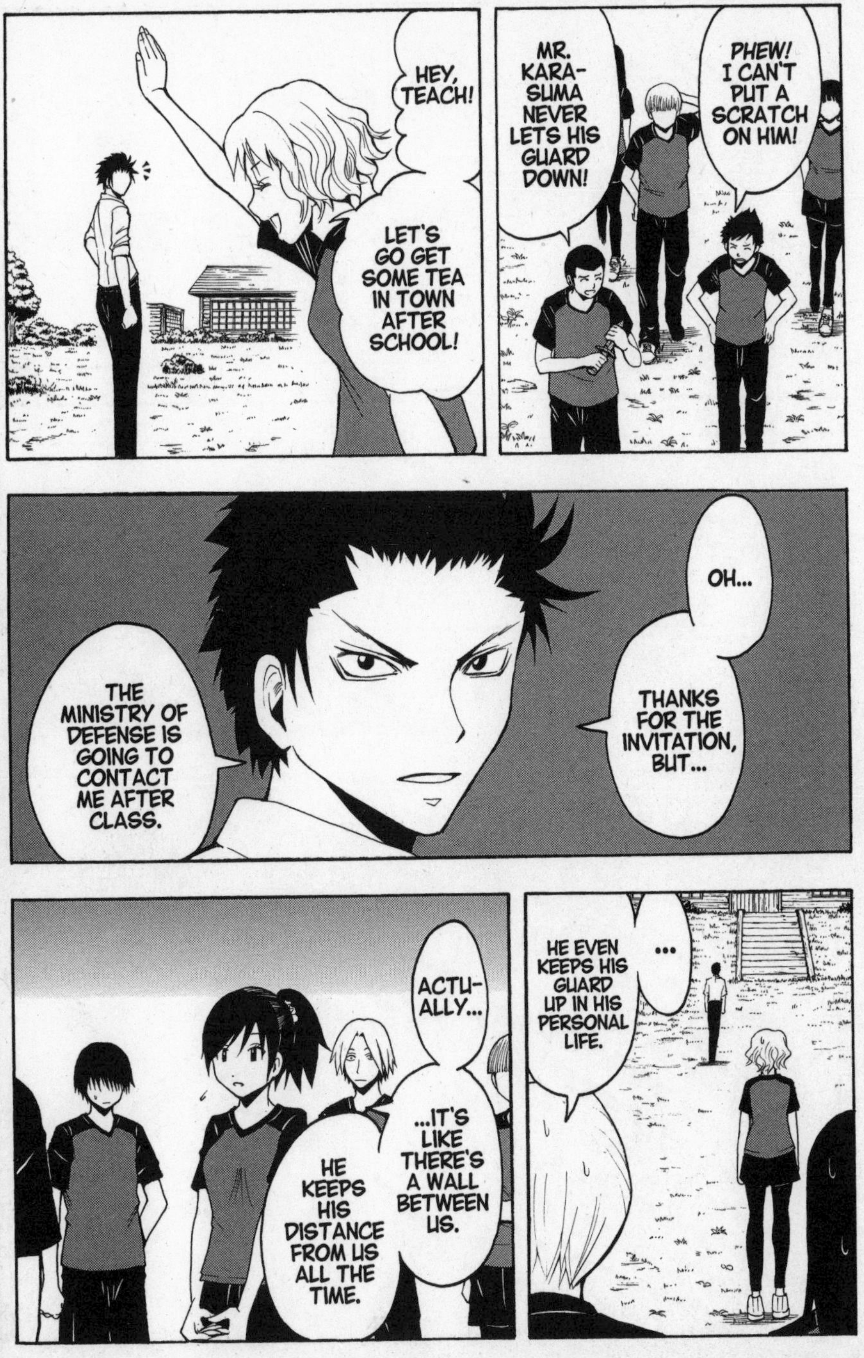
PHEW! I CAN'T PUT A SCRATCH ON HIM!
MR. KARA-SUMA NEVER LETS HIS GUARD DOWN!
HEY, TEACH!
LET'S GO GET SOME TEA IN TOWN AFTER SCHOOL!
OH...
THANKS FOR THE INVITATION, BUT...
THE MINISTRY OF DEFENSE IS GOING TO CONTACT ME AFTER CLASS.
...
HE EVEN KEEPS HIS GUARD UP IN HIS PERSONAL LIFE.
ACTU-ALLY...
...IT'S LIKE THERE'S A WALL BETWEEN US.
HE KEEPS HIS DISTANCE FROM US ALL THE TIME.

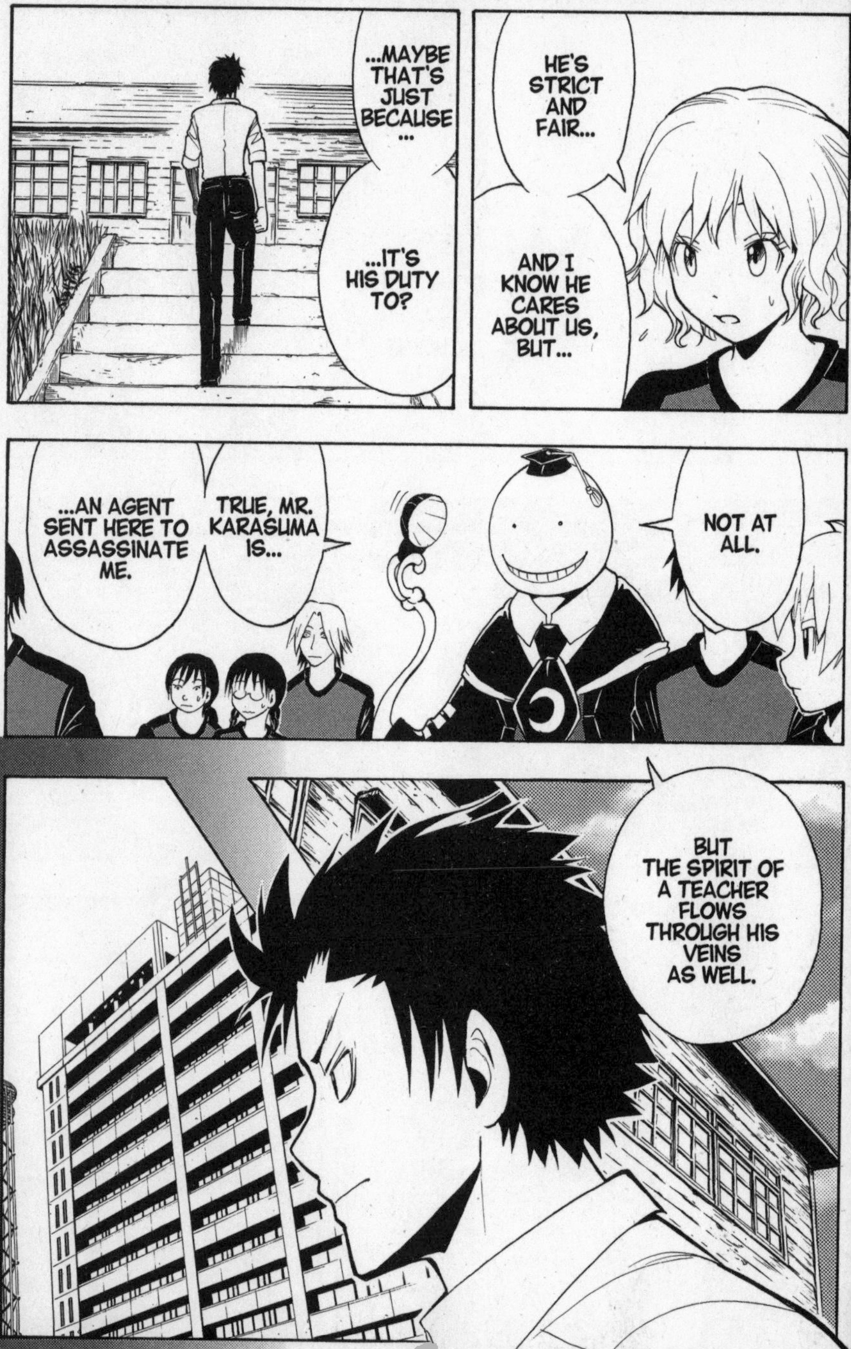
HE'S STRICT AND FAIR...
AND I KNOW HE CARES ABOUT US, BUT...
...MAYBE THAT'S JUST BECAUSE ...
...IT'S HIS DUTY TO?
NOT AT ALL.
TRUE, MR. KARASUMA IS...
...AN AGENT SENT HERE TO ASSASSINATE ME.
BUT THE SPIRIT OF A TEACHER FLOWS THROUGH HIS VEINS AS WELL.

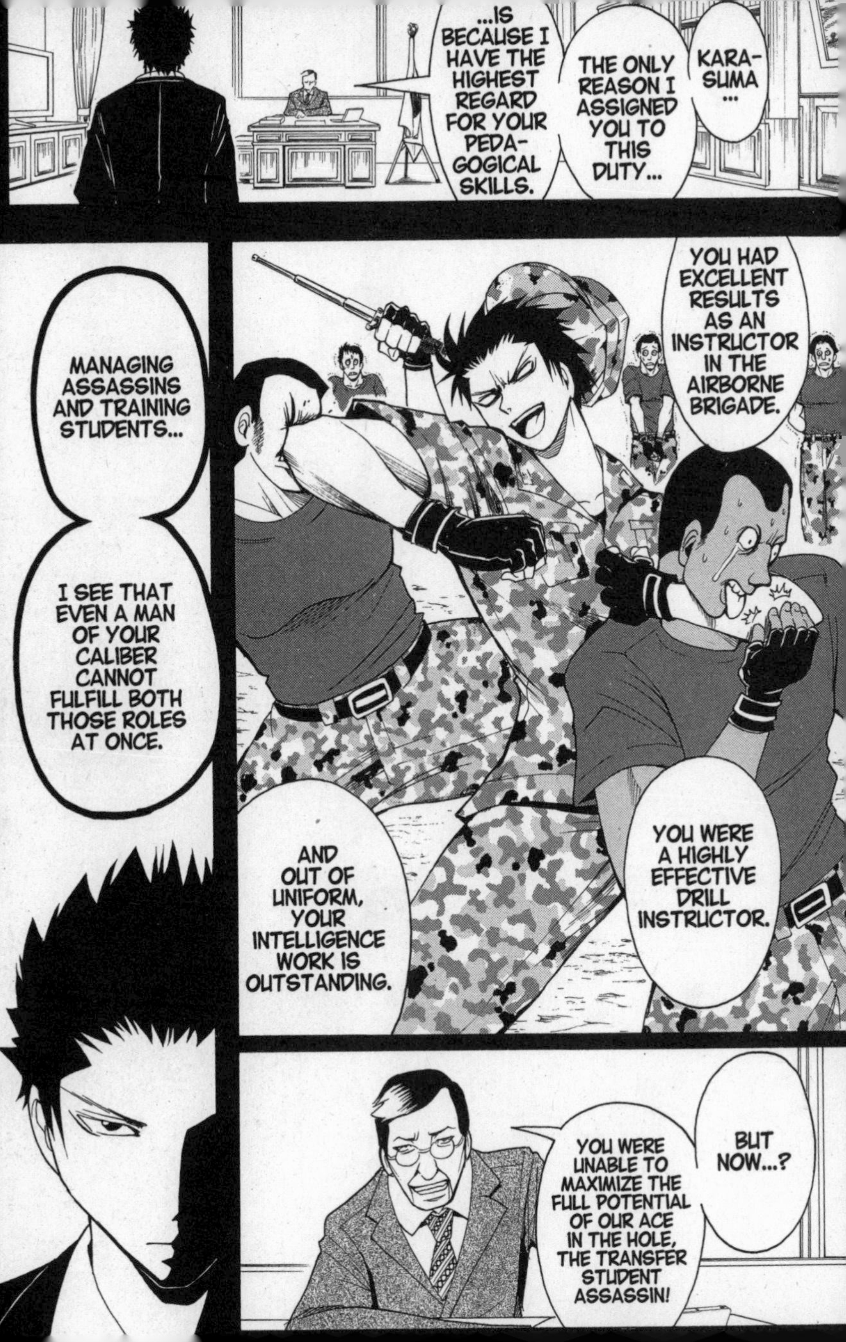
KARA-SUMA...
THE ONLY REASON I ASSIGNED YOU TO THIS DUTY...
...IS BECAUSE I HAVE THE HIGHEST REGARD FOR YOUR PEDA-GOGICAL SKILLS.
YOU HAD EXCELLENT RESULTS AS AN INSTRUCTOR IN THE AIRBORNE BRIGADE.
YOU WERE A HIGHLY EFFECTIVE DRILL INSTRUCTOR.
AND OUT OF UNIFORM, YOUR INTELLIGENCE WORK IS OUTSTANDING.
BUT NOW...?
YOU WERE UNABLE TO MAXIMIZE THE FULL POTENTIAL OF OUR ACE IN THE HOLE, THE TRANSFER STUDENT ASSASSIN!
MANAGING ASSASSINS AND TRAINING STUDENTS...
I SEE THAT EVEN A MAN OF YOUR CALIBER CANNOT FULFILL BOTH THOSE ROLES AT ONCE.

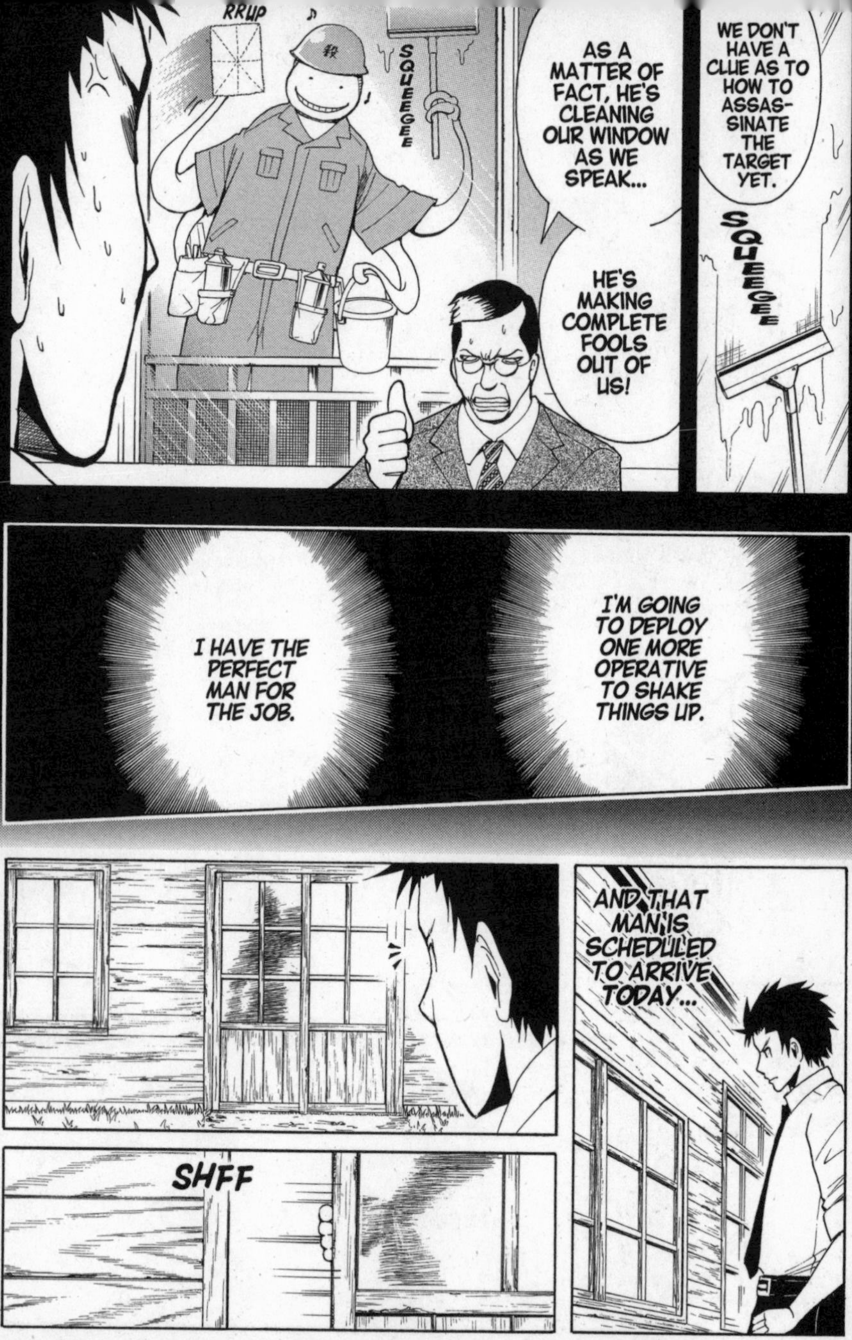
WE DON'T HAVE A CLUE AS TO HOW TO ASSAS-SINATE THE TARGET YET.
SQUEEGEE
AS A MATTER OF FACT, HE'S CLEANING OUR WINDOW AS WE SPEAK...
SQUEEGEE
RRUP
HE'S MAKING COMPLETE FOOLS OUT OF US!
I'M GOING TO DEPLOY ONE MORE OPERATIVE TO SHAKE THINGS UP.
I HAVE THE PERFECT MAN FOR THE JOB.
AND THAT MAN IS SCHEDULED TO ARRIVE TODAY...
SHFF

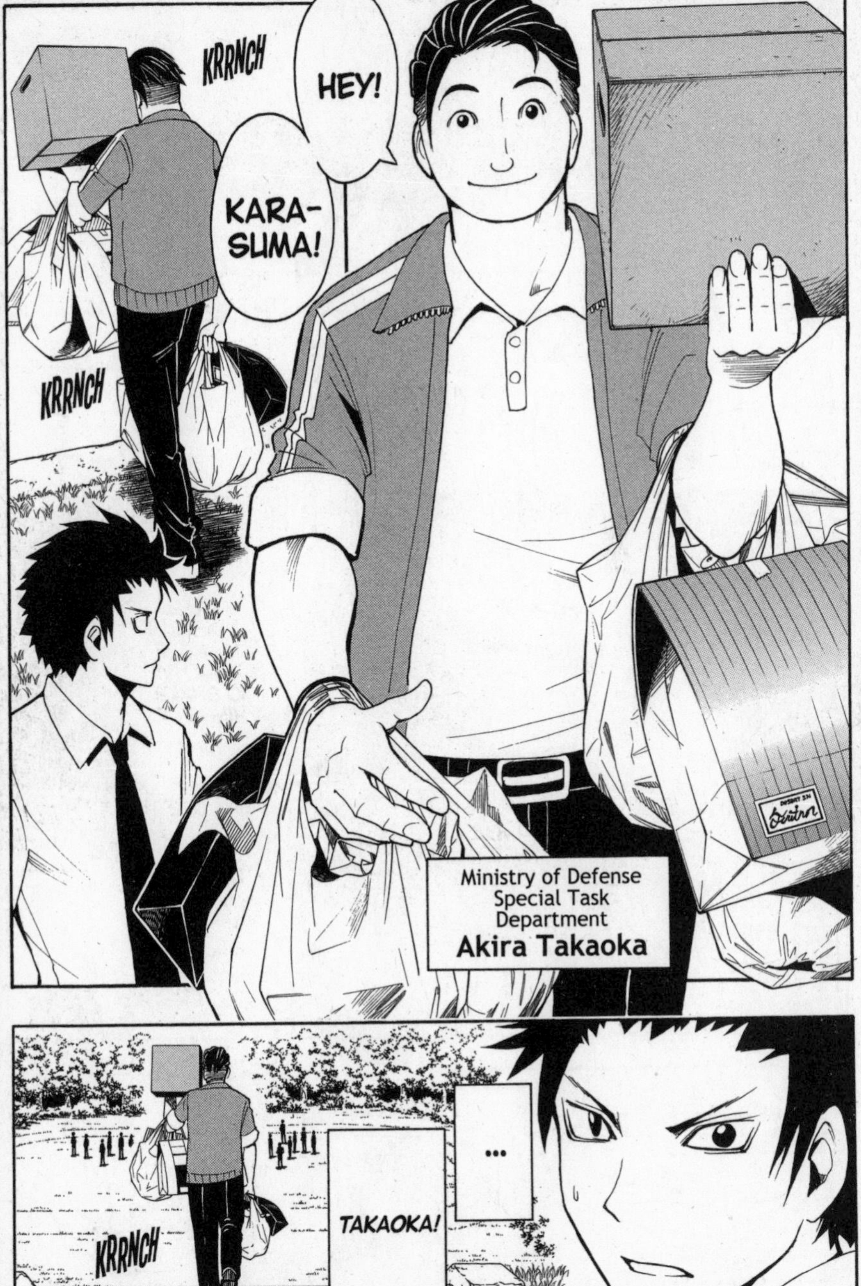
HEY!
KARA-SUMA!
KRRNCH
KRRNCH
Ministry of Defense Special Task Department
Akira Takaoka
...
TAKAOKA!
KRRNCH

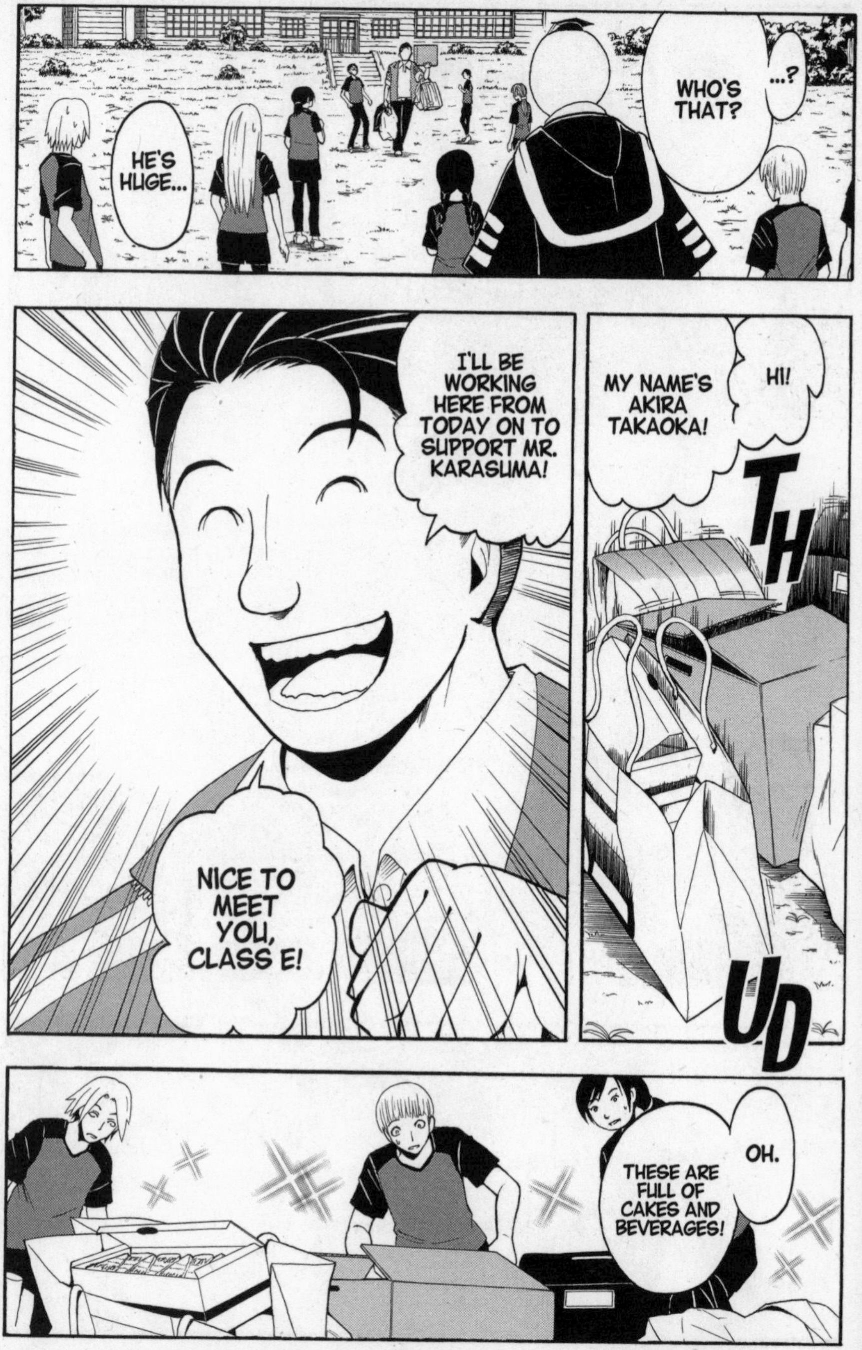
...?
WHO'S THAT?
HE'S HUGE...
HI!
MY NAME'S AKIRA TAKAOKA!
THUD
I'LL BE WORKING HERE FROM TODAY ON TO SUPPORT MR. KARASUMA!
NICE TO MEET YOU, CLASS E!
OH.
THESE ARE FULL OF CAKES AND BEVERAGES!

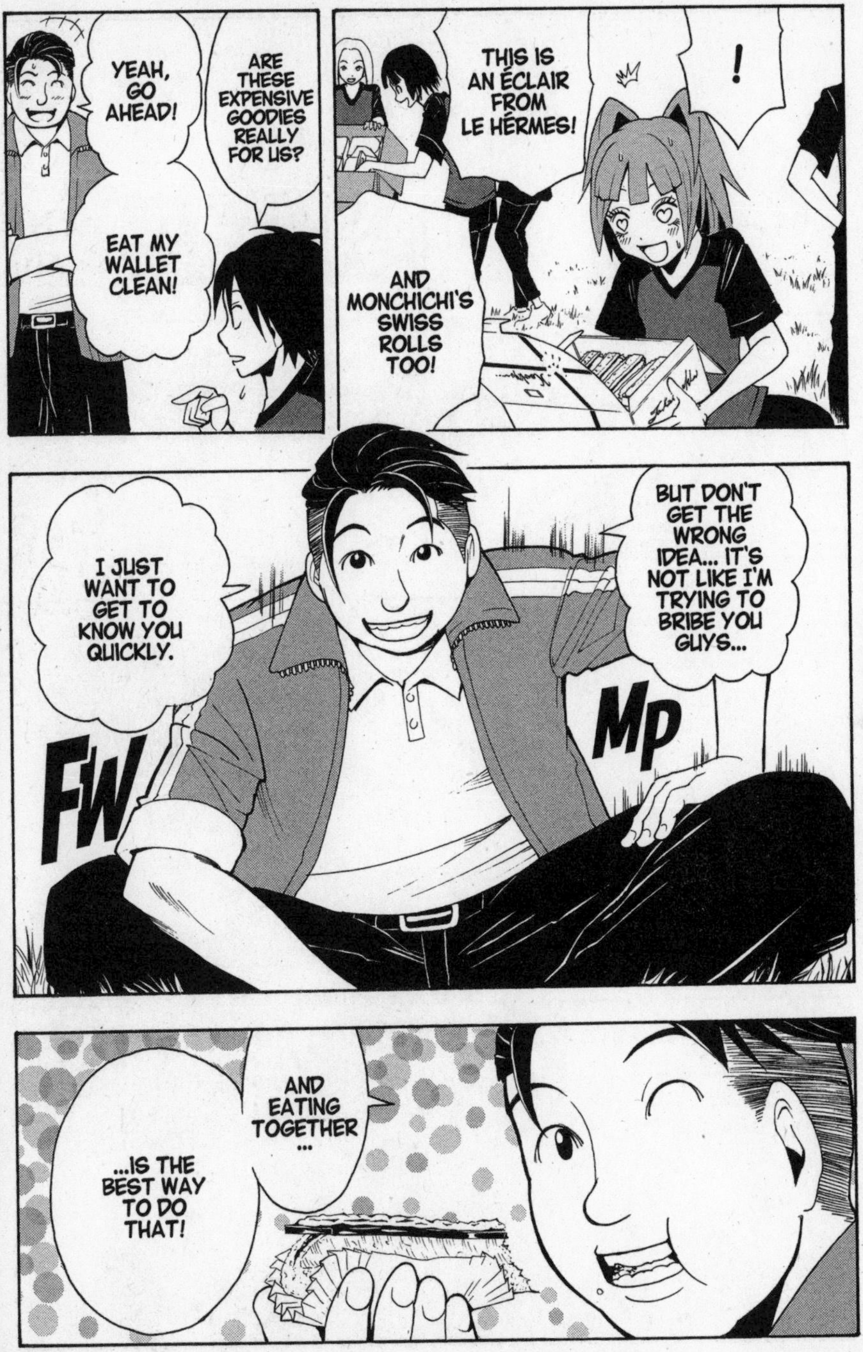
!
THIS IS AN ÉCLAIR FROM LE HÉRMES!
AND MONCHICHI'S SWISS ROLLS TOO!
ARE THESE EXPENSIVE GOODIES REALLY FOR US?
YEAH, GO AHEAD!
EAT MY WALLET CLEAN!
BUT DON'T GET THE WRONG IDEA... IT'S NOT LIKE I'M TRYING TO BRIBE YOU GUYS...
MP
I JUST WANT TO GET TO KNOW YOU QUICKLY.
FW
AND EATING TOGETHER ...
...IS THE BEST WAY TO DO THAT!

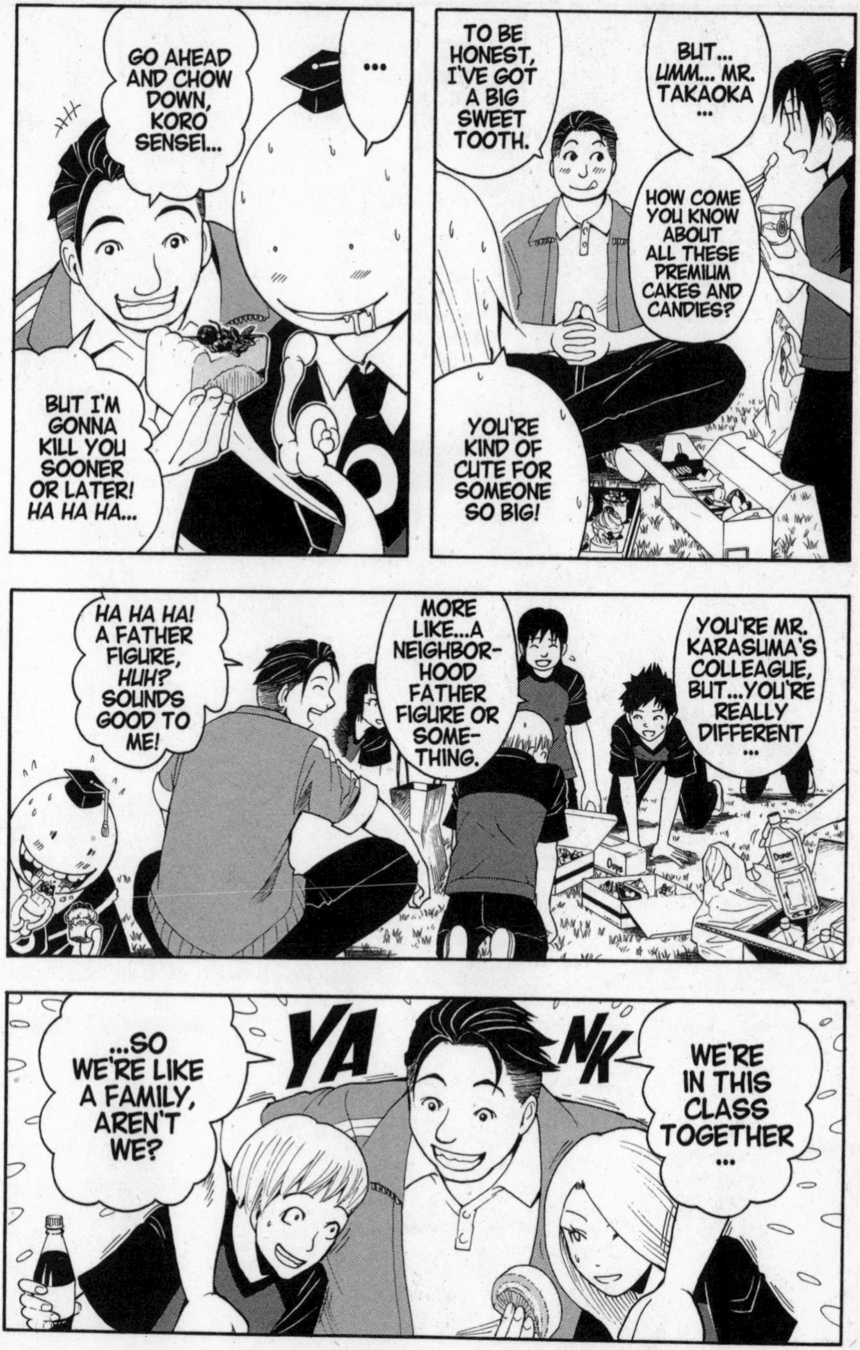
BUT... UMM... MR. TAKAOKA ...
HOW COME YOU KNOW ABOUT ALL THESE PREMIUM CAKES AND CANDIES?
TO BE HONEST, I'VE GOT A BIG SWEET TOOTH.
YOU'RE KIND OF CUTE FOR SOMEONE SO BIG!
...
GO AHEAD AND CHOW DOWN, KORO SENSEI...
BUT I'M GONNA KILL YOU SOONER OR LATER! HA HA HA...
YOU'RE MR. KARASUMA'S COLLEAGUE, BUT...YOU'RE REALLY DIFFERENT ...
MORE LIKE...A NEIGHBOR-HOOD FATHER FIGURE OR SOME-THING.
HA HA HA! A FATHER FIGURE, HUH? SOUNDS GOOD TO ME!
WE'RE IN THIS CLASS TOGETHER ...
YANK
...SO WE'RE LIKE A FAMILY, AREN'T WE?

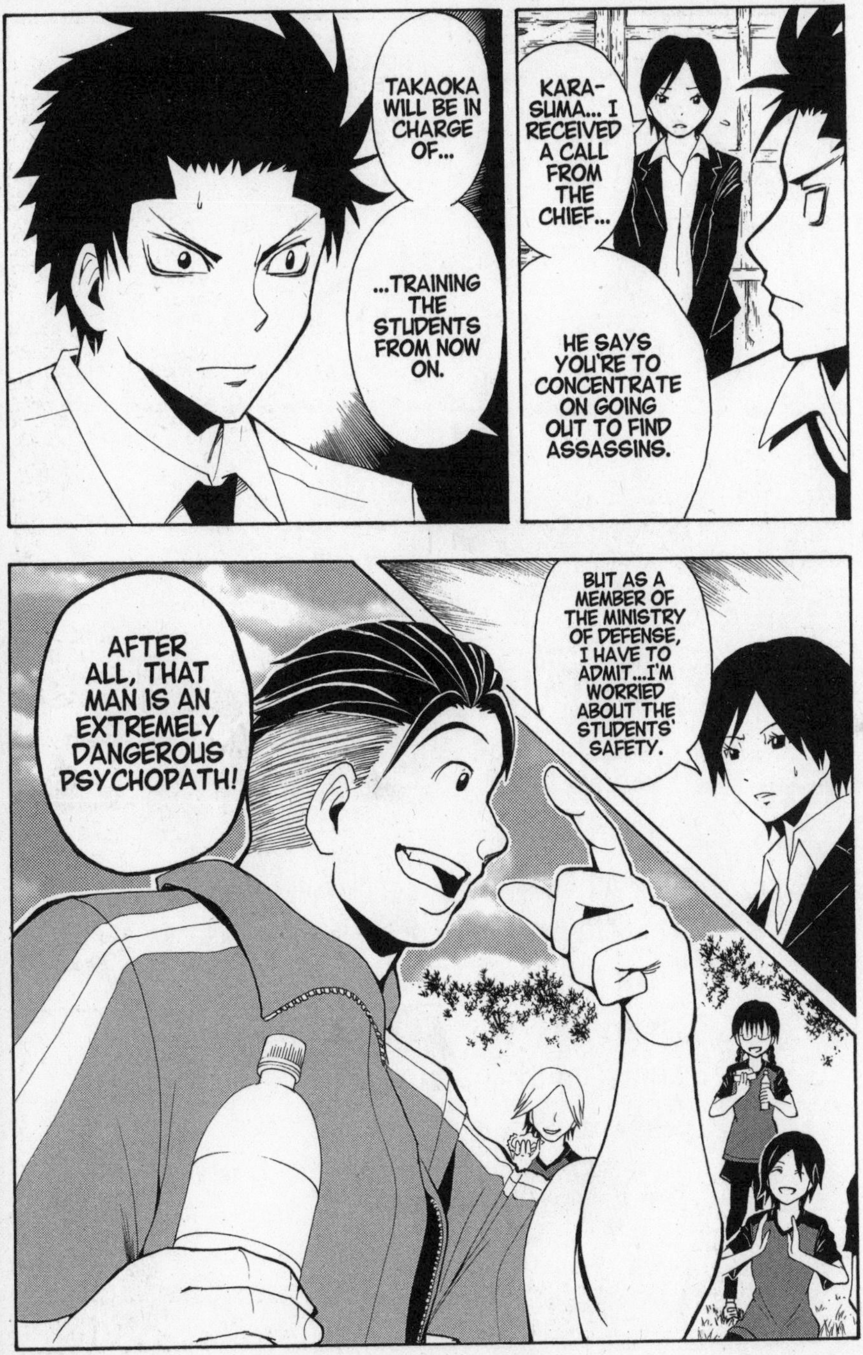
KARA-SUMA... I RECEIVED A CALL FROM THE CHIEF...
HE SAYS YOU'RE TO CONCENTRATE ON GOING OUT TO FIND ASSASSINS.
TAKAOKA WILL BE IN CHARGE OF...
...TRAINING THE STUDENTS FROM NOW ON.
BUT AS A MEMBER OF THE MINISTRY OF DEFENSE, I HAVE TO ADMIT...I'M WORRIED ABOUT THE STUDENTS' SAFETY.
AFTER ALL, THAT MAN IS AN EXTREMELY DANGEROUS PSYCHOPATH!

E-2 TAIGA OKAJIMA

- 🌑 BIRTHDAY: JUNE 9
- 🌑 HEIGHT: 5' 6"
- 🌑 WEIGHT: 127 LBS.
- 🌑 FAVORITE SUBJECT: HEALTH AND PHYSICAL EDUCATION
- 🌑 LEAST FAVORITE SUBJECT: MATH
- 🌑 HOBBY/SKILL: COLLECTING BOOKS
- 🌑 FUTURE GOAL: PHOTOGRAPHER
- 🌑 HIS WORDS OF WISDOM:

    "DON'T HOLD YOUR LECHEROUS THOUGHTS PRISONER.
    LET THEM FLY FREE LIKE A BIRD."

Class 39 Time to Kill Them with Kindness

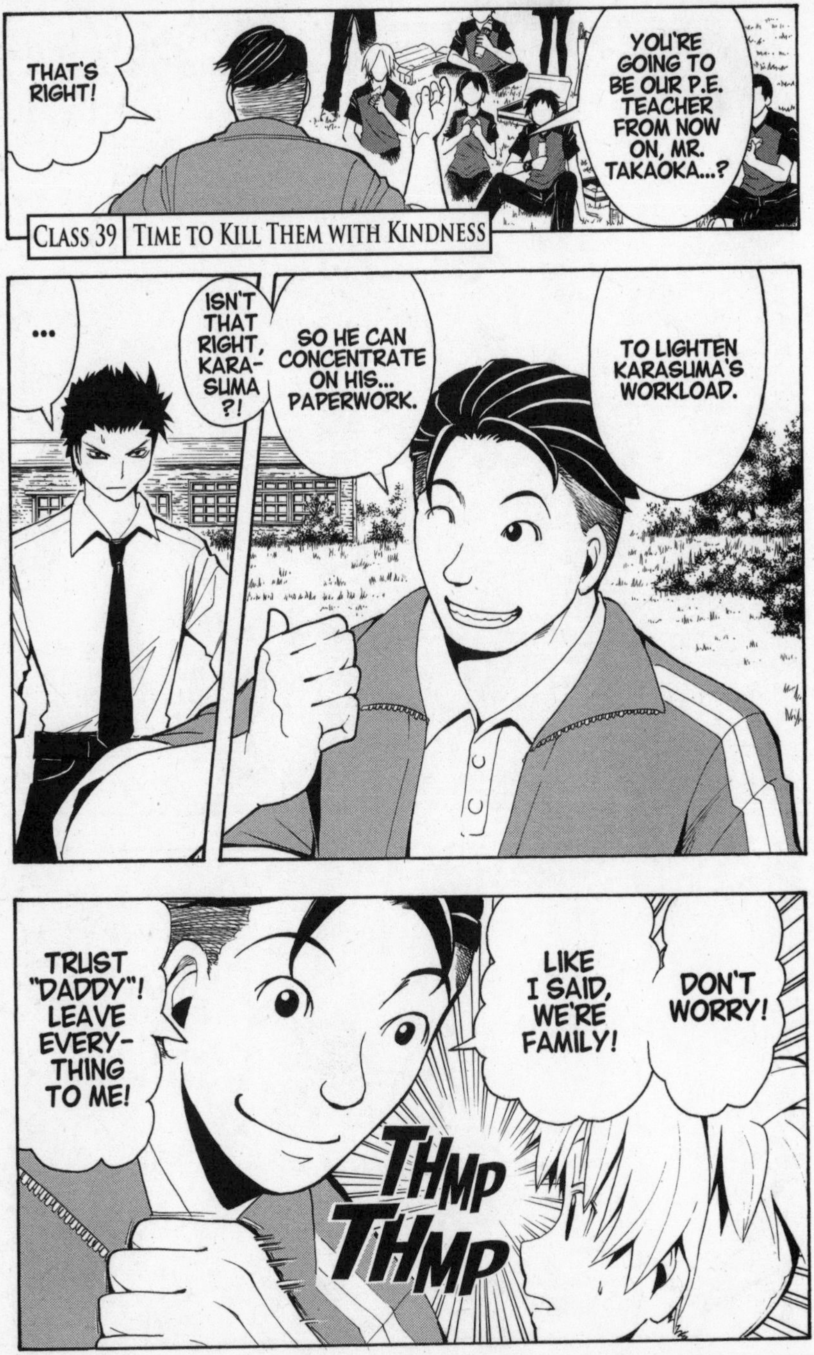

YOU'RE GOING TO BE OUR P.E. TEACHER FROM NOW ON, MR. TAKAOKA...?
THAT'S RIGHT!
TO LIGHTEN KARASUMA'S WORKLOAD.
SO HE CAN CONCENTRATE ON HIS... PAPERWORK.
ISN'T THAT RIGHT, KARA-SUMA?!
...
DON'T WORRY!
LIKE I SAID, WE'RE FAMILY!
TRUST "DADDY"! LEAVE EVERY-THING TO ME!
THMP THMP

CLASS 39 TIME TO KILL THEM WITH KINDNESS

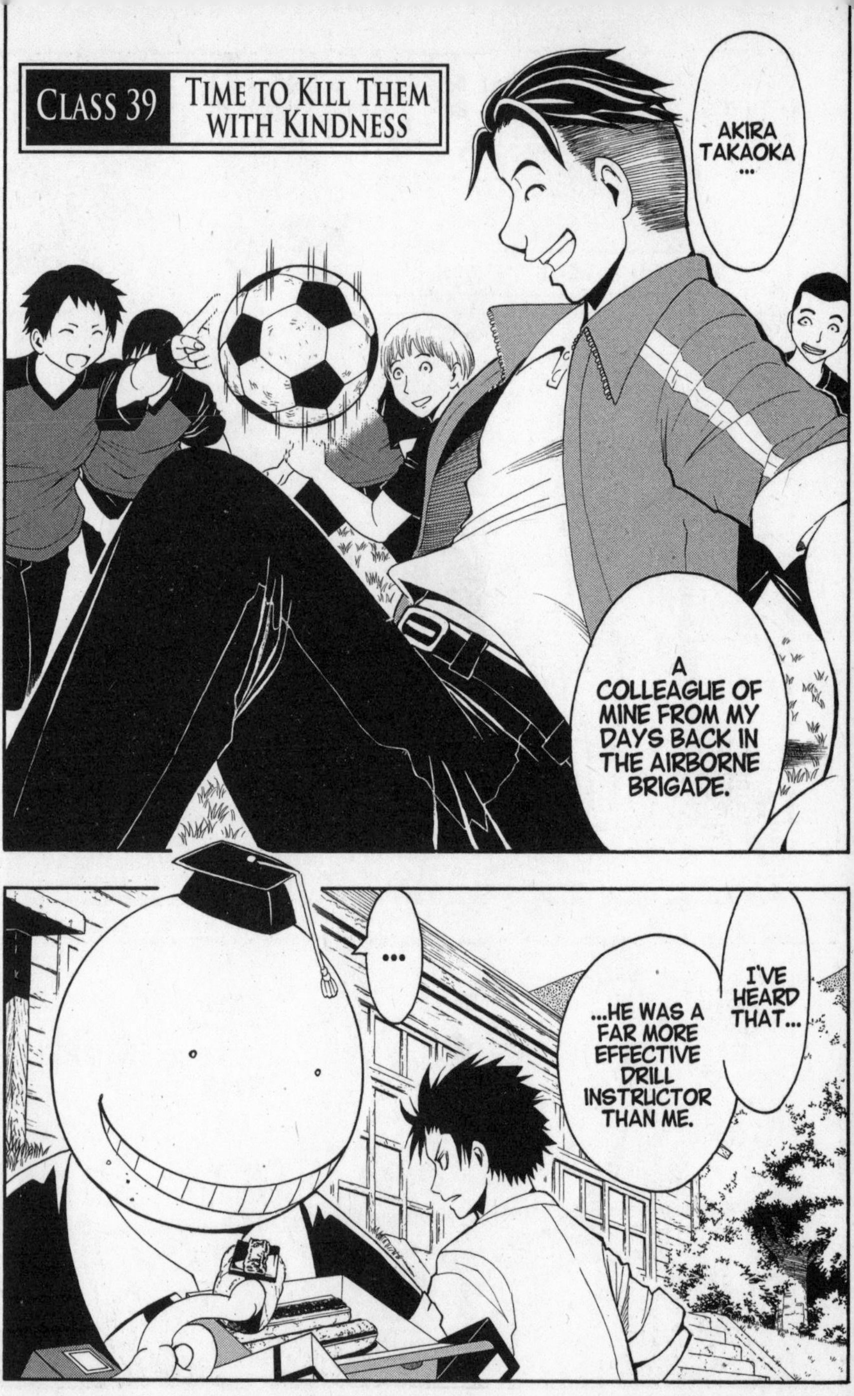
AKIRA TAKAOKA...
A COLLEAGUE OF MINE FROM MY DAYS BACK IN THE AIRBORNE BRIGADE.
I'VE HEARD THAT...
...HE WAS A FAR MORE EFFECTIVE DRILL INSTRUCTOR THAN ME.
...

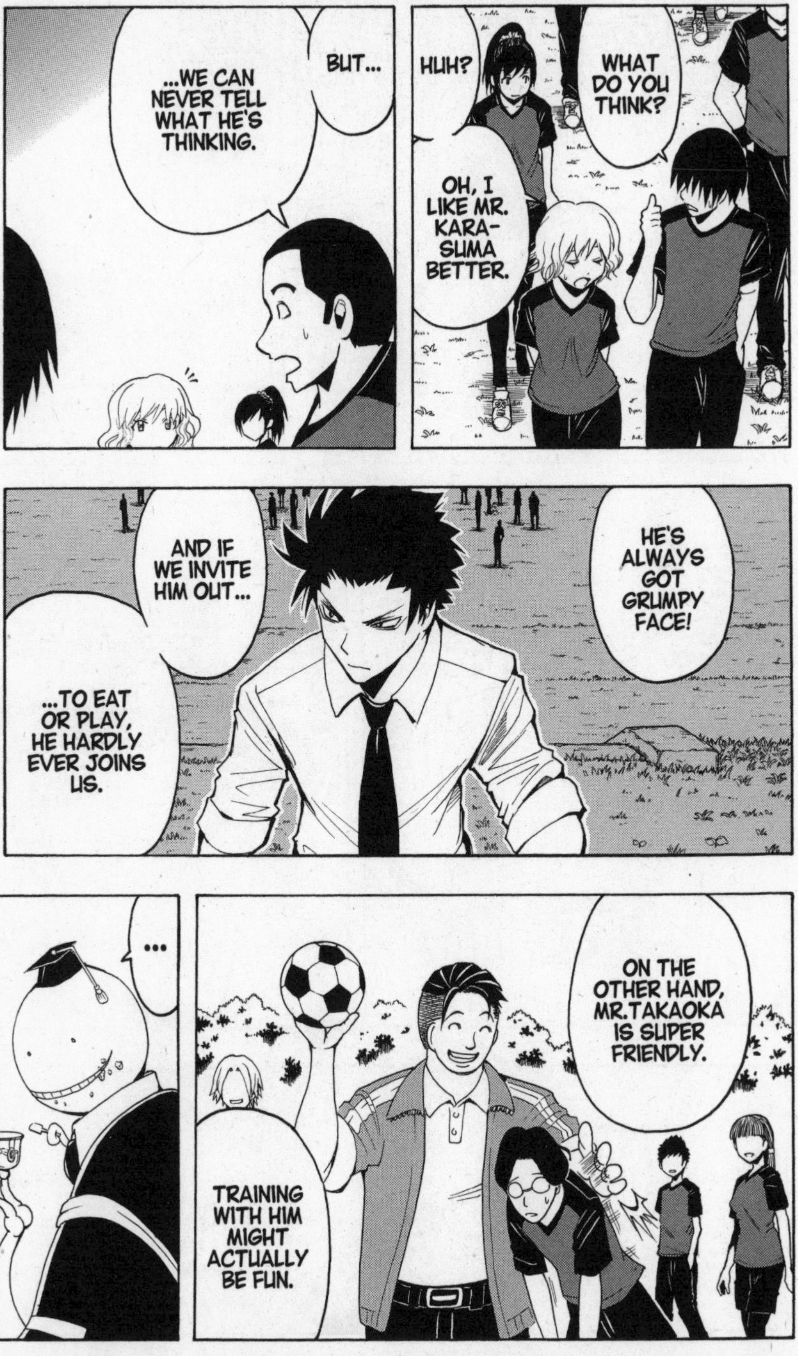
WHAT DO YOU THINK?
HUH?
OH, I LIKE MR. KARA-SUMA BETTER.
BUT...
...WE CAN NEVER TELL WHAT HE'S THINKING.
HE'S ALWAYS GOT GRUMPY FACE!
AND IF WE INVITE HIM OUT...
...TO EAT OR PLAY, HE HARDLY EVER JOINS US.
ON THE OTHER HAND, MR.TAKAOKA IS SUPER FRIENDLY.
TRAINING WITH HIM MIGHT ACTUALLY BE FUN.
...

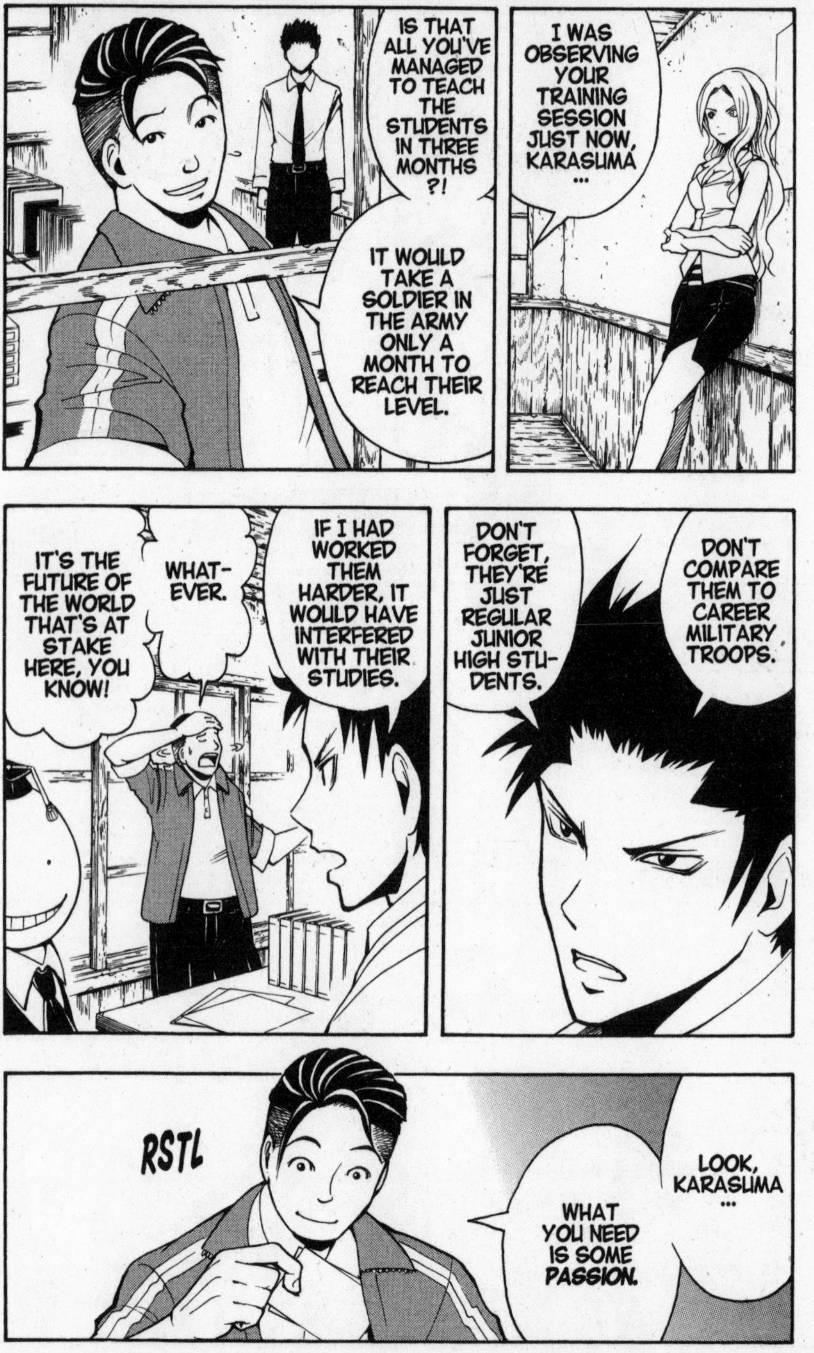
I WAS OBSERVING YOUR TRAINING SESSION JUST NOW, KARASUMA...
IS THAT ALL YOU'VE MANAGED TO TEACH THE STUDENTS IN THREE MONTHS?!
IT WOULD TAKE A SOLDIER IN THE ARMY ONLY A MONTH TO REACH THEIR LEVEL.
DON'T COMPARE THEM TO CAREER MILITARY TROOPS.
DON'T FORGET, THEY'RE JUST REGULAR JUNIOR HIGH STU-DENTS.
IF I HAD WORKED THEM HARDER, IT WOULD HAVE INTERFERED WITH THEIR STUDIES.
WHAT-EVER.
IT'S THE FUTURE OF THE WORLD THAT'S AT STAKE HERE, YOU KNOW!
LOOK, KARASUMA...
WHAT YOU NEED IS SOME PASSION.
RSTL

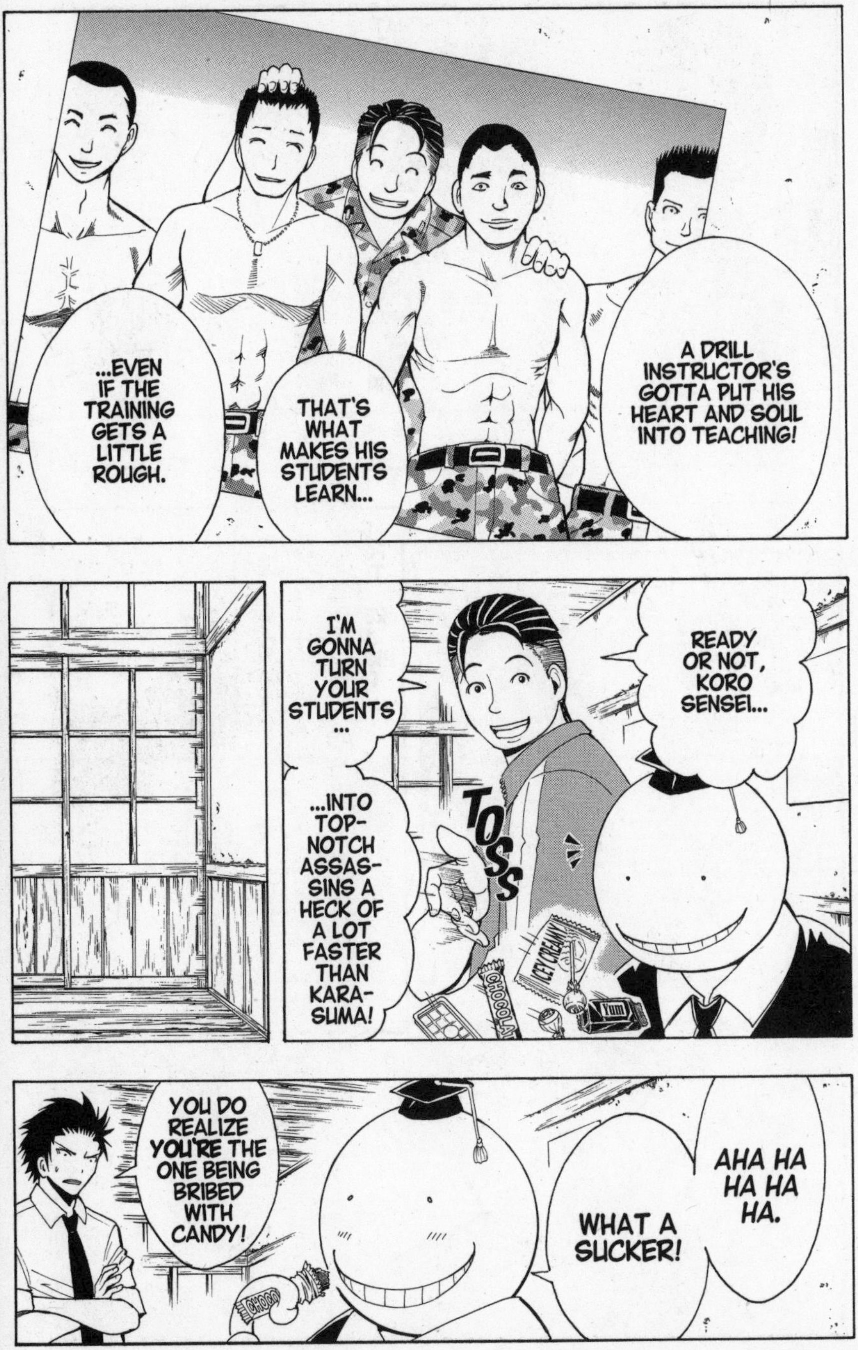
A DRILL INSTRUCTOR'S GOTTA PUT HIS HEART AND SOUL INTO TEACHING!
THAT'S WHAT MAKES HIS STUDENTS LEARN...
...EVEN IF THE TRAINING GETS A LITTLE ROUGH.
READY OR NOT, KORO SENSEI...
I'M GONNA TURN YOUR STUDENTS ...
...INTO TOP-NOTCH ASSAS-SINS A HECK OF A LOT FASTER THAN KARA-SUMA!
TOSS
ICEY CREAM!
CHOCOLAT
Yum
AHA HA HA HA HA.
WHAT A SUCKER!
YOU DO REALIZE YOU'RE THE ONE BEING BRIBED WITH CANDY!
CHOCO

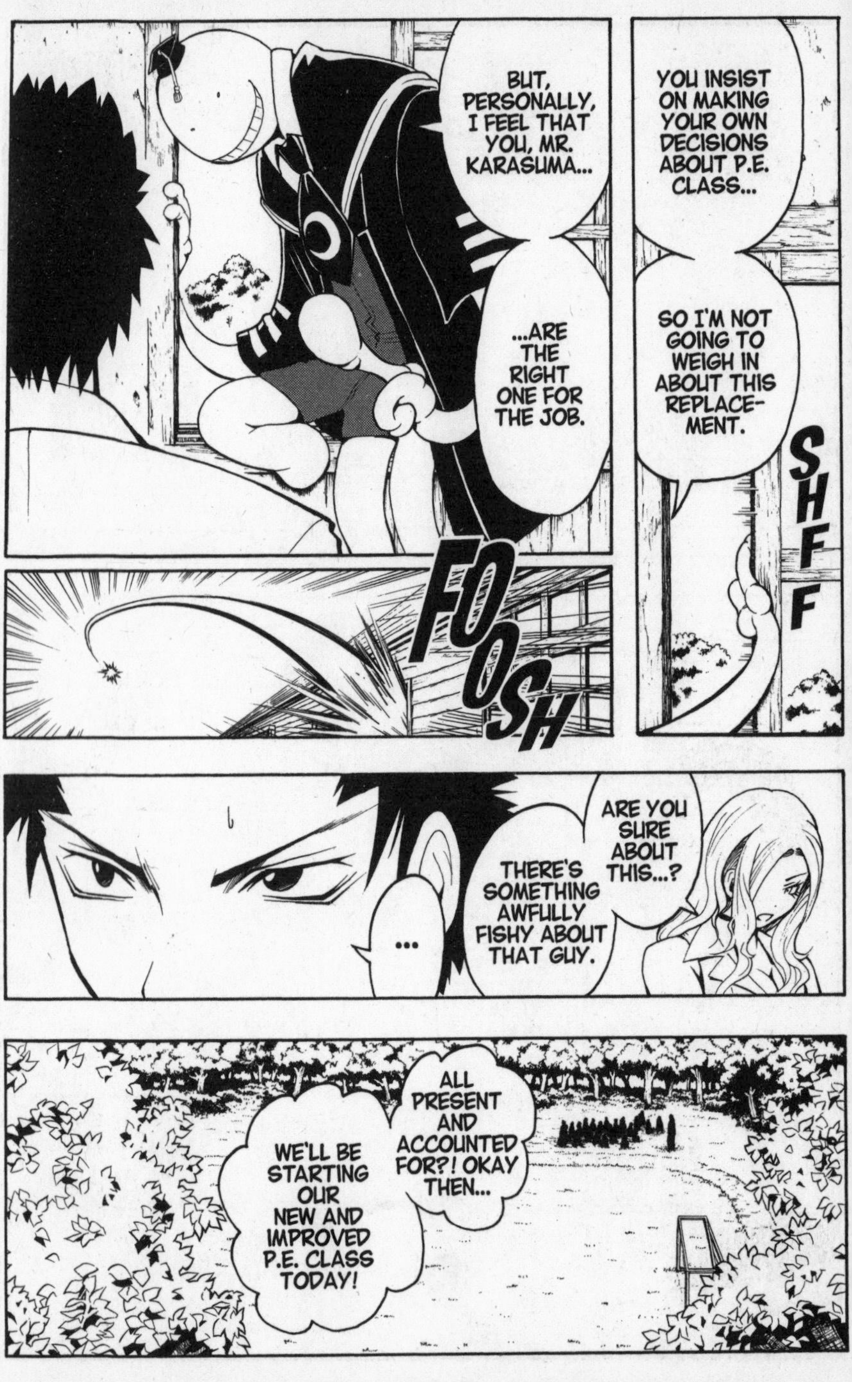
YOU INSIST ON MAKING YOUR OWN DECISIONS ABOUT P.E. CLASS...
SO I'M NOT GOING TO WEIGH IN ABOUT THIS REPLACE-MENT.
SHFF
BUT, PERSONALLY, I FEEL THAT YOU, MR. KARASUMA...
...ARE THE RIGHT ONE FOR THE JOB.
FOOSH
ARE YOU SURE ABOUT THIS...?
THERE'S SOMETHING AWFULLY FISHY ABOUT THAT GUY.
...
ALL PRESENT AND ACCOUNTED FOR?! OKAY THEN...
WE'LL BE STARTING OUR NEW AND IMPROVED P.E. CLASS TODAY!

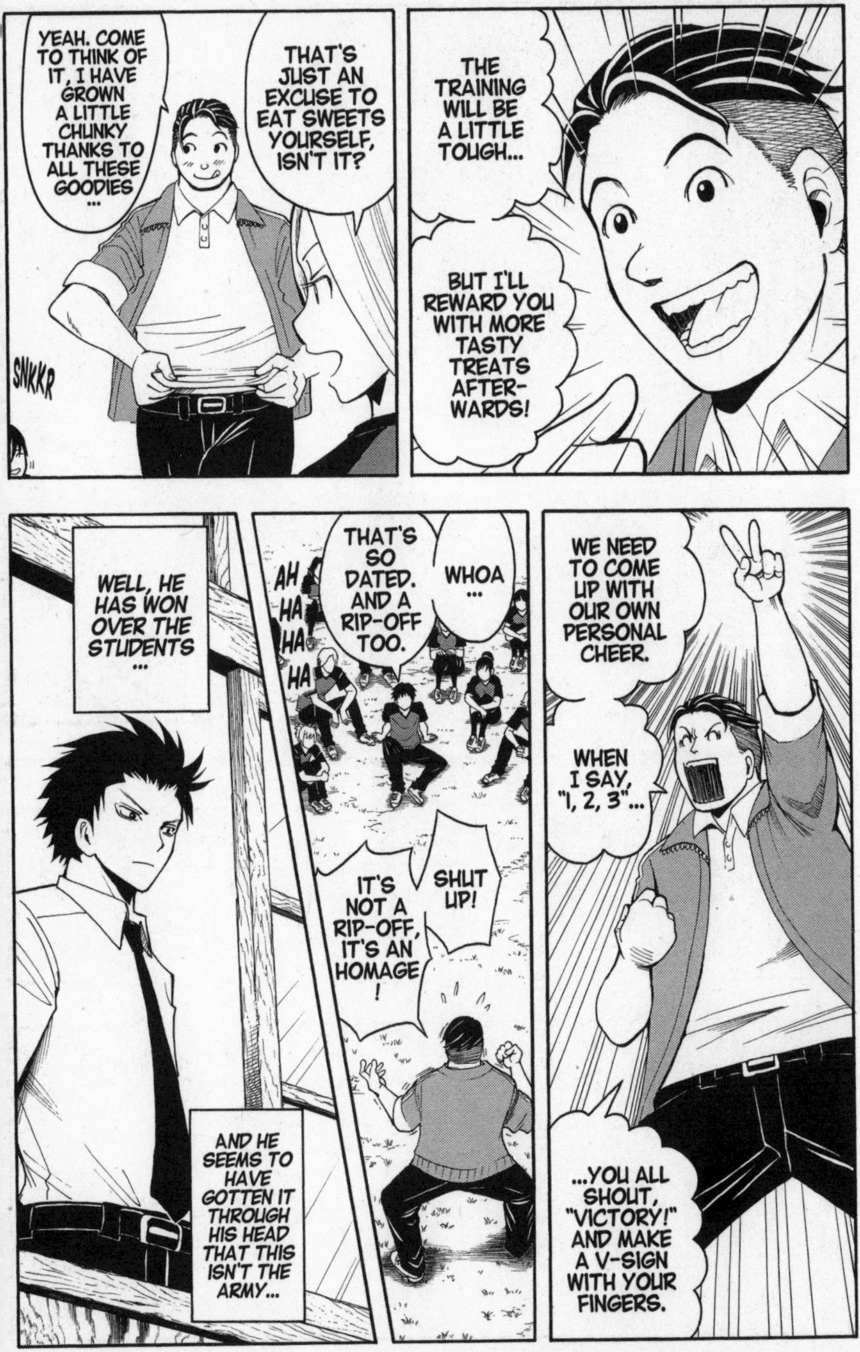
THE TRAINING WILL BE A LITTLE TOUGH...
BUT I'LL REWARD YOU WITH MORE TASTY TREATS AFTER-WARDS!
THAT'S JUST AN EXCUSE TO EAT SWEETS YOURSELF, ISN'T IT?
YEAH. COME TO THINK OF IT, I HAVE GROWN A LITTLE CHUNKY THANKS TO ALL THESE GOODIES ...
SNKKR
WE NEED TO COME UP WITH OUR OWN PERSONAL CHEER.
WHEN I SAY, "1, 2, 3"...
...YOU ALL SHOUT, "VICTORY!" AND MAKE A V-SIGN WITH YOUR FINGERS.
WHOA ...
THAT'S SO DATED. AND A RIP-OFF TOO.
AH HA HA HA
SHUT UP!
IT'S NOT A RIP-OFF, IT'S AN HOMAGE!
WELL, HE HAS WON OVER THE STUDENTS ...
AND HE SEEMS TO HAVE GOTTEN IT THROUGH HIS HEAD THAT THIS ISN'T THE ARMY...

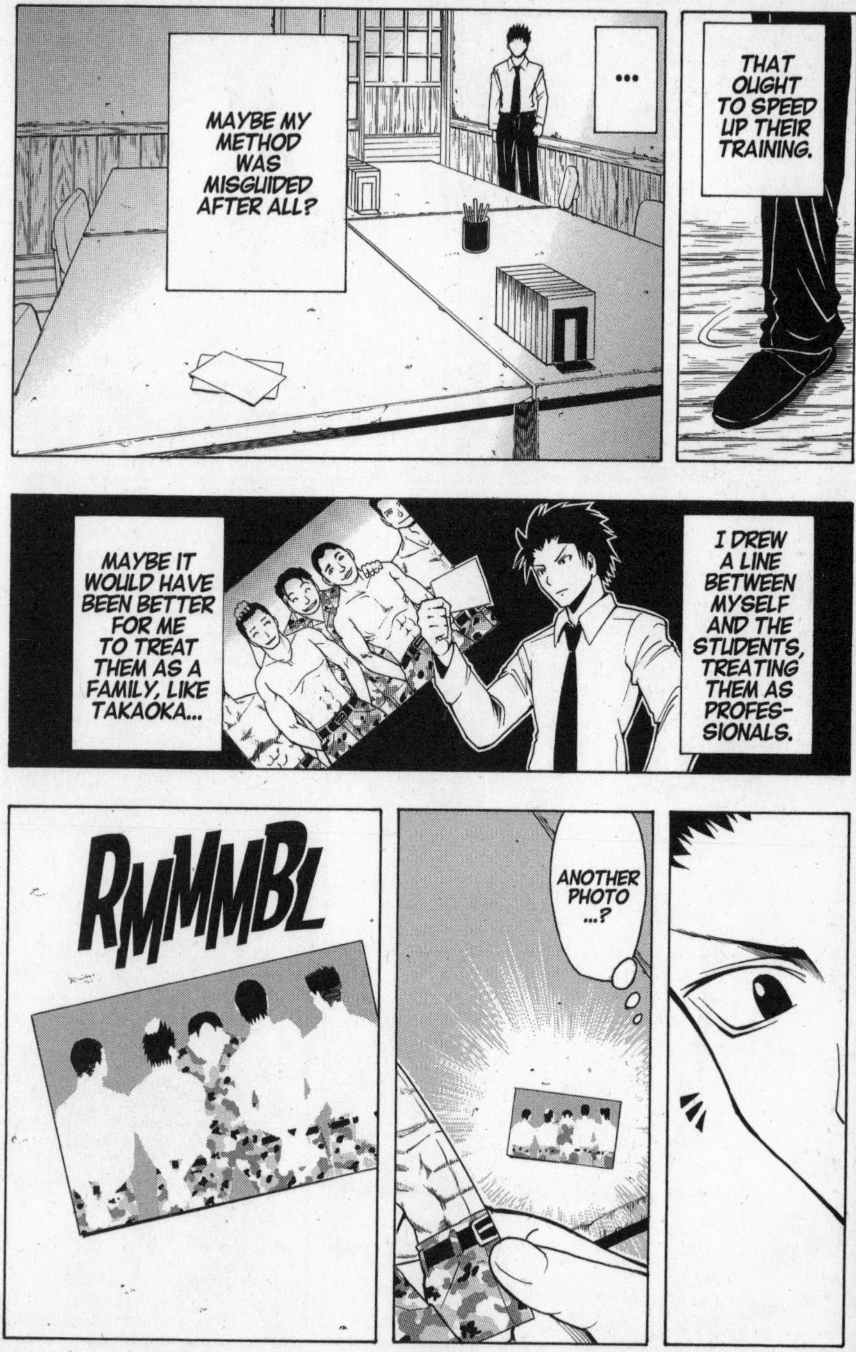
THAT OUGHT TO SPEED UP THEIR TRAINING.
...
MAYBE MY METHOD WAS MISGUIDED AFTER ALL?
I DREW A LINE BETWEEN MYSELF AND THE STUDENTS, TREATING THEM AS PROFES-SIONALS.
MAYBE IT WOULD HAVE BEEN BETTER FOR ME TO TREAT THEM AS A FAMILY, LIKE TAKAOKA...
ANOTHER PHOTO ...?
RMMMBL

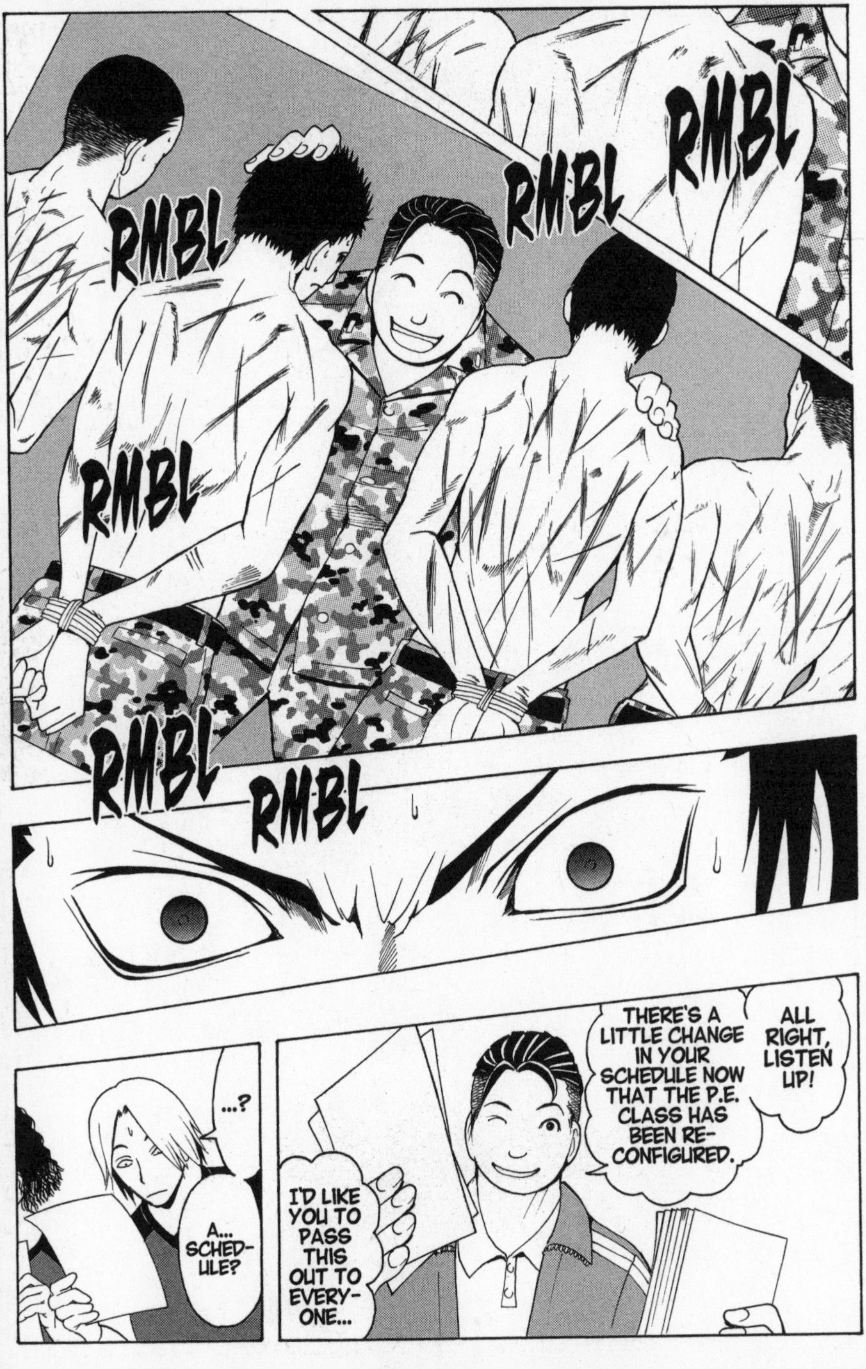
RMBL
RMBL
RMBL
RMBL
RMBL
RMBL
ALL RIGHT, LISTEN UP!
THERE'S A LITTLE CHANGE IN YOUR SCHEDULE NOW THAT THE P.E. CLASS HAS BEEN RE-CONFIGURED.
I'D LIKE YOU TO PASS THIS OUT TO EVERY-ONE...
...?
A... SCHED-ULE?

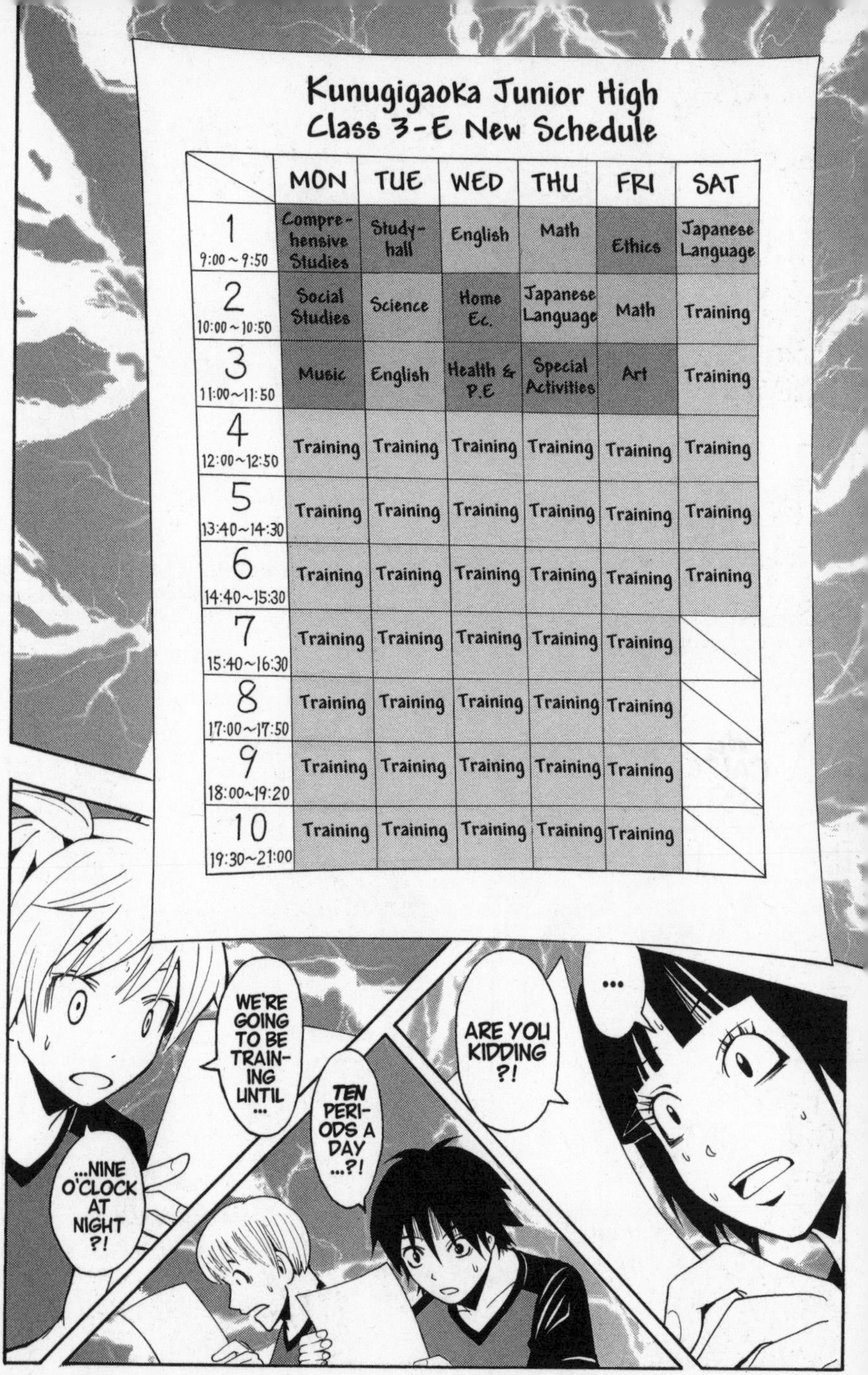
Kunugigaoka Junior High
Class 3-E New Schedule

	MON	TUE	WED	THU	FRI	SAT
1 9:00~9:50	Compre-hensive Studies	Study-hall	English	Math	Ethics	Japanese Language
2 10:00~10:50	Social Studies	Science	Home Ec.	Japanese Language	Math	Training
3 11:00~11:50	Music	English	Health & P.E	Special Activities	Art	Training
4 12:00~12:50	Training	Training	Training	Training	Training	Training
5 13:40~14:30	Training	Training	Training	Training	Training	Training
6 14:40~15:30	Training	Training	Training	Training	Training	Training
7 15:40~16:30	Training	Training	Training	Training	Training	
8 17:00~17:50	Training	Training	Training	Training	Training	
9 18:00~19:20	Training	Training	Training	Training	Training	
10 19:30~21:00	Training	Training	Training	Training	Training	

...
ARE YOU KIDDING?!
TEN PERIODS A DAY...?!
WE'RE GOING TO BE TRAINING UNTIL...
...NINE O'CLOCK AT NIGHT?!

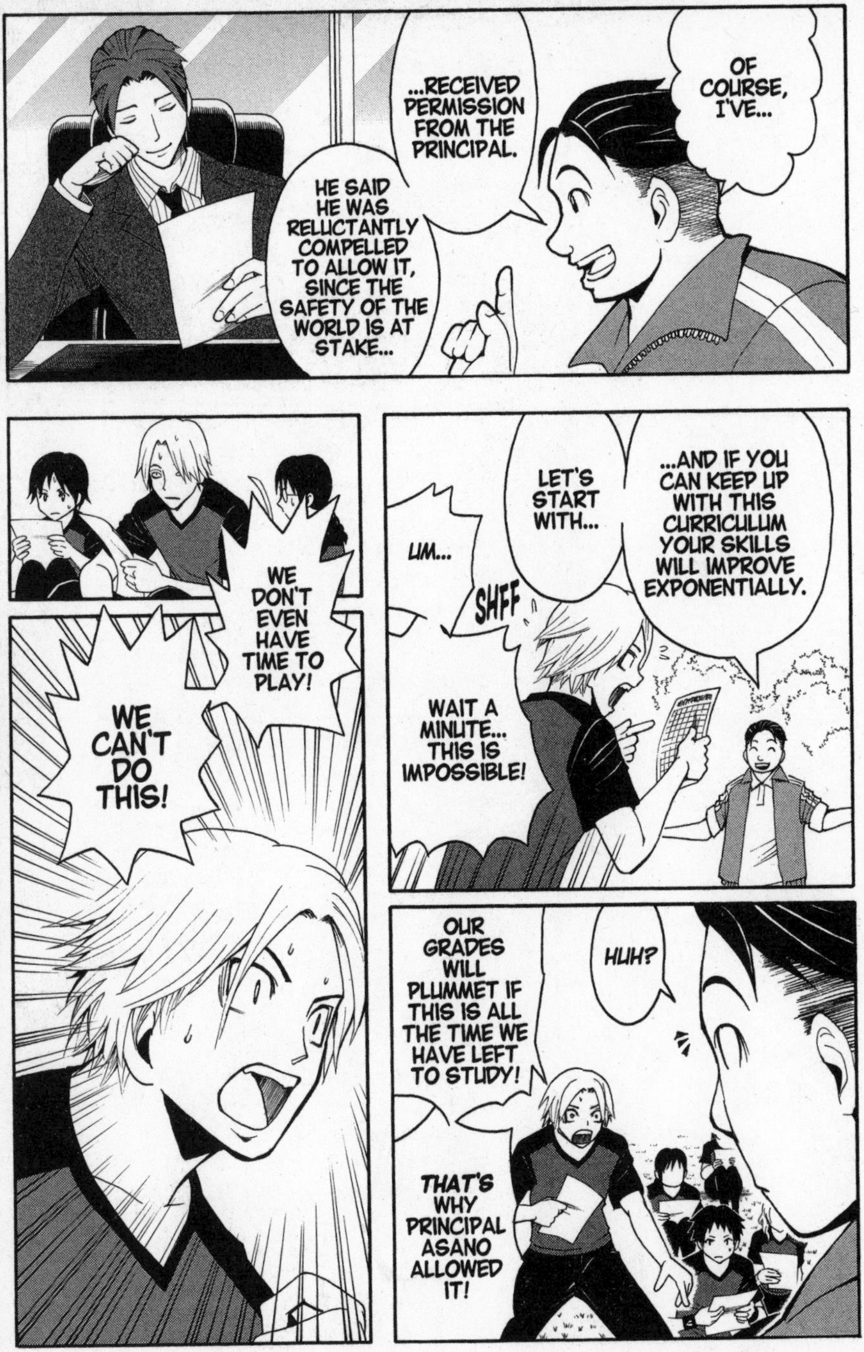

OF COURSE, I'VE...
...RECEIVED PERMISSION FROM THE PRINCIPAL.
HE SAID HE WAS RELUCTANTLY COMPELLED TO ALLOW IT, SINCE THE SAFETY OF THE WORLD IS AT STAKE...
...AND IF YOU CAN KEEP UP WITH THIS CURRICULUM YOUR SKILLS WILL IMPROVE EXPONENTIALLY.
LET'S START WITH...
UM...
SHFF
WAIT A MINUTE... THIS IS IMPOSSIBLE!
WE DON'T EVEN HAVE TIME TO PLAY!
WE CAN'T DO THIS!
HUH?
OUR GRADES WILL PLUMMET IF THIS IS ALL THE TIME WE HAVE LEFT TO STUDY!
THAT'S WHY PRINCIPAL ASANO ALLOWED IT!

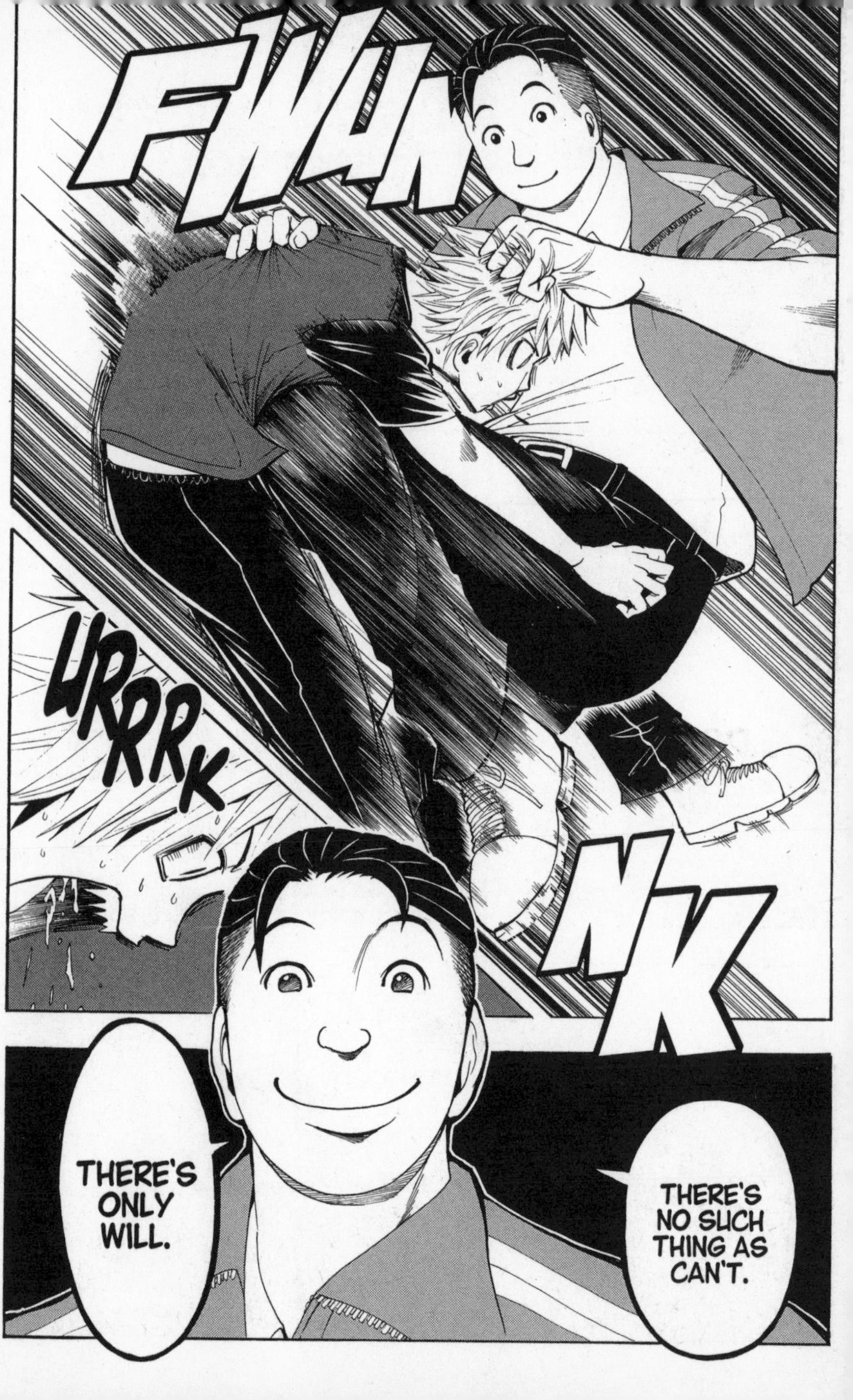
F-WUM
URRRK
NK
THERE'S NO SUCH THING AS CAN'T.
THERE'S ONLY WILL.

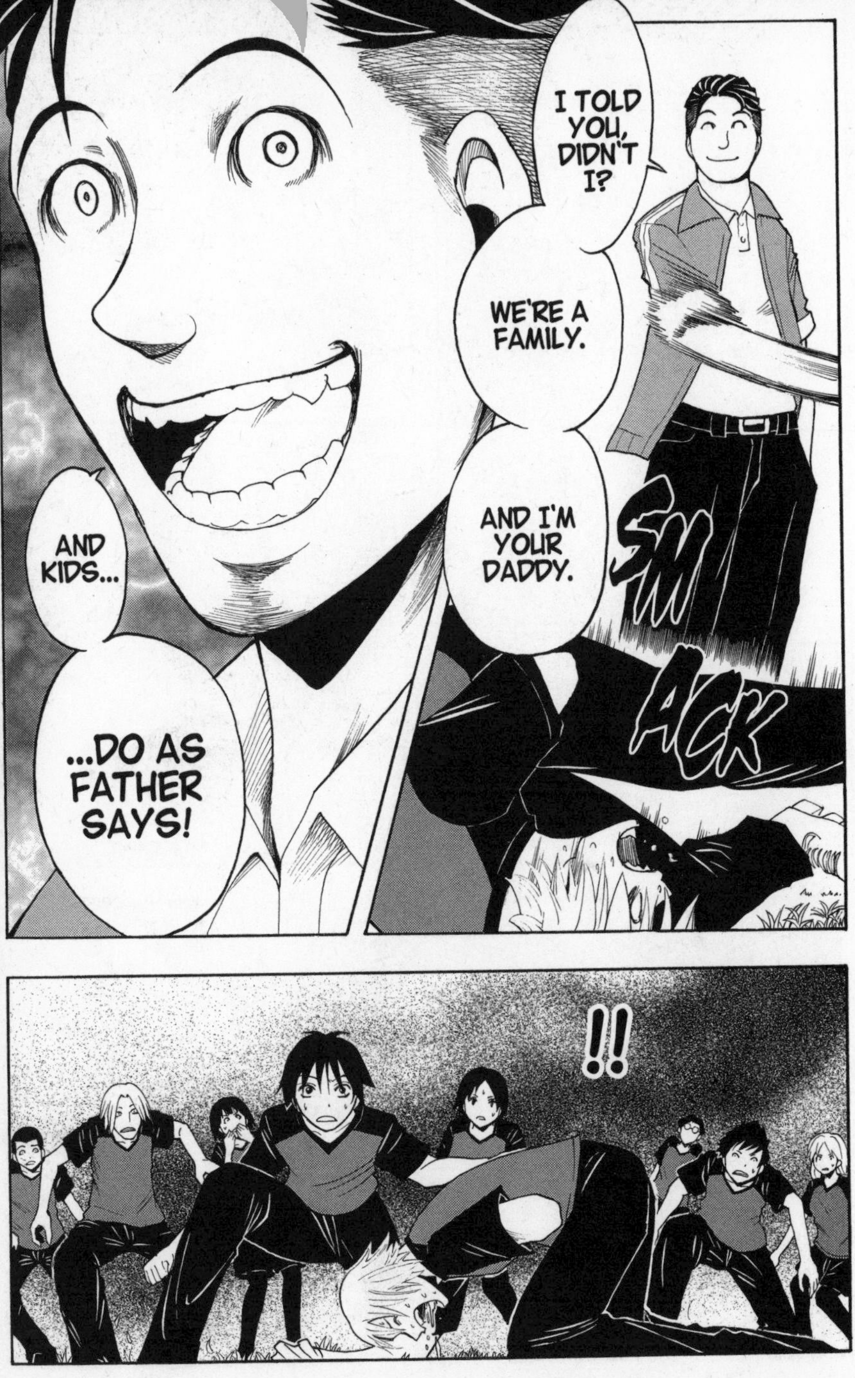
I TOLD YOU, DIDN'T I?
WE'RE A FAMILY.
AND I'M YOUR DADDY.
SMACK
AND KIDS...
...DO AS FATHER SAYS!
!!

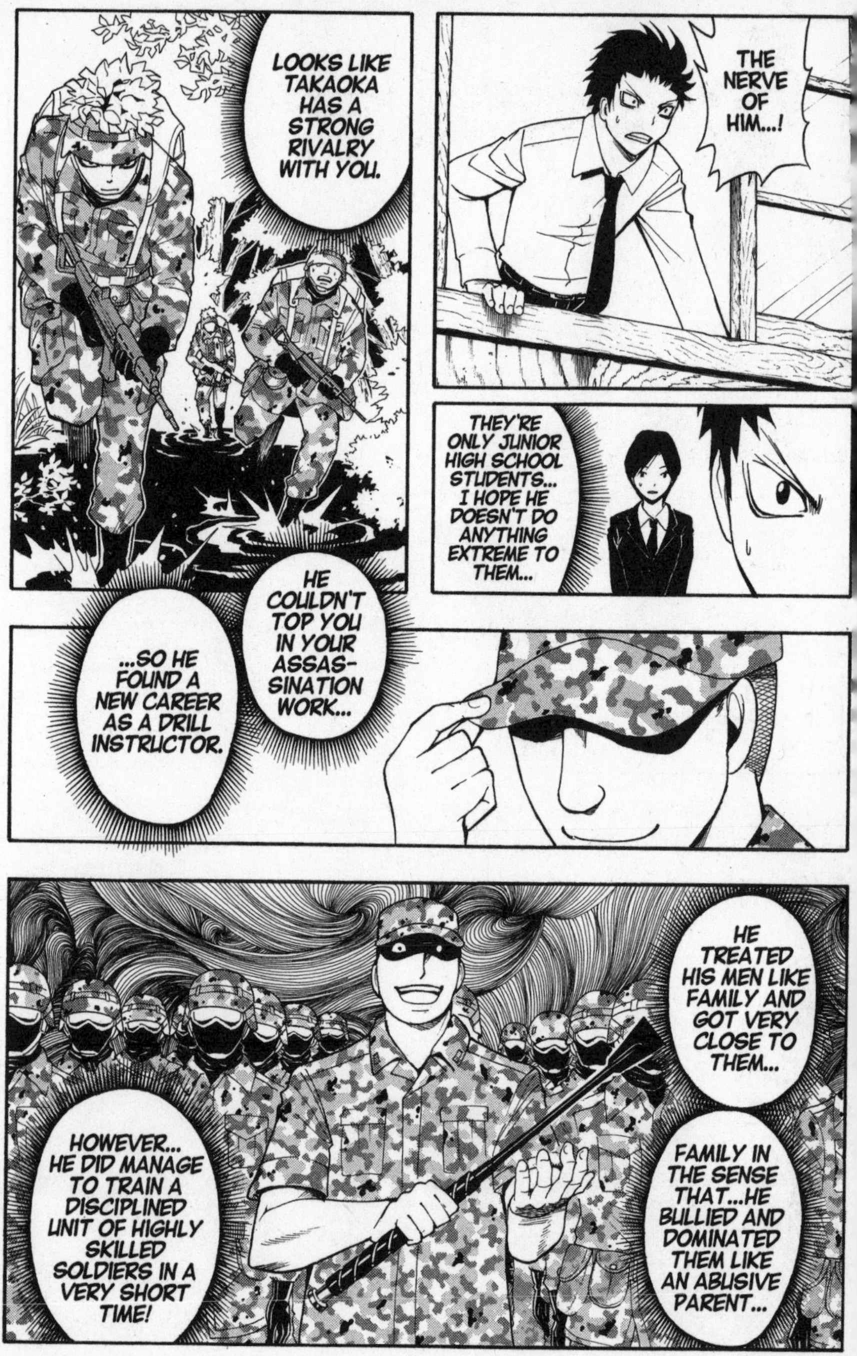
THE NERVE OF HIM...!
THEY'RE ONLY JUNIOR HIGH SCHOOL STUDENTS... I HOPE HE DOESN'T DO ANYTHING EXTREME TO THEM...
LOOKS LIKE TAKAOKA HAS A STRONG RIVALRY WITH YOU.
HE COULDN'T TOP YOU IN YOUR ASSAS-SINATION WORK...
...SO HE FOUND A NEW CAREER AS A DRILL INSTRUCTOR.
HE TREATED HIS MEN LIKE FAMILY AND GOT VERY CLOSE TO THEM...
FAMILY IN THE SENSE THAT...HE BULLIED AND DOMINATED THEM LIKE AN ABUSIVE PARENT...
HOWEVER... HE DID MANAGE TO TRAIN A DISCIPLINED UNIT OF HIGHLY SKILLED SOLDIERS IN A VERY SHORT TIME!

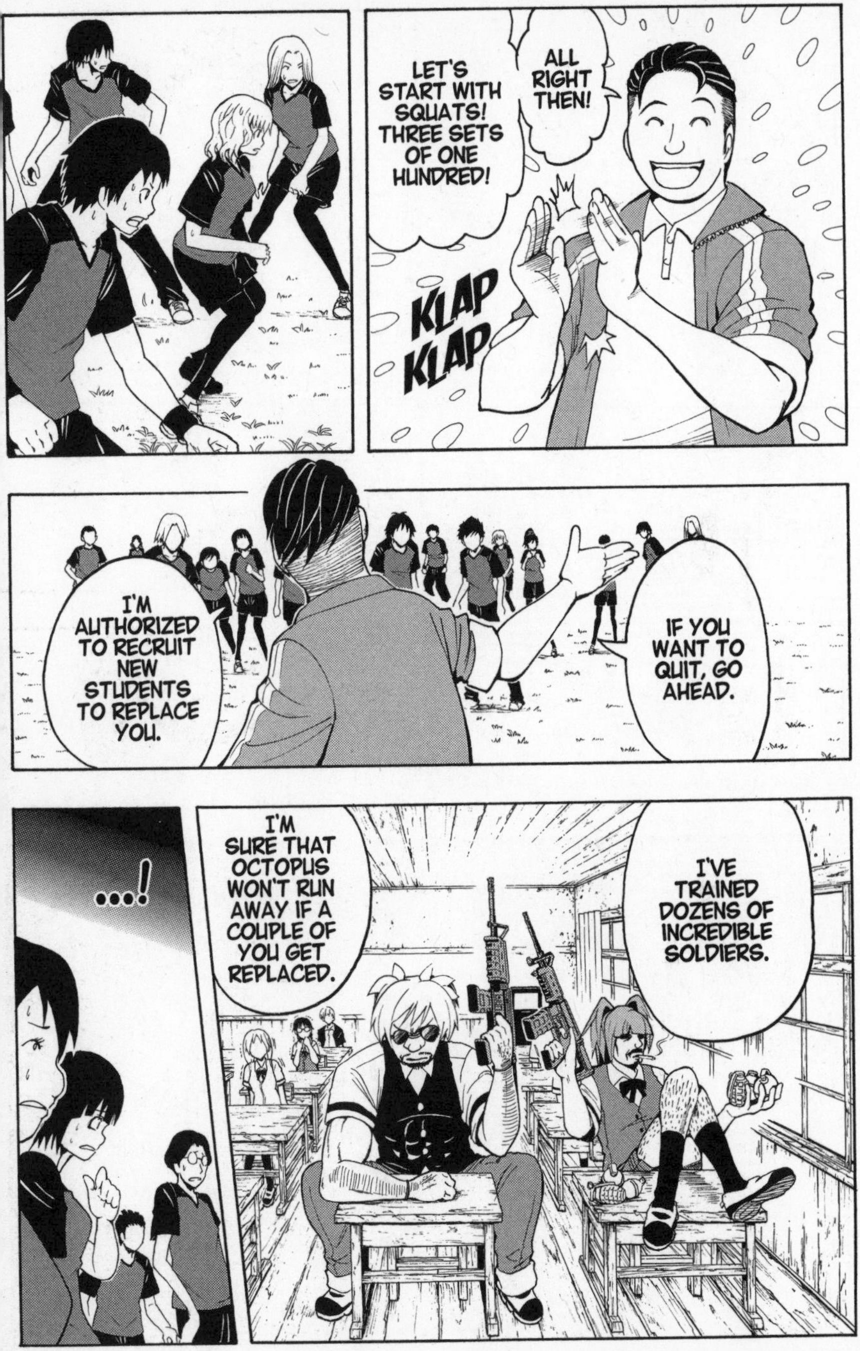
ALL RIGHT THEN!
LET'S START WITH SQUATS! THREE SETS OF ONE HUNDRED!
KLAP KLAP
IF YOU WANT TO QUIT, GO AHEAD.
I'M AUTHORIZED TO RECRUIT NEW STUDENTS TO REPLACE YOU.
I'VE TRAINED DOZENS OF INCREDIBLE SOLDIERS.
I'M SURE THAT OCTOPUS WON'T RUN AWAY IF A COUPLE OF YOU GET REPLACED.
...!

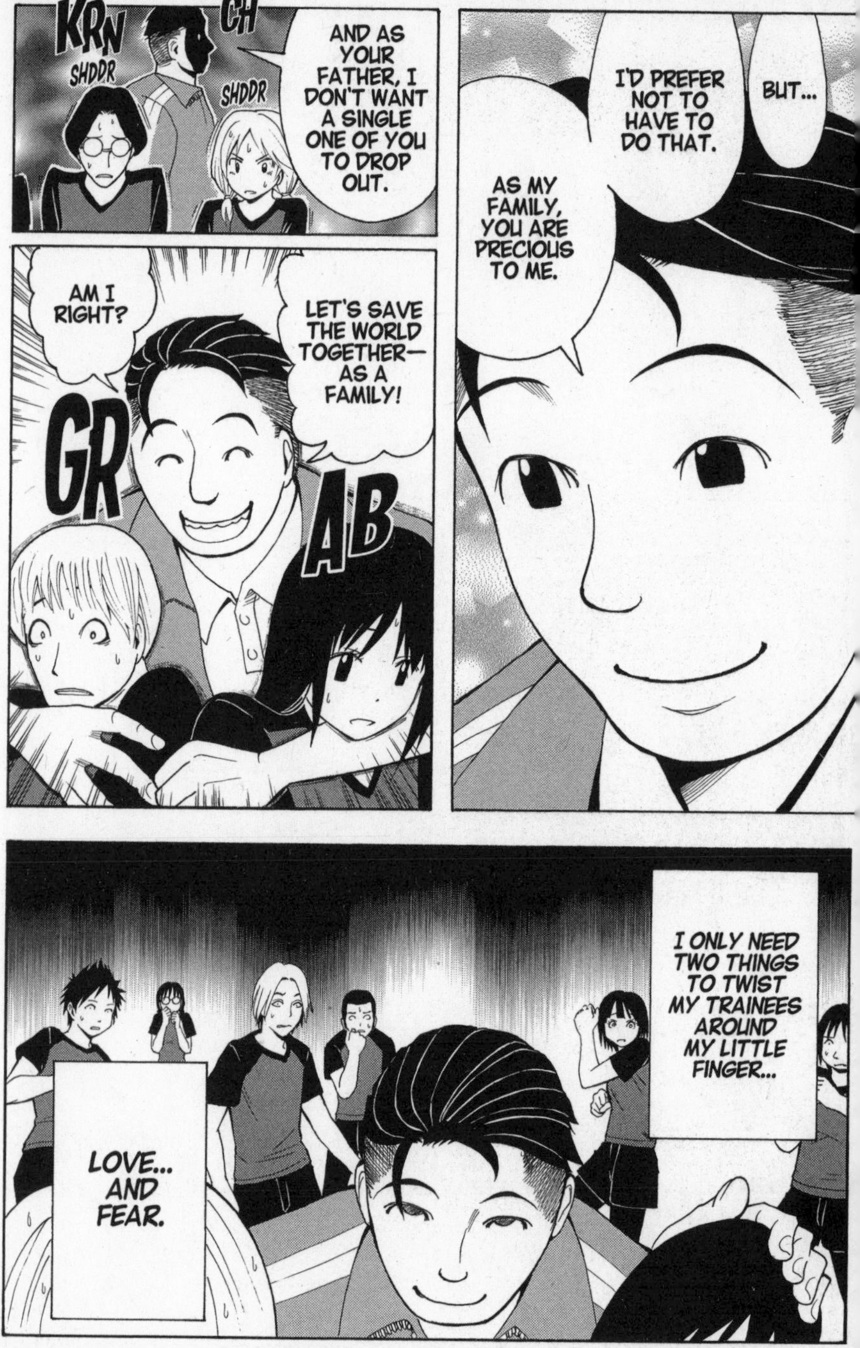
BUT...
I'D PREFER NOT TO HAVE TO DO THAT.
AS MY FAMILY, YOU ARE PRECIOUS TO ME.
AND AS YOUR FATHER, I DON'T WANT A SINGLE ONE OF YOU TO DROP OUT.
KRNCH
SHDDR
SHDDR
LET'S SAVE THE WORLD TOGETHER—AS A FAMILY!
AM I RIGHT?
GRAB
I ONLY NEED TWO THINGS TO TWIST MY TRAINEES AROUND MY LITTLE FINGER...
LOVE... AND FEAR.

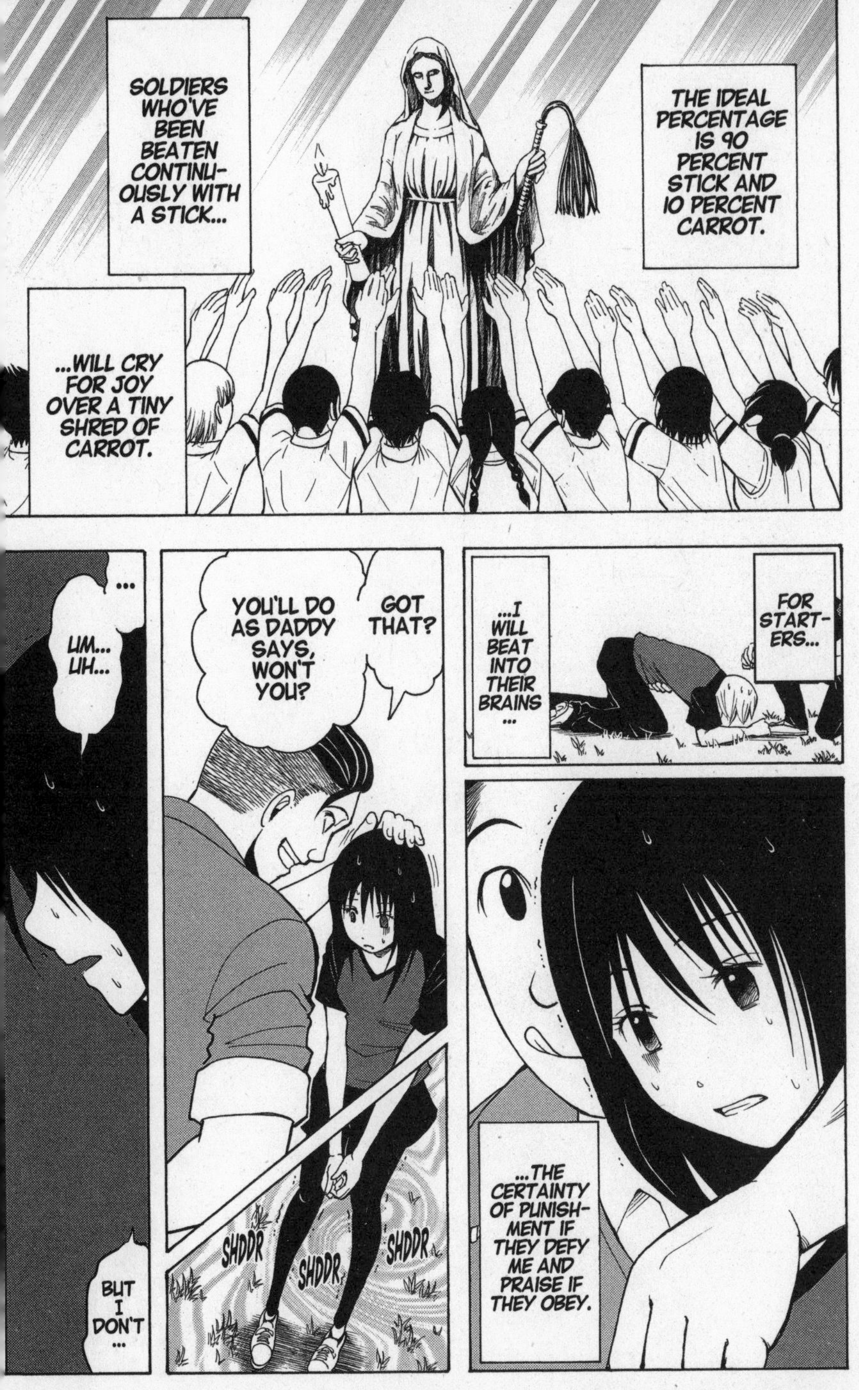

THE IDEAL PERCENTAGE IS 90 PERCENT STICK AND 10 PERCENT CARROT.
SOLDIERS WHO'VE BEEN BEATEN CONTINU-OUSLY WITH A STICK...
...WILL CRY FOR JOY OVER A TINY SHRED OF CARROT.
FOR STARTERS...
...I WILL BEAT INTO THEIR BRAINS...
...THE CERTAINTY OF PUNISH-MENT IF THEY DEFY ME AND PRAISE IF THEY OBEY.
GOT THAT?
YOU'LL DO AS DADDY SAYS, WON'T YOU?
SHDDR
SHDDR
SHDDR
...
UM... UH...
BUT I DON'T...

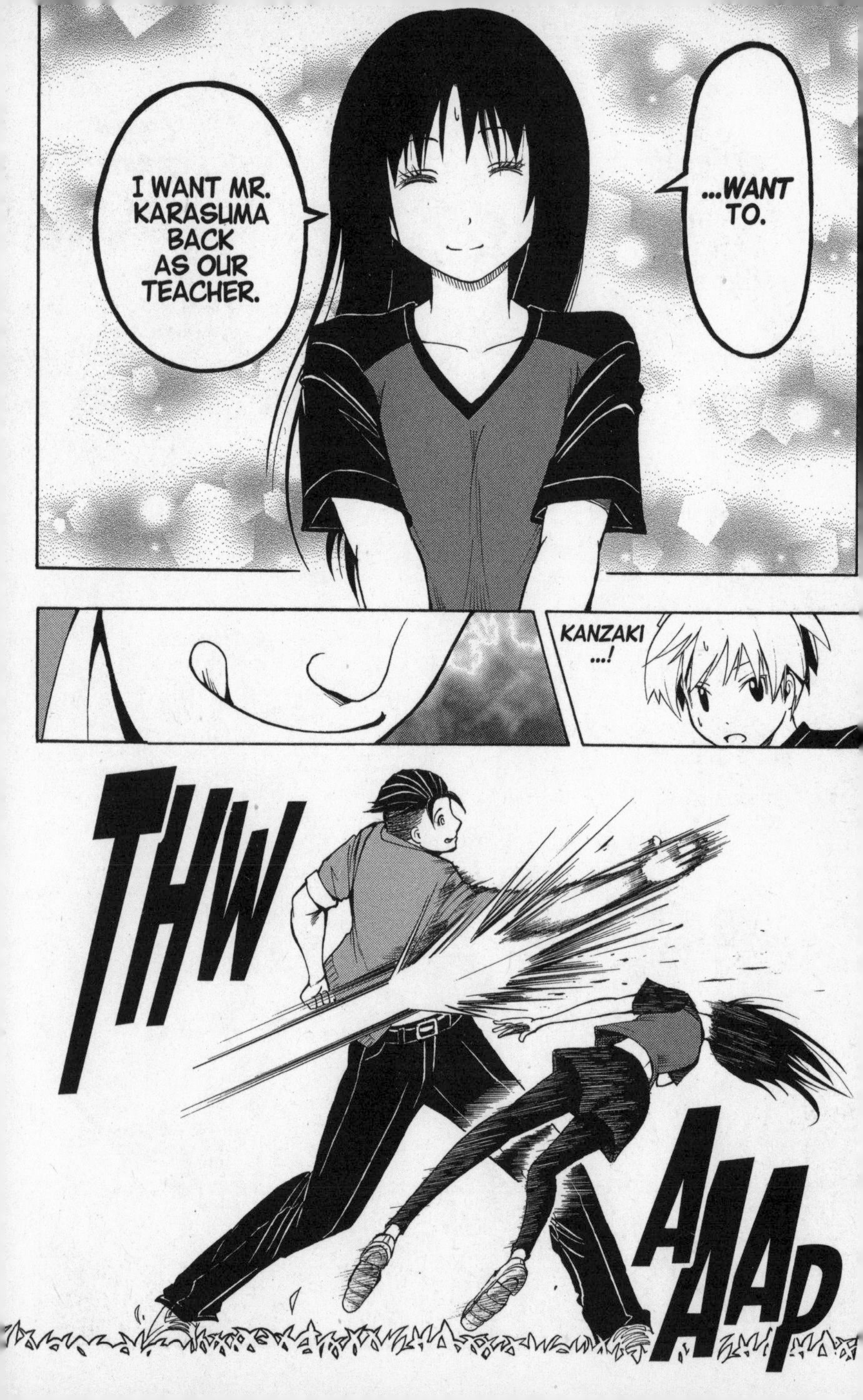
I WANT MR. KARASUMA BACK AS OUR TEACHER.
...WANT TO.
KANZAKI ...!
THWAAAP

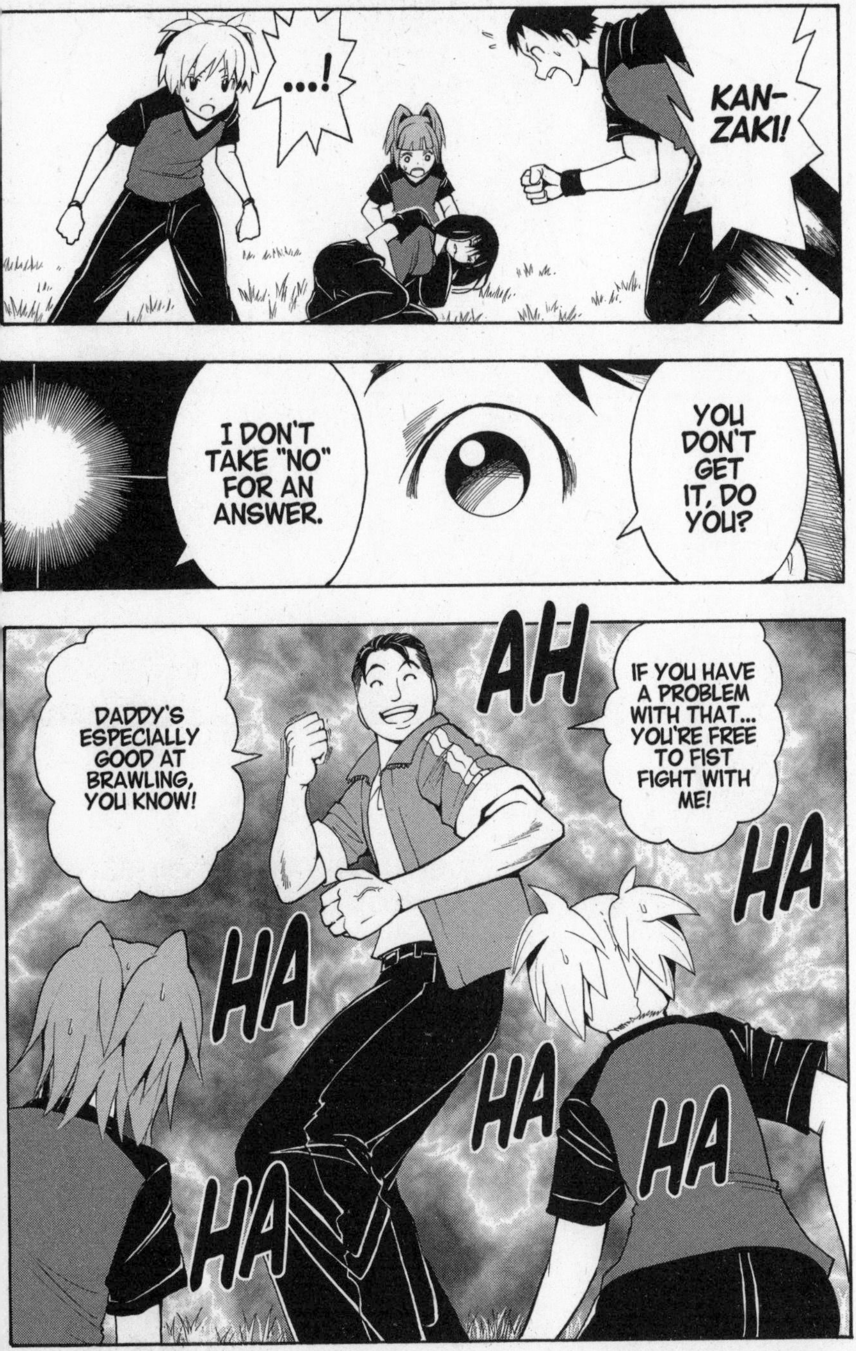
KAN-ZAKI!
...!
YOU DON'T GET IT, DO YOU?
I DON'T TAKE "NO" FOR AN ANSWER.
IF YOU HAVE A PROBLEM WITH THAT... YOU'RE FREE TO FIST FIGHT WITH ME!
DADDY'S ESPECIALLY GOOD AT BRAWLING, YOU KNOW!
AH HA HA HA HA HA

A Taste of
Daddy's Medicine

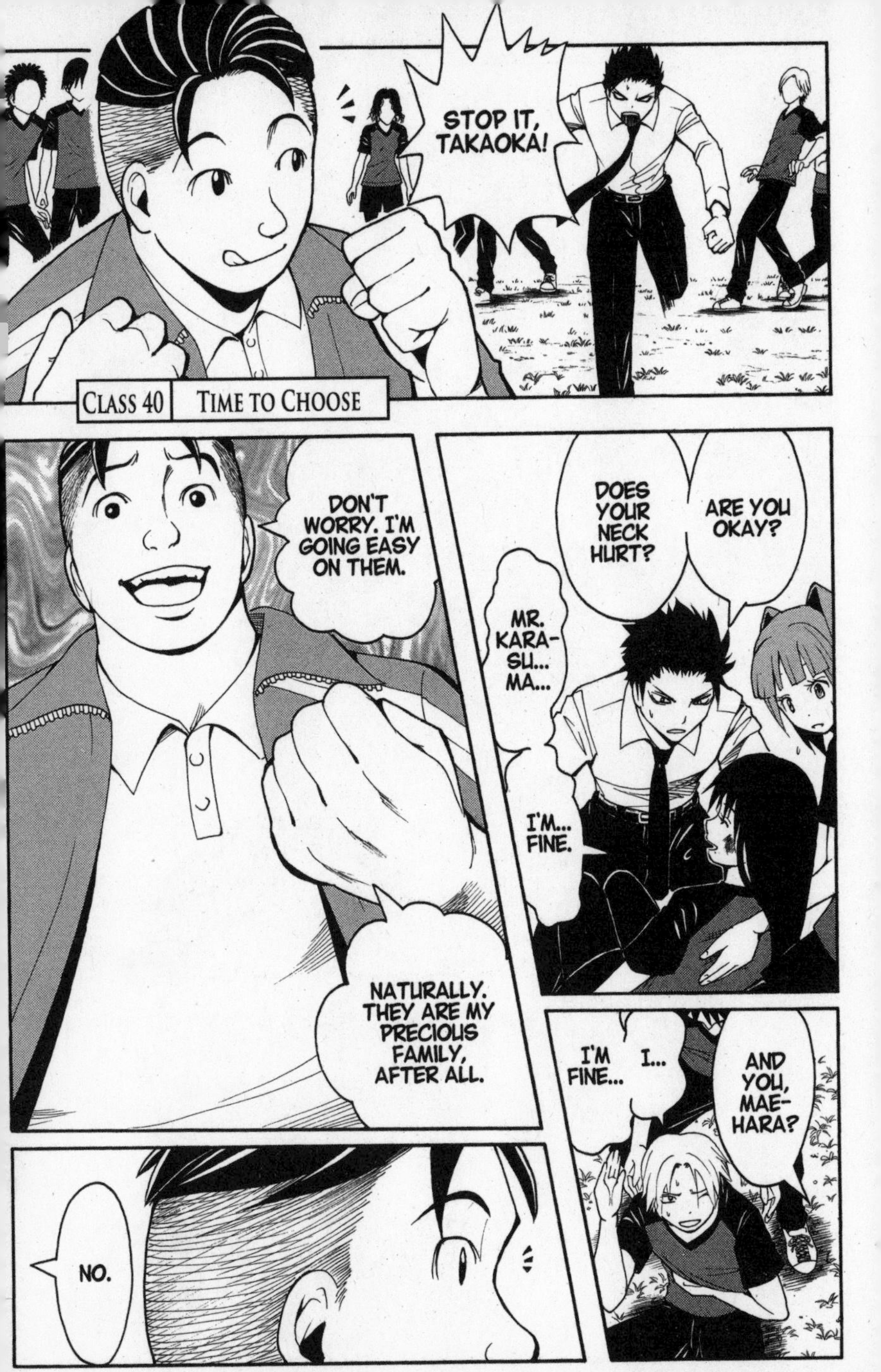
STOP IT, TAKAOKA!
CLASS 40 TIME TO CHOOSE
ARE YOU OKAY?
DOES YOUR NECK HURT?
MR. KARA-SU... MA...
I'M... FINE.
AND YOU, MAE-HARA?
I...
I'M FINE...
DON'T WORRY. I'M GOING EASY ON THEM.
NATURALLY. THEY ARE MY PRECIOUS FAMILY, AFTER ALL.
NO.

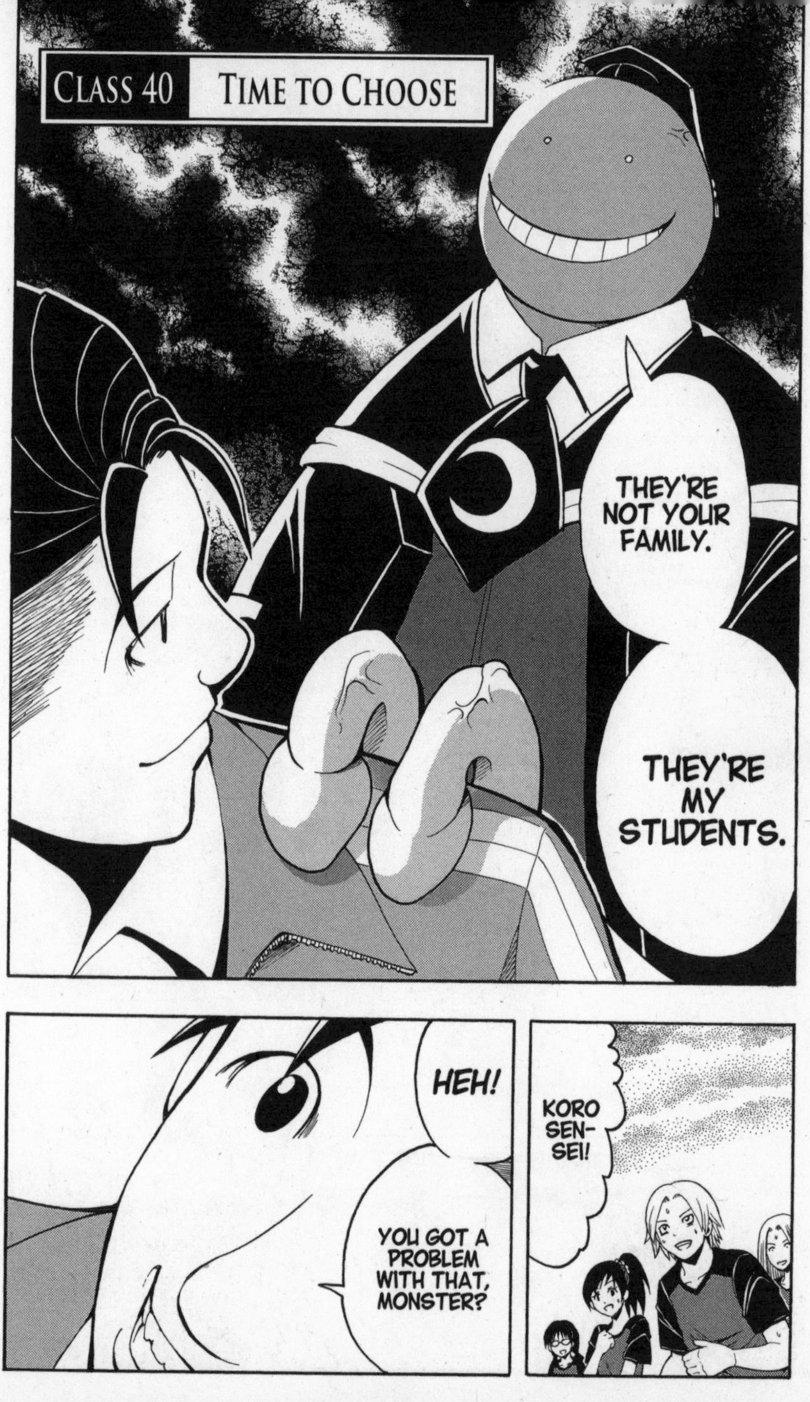
CLASS 40 TIME TO CHOOSE
THEY'RE NOT YOUR FAMILY.
THEY'RE MY STUDENTS.
KORO SEN-SEI!
HEH!
YOU GOT A PROBLEM WITH THAT, MONSTER?

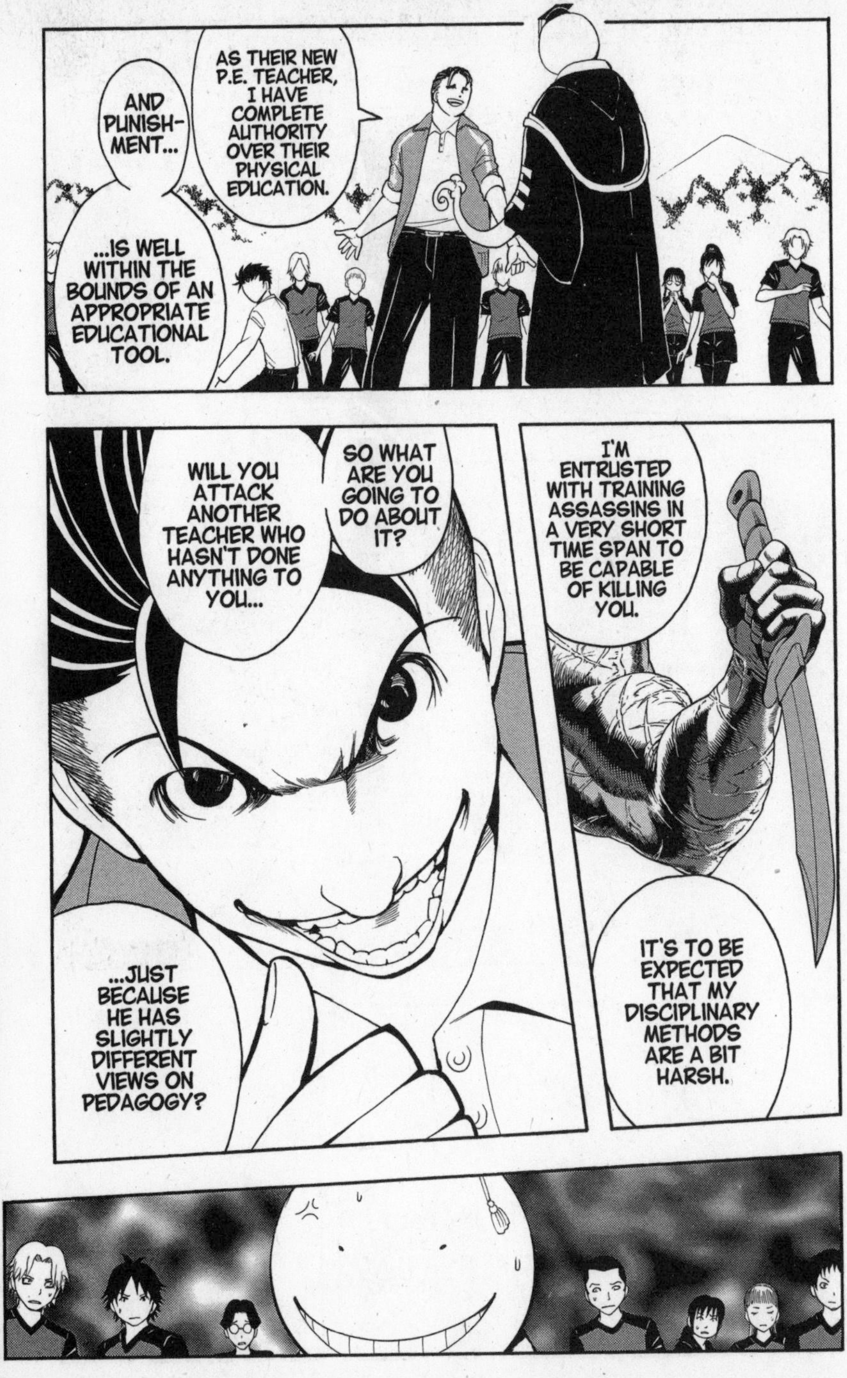
AS THEIR NEW P.E. TEACHER, I HAVE COMPLETE AUTHORITY OVER THEIR PHYSICAL EDUCATION.
AND PUNISHMENT...
...IS WELL WITHIN THE BOUNDS OF AN APPROPRIATE EDUCATIONAL TOOL.
I'M ENTRUSTED WITH TRAINING ASSASSINS IN A VERY SHORT TIME SPAN TO BE CAPABLE OF KILLING YOU.
IT'S TO BE EXPECTED THAT MY DISCIPLINARY METHODS ARE A BIT HARSH.
SO WHAT ARE YOU GOING TO DO ABOUT IT?
WILL YOU ATTACK ANOTHER TEACHER WHO HASN'T DONE ANYTHING TO YOU...
...JUST BECAUSE HE HAS SLIGHTLY DIFFERENT VIEWS ON PEDAGOGY?

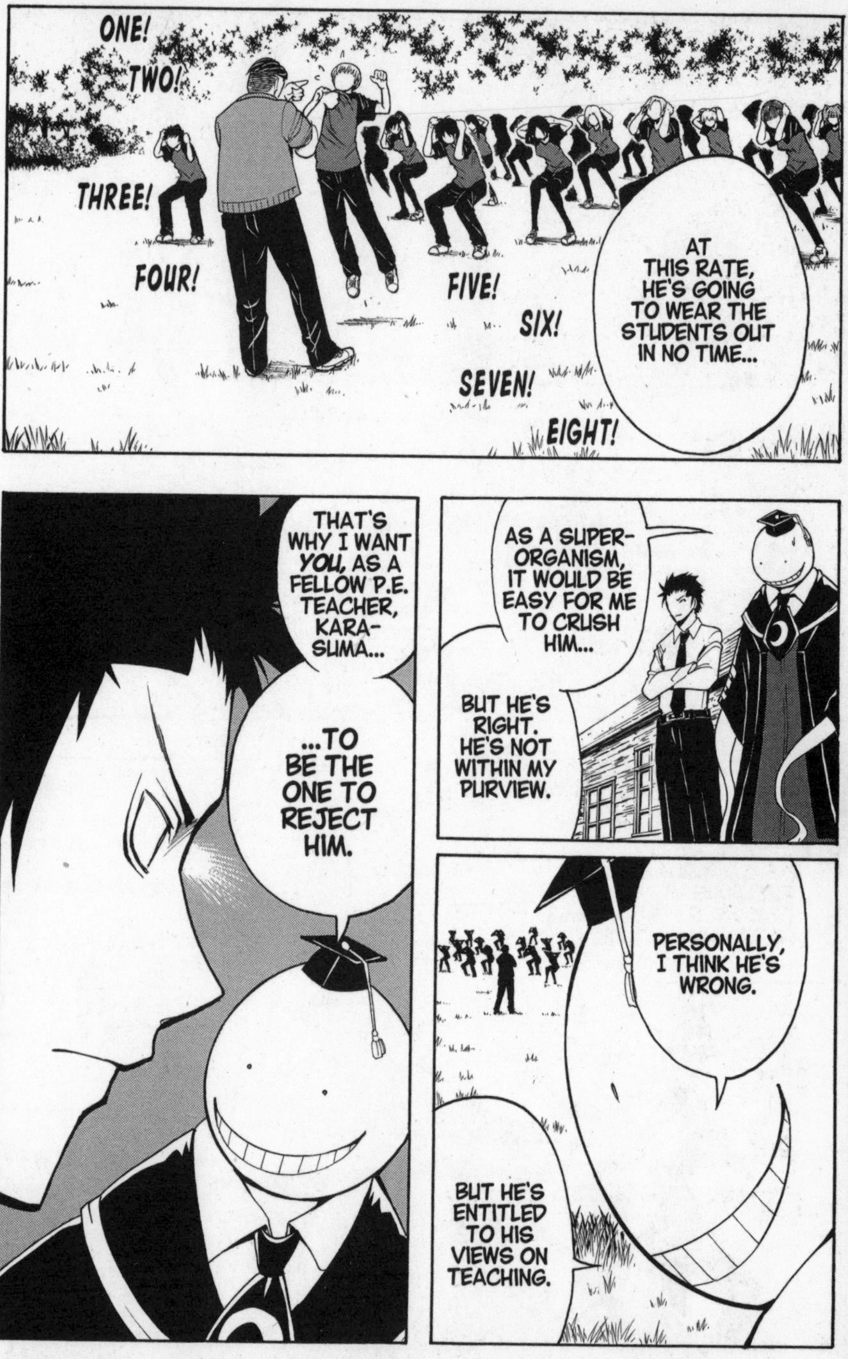
AT THIS RATE, HE'S GOING TO WEAR THE STUDENTS OUT IN NO TIME...
ONE!
TWO!
THREE!
FOUR!
FIVE!
SIX!
SEVEN!
EIGHT!
AS A SUPER-ORGANISM, IT WOULD BE EASY FOR ME TO CRUSH HIM...
BUT HE'S RIGHT. HE'S NOT WITHIN MY PURVIEW.
PERSONALLY, I THINK HE'S WRONG.
BUT HE'S ENTITLED TO HIS VIEWS ON TEACHING.
THAT'S WHY I WANT *YOU*, AS A FELLOW P.E. TEACHER, KARASUMA...
...TO BE THE ONE TO REJECT HIM.

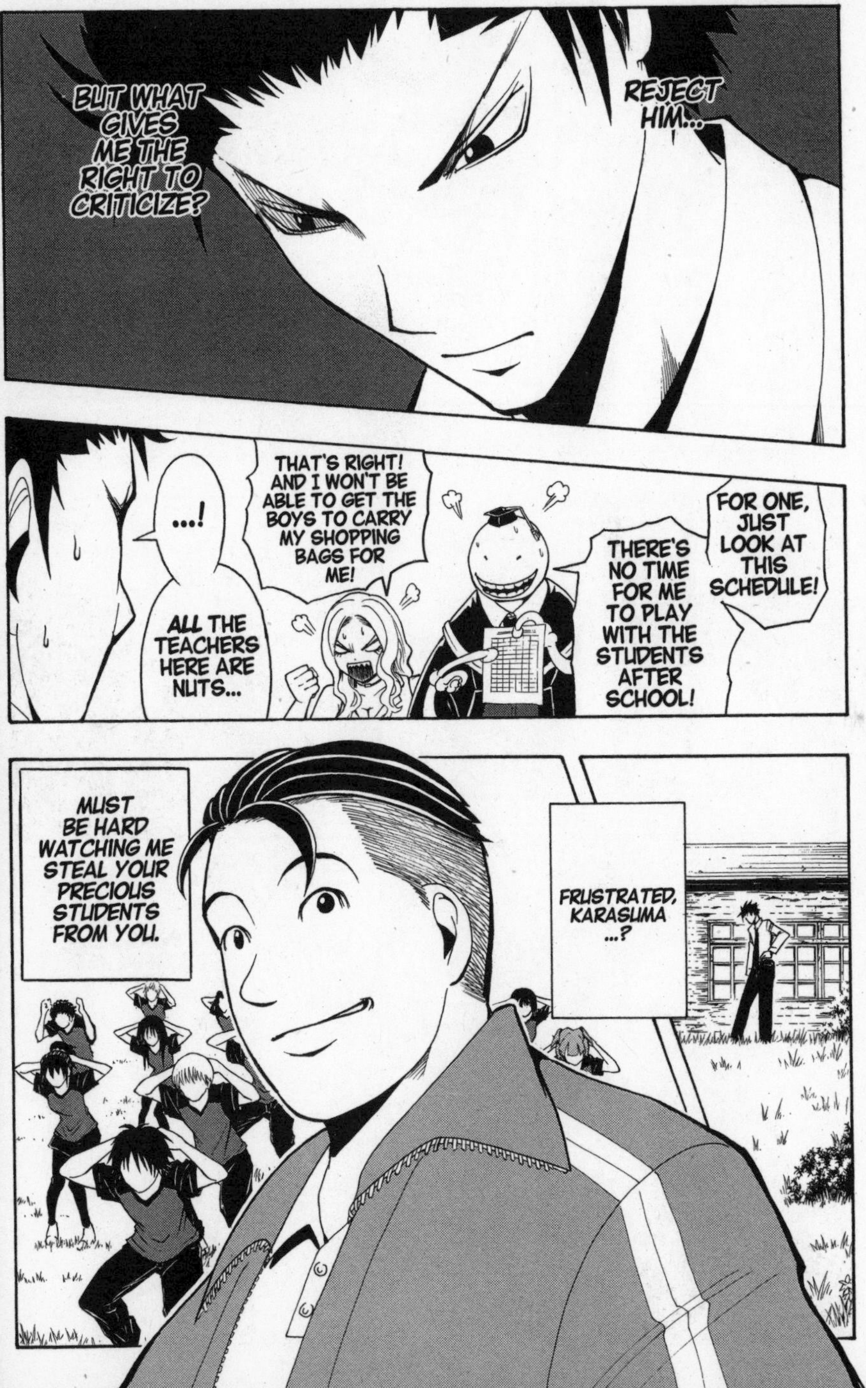
REJECT HIM...
BUT WHAT GIVES ME THE RIGHT TO CRITICIZE?
FOR ONE, JUST LOOK AT THIS SCHEDULE!
THERE'S NO TIME FOR ME TO PLAY WITH THE STUDENTS AFTER SCHOOL!
THAT'S RIGHT! AND I WON'T BE ABLE TO GET THE BOYS TO CARRY MY SHOPPING BAGS FOR ME!
...!
ALL THE TEACHERS HERE ARE NUTS...
FRUSTRATED, KARASUMA ...?
MUST BE HARD WATCHING ME STEAL YOUR PRECIOUS STUDENTS FROM YOU.

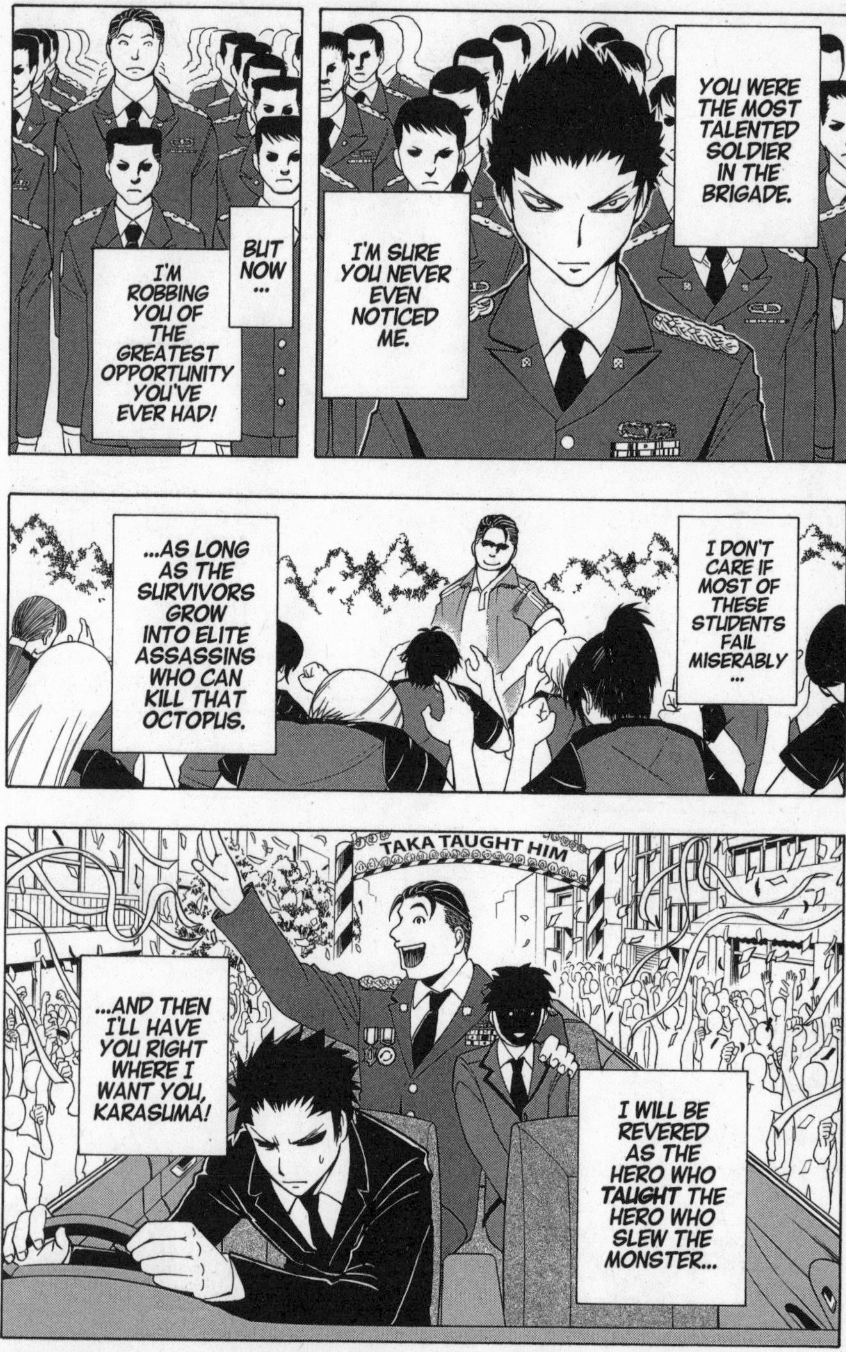
YOU WERE THE MOST TALENTED SOLDIER IN THE BRIGADE.
I'M SURE YOU NEVER EVEN NOTICED ME.
BUT NOW...
I'M ROBBING YOU OF THE GREATEST OPPORTUNITY YOU'VE EVER HAD!
I DON'T CARE IF MOST OF THESE STUDENTS FAIL MISERABLY...
...AS LONG AS THE SURVIVORS GROW INTO ELITE ASSASSINS WHO CAN KILL THAT OCTOPUS.
TAKA TAUGHT HIM
I WILL BE REVERED AS THE HERO WHO TAUGHT THE HERO WHO SLEW THE MONSTER...
...AND THEN I'LL HAVE YOU RIGHT WHERE I WANT YOU, KARASUMA!

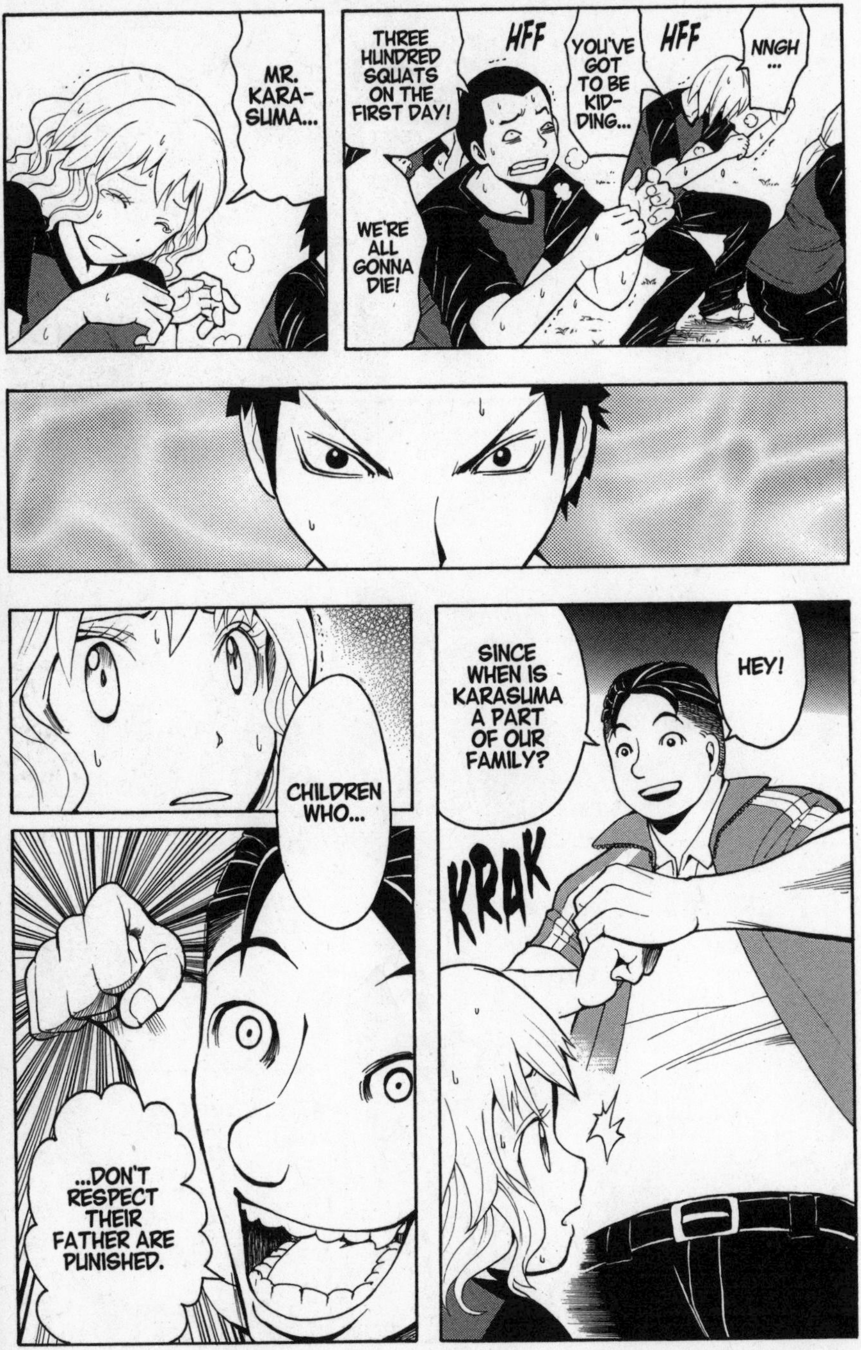
NNGH...
HFF
YOU'VE GOT TO BE KID-DING...
HFF
THREE HUNDRED SQUATS ON THE FIRST DAY!
WE'RE ALL GONNA DIE!
MR. KARA-SUMA...
HEY!
SINCE WHEN IS KARASUMA A PART OF OUR FAMILY?
KRAK
CHILDREN WHO...
...DON'T RESPECT THEIR FATHER ARE PUNISHED.

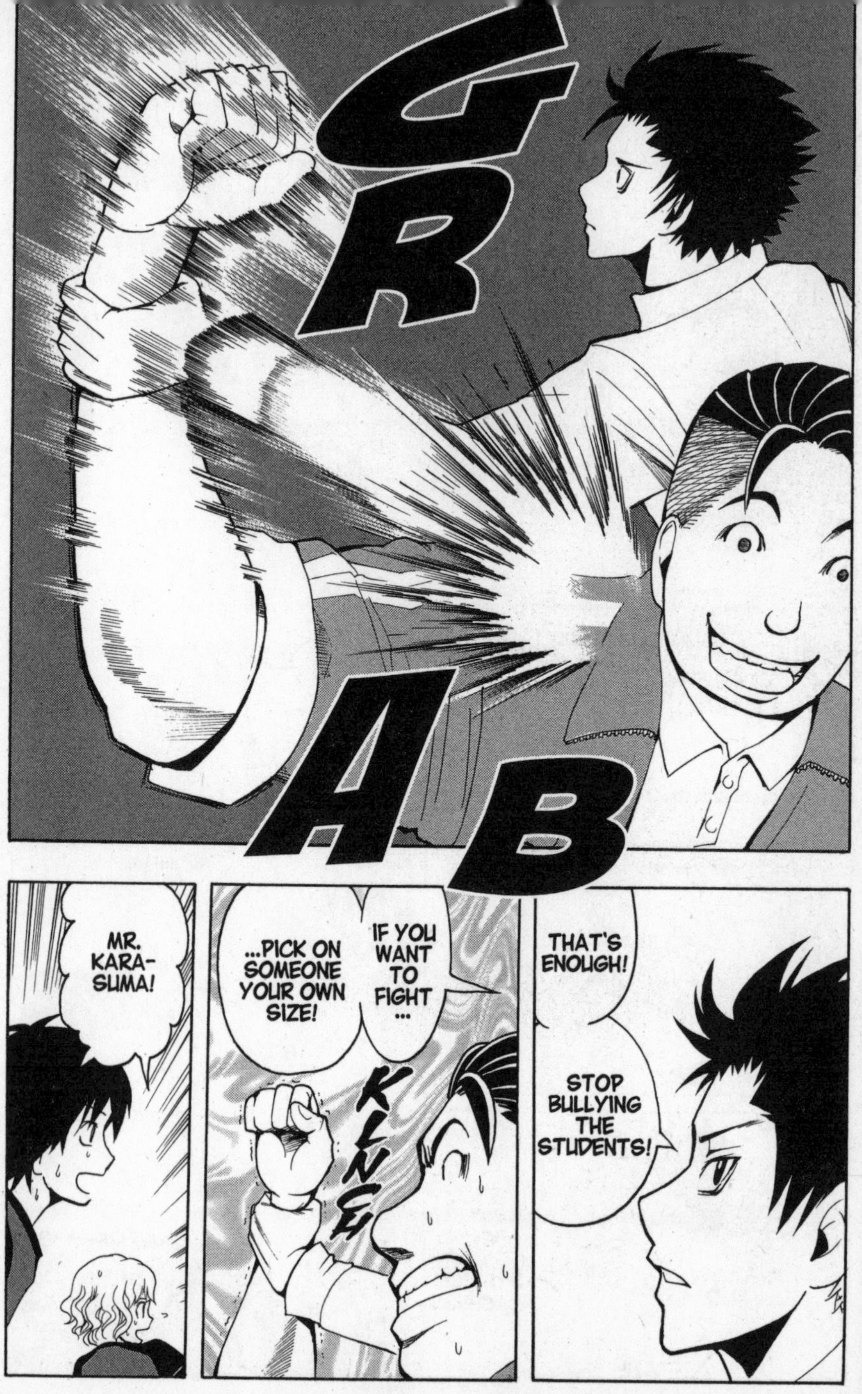
GRAB
THAT'S ENOUGH!
STOP BULLYING THE STUDENTS!
IF YOU WANT TO FIGHT ...
...PICK ON SOMEONE YOUR OWN SIZE!
MR. KARA-SUMA!

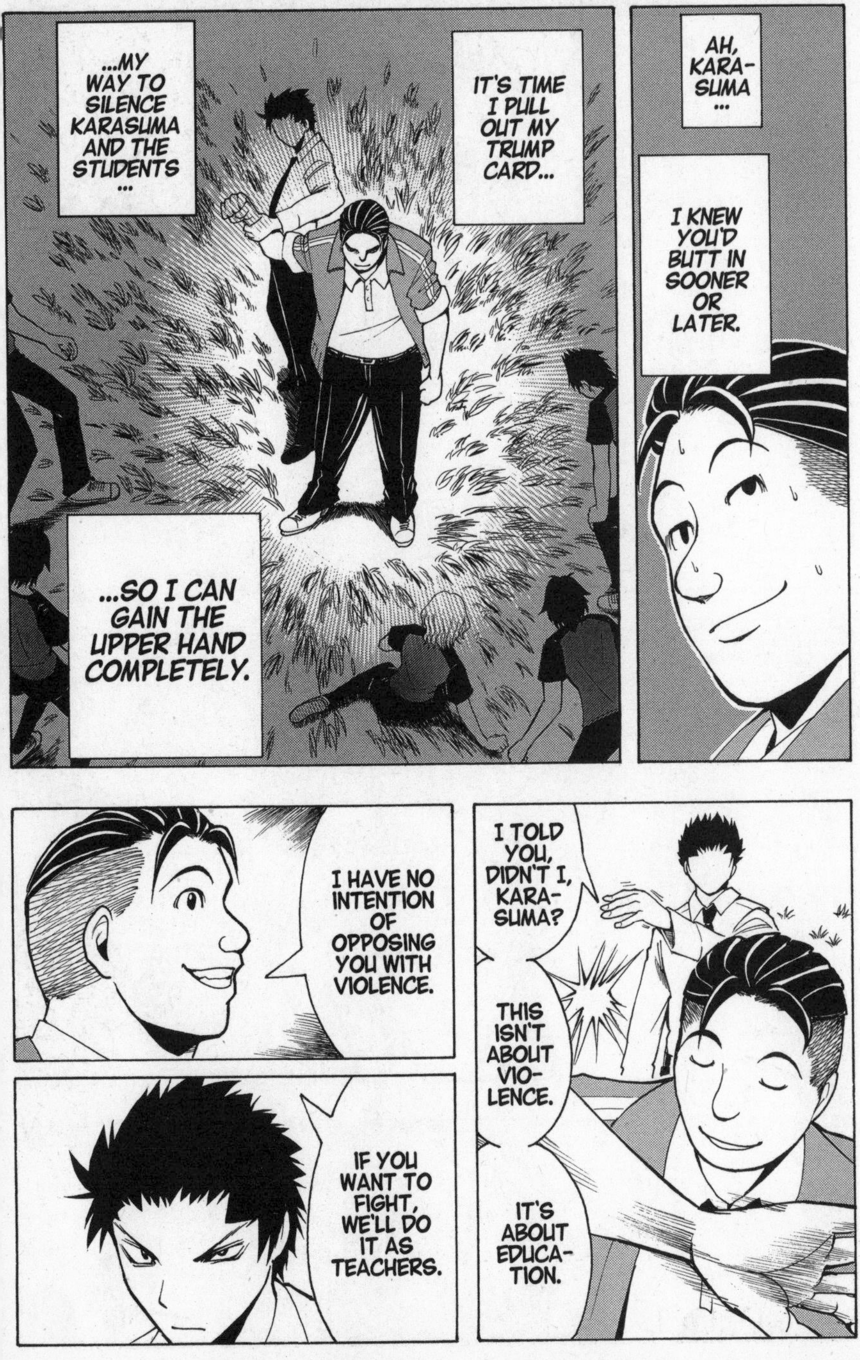
AH, KARA-SUMA...
I KNEW YOU'D BUTT IN SOONER OR LATER.
IT'S TIME I PULL OUT MY TRUMP CARD...
...MY WAY TO SILENCE KARASUMA AND THE STUDENTS...
...SO I CAN GAIN THE UPPER HAND COMPLETELY.
I TOLD YOU, DIDN'T I, KARA-SUMA?
THIS ISN'T ABOUT VIO-LENCE.
IT'S ABOUT EDUCA-TION.
I HAVE NO INTENTION OF OPPOSING YOU WITH VIOLENCE.
IF YOU WANT TO FIGHT, WE'LL DO IT AS TEACHERS.

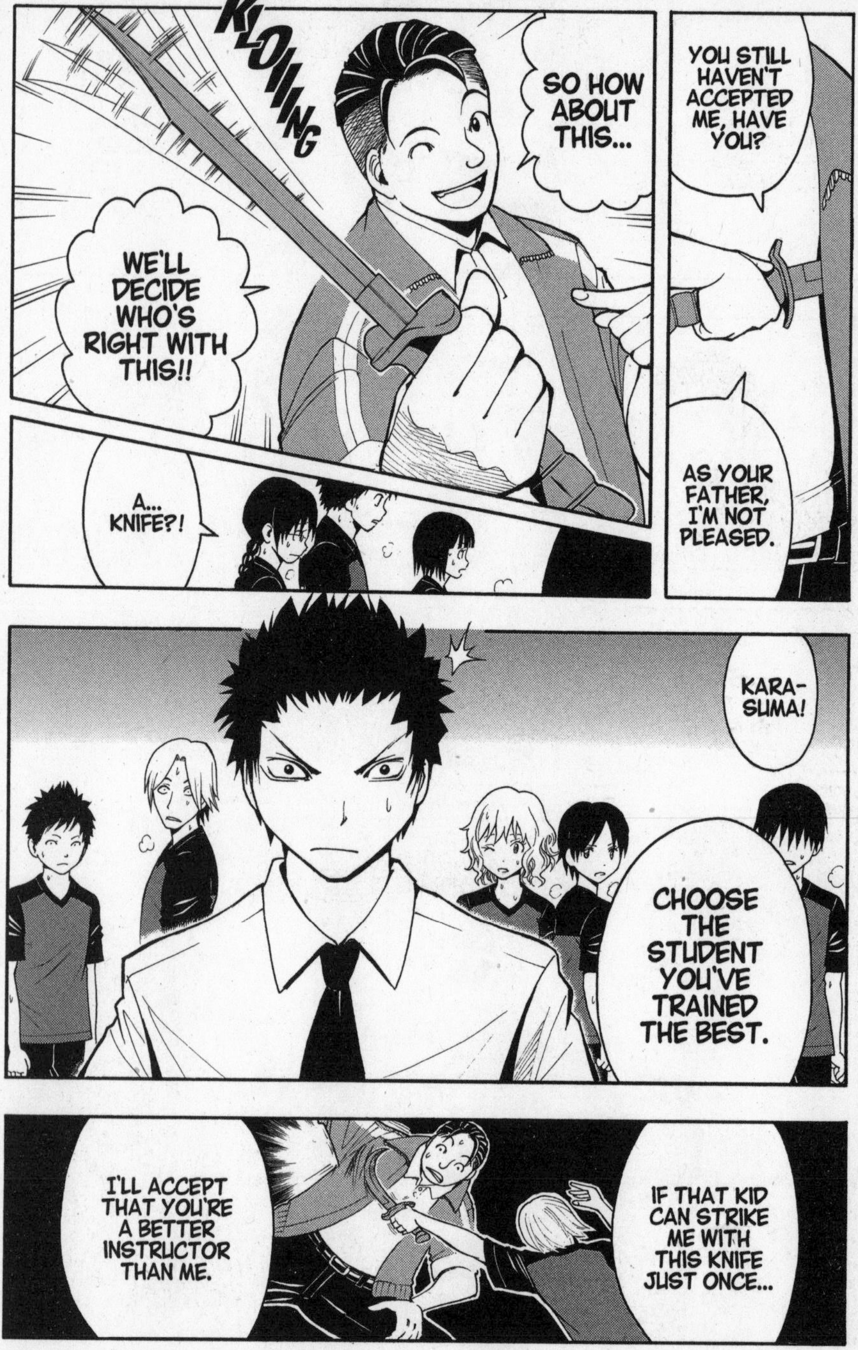
YOU STILL HAVEN'T ACCEPTED ME, HAVE YOU?
AS YOUR FATHER, I'M NOT PLEASED.
KLOIING
SO HOW ABOUT THIS...
WE'LL DECIDE WHO'S RIGHT WITH THIS!!
A... KNIFE?!
KARA-SUMA!
CHOOSE THE STUDENT YOU'VE TRAINED THE BEST.
IF THAT KID CAN STRIKE ME WITH THIS KNIFE JUST ONCE...
I'LL ACCEPT THAT YOU'RE A BETTER INSTRUCTOR THAN ME.

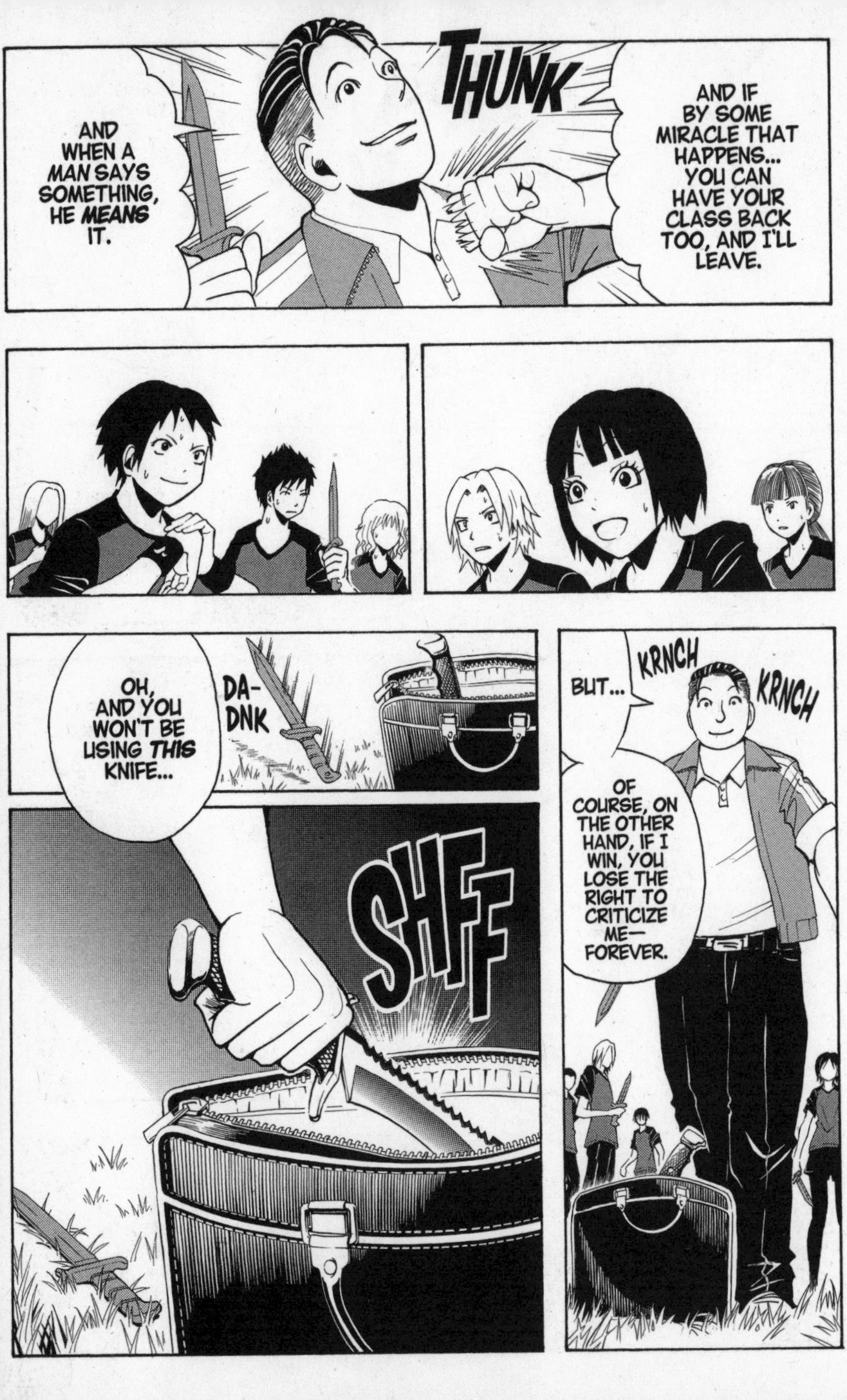
AND IF BY SOME MIRACLE THAT HAPPENS... YOU CAN HAVE YOUR CLASS BACK TOO, AND I'LL LEAVE.
THUNK
AND WHEN A MAN SAYS SOMETHING, HE MEANS IT.
KRNCH
KRNCH
BUT...
OF COURSE, ON THE OTHER HAND, IF I WIN, YOU LOSE THE RIGHT TO CRITICIZE ME—FOREVER.
DA-DNK
OH, AND YOU WON'T BE USING THIS KNIFE...
SHFF

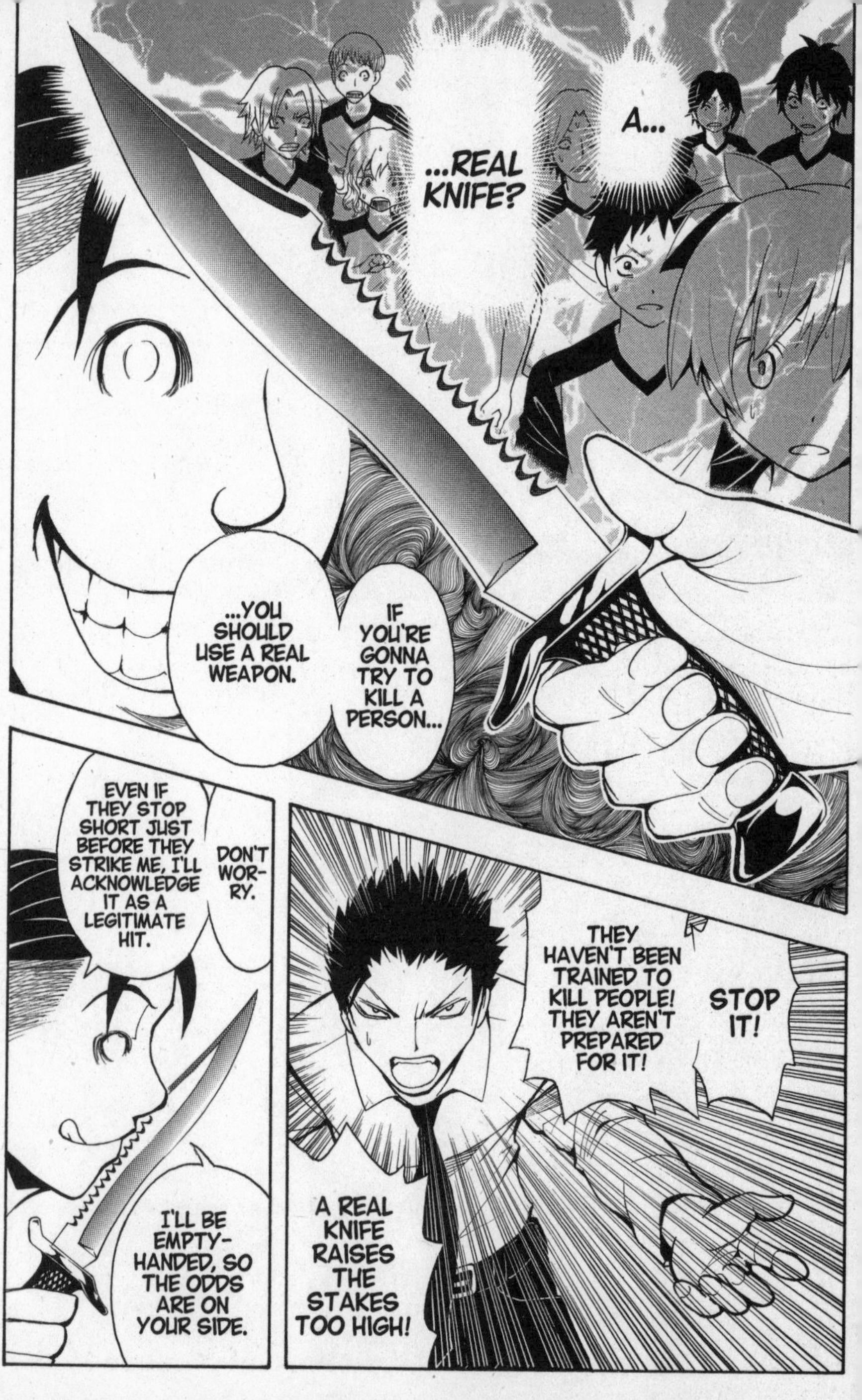
A...
...REAL KNIFE?
IF YOU'RE GONNA TRY TO KILL A PERSON...
...YOU SHOULD USE A REAL WEAPON.
STOP IT!
THEY HAVEN'T BEEN TRAINED TO KILL PEOPLE! THEY AREN'T PREPARED FOR IT!
A REAL KNIFE RAISES THE STAKES TOO HIGH!
DON'T WORRY.
EVEN IF THEY STOP SHORT JUST BEFORE THEY STRIKE ME, I'LL ACKNOWLEDGE IT AS A LEGITIMATE HIT.
I'LL BE EMPTY-HANDED, SO THE ODDS ARE ON YOUR SIDE.

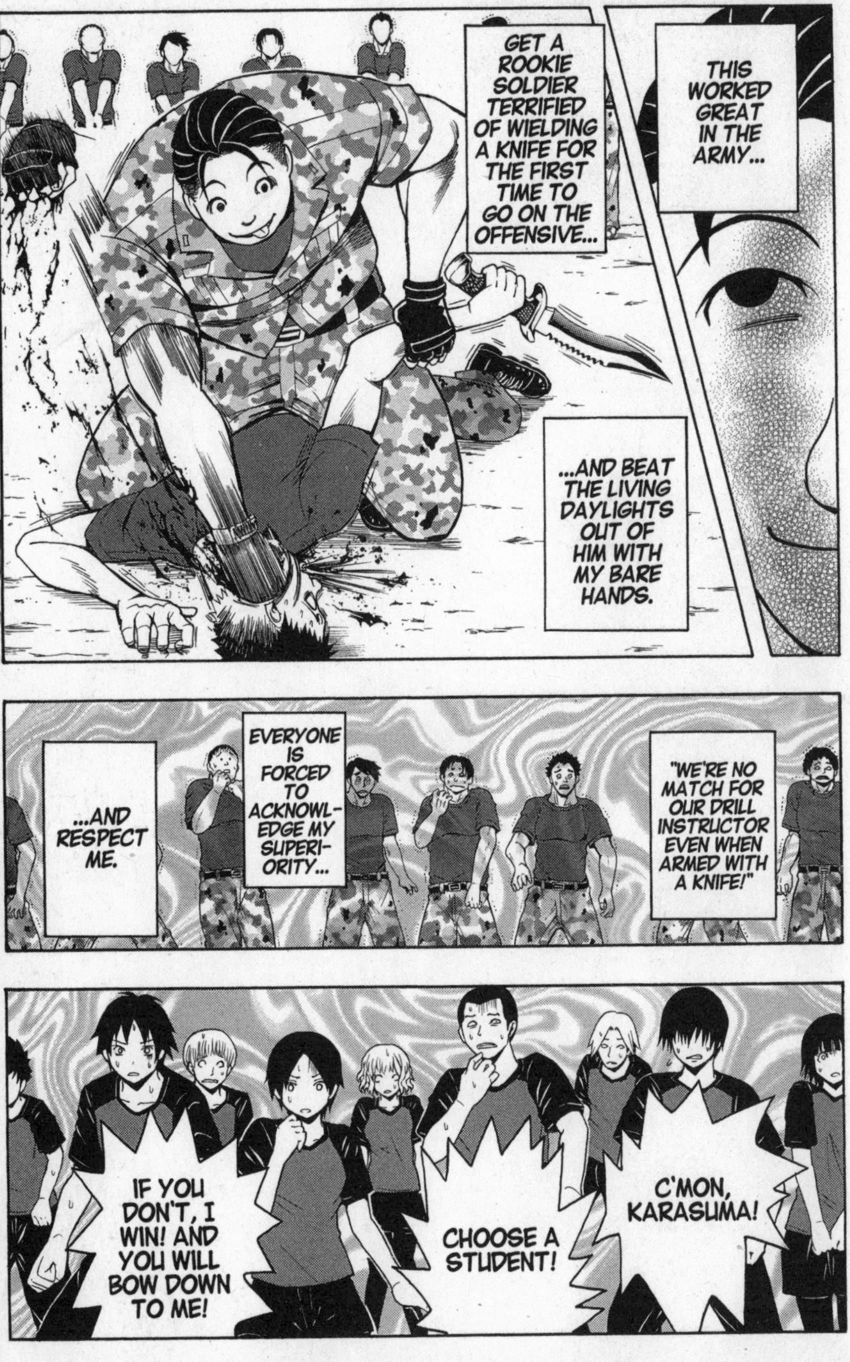
THIS WORKED GREAT IN THE ARMY...
GET A ROOKIE SOLDIER TERRIFIED OF WIELDING A KNIFE FOR THE FIRST TIME TO GO ON THE OFFENSIVE...
...AND BEAT THE LIVING DAYLIGHTS OUT OF HIM WITH MY BARE HANDS.
"WE'RE NO MATCH FOR OUR DRILL INSTRUCTOR EVEN WHEN ARMED WITH A KNIFE!"
EVERYONE IS FORCED TO ACKNOWL-EDGE MY SUPERI-ORITY...
...AND RESPECT ME.
C'MON, KARASUMA!
CHOOSE A STUDENT!
IF YOU DON'T, I WIN! AND YOU WILL BOW DOWN TO ME!

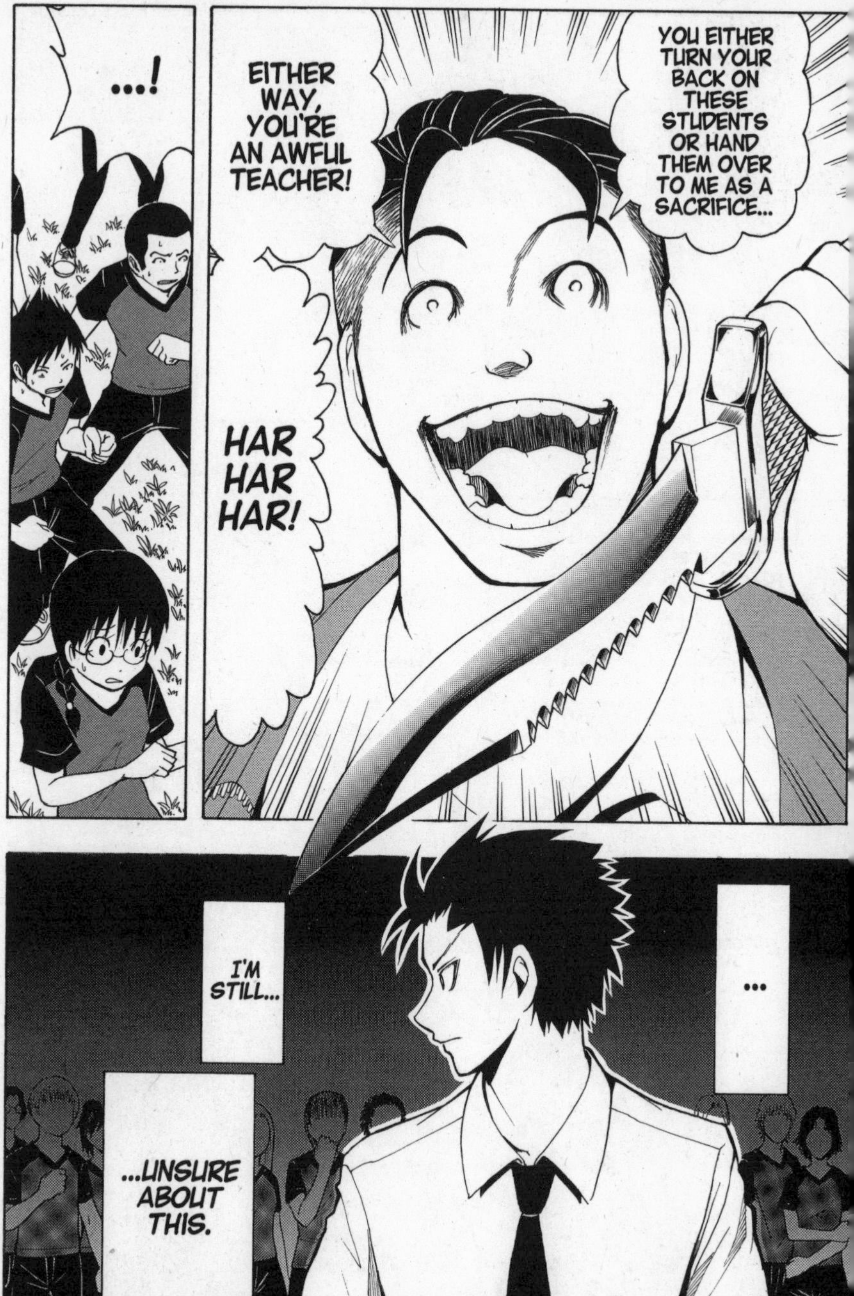
YOU EITHER TURN YOUR BACK ON THESE STUDENTS OR HAND THEM OVER TO ME AS A SACRIFICE...
EITHER WAY, YOU'RE AN AWFUL TEACHER!
HAR HAR HAR!
...!
...
I'M STILL...
...UNSURE ABOUT THIS.

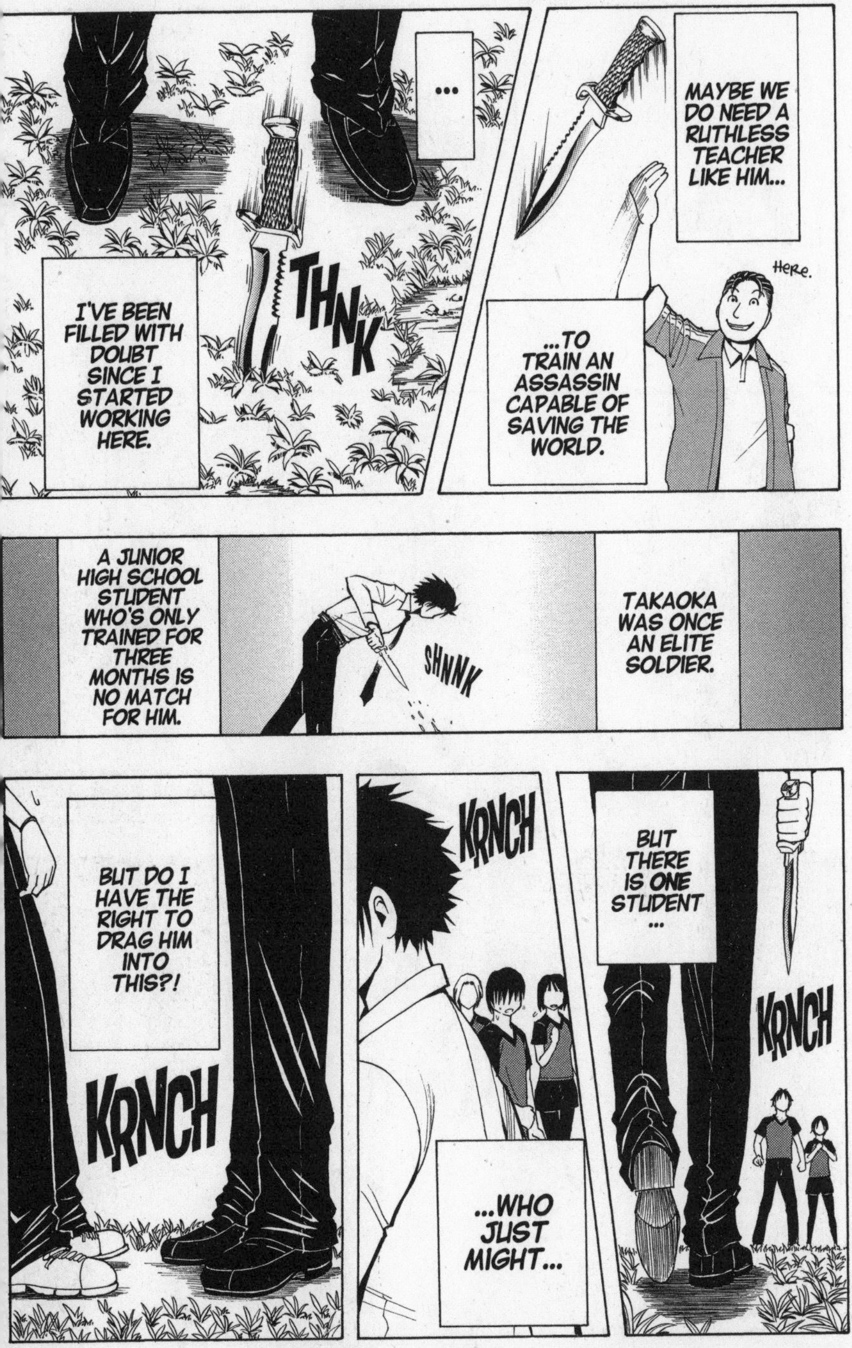
MAYBE WE DO NEED A RUTHLESS TEACHER LIKE HIM...
Here.
...TO TRAIN AN ASSASSIN CAPABLE OF SAVING THE WORLD.
...
THNK
I'VE BEEN FILLED WITH DOUBT SINCE I STARTED WORKING HERE.
TAKAOKA WAS ONCE AN ELITE SOLDIER.
SHNNK
A JUNIOR HIGH SCHOOL STUDENT WHO'S ONLY TRAINED FOR THREE MONTHS IS NO MATCH FOR HIM.
BUT THERE IS ONE STUDENT ...
KRNCH
KRNCH
...WHO JUST MIGHT...
BUT DO I HAVE THE RIGHT TO DRAG HIM INTO THIS?!
KRNCH

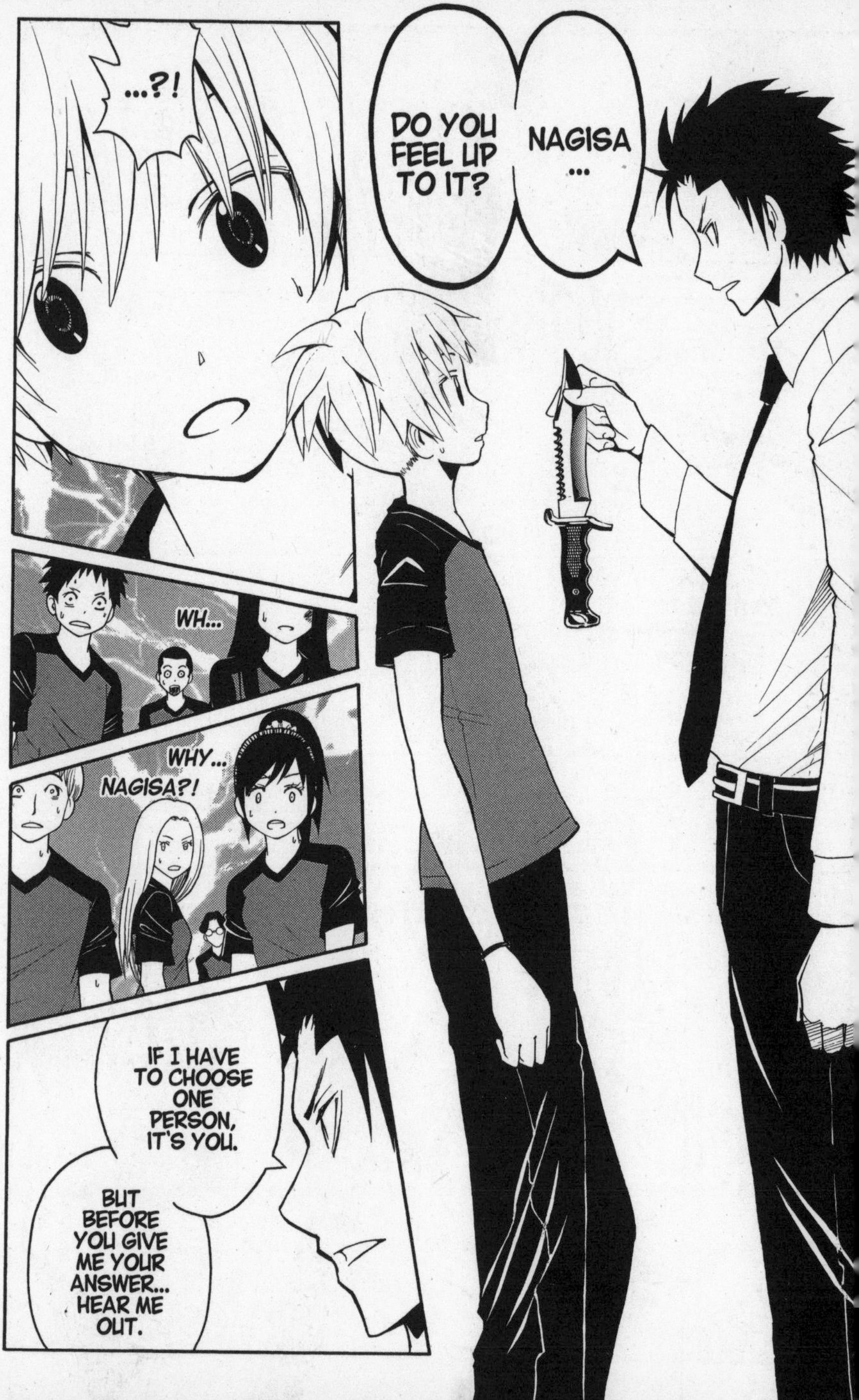
NAGISA ...
DO YOU FEEL UP TO IT?
...?!
WH...
WHY...
NAGISA?!
IF I HAVE TO CHOOSE ONE PERSON, IT'S YOU.
BUT BEFORE YOU GIVE ME YOUR ANSWER... HEAR ME OUT.

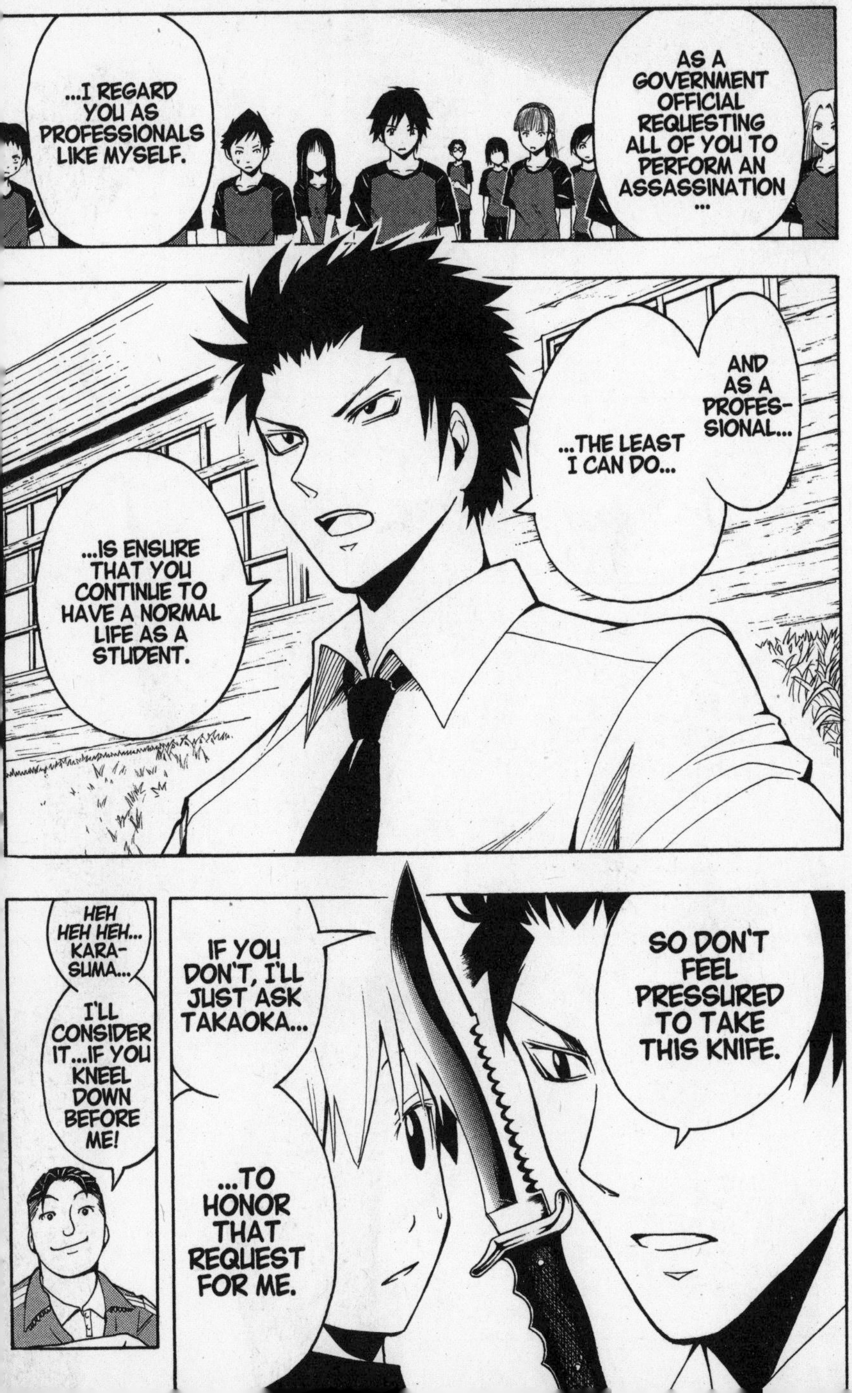
AS A GOVERNMENT OFFICIAL REQUESTING ALL OF YOU TO PERFORM AN ASSASSINATION ...
...I REGARD YOU AS PROFESSIONALS LIKE MYSELF.
AND AS A PROFES-SIONAL...
...THE LEAST I CAN DO...
...IS ENSURE THAT YOU CONTINUE TO HAVE A NORMAL LIFE AS A STUDENT.
SO DON'T FEEL PRESSURED TO TAKE THIS KNIFE.
IF YOU DON'T, I'LL JUST ASK TAKAOKA...
...TO HONOR THAT REQUEST FOR ME.
HEH HEH HEH... KARA-SUMA...
I'LL CONSIDER IT...IF YOU KNEEL DOWN BEFORE ME!

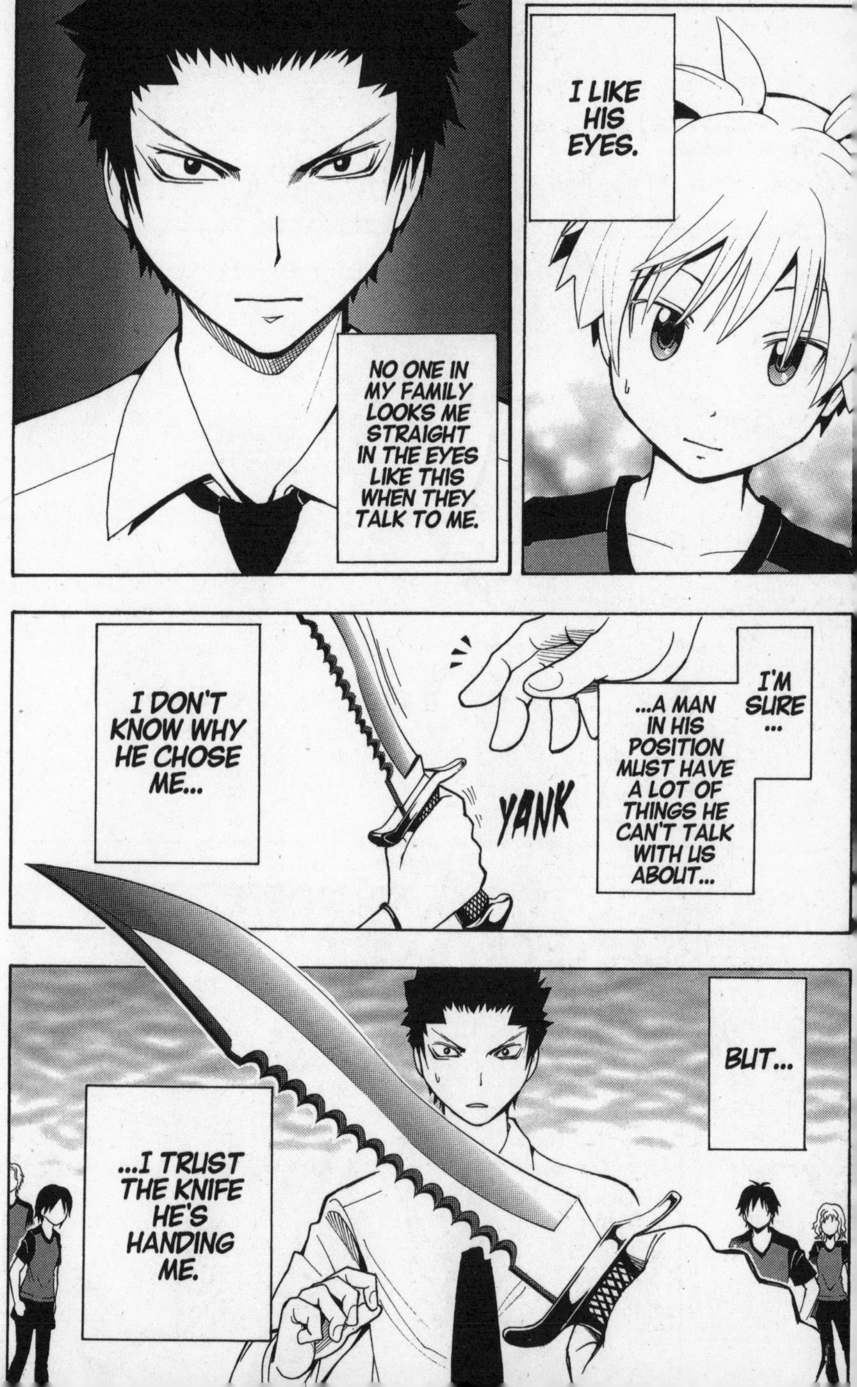
I LIKE HIS EYES.
NO ONE IN MY FAMILY LOOKS ME STRAIGHT IN THE EYES LIKE THIS WHEN THEY TALK TO ME.
I'M SURE...
...A MAN IN HIS POSITION MUST HAVE A LOT OF THINGS HE CAN'T TALK WITH US ABOUT...
YANK
I DON'T KNOW WHY HE CHOSE ME...
BUT...
...I TRUST THE KNIFE HE'S HANDING ME.

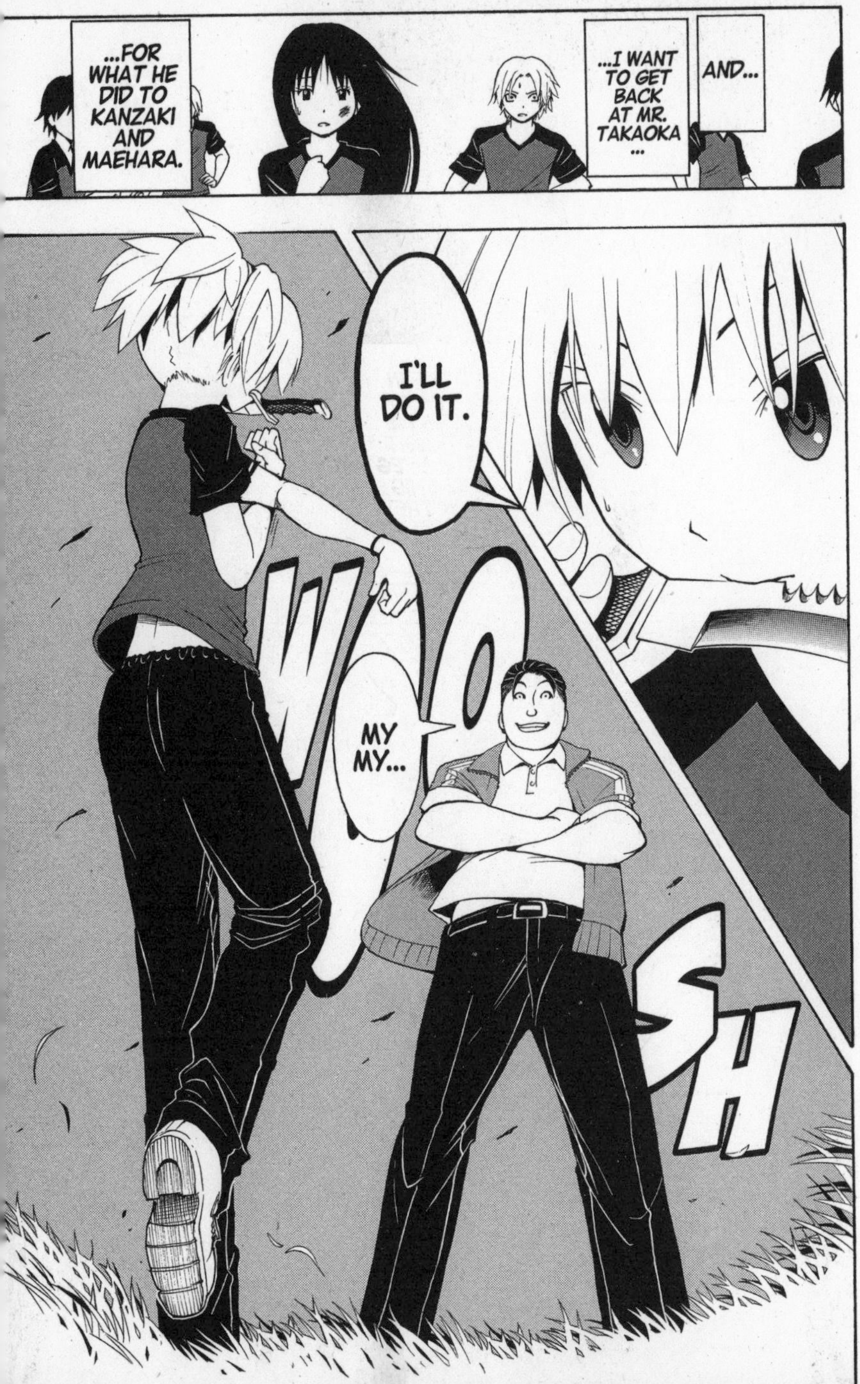
AND...
...I WANT TO GET BACK AT MR. TAKAOKA...
...FOR WHAT HE DID TO KANZAKI AND MAEHARA.
I'LL DO IT.
WOOSH
MY MY...

I have to do
it, don't I?

I'll do it.

I want to do it,
but...

I don't think I can
do it.

Let's just say I tried
to do it. Isn't that
good enough?

The Five Levels of "I'll Do It."

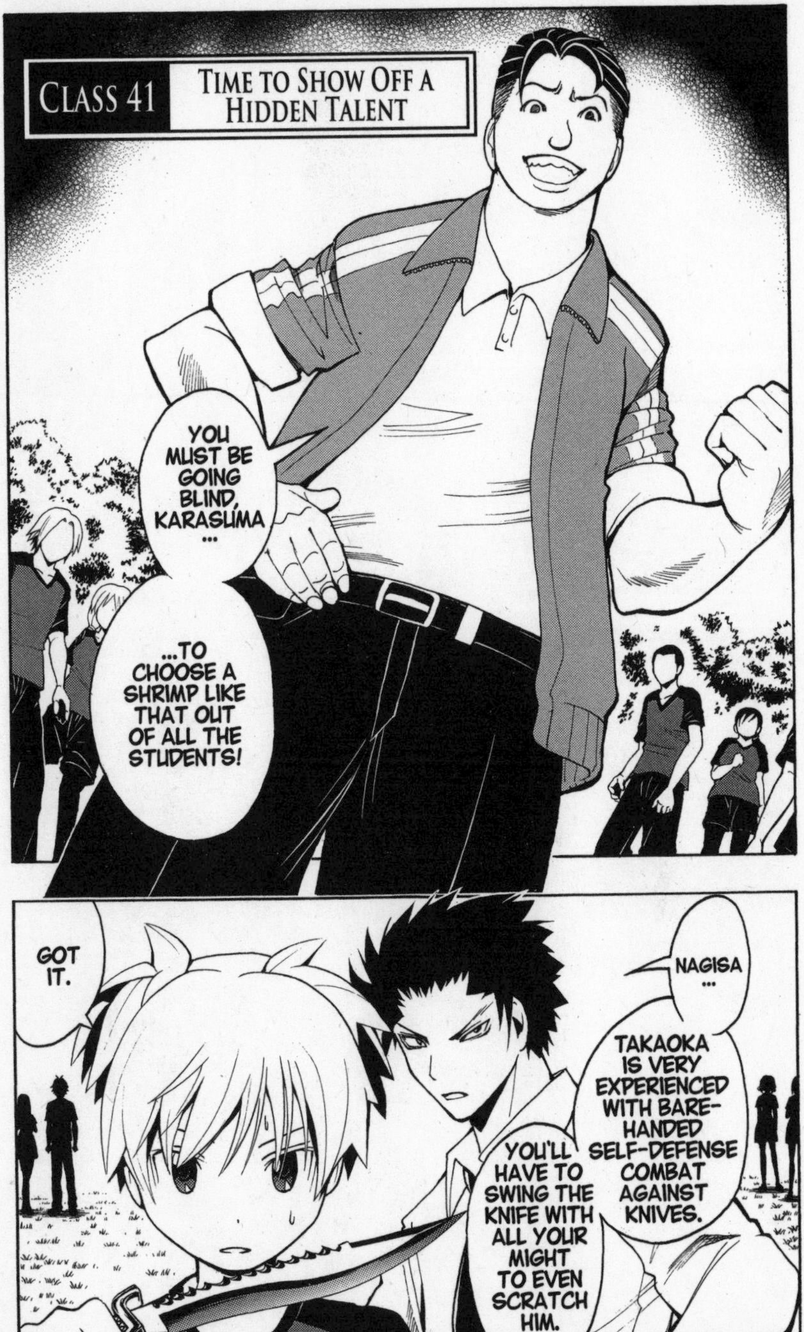
CLASS 41
TIME TO SHOW OFF A HIDDEN TALENT
YOU MUST BE GOING BLIND, KARASUMA...
...TO CHOOSE A SHRIMP LIKE THAT OUT OF ALL THE STUDENTS!
NAGISA...
TAKAOKA IS VERY EXPERIENCED WITH BARE-HANDED SELF-DEFENSE COMBAT AGAINST KNIVES.
YOU'LL HAVE TO SWING THE KNIFE WITH ALL YOUR MIGHT TO EVEN SCRATCH HIM.
GOT IT.

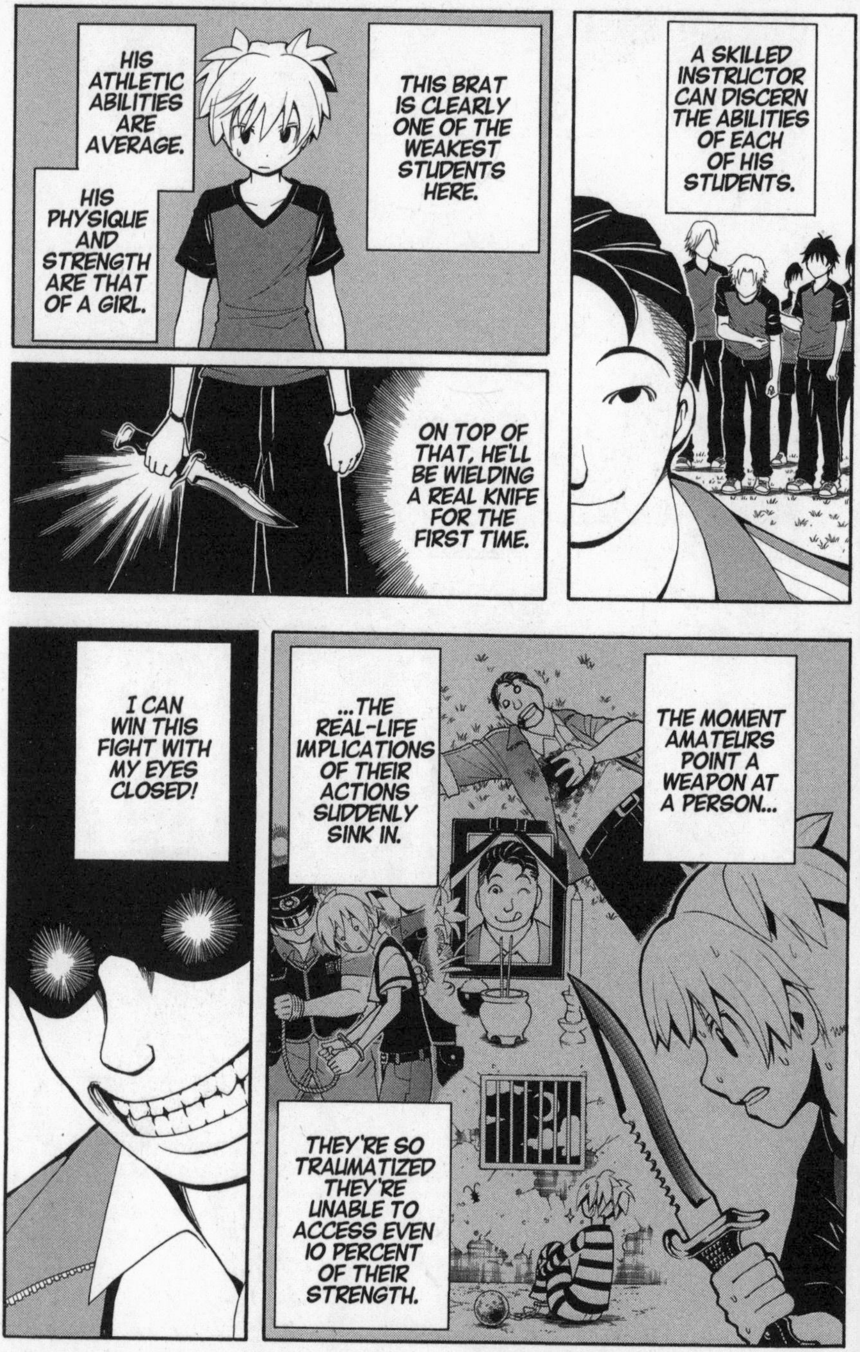
A SKILLED INSTRUCTOR CAN DISCERN THE ABILITIES OF EACH OF HIS STUDENTS.
THIS BRAT IS CLEARLY ONE OF THE WEAKEST STUDENTS HERE.
HIS ATHLETIC ABILITIES ARE AVERAGE.
HIS PHYSIQUE AND STRENGTH ARE THAT OF A GIRL.
ON TOP OF THAT, HE'LL BE WIELDING A REAL KNIFE FOR THE FIRST TIME.
THE MOMENT AMATEURS POINT A WEAPON AT A PERSON...
...THE REAL-LIFE IMPLICATIONS OF THEIR ACTIONS SUDDENLY SINK IN.
THEY'RE SO TRAUMATIZED THEY'RE UNABLE TO ACCESS EVEN 10 PERCENT OF THEIR STRENGTH.
I CAN WIN THIS FIGHT WITH MY EYES CLOSED!

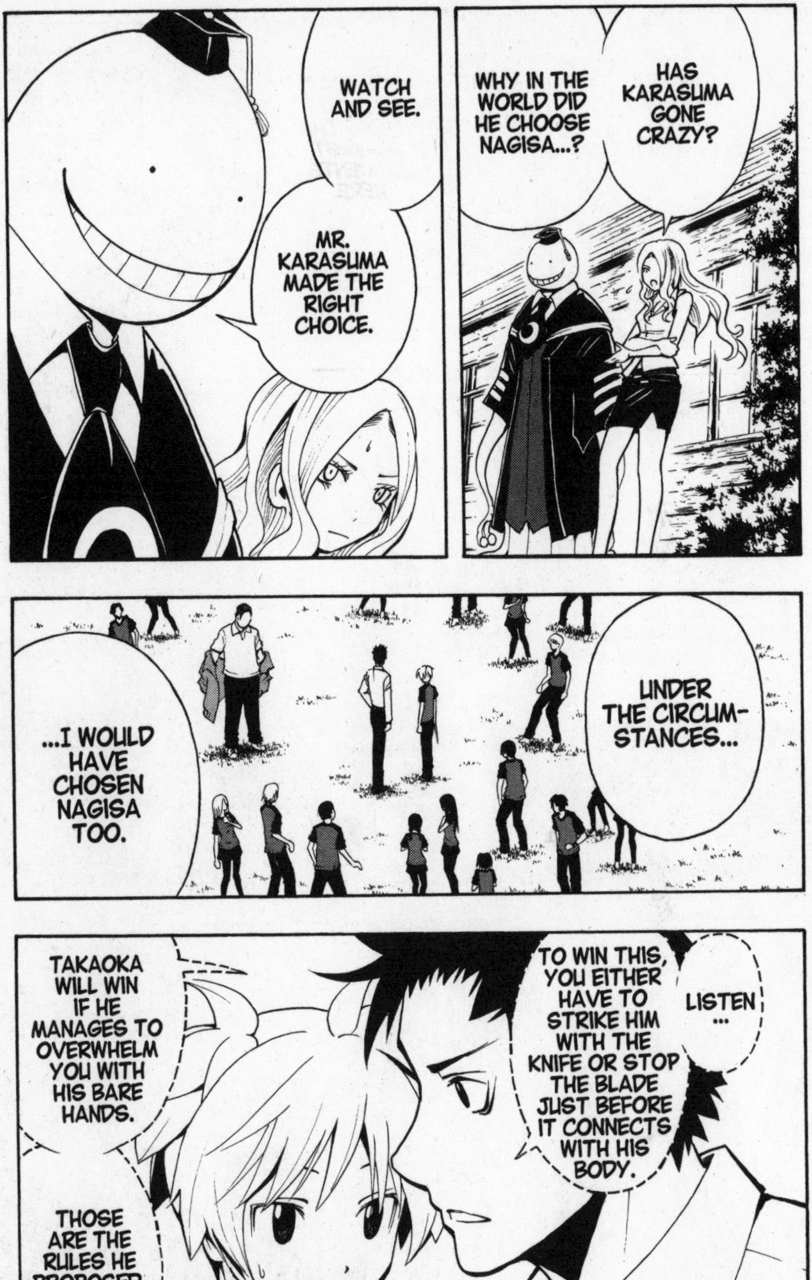
HAS KARASUMA GONE CRAZY?
WHY IN THE WORLD DID HE CHOOSE NAGISA...?
WATCH AND SEE.
MR. KARASUMA MADE THE RIGHT CHOICE.
UNDER THE CIRCUMSTANCES...
...I WOULD HAVE CHOSEN NAGISA TOO.
LISTEN...
TO WIN THIS, YOU EITHER HAVE TO STRIKE HIM WITH THE KNIFE OR STOP THE BLADE JUST BEFORE IT CONNECTS WITH HIS BODY.
TAKAOKA WILL WIN IF HE MANAGES TO OVERWHELM YOU WITH HIS BARE HANDS.
THOSE ARE THE RULES HE PROPOSED.

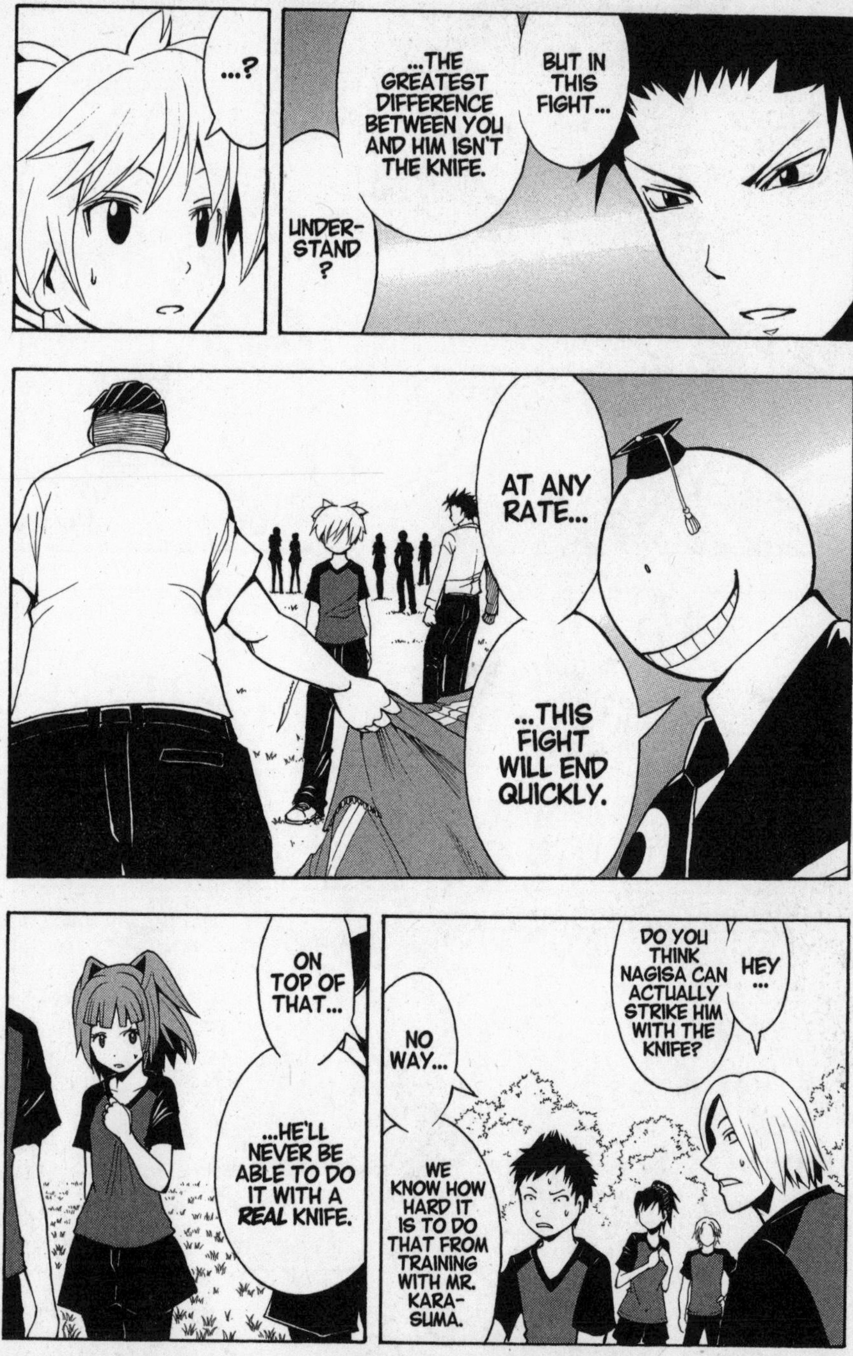
BUT IN THIS FIGHT...
...THE GREATEST DIFFERENCE BETWEEN YOU AND HIM ISN'T THE KNIFE.
UNDER-STAND?
...?
AT ANY RATE...
...THIS FIGHT WILL END QUICKLY.
HEY...
DO YOU THINK NAGISA CAN ACTUALLY STRIKE HIM WITH THE KNIFE?
NO WAY...
WE KNOW HOW HARD IT IS TO DO THAT FROM TRAINING WITH MR. KARA-SUMA.
ON TOP OF THAT...
...HE'LL NEVER BE ABLE TO DO IT WITH A *REAL* KNIFE.

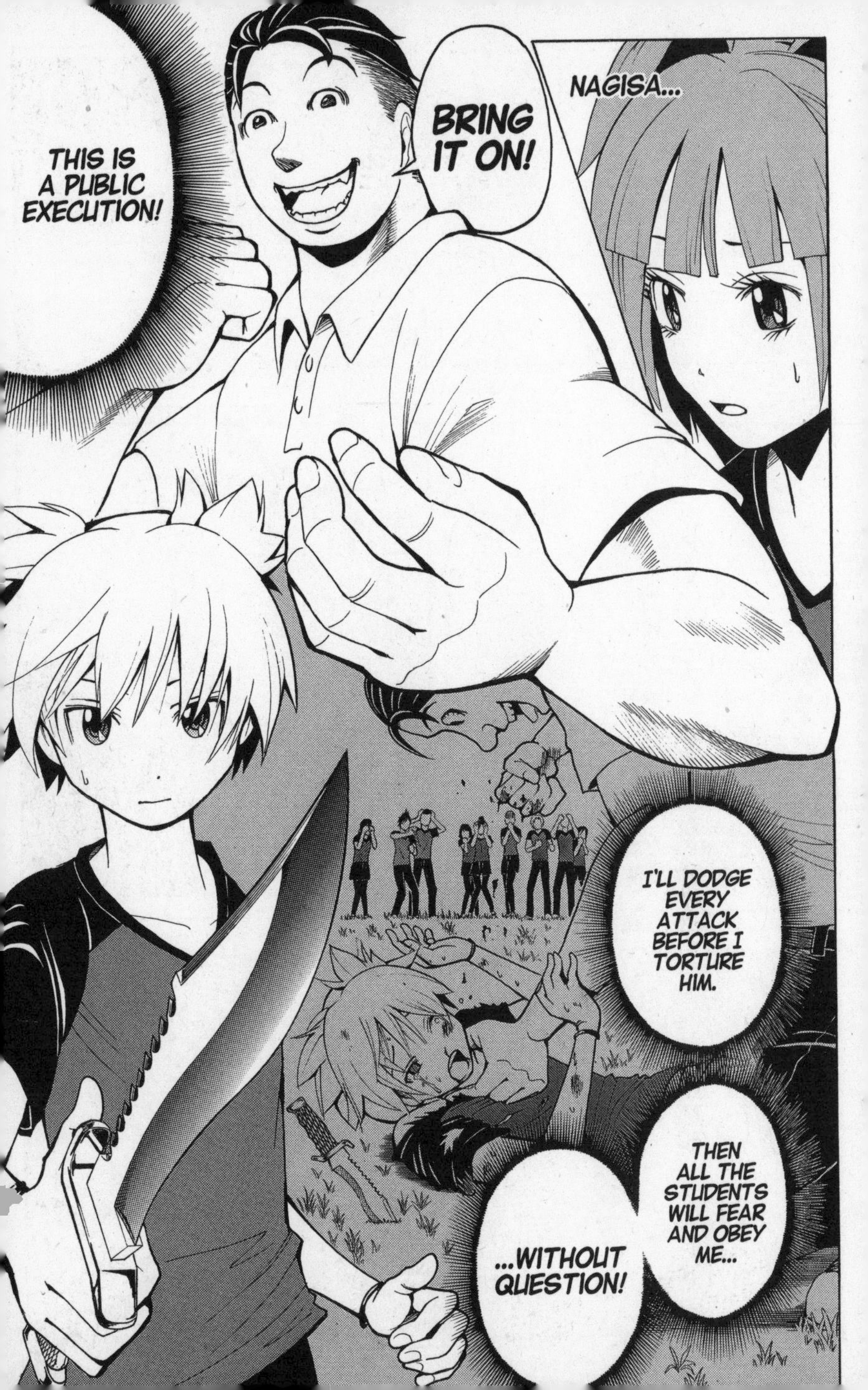
NAGISA...
BRING IT ON!
THIS IS A PUBLIC EXECUTION!
I'LL DODGE EVERY ATTACK BEFORE I TORTURE HIM.
THEN ALL THE STUDENTS WILL FEAR AND OBEY ME...
...WITHOUT QUESTION!

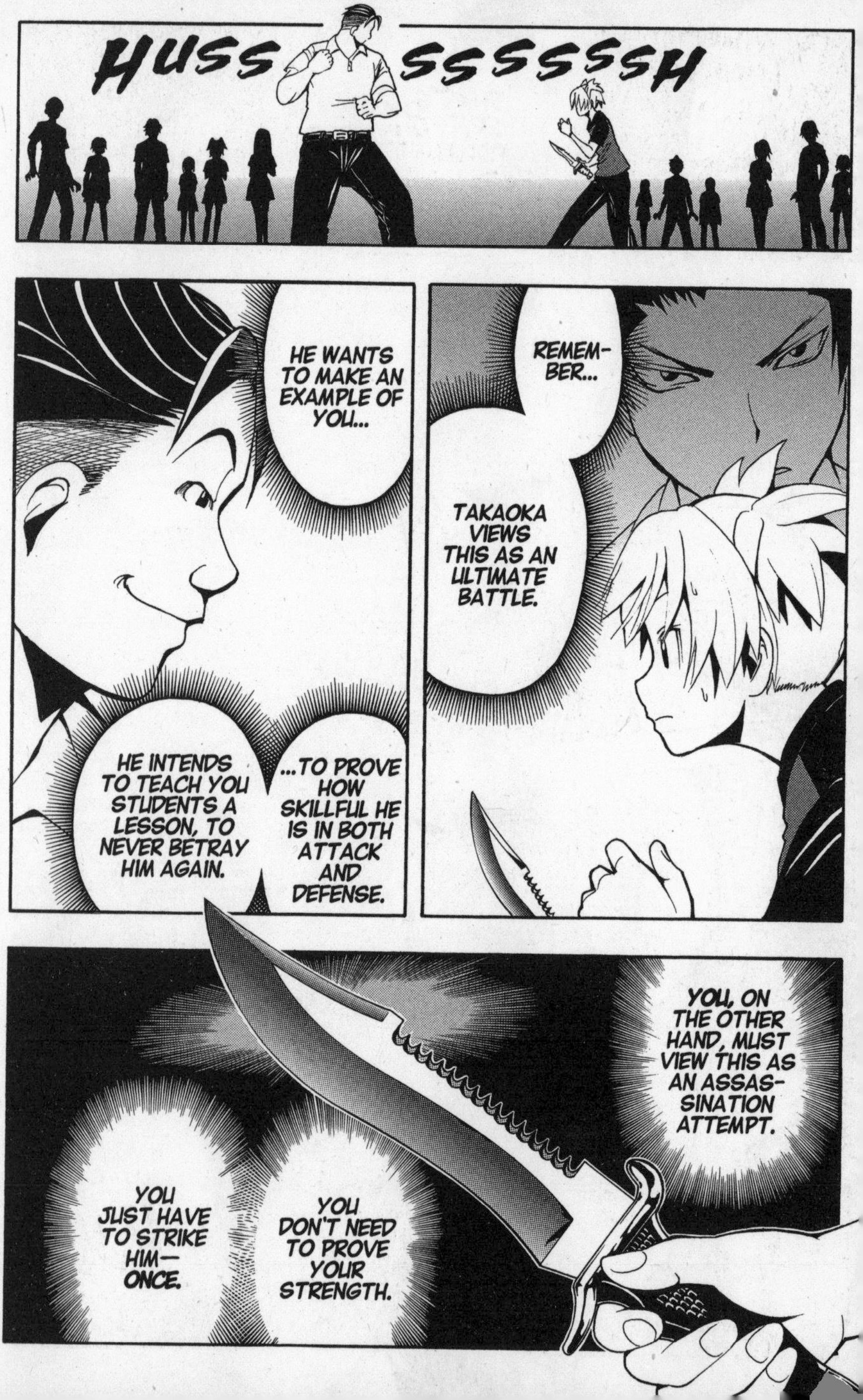
HUSS SSSSSSH
REMEMBER...
TAKAOKA VIEWS THIS AS AN ULTIMATE BATTLE.
HE WANTS TO MAKE AN EXAMPLE OF YOU...
...TO PROVE HOW SKILLFUL HE IS IN BOTH ATTACK AND DEFENSE.
HE INTENDS TO TEACH YOU STUDENTS A LESSON, TO NEVER BETRAY HIM AGAIN.
YOU, ON THE OTHER HAND, MUST VIEW THIS AS AN ASSASSINATION ATTEMPT.
YOU DON'T NEED TO PROVE YOUR STRENGTH.
YOU JUST HAVE TO STRIKE HIM—ONCE.

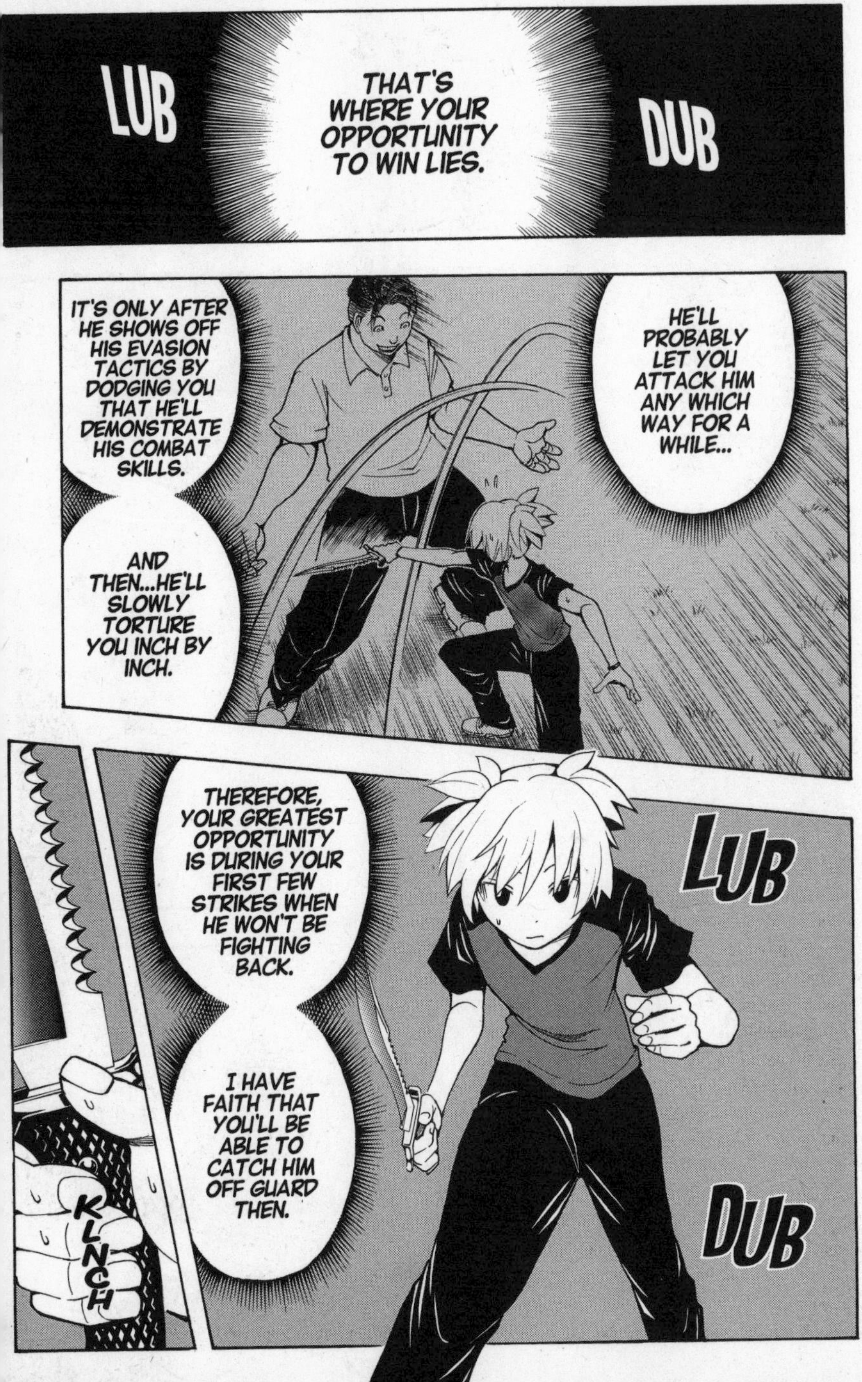
DUB
THAT'S WHERE YOUR OPPORTUNITY TO WIN LIES.
LUB
HE'LL PROBABLY LET YOU ATTACK HIM ANY WHICH WAY FOR A WHILE...
IT'S ONLY AFTER HE SHOWS OFF HIS EVASION TACTICS BY DODGING YOU THAT HE'LL DEMONSTRATE HIS COMBAT SKILLS.
AND THEN...HE'LL SLOWLY TORTURE YOU INCH BY INCH.
LUB
THEREFORE, YOUR GREATEST OPPORTUNITY IS DURING YOUR FIRST FEW STRIKES WHEN HE WON'T BE FIGHTING BACK.
I HAVE FAITH THAT YOU'LL BE ABLE TO CATCH HIM OFF GUARD THEN.
DUB
KLNCH

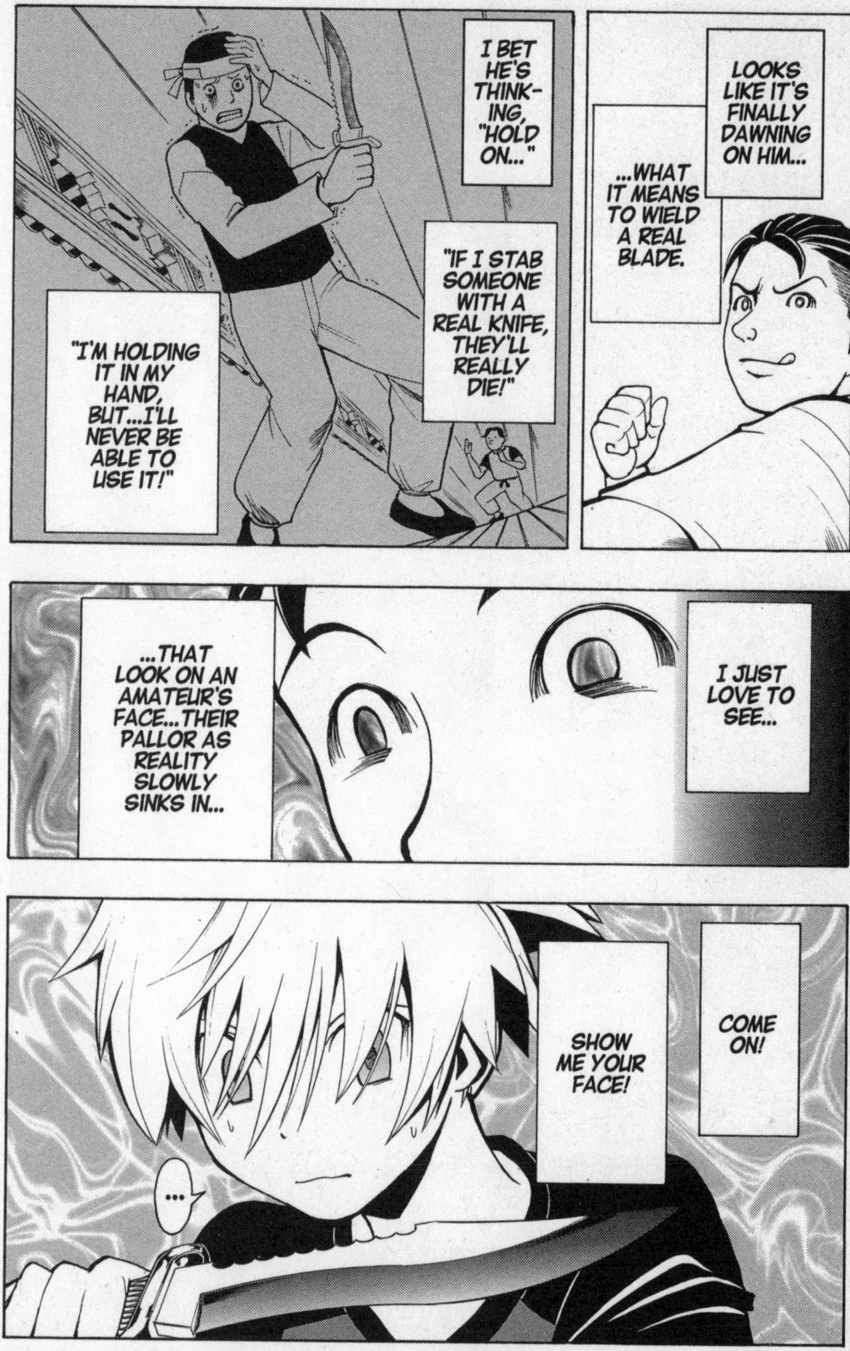
LOOKS LIKE IT'S FINALLY DAWNING ON HIM...
...WHAT IT MEANS TO WIELD A REAL BLADE.
I BET HE'S THINKING, "HOLD ON..."
"IF I STAB SOMEONE WITH A REAL KNIFE, THEY'LL REALLY DIE!"
"I'M HOLDING IT IN MY HAND, BUT...I'LL NEVER BE ABLE TO USE IT!"
I JUST LOVE TO SEE...
...THAT LOOK ON AN AMATEUR'S FACE...THEIR PALLOR AS REALITY SLOWLY SINKS IN...
COME ON!
SHOW ME YOUR FACE!
...

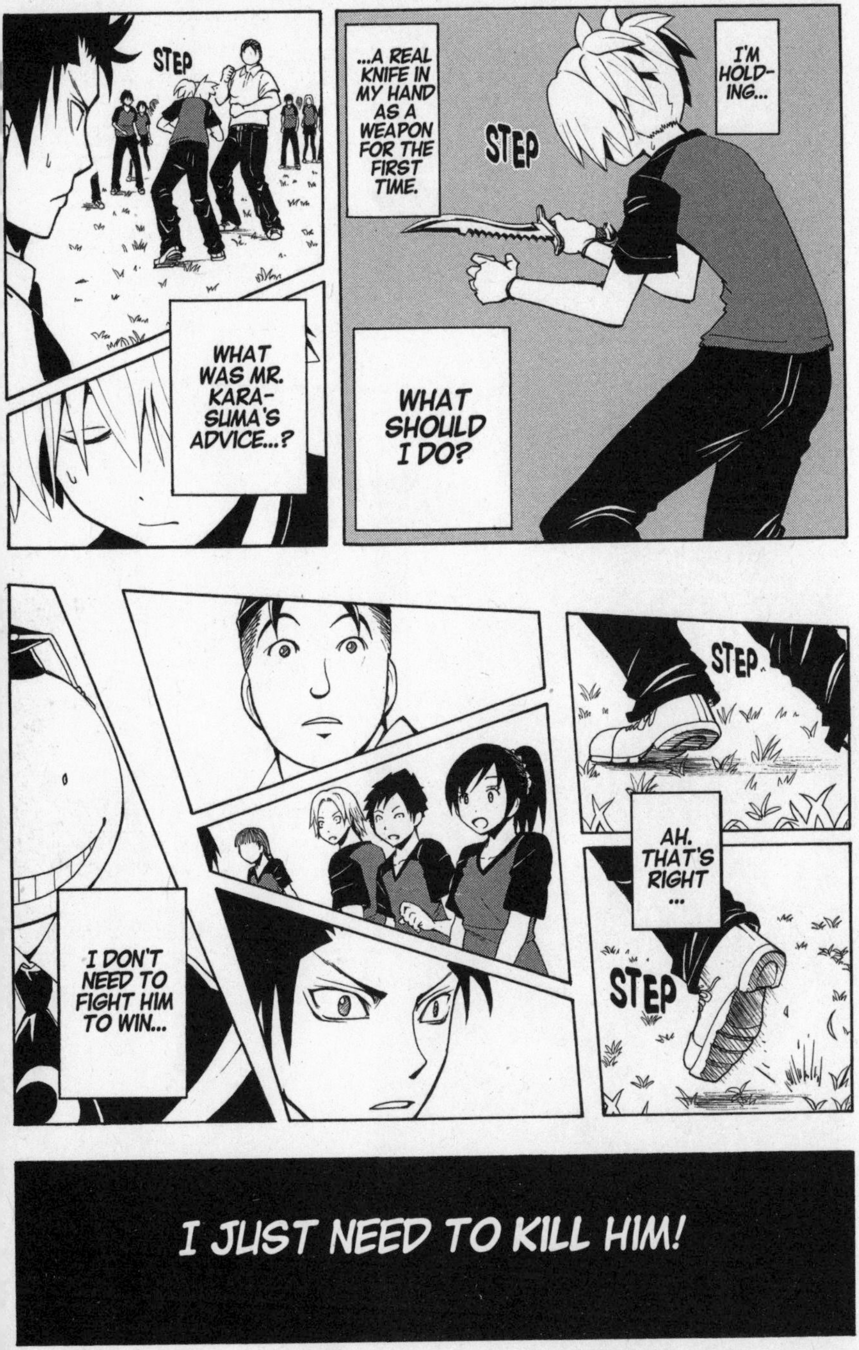
I'M HOLDING...
...A REAL KNIFE IN MY HAND AS A WEAPON FOR THE FIRST TIME.
STEP
WHAT SHOULD I DO?
STEP
WHAT WAS MR. KARASUMA'S ADVICE...?
STEP
AH. THAT'S RIGHT ...
STEP
I DON'T NEED TO FIGHT HIM TO WIN...
I JUST NEED TO KILL HIM!

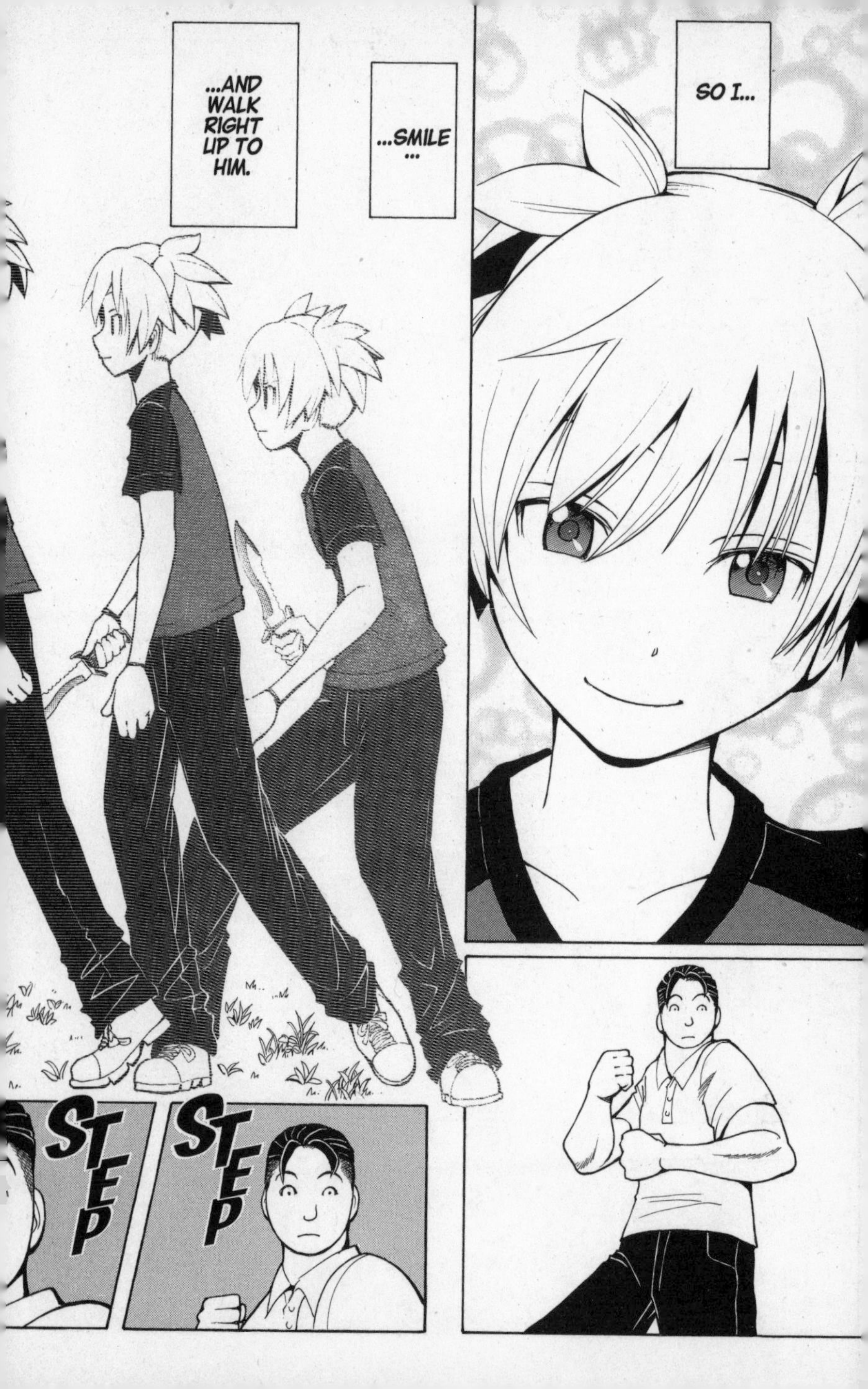
SO I...
...SMILE ...
...AND WALK RIGHT UP TO HIM.
STEP
STEP

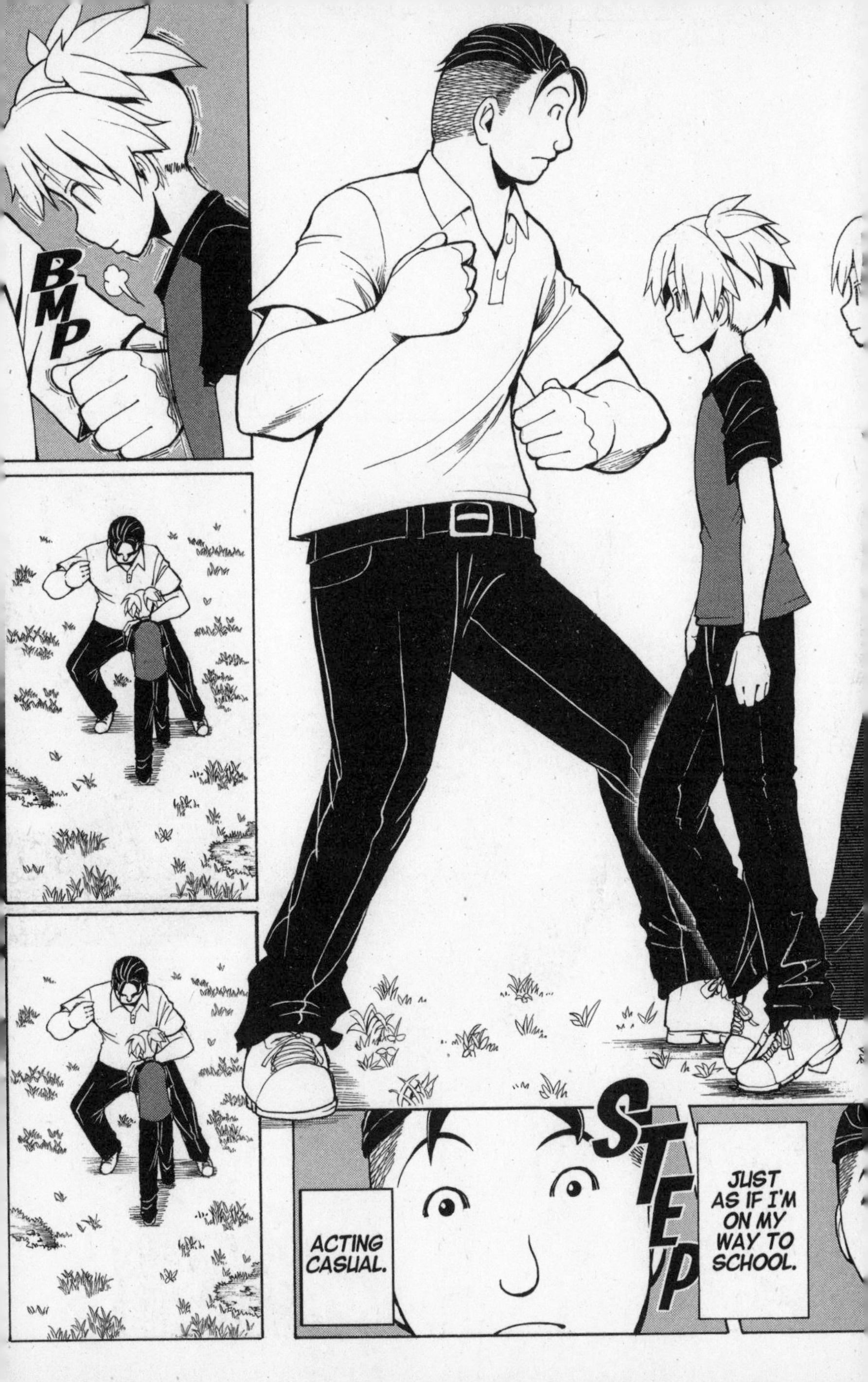
JUST AS IF I'M ON MY WAY TO SCHOOL.
STEP
ACTING CASUAL.
BMP

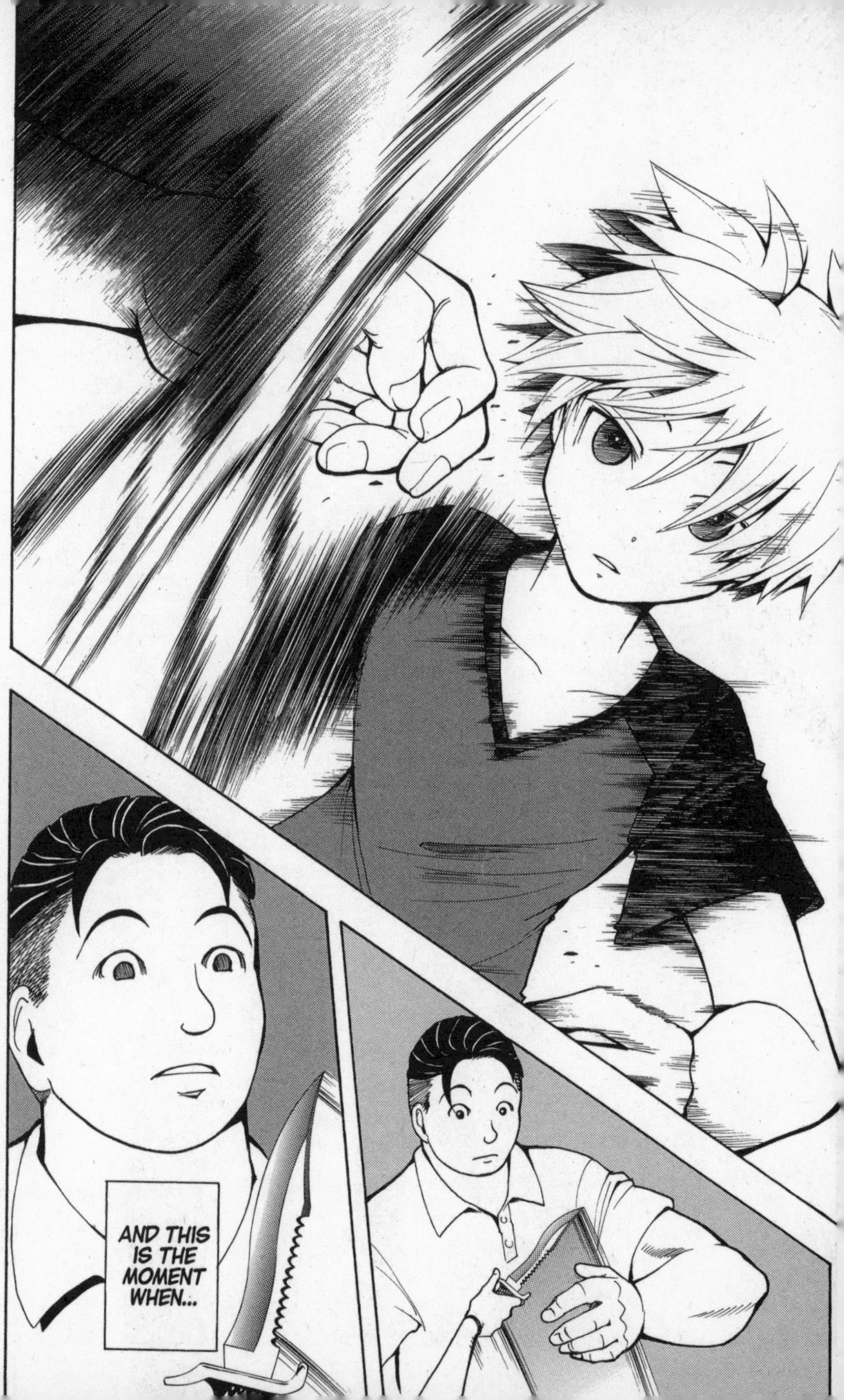
AND THIS IS THE MOMENT WHEN...

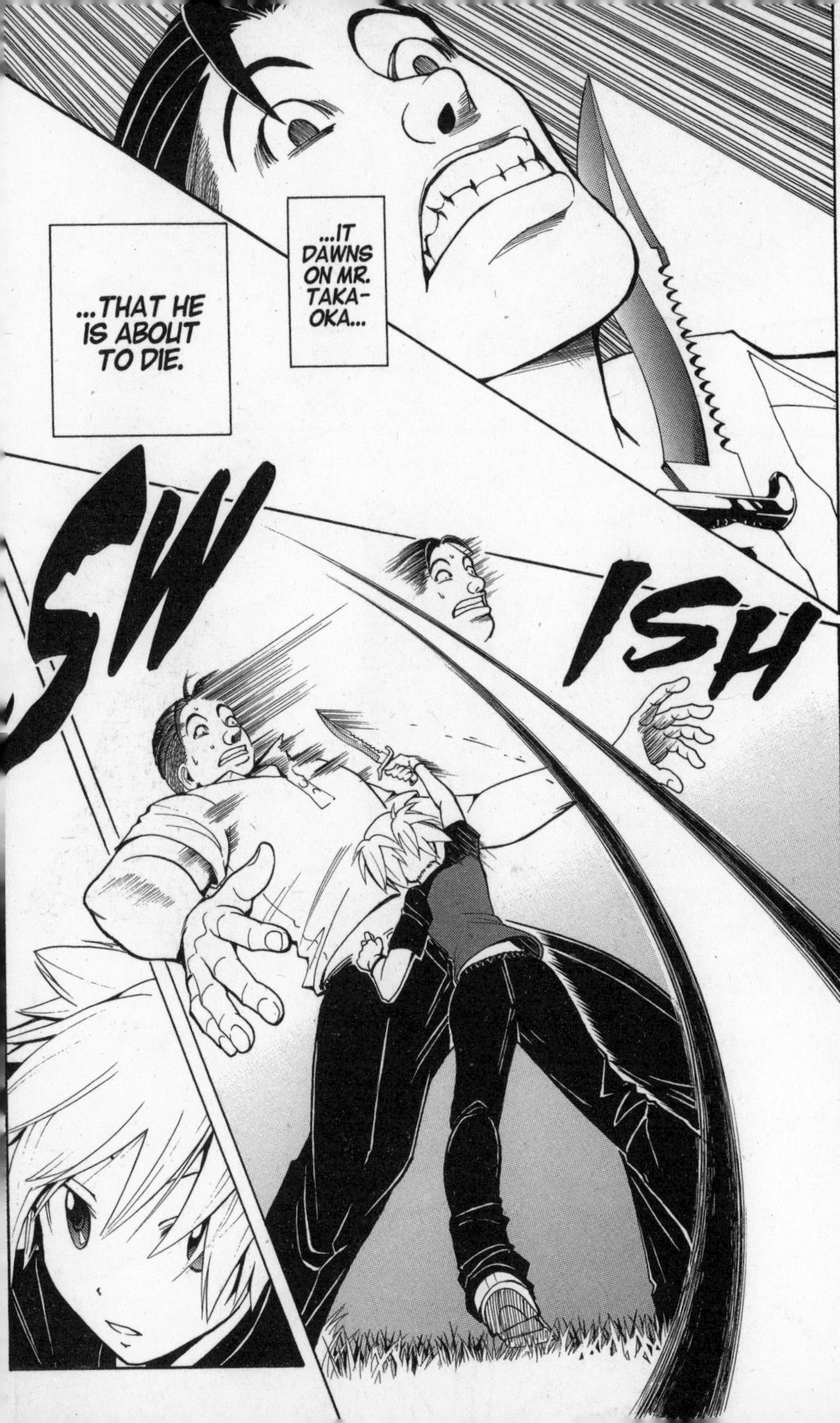
...IT DAWNS ON MR. TAKA-OKA...
...THAT HE IS ABOUT TO DIE.
SWISH

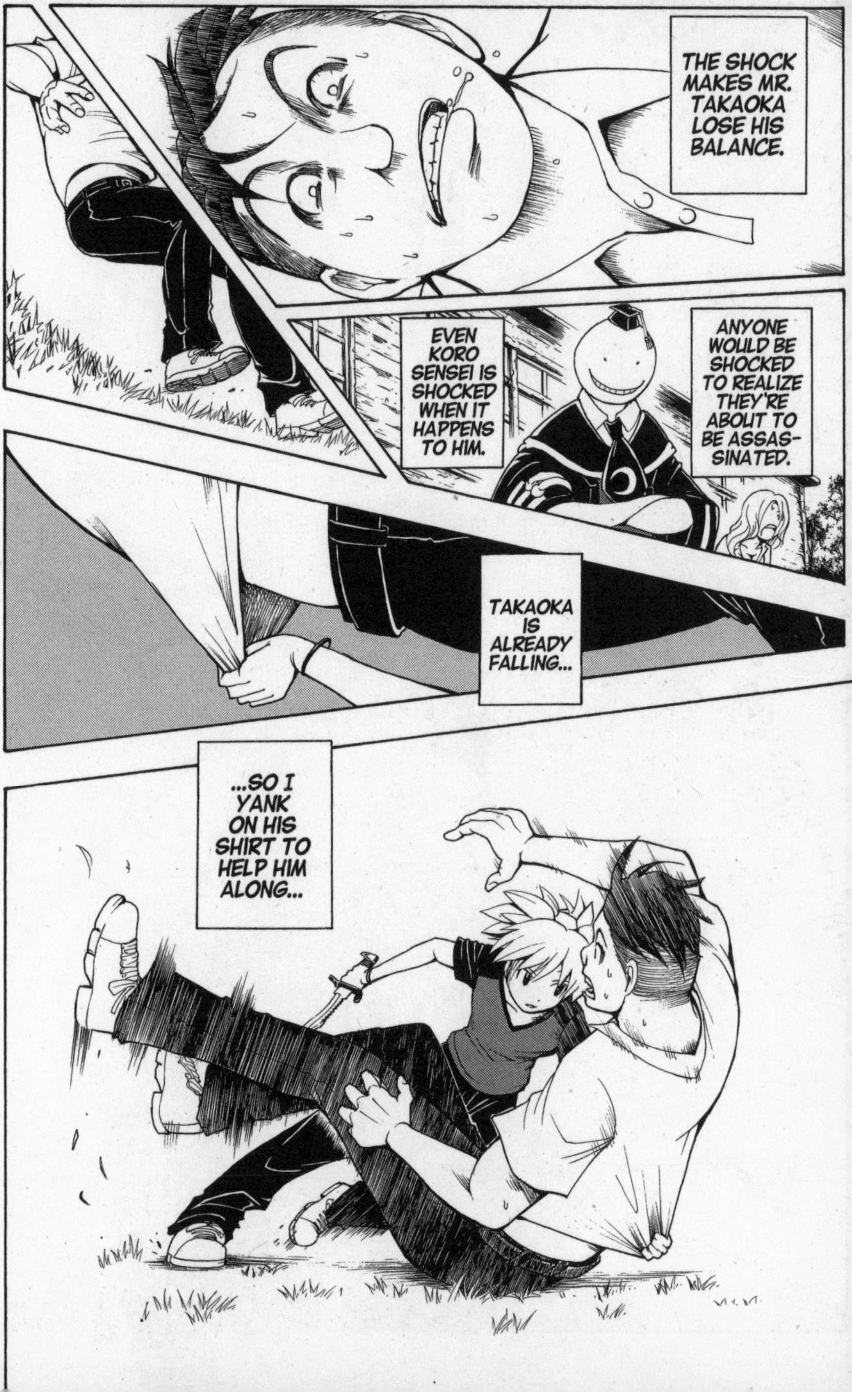
THE SHOCK MAKES MR. TAKAOKA LOSE HIS BALANCE.
ANYONE WOULD BE SHOCKED TO REALIZE THEY'RE ABOUT TO BE ASSAS-SINATED.
EVEN KORO SENSEI IS SHOCKED WHEN IT HAPPENS TO HIM.
TAKAOKA IS ALREADY FALLING...
...SO I YANK ON HIS SHIRT TO HELP HIM ALONG...

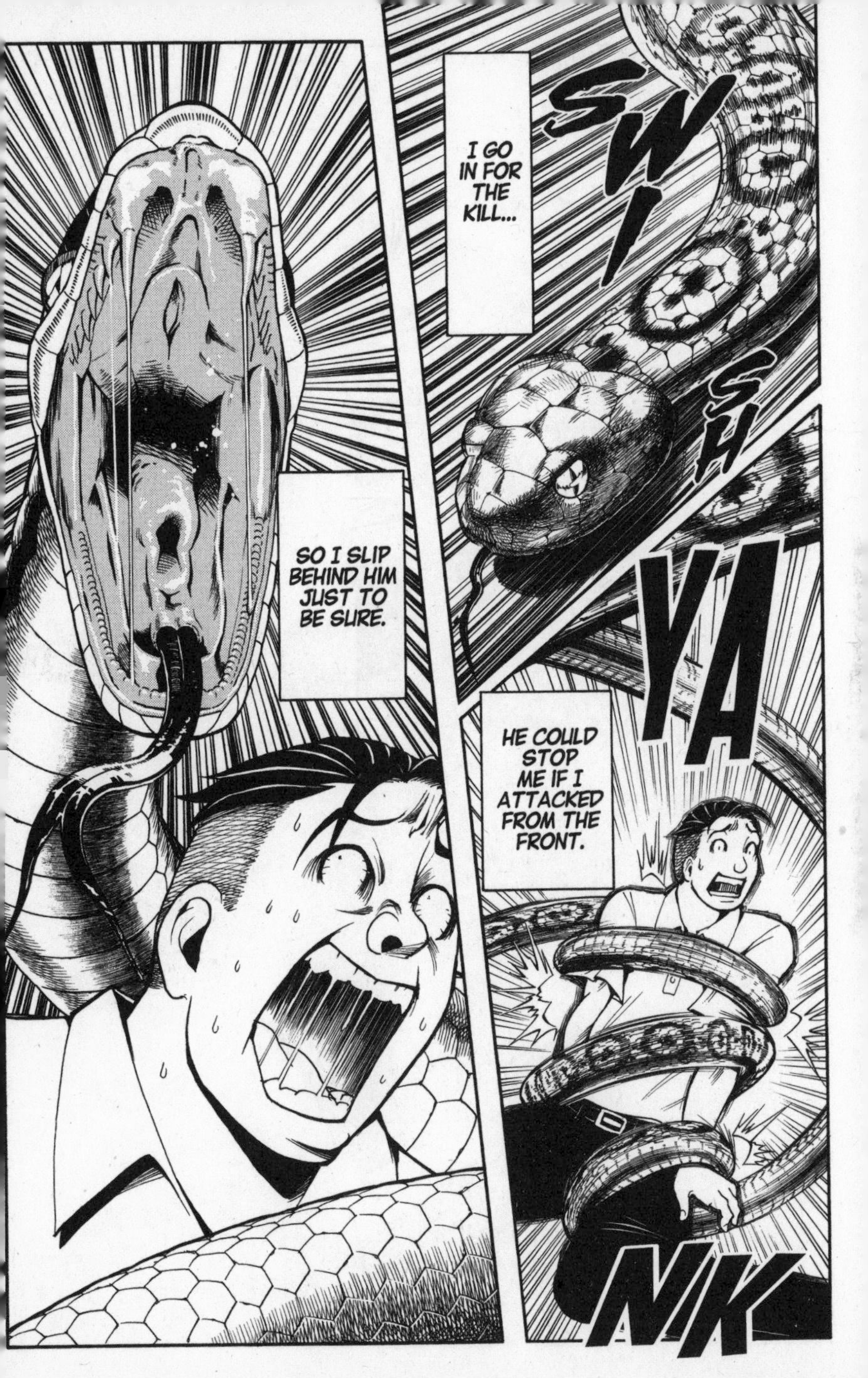
I GO IN FOR THE KILL...
SWISH
HE COULD STOP ME IF I ATTACKED FROM THE FRONT.
YANK
SO I SLIP BEHIND HIM JUST TO BE SURE.

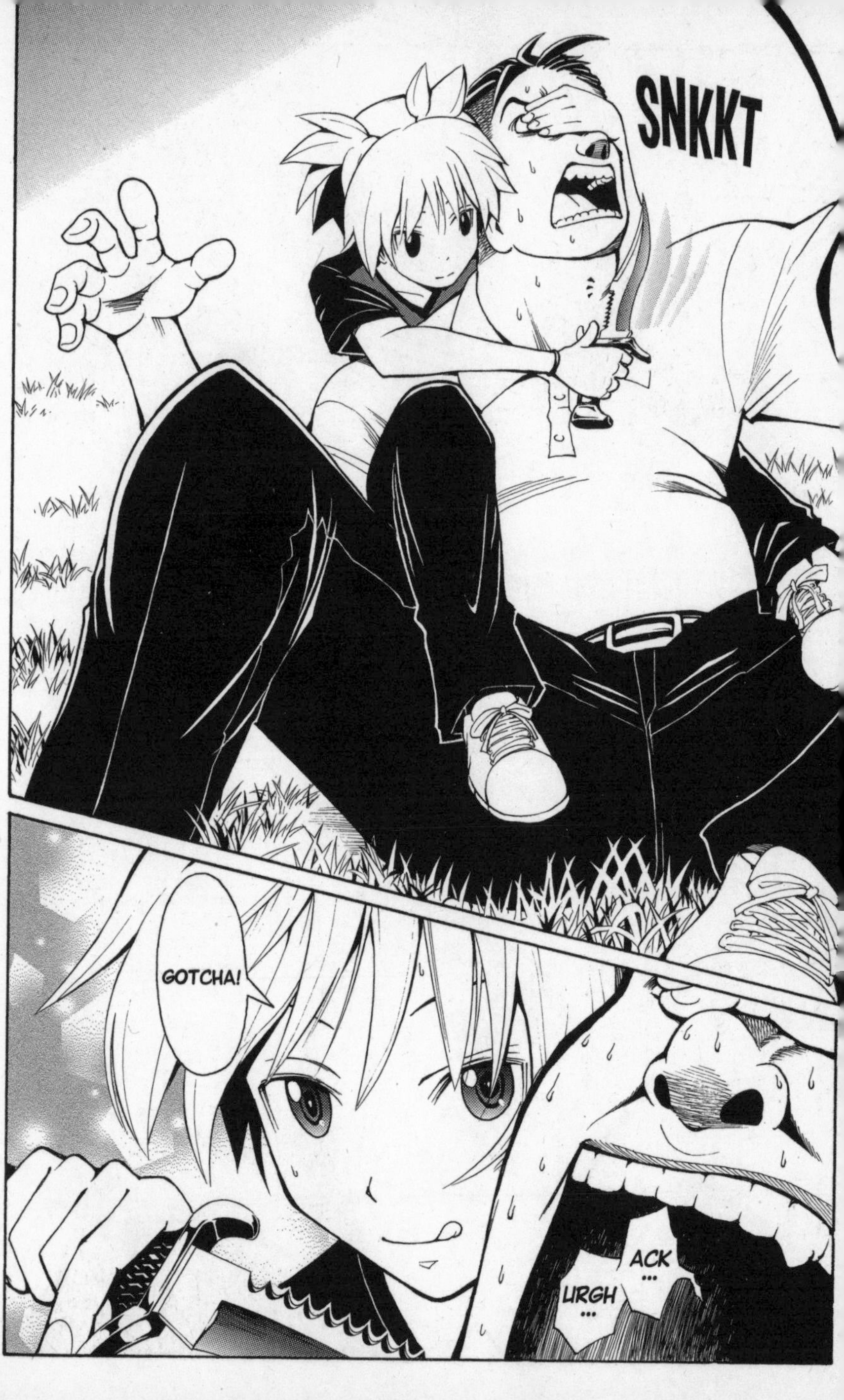
SNKKT
GOTCHA!
ACK...
URGH...

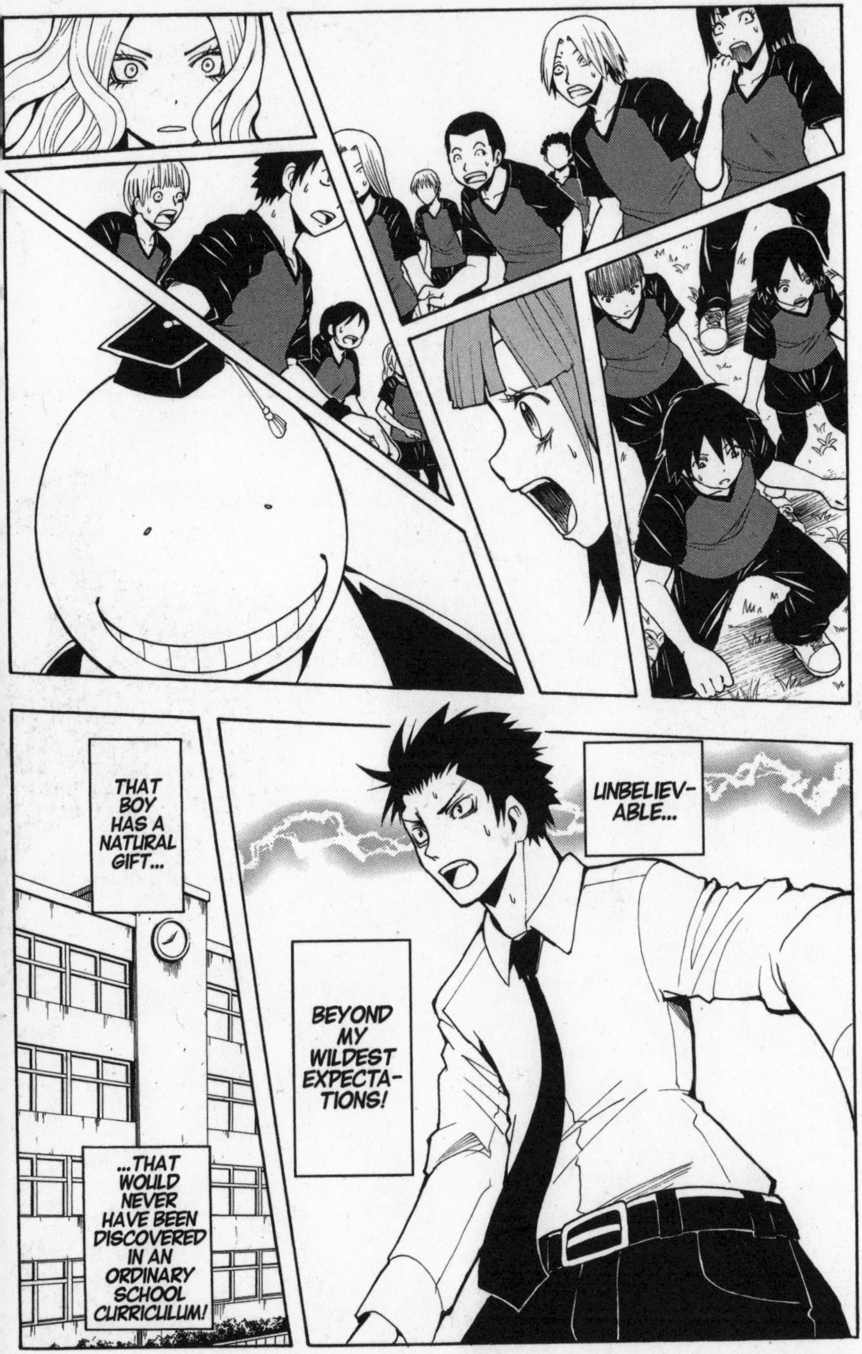
UNBELIEVABLE...
BEYOND MY WILDEST EXPECTATIONS!
THAT BOY HAS A NATURAL GIFT...
...THAT WOULD NEVER HAVE BEEN DISCOVERED IN AN ORDINARY SCHOOL CURRICULUM!

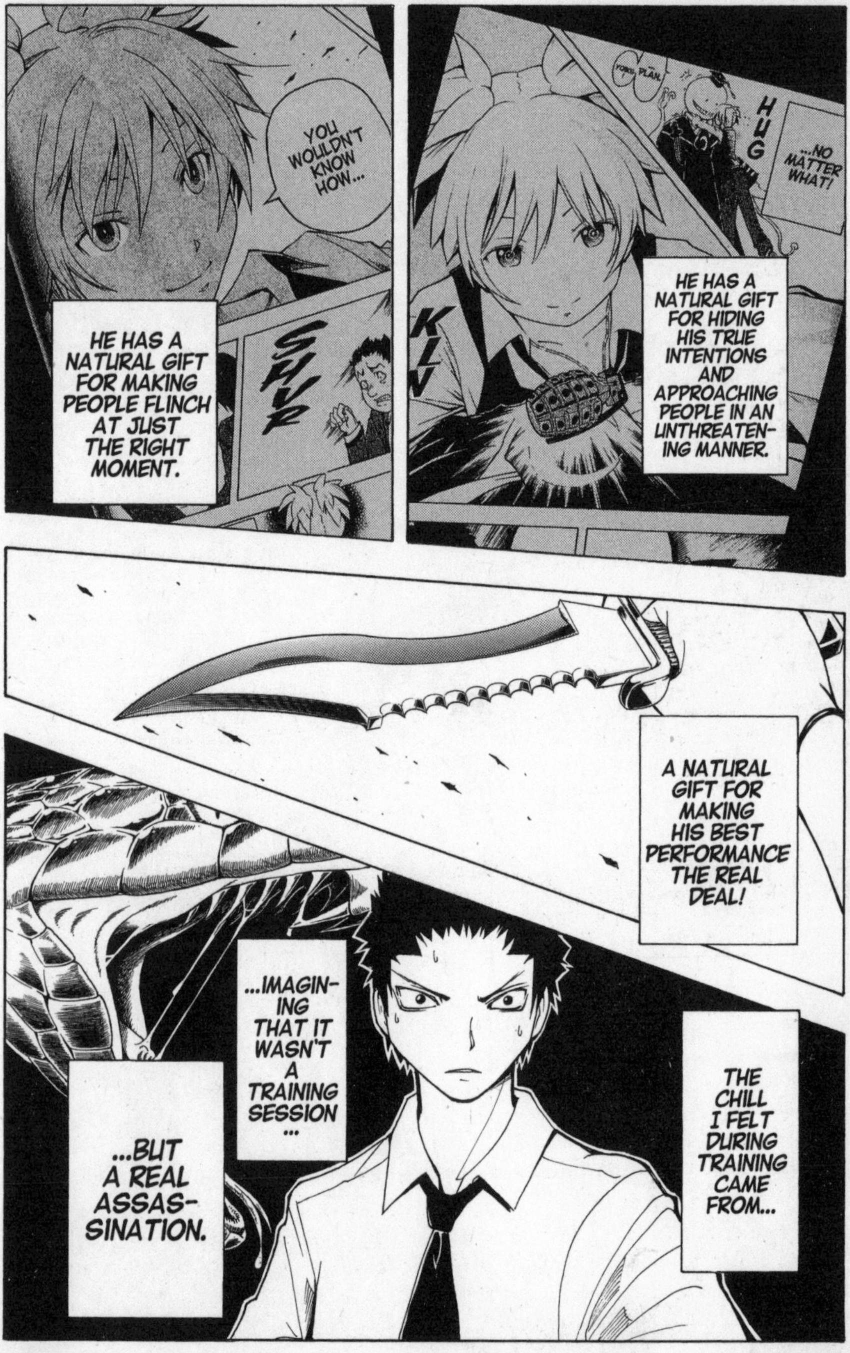
PLAN.
HUG
...NO MATTER WHAT!
KIN
HE HAS A NATURAL GIFT FOR HIDING HIS TRUE INTENTIONS AND APPROACHING PEOPLE IN AN UNTHREATENING MANNER.
YOU WOULDN'T KNOW HOW...
SHUR
HE HAS A NATURAL GIFT FOR MAKING PEOPLE FLINCH AT JUST THE RIGHT MOMENT.
A NATURAL GIFT FOR MAKING HIS BEST PERFORMANCE THE REAL DEAL!
THE CHILL I FELT DURING TRAINING CAME FROM...
...IMAGINING THAT IT WASN'T A TRAINING SESSION...
...BUT A REAL ASSASSINATION.

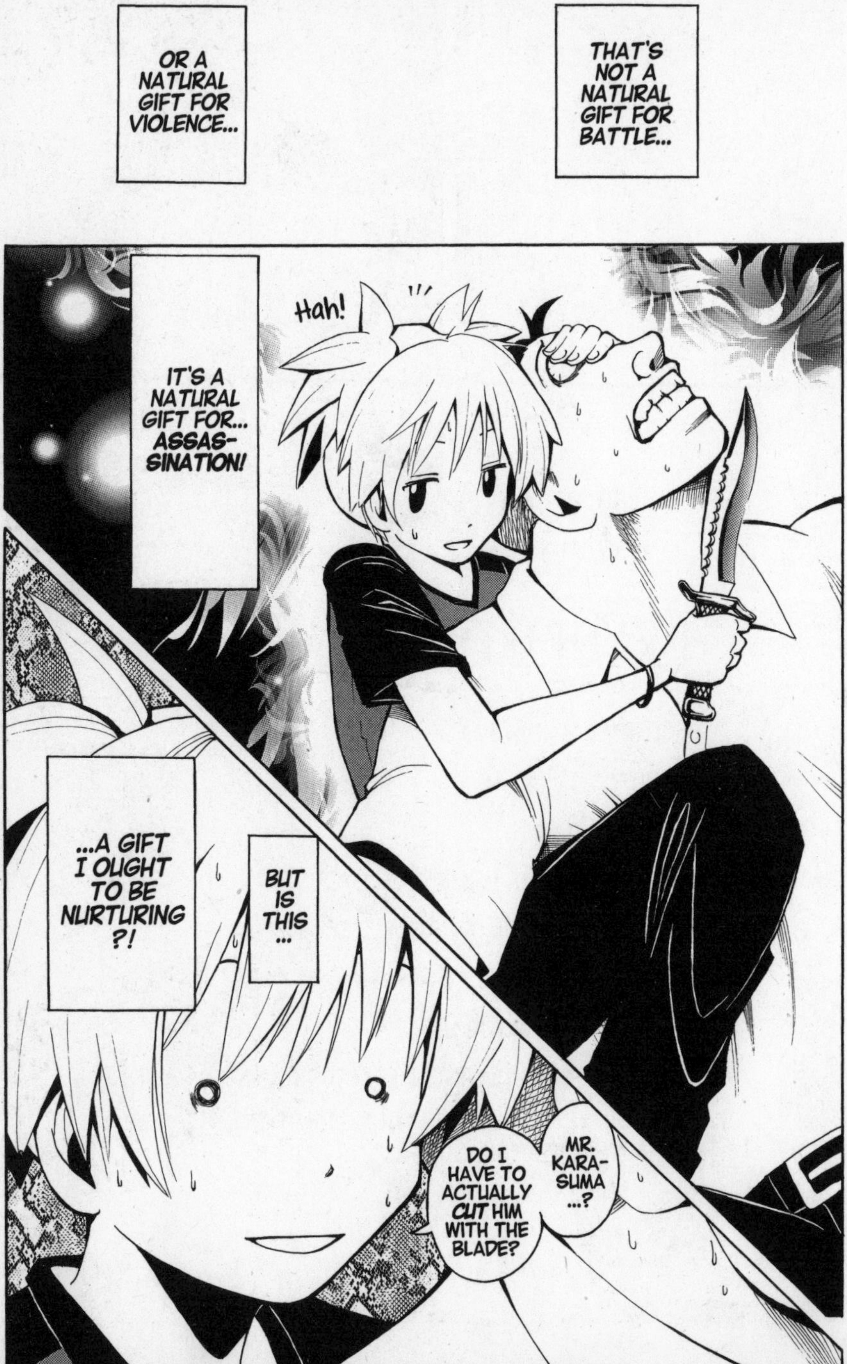
THAT'S NOT A NATURAL GIFT FOR BATTLE...
OR A NATURAL GIFT FOR VIOLENCE...
Hah!
IT'S A NATURAL GIFT FOR... ASSASSINATION!
MR. KARASUMA...?
DO I HAVE TO ACTUALLY CUT HIM WITH THE BLADE?
BUT IS THIS...
...A GIFT I OUGHT TO BE NURTURING?!

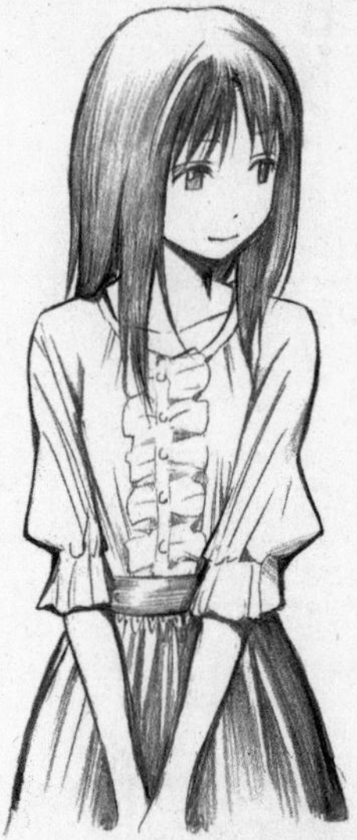

E-8 Yukiko Kanzaki

- Birthday: March 3
- Height: 5' 1"
- Weight: 101.4 lbs.
- Favorite Subject: Japanese Classics
- Least Favorite Subject: Chemistry
- Hobby/Skill: Computer Games
- Future Goal: Caregiver
- A type of game she's recently begun playing: Online FPS
- Her online nickname on the battlefield after a month: Yuki-ogre-ko

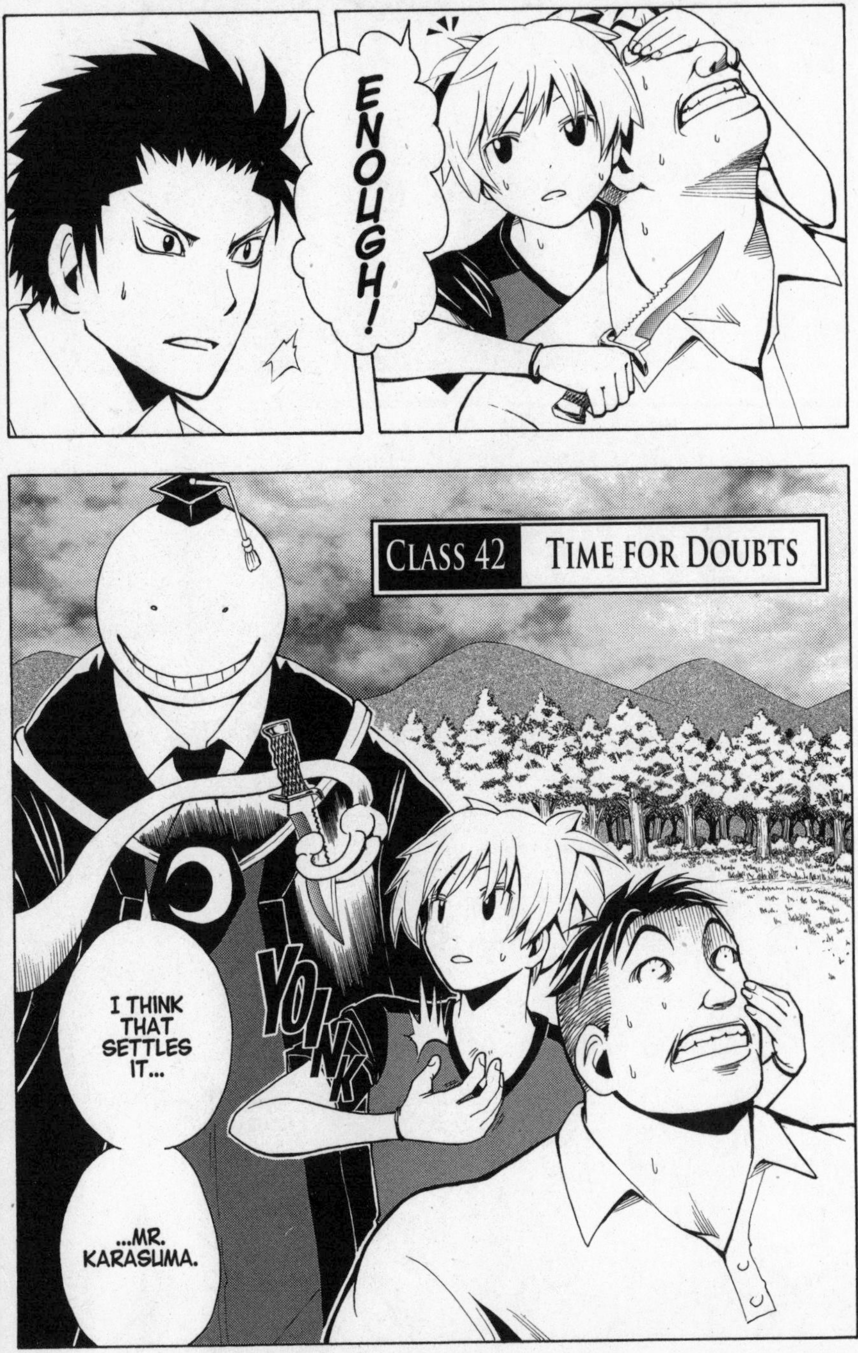
ENOUGH!
CLASS 42 TIME FOR DOUBTS
YOINK
I THINK THAT SETTLES IT...
...MR. KARASUMA.

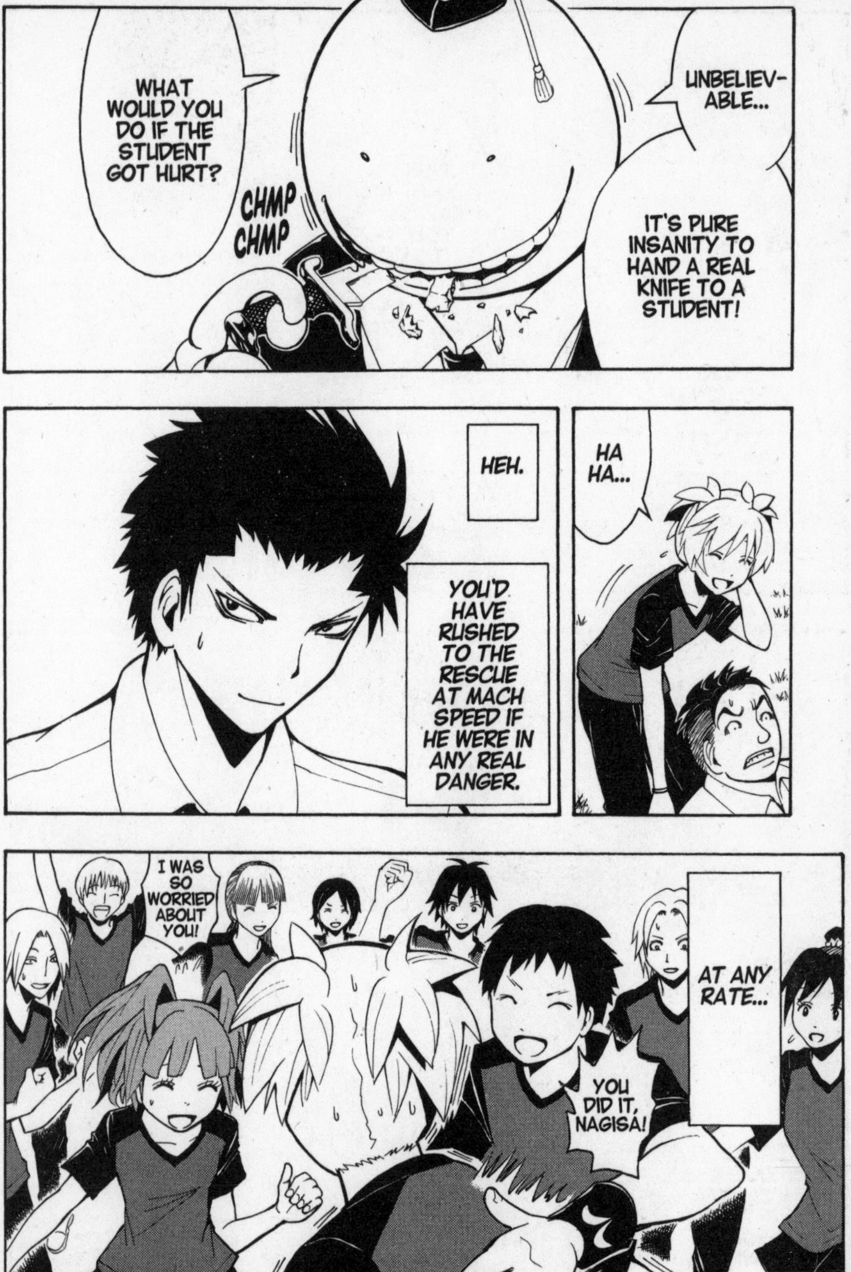
UNBELIEVABLE...
IT'S PURE INSANITY TO HAND A REAL KNIFE TO A STUDENT!
WHAT WOULD YOU DO IF THE STUDENT GOT HURT?
CHMP CHMP
HA HA...
HEH.
YOU'D HAVE RUSHED TO THE RESCUE AT MACH SPEED IF HE WERE IN ANY REAL DANGER.
AT ANY RATE...
YOU DID IT, NAGISA!
I WAS SO WORRIED ABOUT YOU!

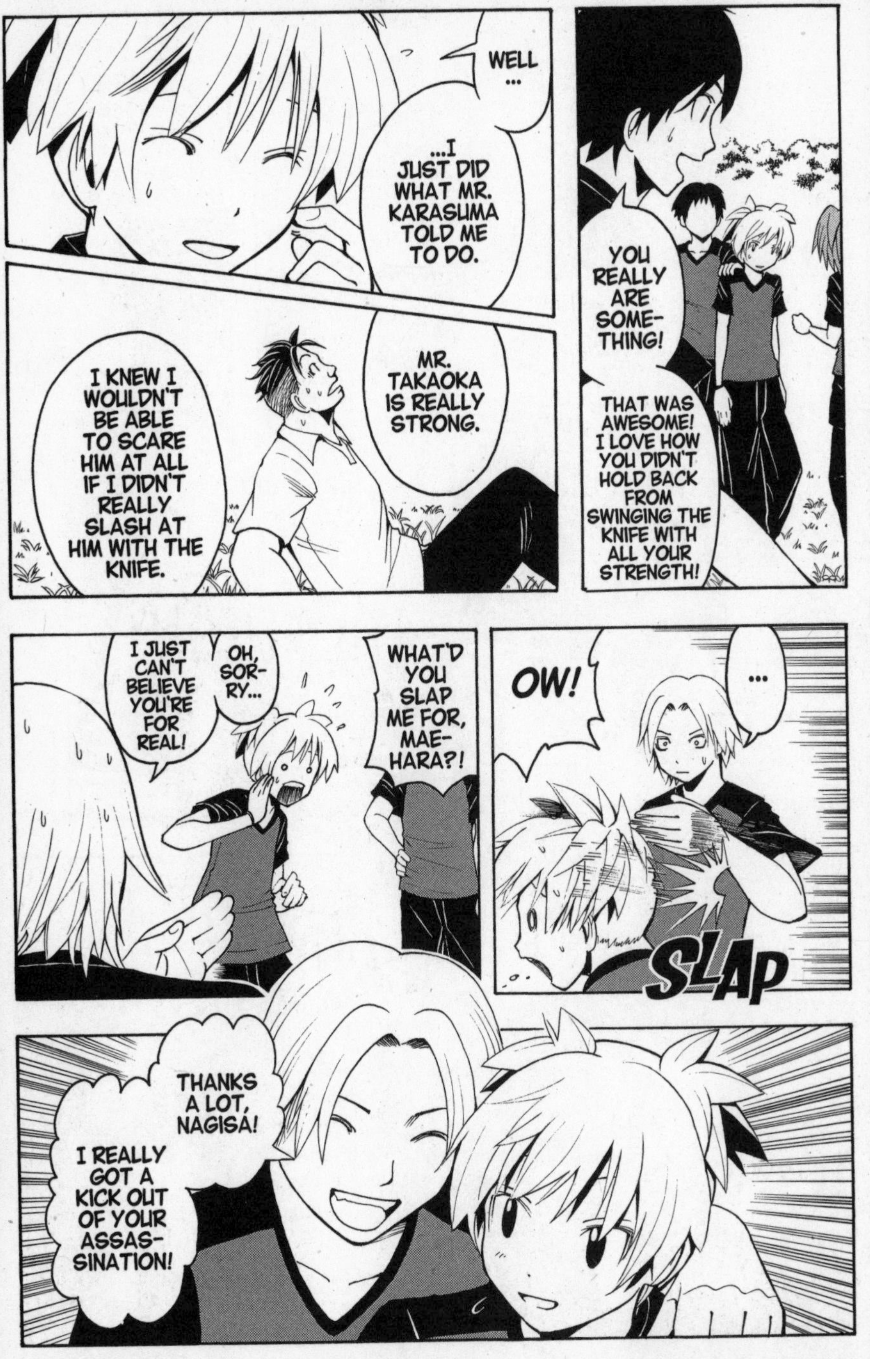
YOU REALLY ARE SOME-THING!
THAT WAS AWESOME! I LOVE HOW YOU DIDN'T HOLD BACK FROM SWINGING THE KNIFE WITH ALL YOUR STRENGTH!
WELL ...
...I JUST DID WHAT MR. KARASUMA TOLD ME TO DO.
MR. TAKAOKA IS REALLY STRONG.
I KNEW I WOULDN'T BE ABLE TO SCARE HIM AT ALL IF I DIDN'T REALLY SLASH AT HIM WITH THE KNIFE.
...
OW!
SLAP
WHAT'D YOU SLAP ME FOR, MAE-HARA?!
OH, SOR-RY...
I JUST CAN'T BELIEVE YOU'RE FOR REAL!
THANKS A LOT, NAGISA!
I REALLY GOT A KICK OUT OF YOUR ASSAS-SINATION!

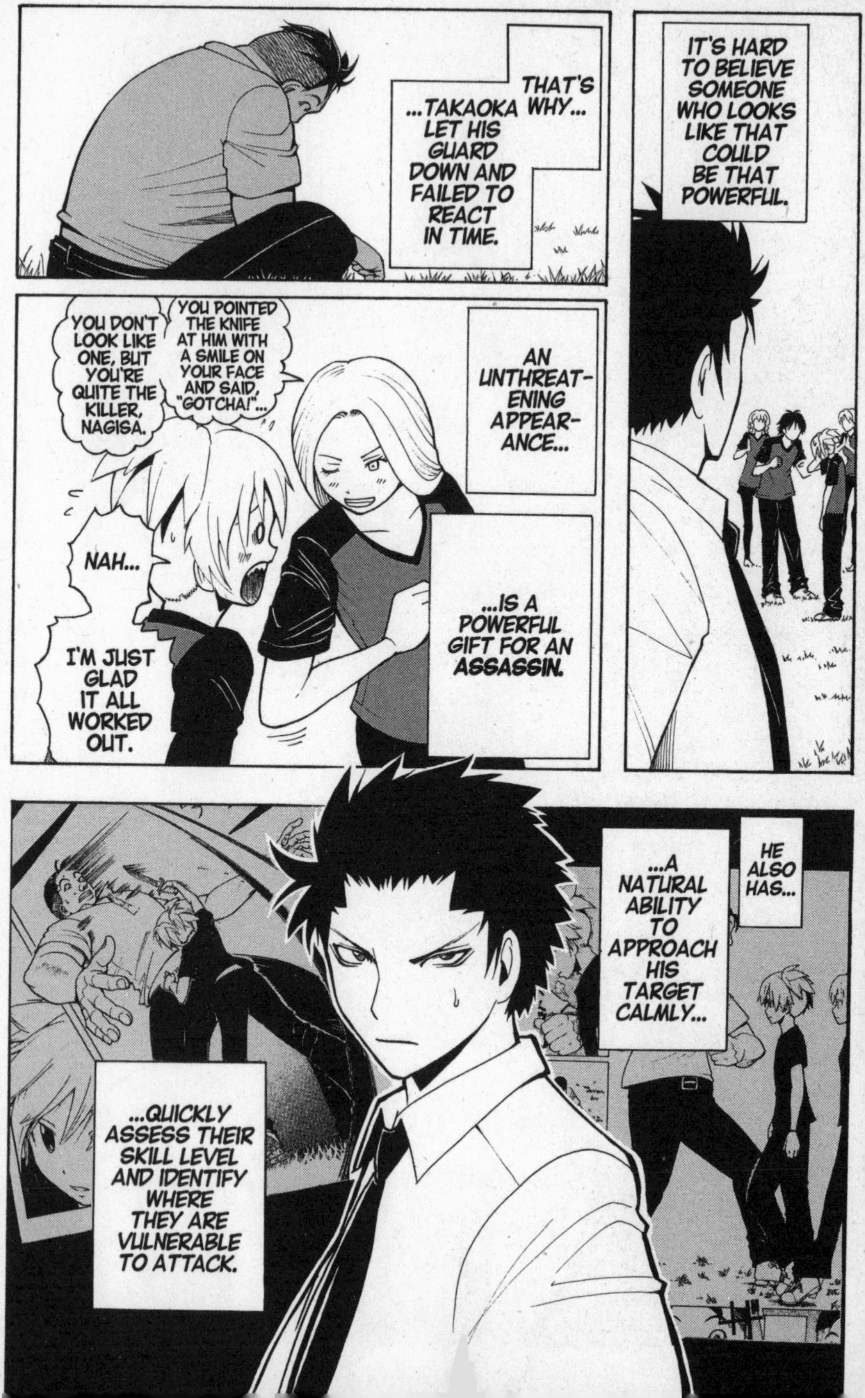
IT'S HARD TO BELIEVE SOMEONE WHO LOOKS LIKE THAT COULD BE THAT POWERFUL.
THAT'S WHY...
...TAKAOKA LET HIS GUARD DOWN AND FAILED TO REACT IN TIME.
AN UNTHREAT-ENING APPEAR-ANCE...
...IS A POWERFUL GIFT FOR AN ASSASSIN.
YOU POINTED THE KNIFE AT HIM WITH A SMILE ON YOUR FACE AND SAID, "GOTCHA!"...
YOU DON'T LOOK LIKE ONE, BUT YOU'RE QUITE THE KILLER, NAGISA.
NAH...
I'M JUST GLAD IT ALL WORKED OUT.
HE ALSO HAS...
...A NATURAL ABILITY TO APPROACH HIS TARGET CALMLY...
...QUICKLY ASSESS THEIR SKILL LEVEL AND IDENTIFY WHERE THEY ARE VULNERABLE TO ATTACK.

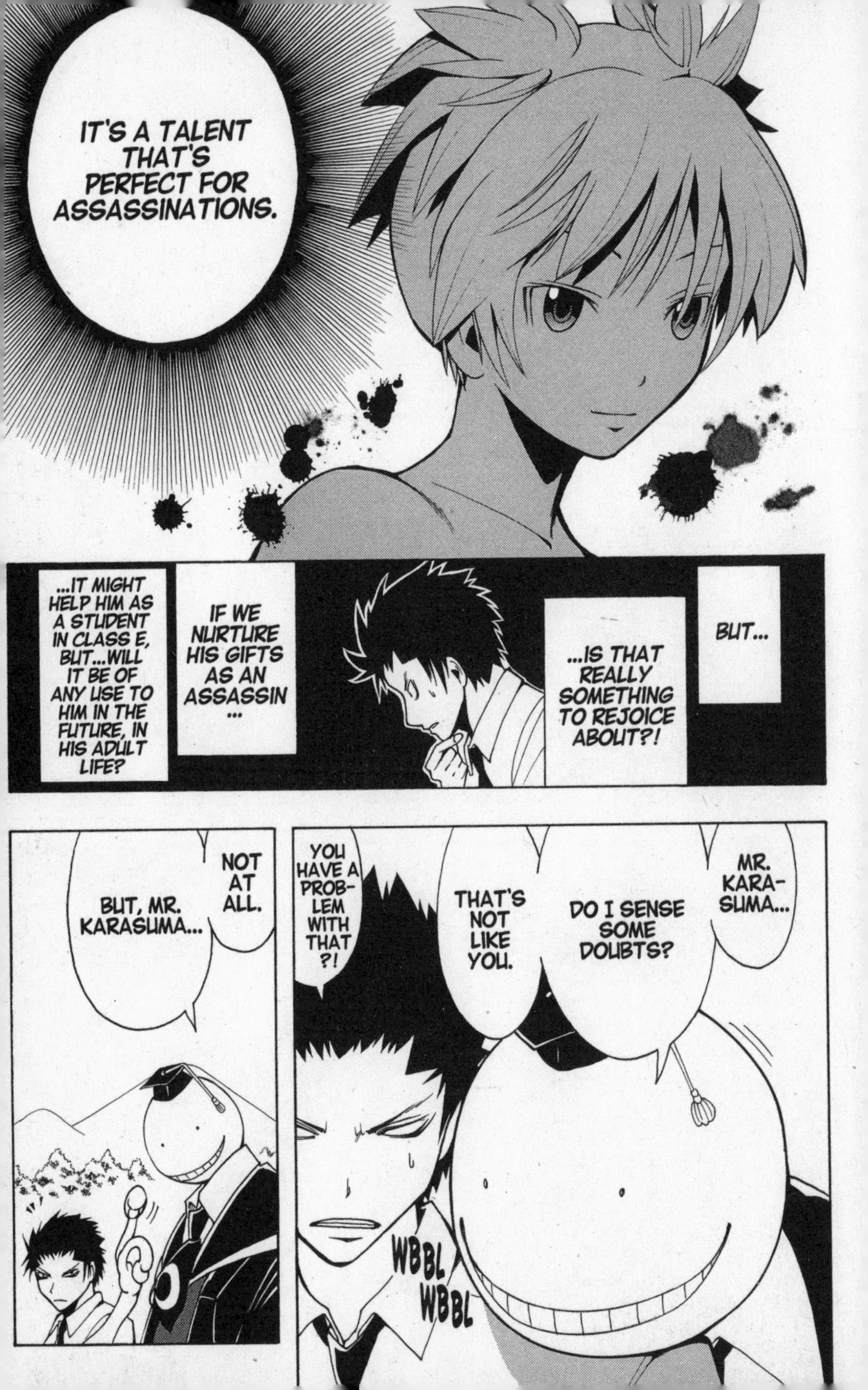
IT'S A TALENT THAT'S PERFECT FOR ASSASSINATIONS.
BUT...
...IS THAT REALLY SOMETHING TO REJOICE ABOUT?!
IF WE NURTURE HIS GIFTS AS AN ASSASSIN ...
...IT MIGHT HELP HIM AS A STUDENT IN CLASS E, BUT...WILL IT BE OF ANY USE TO HIM IN THE FUTURE, IN HIS ADULT LIFE?
MR. KARA-SUMA...
DO I SENSE SOME DOUBTS?
THAT'S NOT LIKE YOU.
YOU HAVE A PROB-LEM WITH THAT?!
WBBL WBBL
NOT AT ALL.
BUT, MR. KARASUMA...

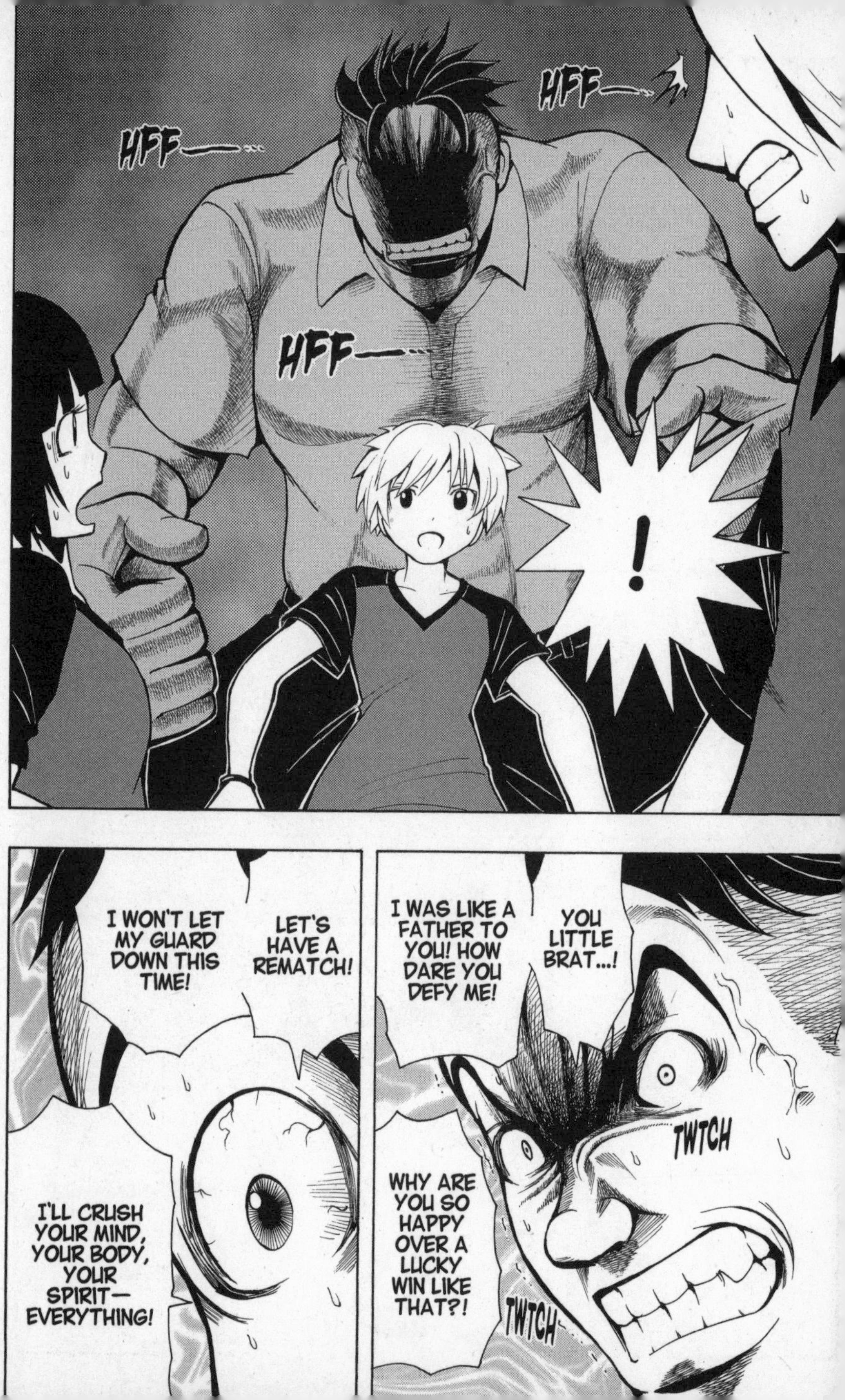
HFF—…
HFF—…
HFF—…
!
YOU LITTLE BRAT...!
I WAS LIKE A FATHER TO YOU! HOW DARE YOU DEFY ME!
TWTCH
WHY ARE YOU SO HAPPY OVER A LUCKY WIN LIKE THAT?!
TWTCH
LET'S HAVE A REMATCH!
I WON'T LET MY GUARD DOWN THIS TIME!
I'LL CRUSH YOUR MIND, YOUR BODY, YOUR SPIRIT—EVERYTHING!

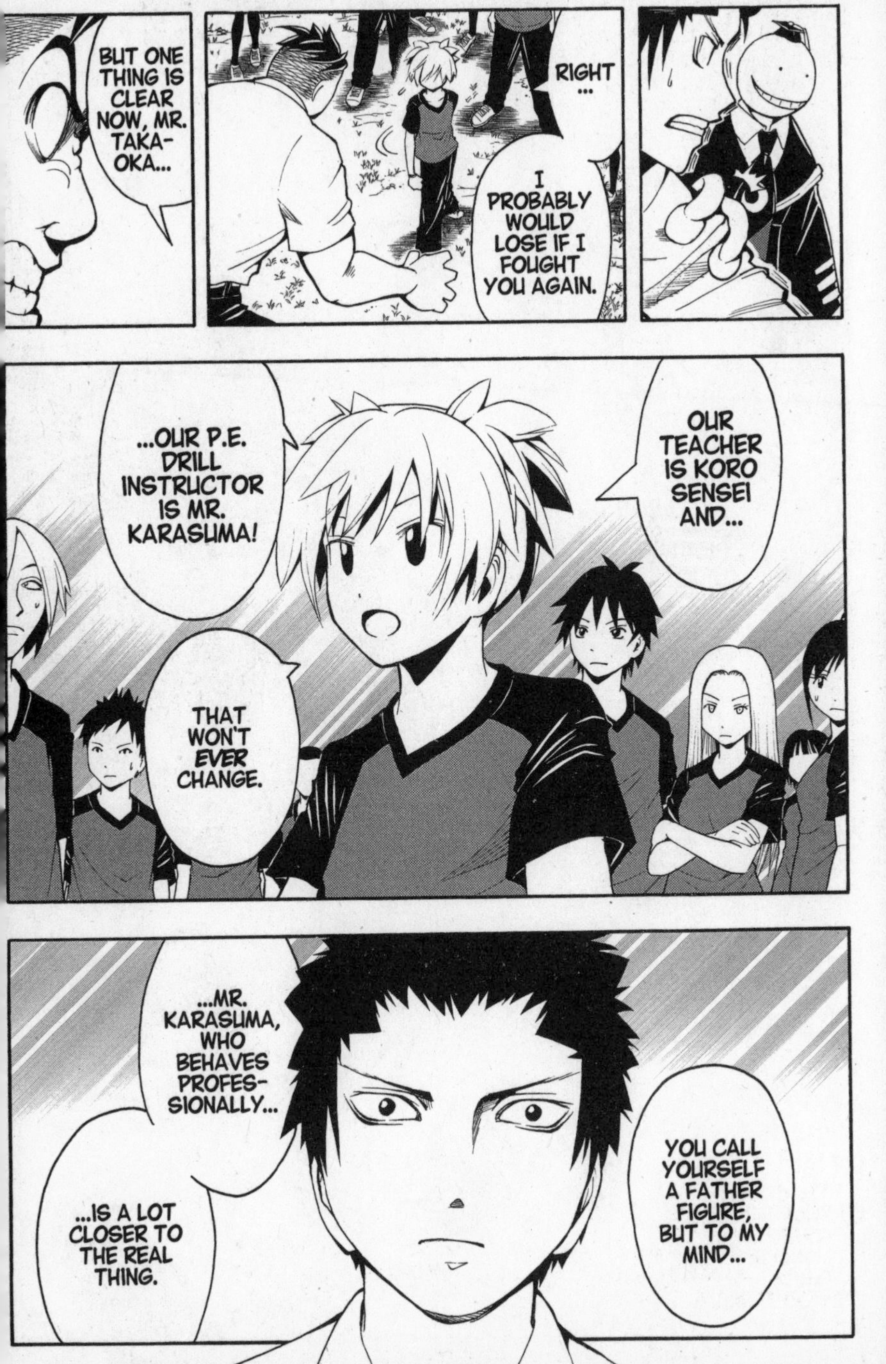
RIGHT...
I PROBABLY WOULD LOSE IF I FOUGHT YOU AGAIN.
BUT ONE THING IS CLEAR NOW, MR. TAKAOKA...
OUR TEACHER IS KORO SENSEI AND...
...OUR P.E. DRILL INSTRUCTOR IS MR. KARASUMA!
THAT WON'T *EVER* CHANGE.
YOU CALL YOURSELF A FATHER FIGURE, BUT TO MY MIND...
...MR. KARASUMA, WHO BEHAVES PROFESSIONALLY...
...IS A LOT CLOSER TO THE REAL THING.

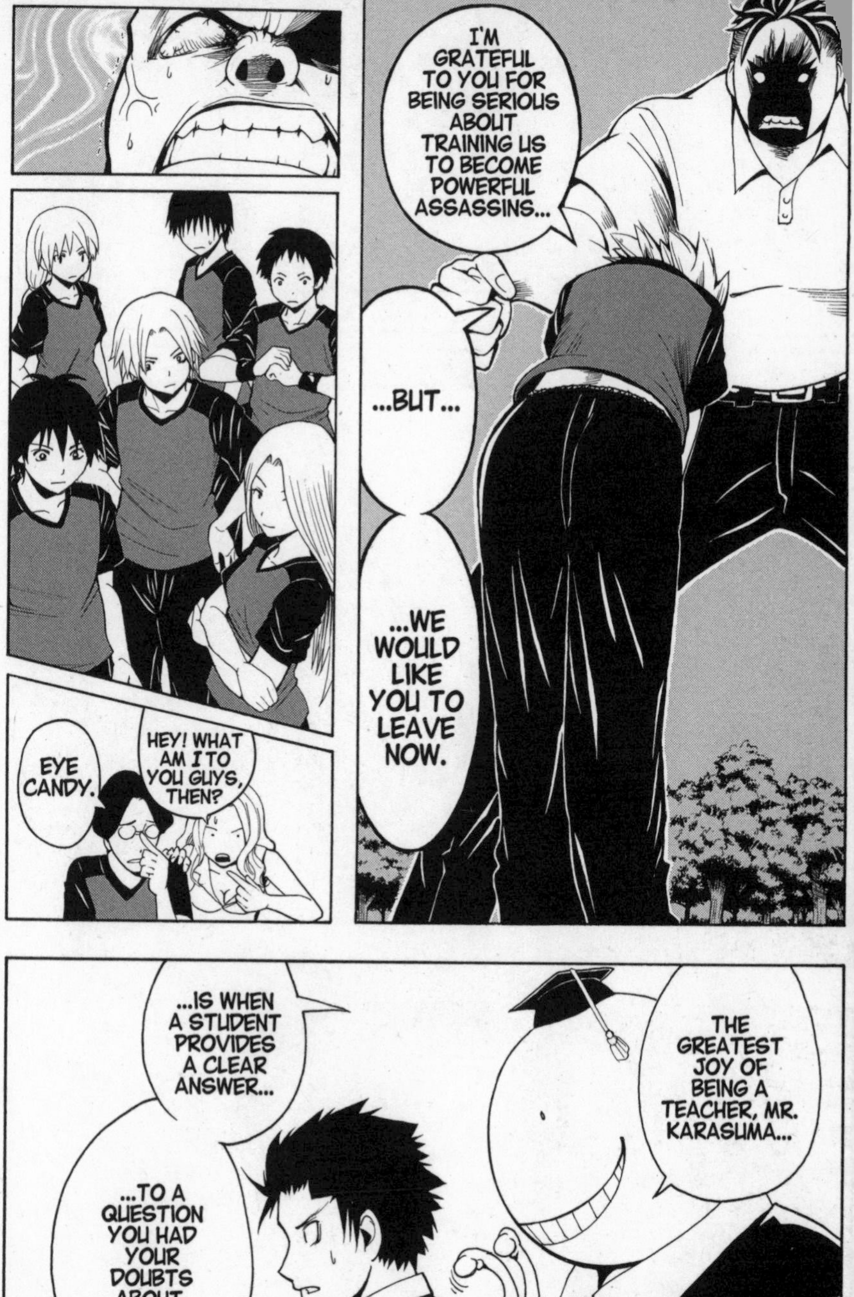
I'M GRATEFUL TO YOU FOR BEING SERIOUS ABOUT TRAINING US TO BECOME POWERFUL ASSASSINS...
...BUT...
...WE WOULD LIKE YOU TO LEAVE NOW.
HEY! WHAT AM I TO YOU GUYS, THEN?
EYE CANDY.
THE GREATEST JOY OF BEING A TEACHER, MR. KARASUMA...
...IS WHEN A STUDENT PROVIDES A CLEAR ANSWER...
...TO A QUESTION YOU HAD YOUR DOUBTS ABOUT.

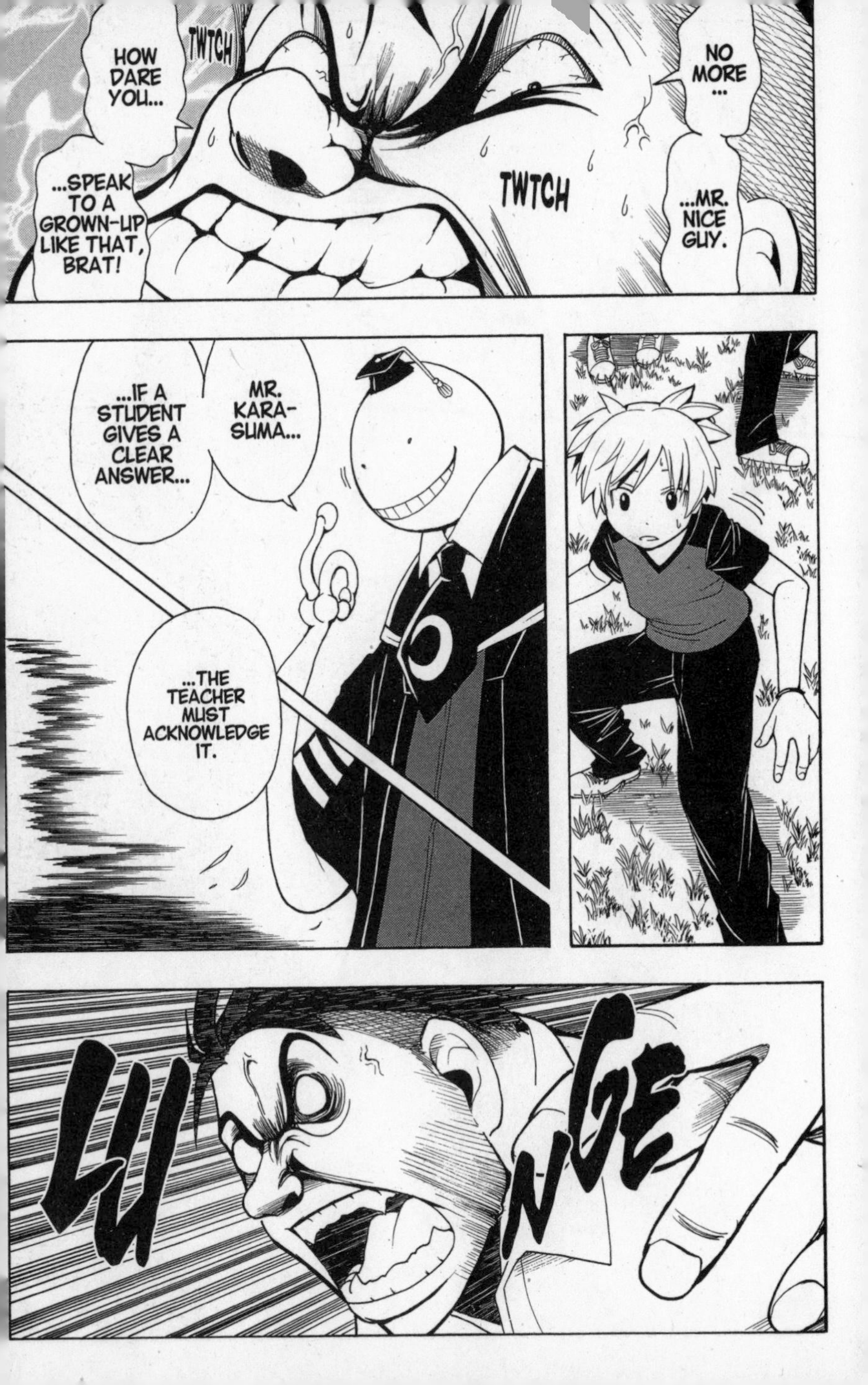
NO MORE...
...MR. NICE GUY.
TWTCH
TWTCH
HOW DARE YOU...
...SPEAK TO A GROWN-UP LIKE THAT, BRAT!
MR. KARA-SUMA...
...IF A STUDENT GIVES A CLEAR ANSWER...
...THE TEACHER MUST ACKNOWLEDGE IT.
LUNGE

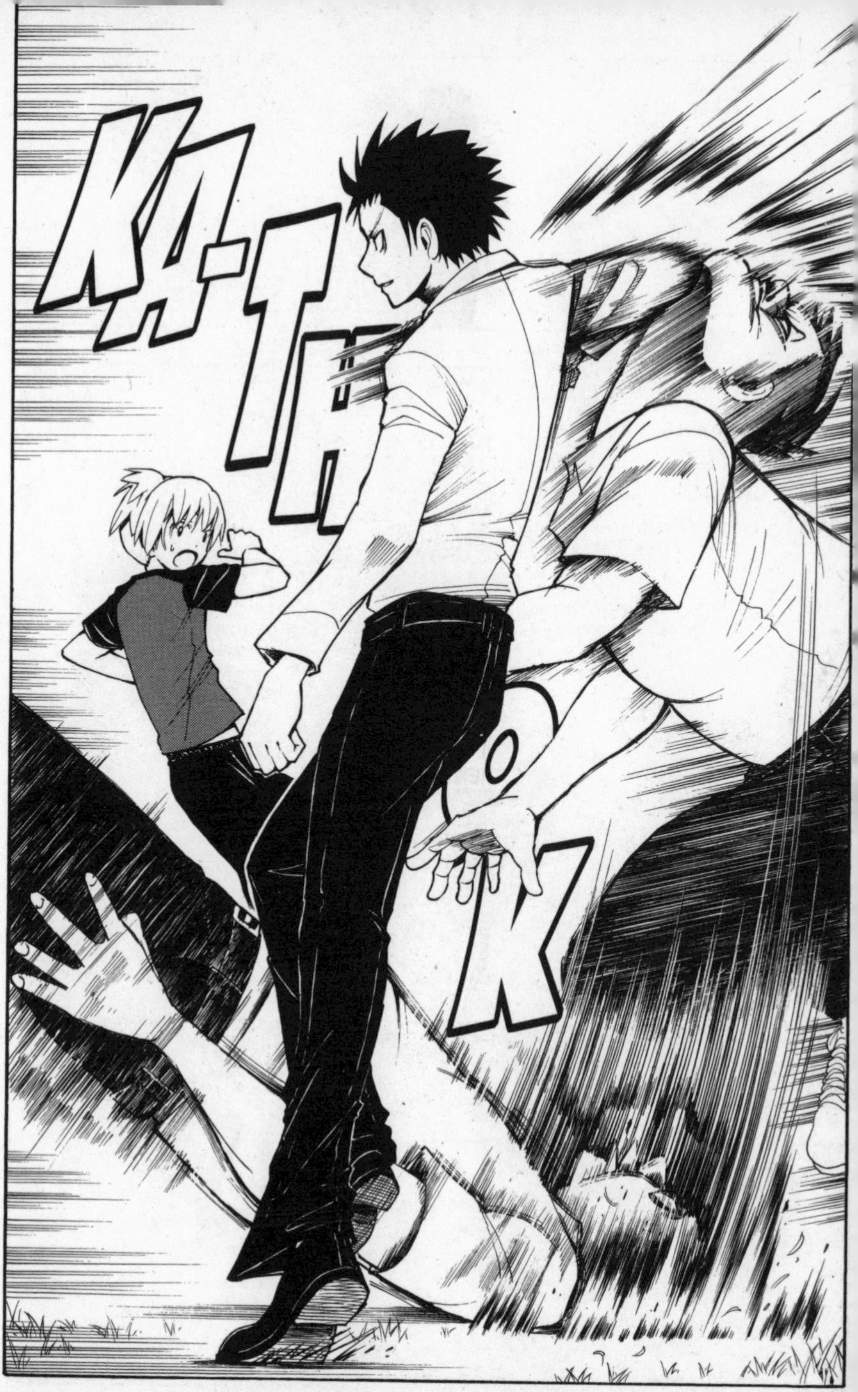
KA-THOK

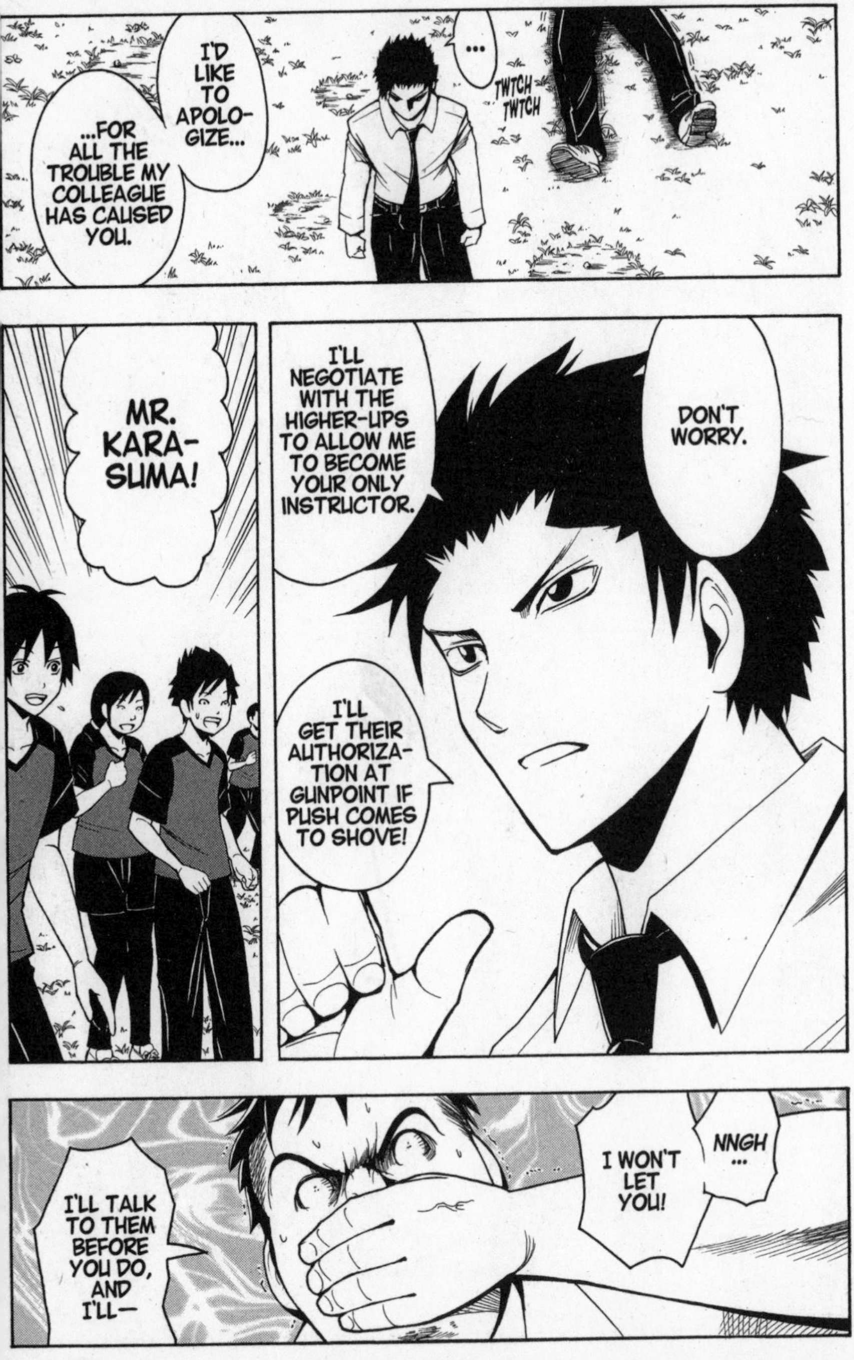
...
TWTCH TWTCH
I'D LIKE TO APOLOGIZE...
...FOR ALL THE TROUBLE MY COLLEAGUE HAS CAUSED YOU.
DON'T WORRY.
I'LL NEGOTIATE WITH THE HIGHER-UPS TO ALLOW ME TO BECOME YOUR ONLY INSTRUCTOR.
I'LL GET THEIR AUTHORIZATION AT GUNPOINT IF PUSH COMES TO SHOVE!
MR. KARASUMA!
NNGH...
I WON'T LET YOU!
I'LL TALK TO THEM BEFORE YOU DO, AND I'LL—

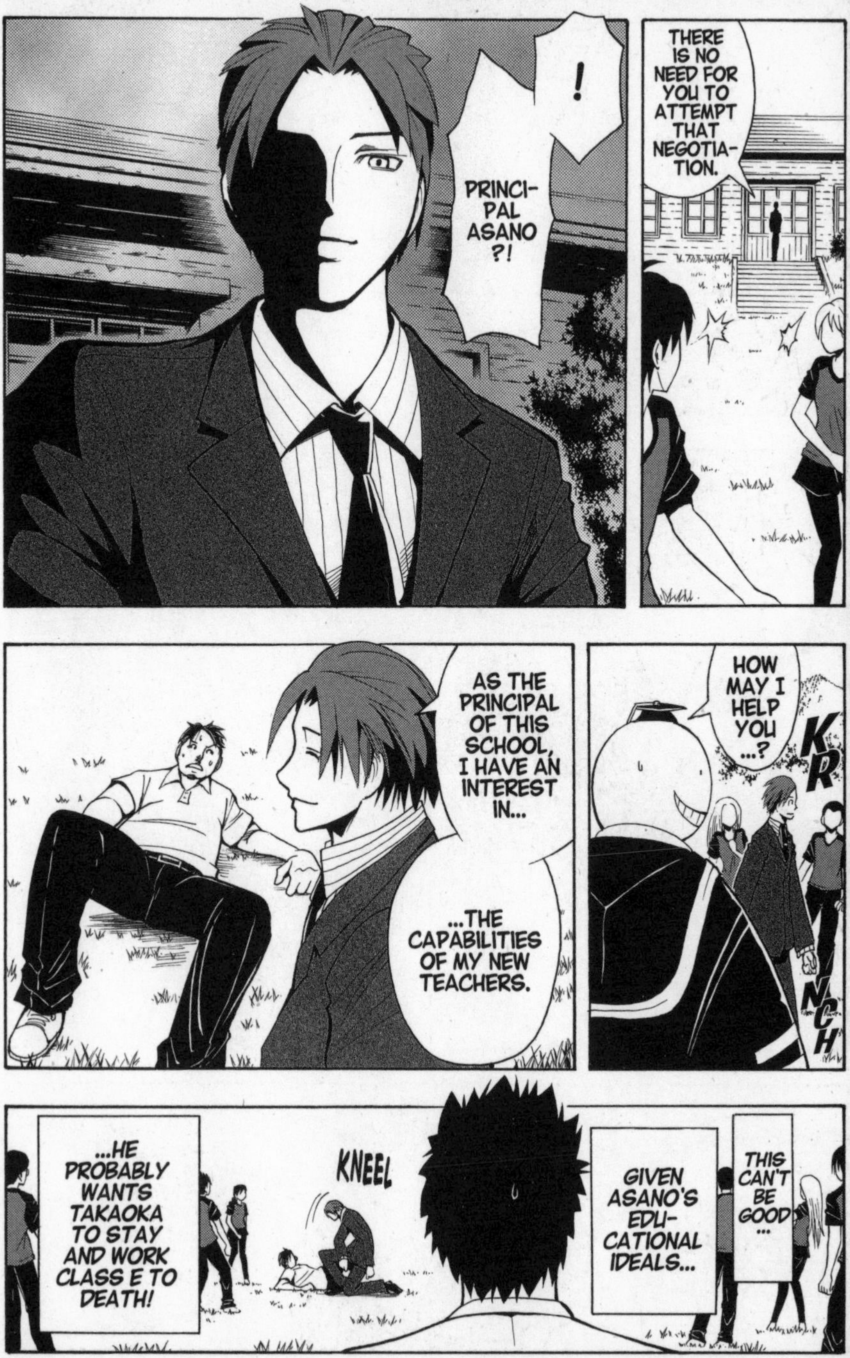

THERE IS NO NEED FOR YOU TO ATTEMPT THAT NEGOTIA-TION.
!
PRINCI-PAL ASANO?!
HOW MAY I HELP YOU...?
KR
NCH
AS THE PRINCIPAL OF THIS SCHOOL, I HAVE AN INTEREST IN...
...THE CAPABILITIES OF MY NEW TEACHERS.
THIS CAN'T BE GOOD...
GIVEN ASANO'S EDU-CATIONAL IDEALS...
KNEEL
...HE PROBABLY WANTS TAKAOKA TO STAY AND WORK CLASS E TO DEATH!

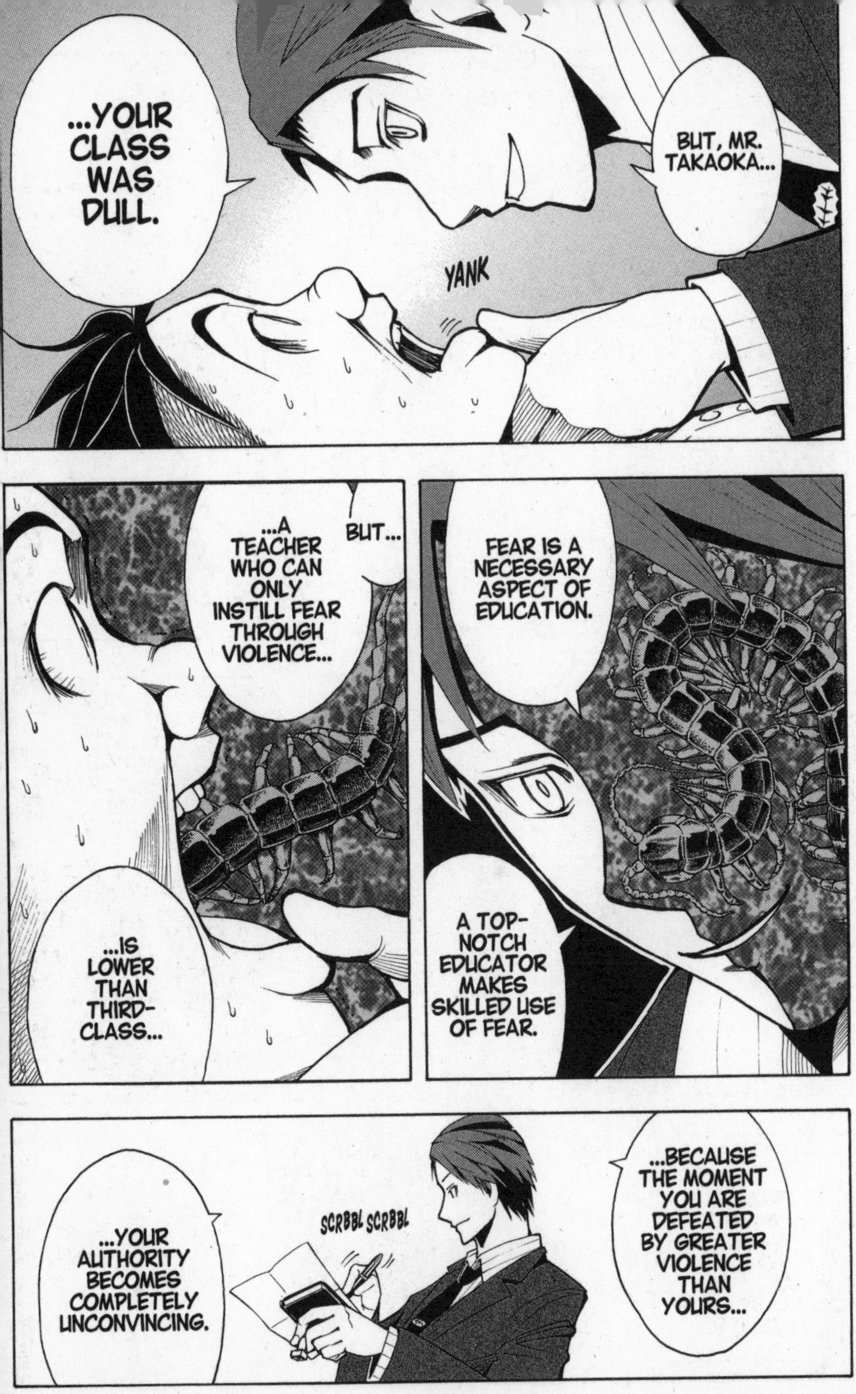
BUT, MR. TAKAOKA...
YANK
...YOUR CLASS WAS DULL.
FEAR IS A NECESSARY ASPECT OF EDUCATION.
A TOP-NOTCH EDUCATOR MAKES SKILLED USE OF FEAR.
BUT...
...A TEACHER WHO CAN ONLY INSTILL FEAR THROUGH VIOLENCE...
...IS LOWER THAN THIRD-CLASS...
...BECAUSE THE MOMENT YOU ARE DEFEATED BY GREATER VIOLENCE THAN YOURS...
SCRBBL SCRBBL
...YOUR AUTHORITY BECOMES COMPLETELY UNCONVINCING.

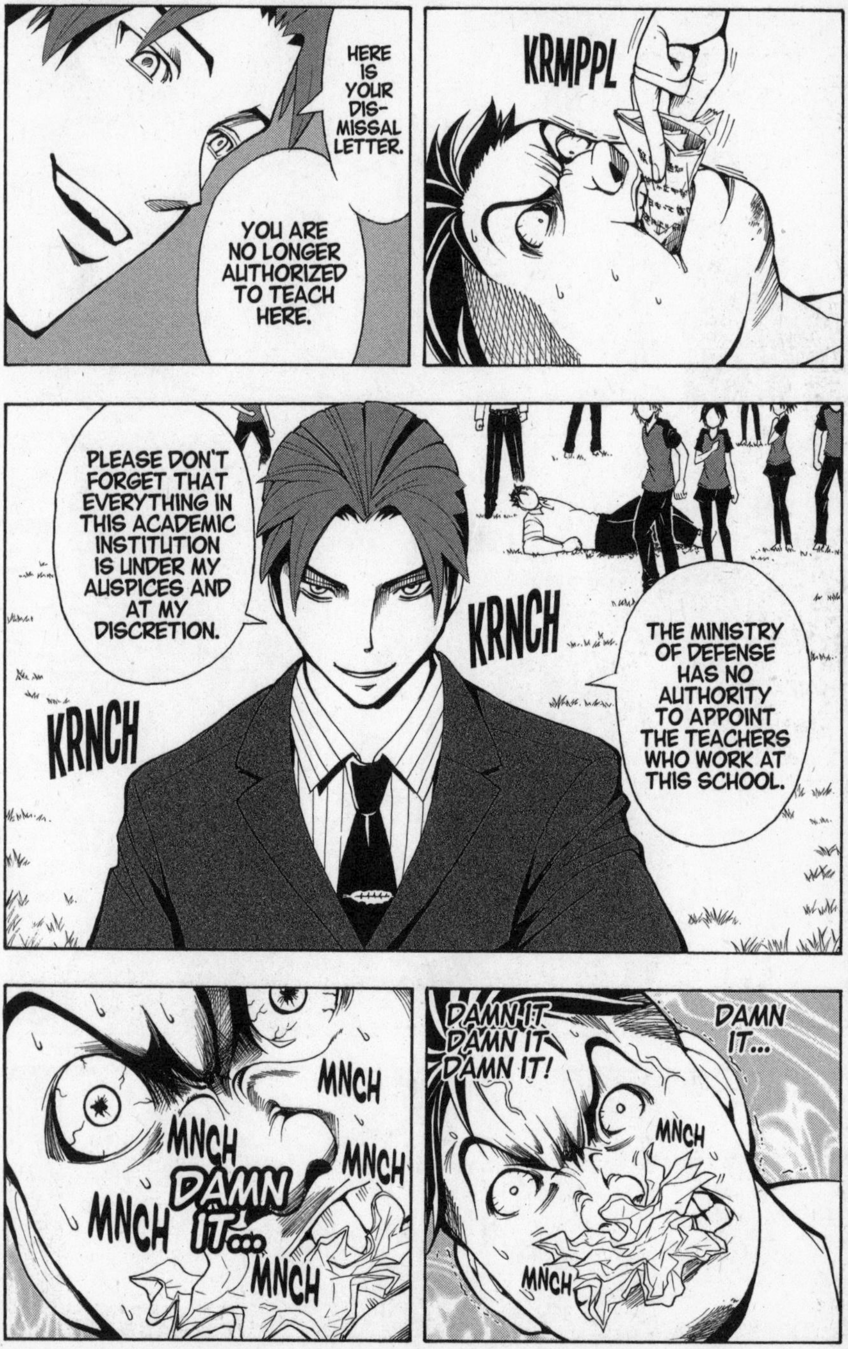
KRMPPL
HERE IS YOUR DIS-MISSAL LETTER.
YOU ARE NO LONGER AUTHORIZED TO TEACH HERE.
THE MINISTRY OF DEFENSE HAS NO AUTHORITY TO APPOINT THE TEACHERS WHO WORK AT THIS SCHOOL.
KRNCH
PLEASE DON'T FORGET THAT EVERYTHING IN THIS ACADEMIC INSTITUTION IS UNDER MY AUSPICES AND AT MY DISCRETION.
KRNCH
DAMN IT...
DAMN IT DAMN IT DAMN IT!
MNCH
MNCH
MNCH
MNCH
MNCH
DAMN IT...
MNCH
MNCH

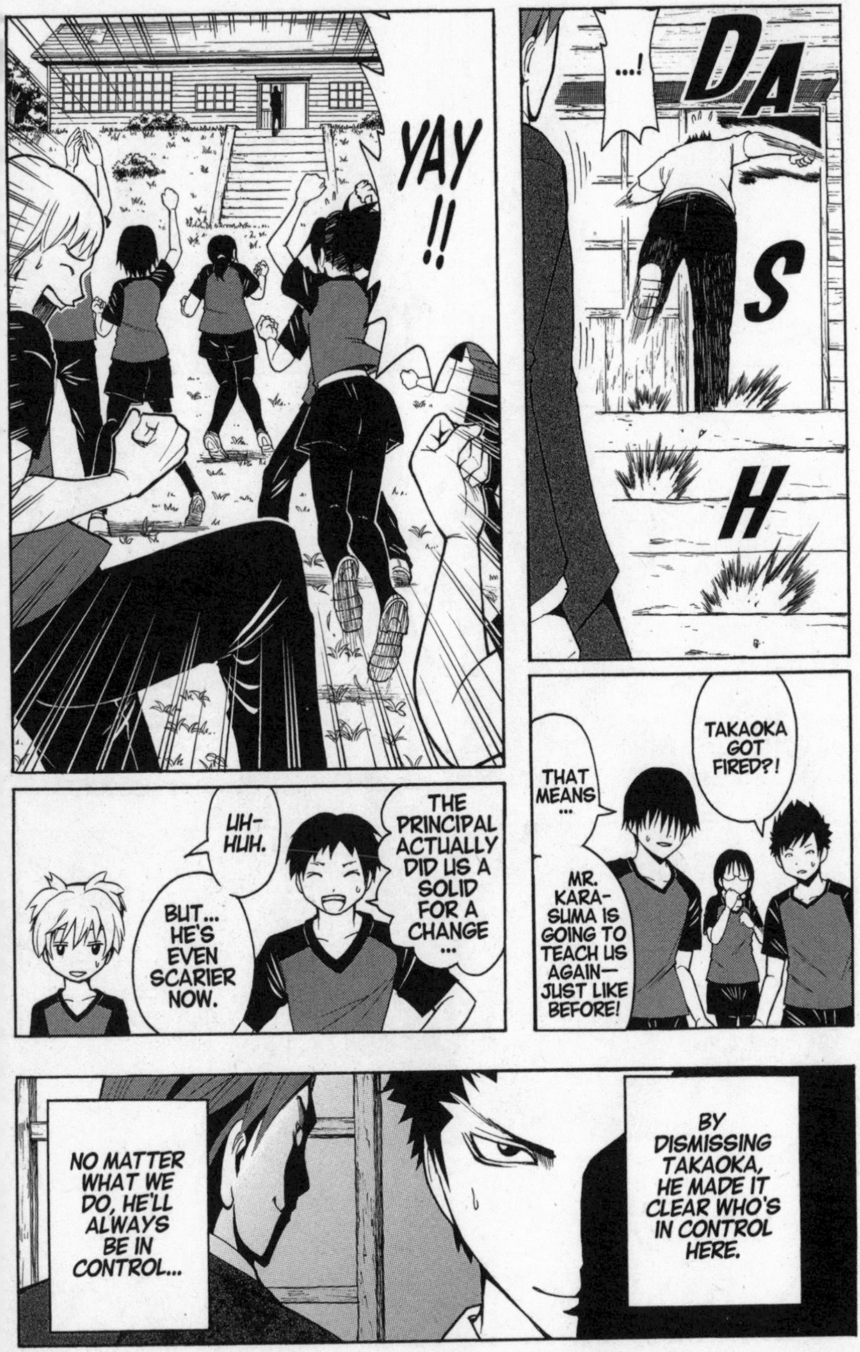
...!
DASH
YAY!!
TAKAOKA GOT FIRED?!
THAT MEANS...
MR. KARASUMA IS GOING TO TEACH US AGAIN—JUST LIKE BEFORE!
THE PRINCIPAL ACTUALLY DID US A SOLID FOR A CHANGE...
UH-HUH.
BUT... HE'S EVEN SCARIER NOW.
BY DISMISSING TAKAOKA, HE MADE IT CLEAR WHO'S IN CONTROL HERE.
NO MATTER WHAT WE DO, HE'LL ALWAYS BE IN CONTROL...

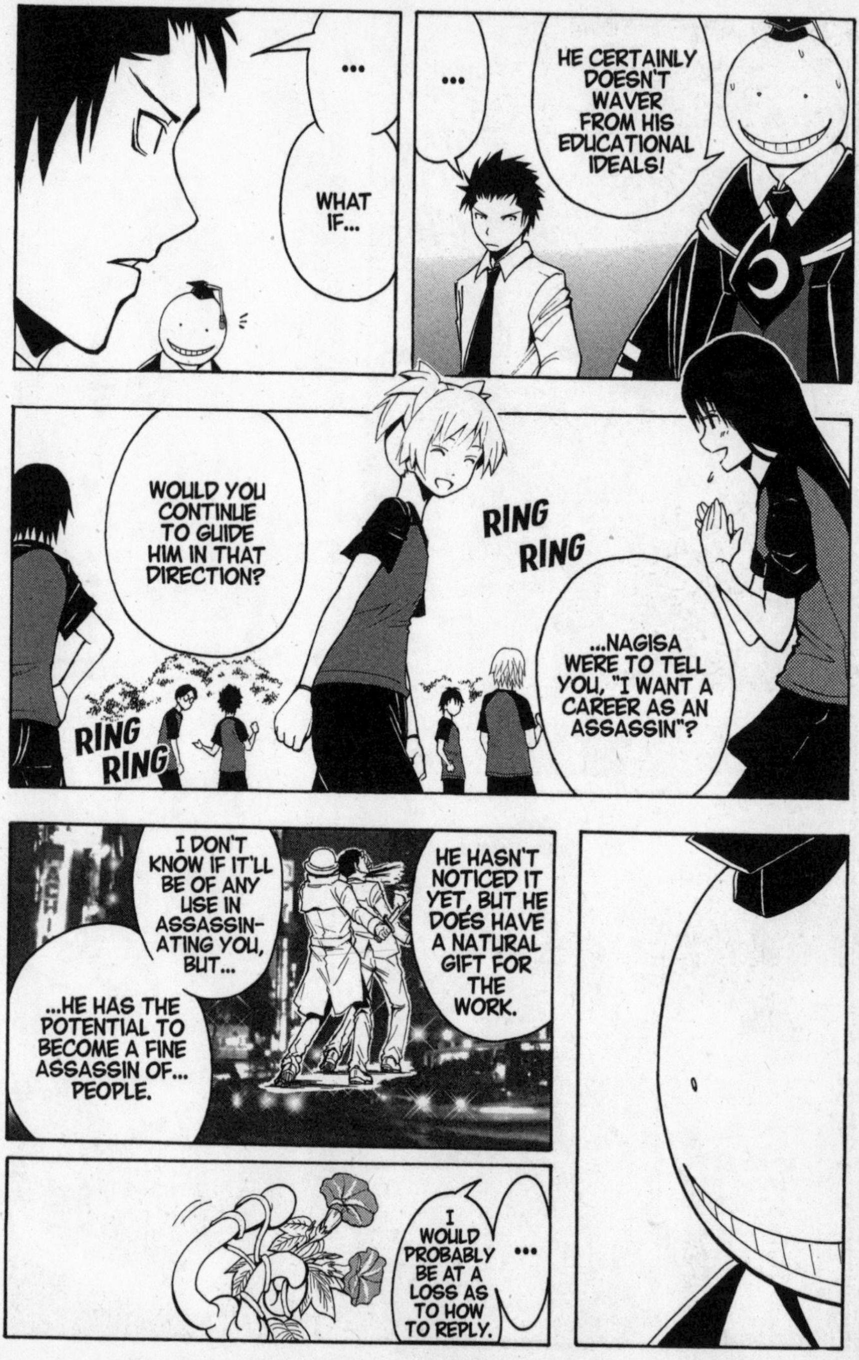
HE CERTAINLY DOESN'T WAVER FROM HIS EDUCATIONAL IDEALS!
...
...
WHAT IF...
RING RING
...NAGISA WERE TO TELL YOU, "I WANT A CAREER AS AN ASSASSIN"?
WOULD YOU CONTINUE TO GUIDE HIM IN THAT DIRECTION?
RING RING
HE HASN'T NOTICED IT YET, BUT HE DOES HAVE A NATURAL GIFT FOR THE WORK.
I DON'T KNOW IF IT'LL BE OF ANY USE IN ASSASSIN-ATING YOU, BUT...
...HE HAS THE POTENTIAL TO BECOME A FINE ASSASSIN OF... PEOPLE.
...
I WOULD PROBABLY BE AT A LOSS AS TO HOW TO REPLY.

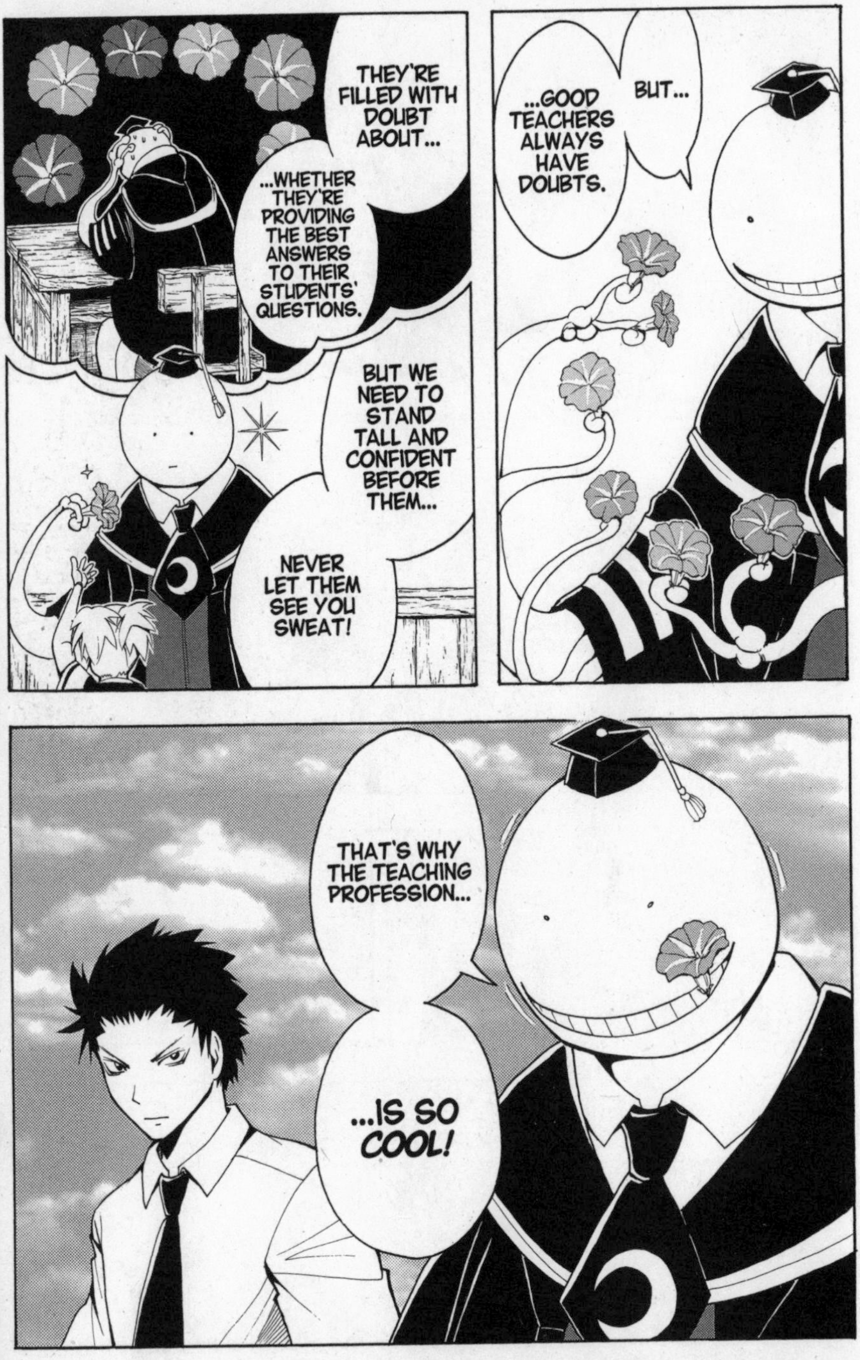
BUT...
...GOOD TEACHERS ALWAYS HAVE DOUBTS.
THEY'RE FILLED WITH DOUBT ABOUT...
...WHETHER THEY'RE PROVIDING THE BEST ANSWERS TO THEIR STUDENTS' QUESTIONS.
BUT WE NEED TO STAND TALL AND CONFIDENT BEFORE THEM...
NEVER LET THEM SEE YOU SWEAT!
THAT'S WHY THE TEACHING PROFESSION...
...IS SO COOL!

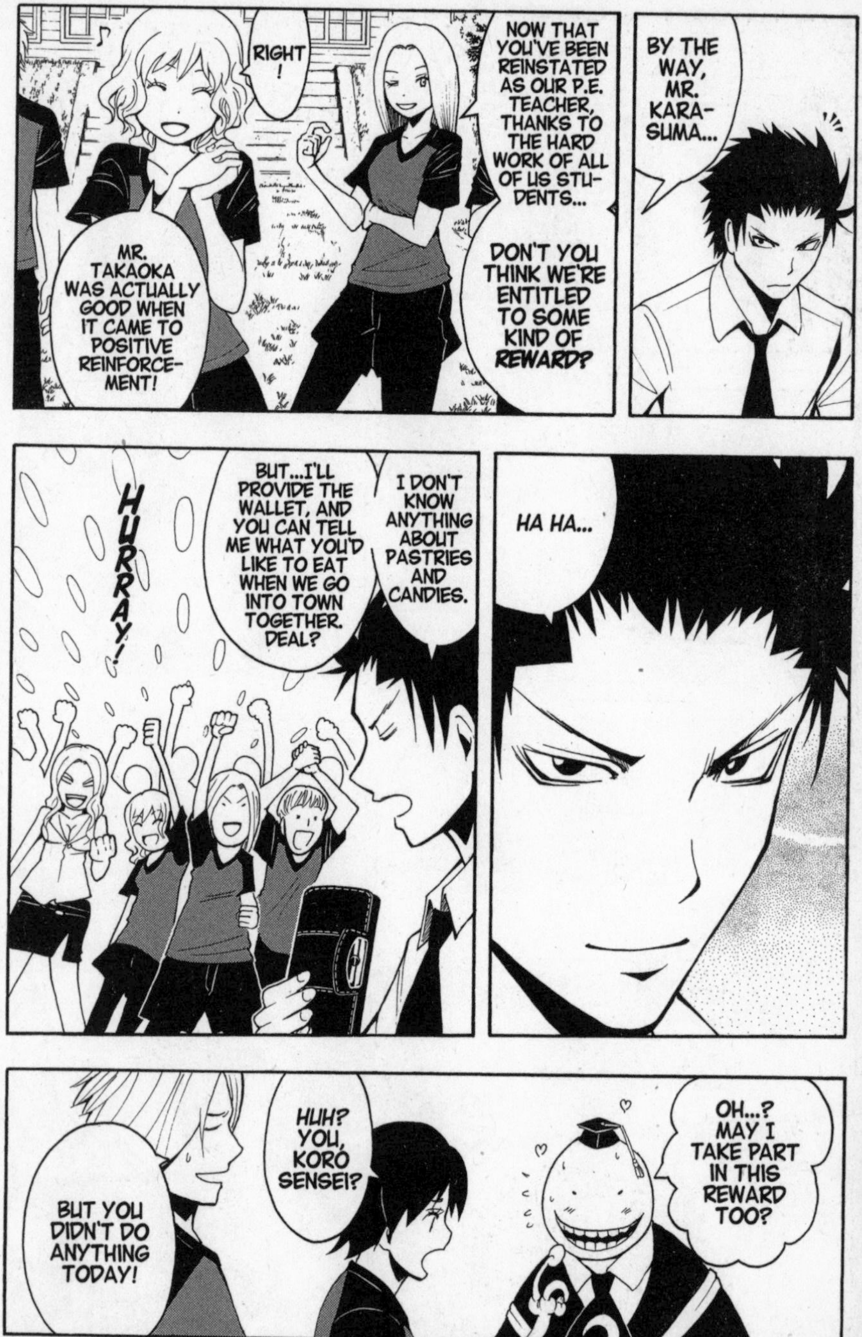
BY THE WAY, MR. KARA-SUMA...
NOW THAT YOU'VE BEEN REINSTATED AS OUR P.E. TEACHER, THANKS TO THE HARD WORK OF ALL OF US STU-DENTS...
DON'T YOU THINK WE'RE ENTITLED TO SOME KIND OF REWARD?
RIGHT!
MR. TAKAOKA WAS ACTUALLY GOOD WHEN IT CAME TO POSITIVE REINFORCE-MENT!
HA HA...
I DON'T KNOW ANYTHING ABOUT PASTRIES AND CANDIES.
BUT...I'LL PROVIDE THE WALLET, AND YOU CAN TELL ME WHAT YOU'D LIKE TO EAT WHEN WE GO INTO TOWN TOGETHER. DEAL?
HURRAY!
OH...? MAY I TAKE PART IN THIS REWARD TOO?
HUH? YOU, KORO SENSEI?
BUT YOU DIDN'T DO ANYTHING TODAY!

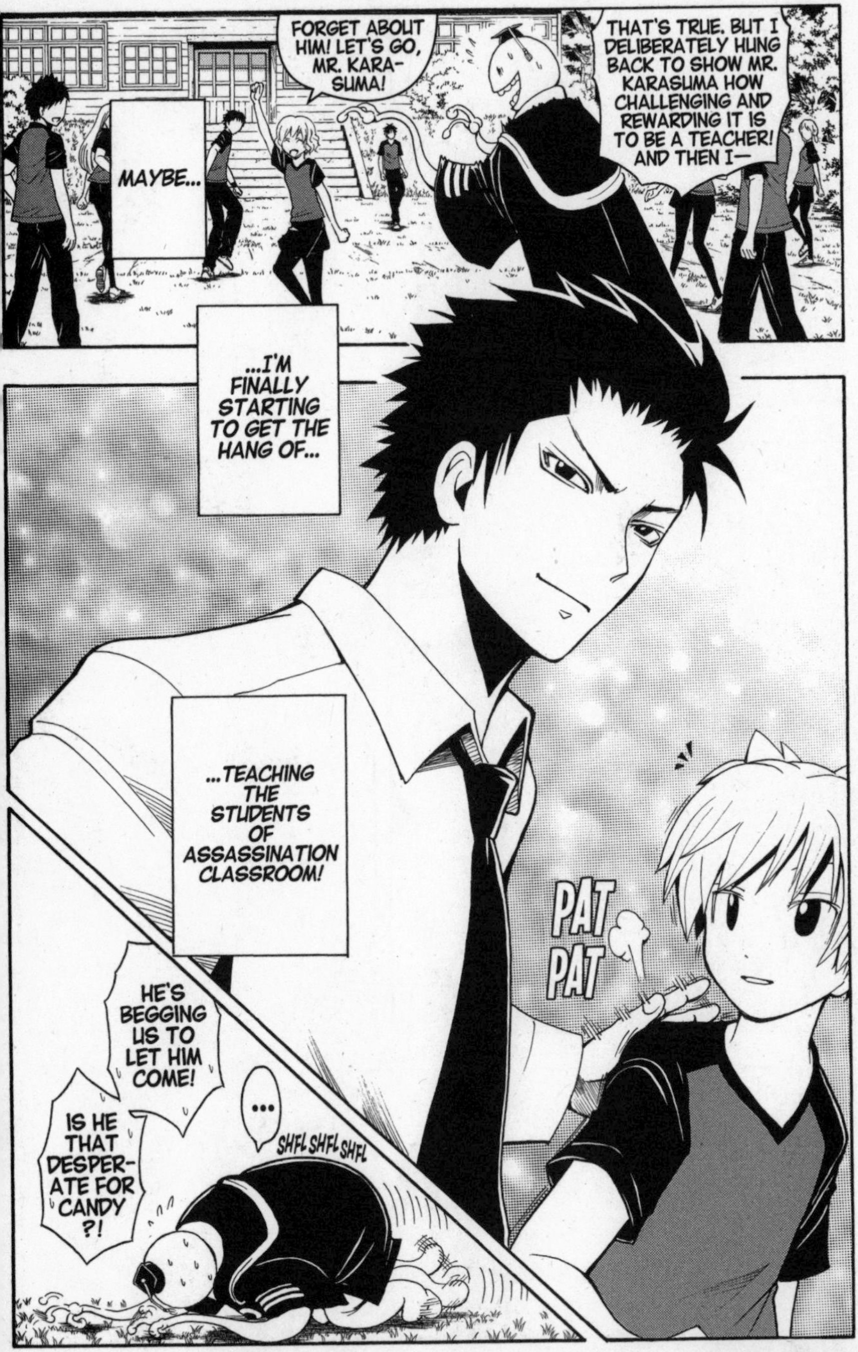
THAT'S TRUE. BUT I DELIBERATELY HUNG BACK TO SHOW MR. KARASUMA HOW CHALLENGING AND REWARDING IT IS TO BE A TEACHER! AND THEN I—
FORGET ABOUT HIM! LET'S GO, MR. KARA-SUMA!
MAYBE...
...I'M FINALLY STARTING TO GET THE HANG OF...
...TEACHING THE STUDENTS OF ASSASSINATION CLASSROOM!
PAT PAT
HE'S BEGGING US TO LET HIM COME!
...
IS HE THAT DESPER-ATE FOR CANDY?!
SHFL SHFL SHFL

And he's off...

Class 43 In the Summertime

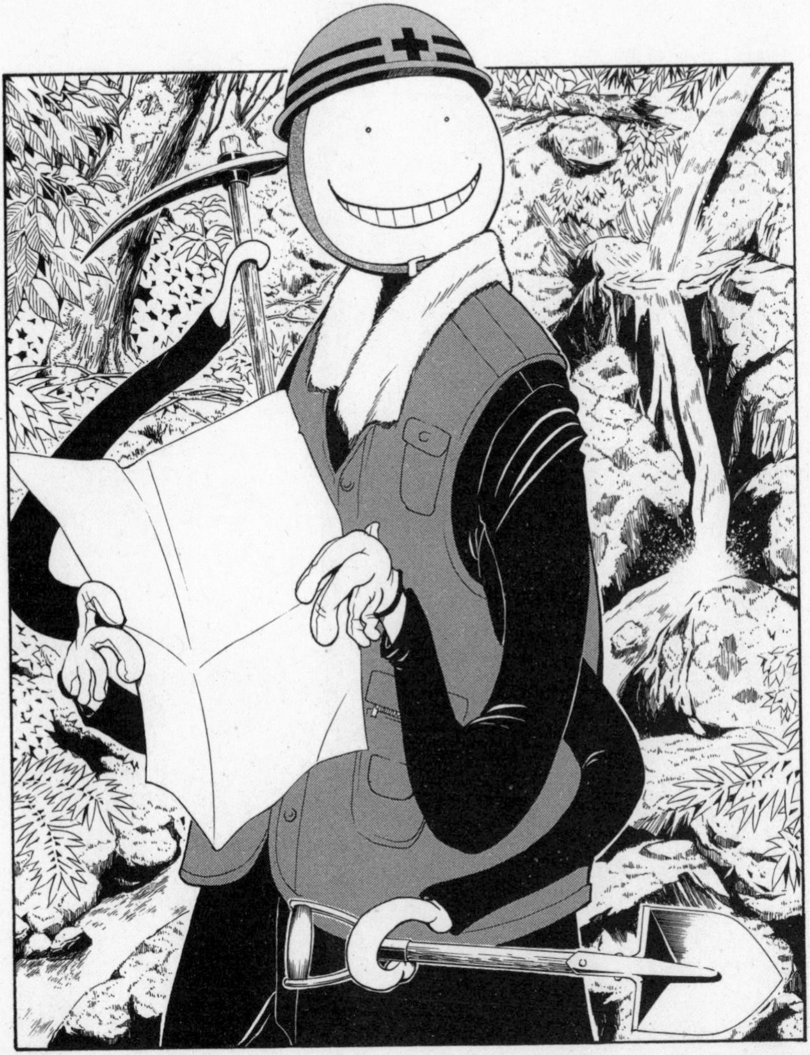

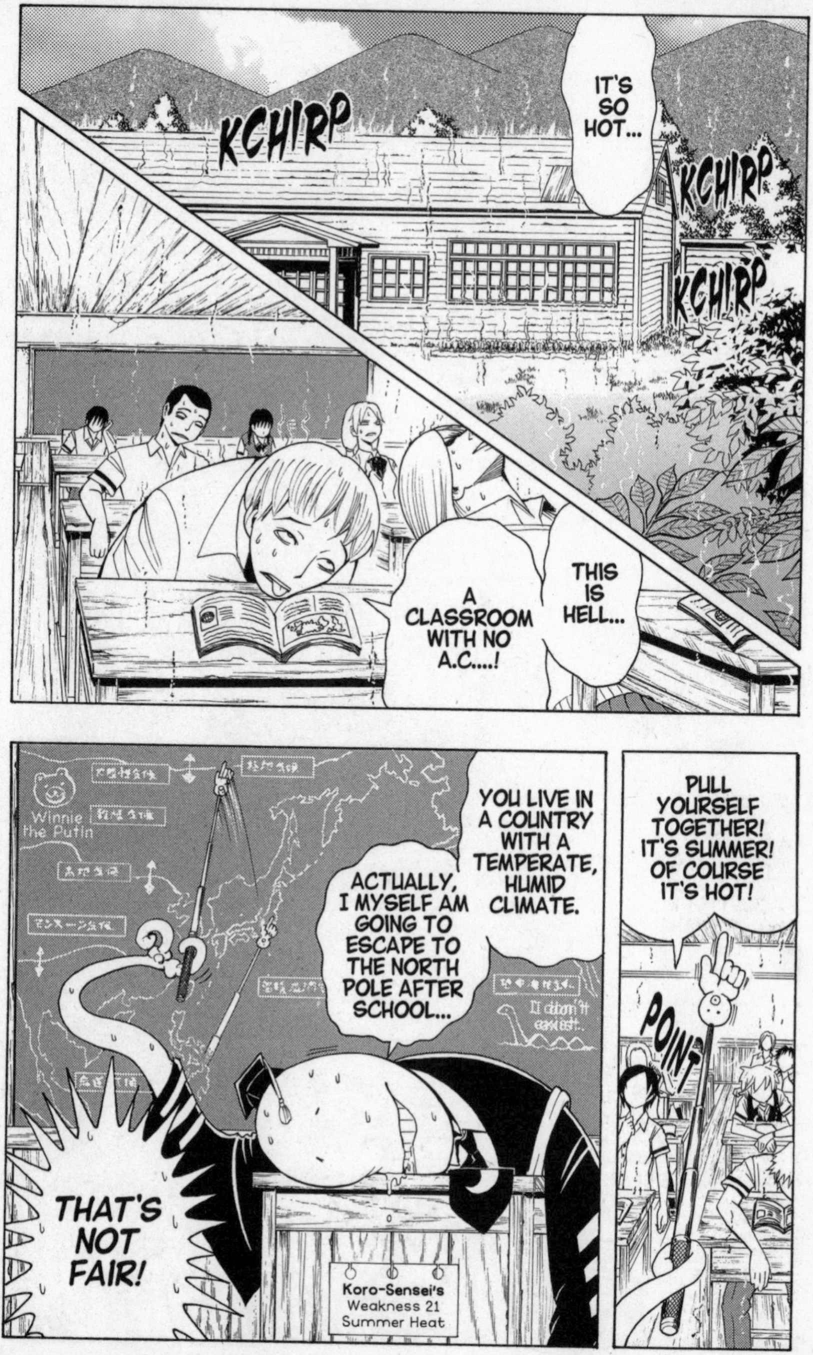
IT'S SO HOT...
KCHIRP
KCHIRP
KCHIRP
THIS IS HELL...
A CLASSROOM WITH NO A.C....!
PULL YOURSELF TOGETHER! IT'S SUMMER! OF COURSE IT'S HOT!
POINT
YOU LIVE IN A COUNTRY WITH A TEMPERATE, HUMID CLIMATE.
Winnie the Putin
ACTUALLY, I MYSELF AM GOING TO ESCAPE TO THE NORTH POLE AFTER SCHOOL...
THAT'S NOT FAIR!
Koro-Sensei's Weakness 21 Summer Heat

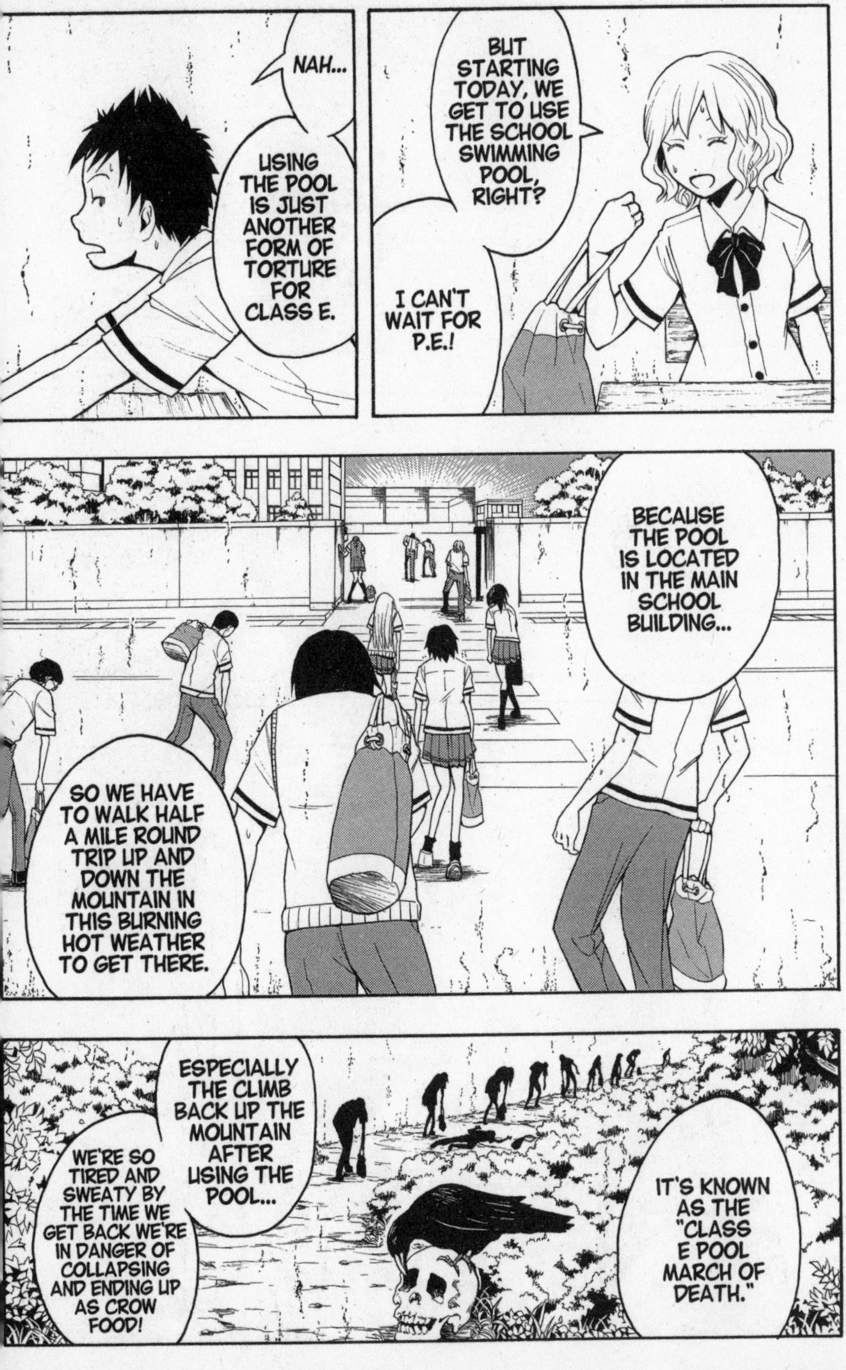
BUT STARTING TODAY, WE GET TO USE THE SCHOOL SWIMMING POOL, RIGHT?
I CAN'T WAIT FOR P.E.!
NAH...
USING THE POOL IS JUST ANOTHER FORM OF TORTURE FOR CLASS E.
BECAUSE THE POOL IS LOCATED IN THE MAIN SCHOOL BUILDING...
SO WE HAVE TO WALK HALF A MILE ROUND TRIP UP AND DOWN THE MOUNTAIN IN THIS BURNING HOT WEATHER TO GET THERE.
ESPECIALLY THE CLIMB BACK UP THE MOUNTAIN AFTER USING THE POOL...
WE'RE SO TIRED AND SWEATY BY THE TIME WE GET BACK WE'RE IN DANGER OF COLLAPSING AND ENDING UP AS CROW FOOD!
IT'S KNOWN AS THE "CLASS E POOL MARCH OF DEATH."

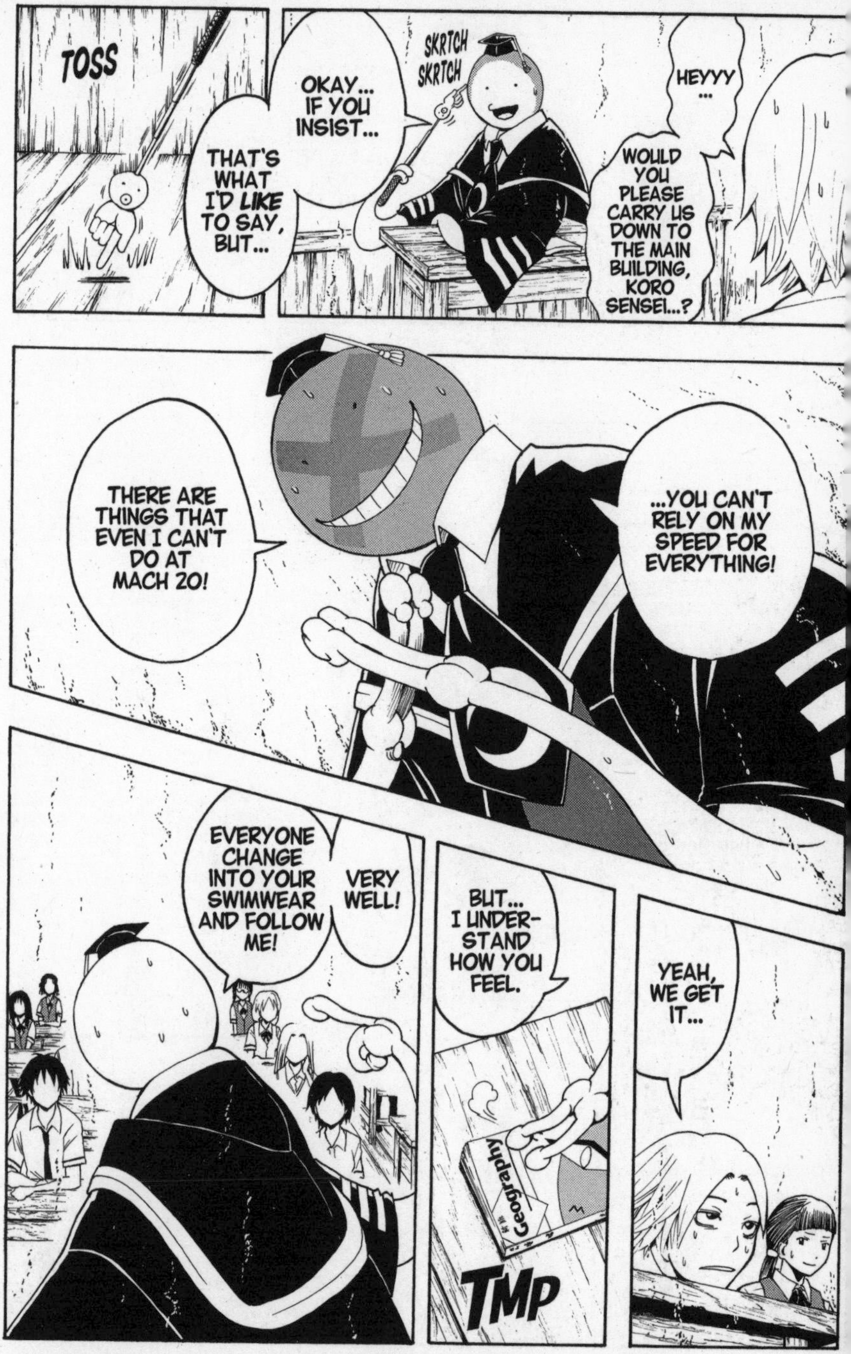
HEYYY ...
WOULD YOU PLEASE CARRY US DOWN TO THE MAIN BUILDING, KORO SENSEI...?
SKRTCH SKRTCH
OKAY... IF YOU INSIST...
THAT'S WHAT I'D *LIKE* TO SAY, BUT...
TOSS
...YOU CAN'T RELY ON MY SPEED FOR EVERYTHING!
THERE ARE THINGS THAT EVEN I CAN'T DO AT MACH 20!
YEAH, WE GET IT...
BUT... I UNDERSTAND HOW YOU FEEL.
Geography
TMP
VERY WELL!
EVERYONE CHANGE INTO YOUR SWIMWEAR AND FOLLOW ME!

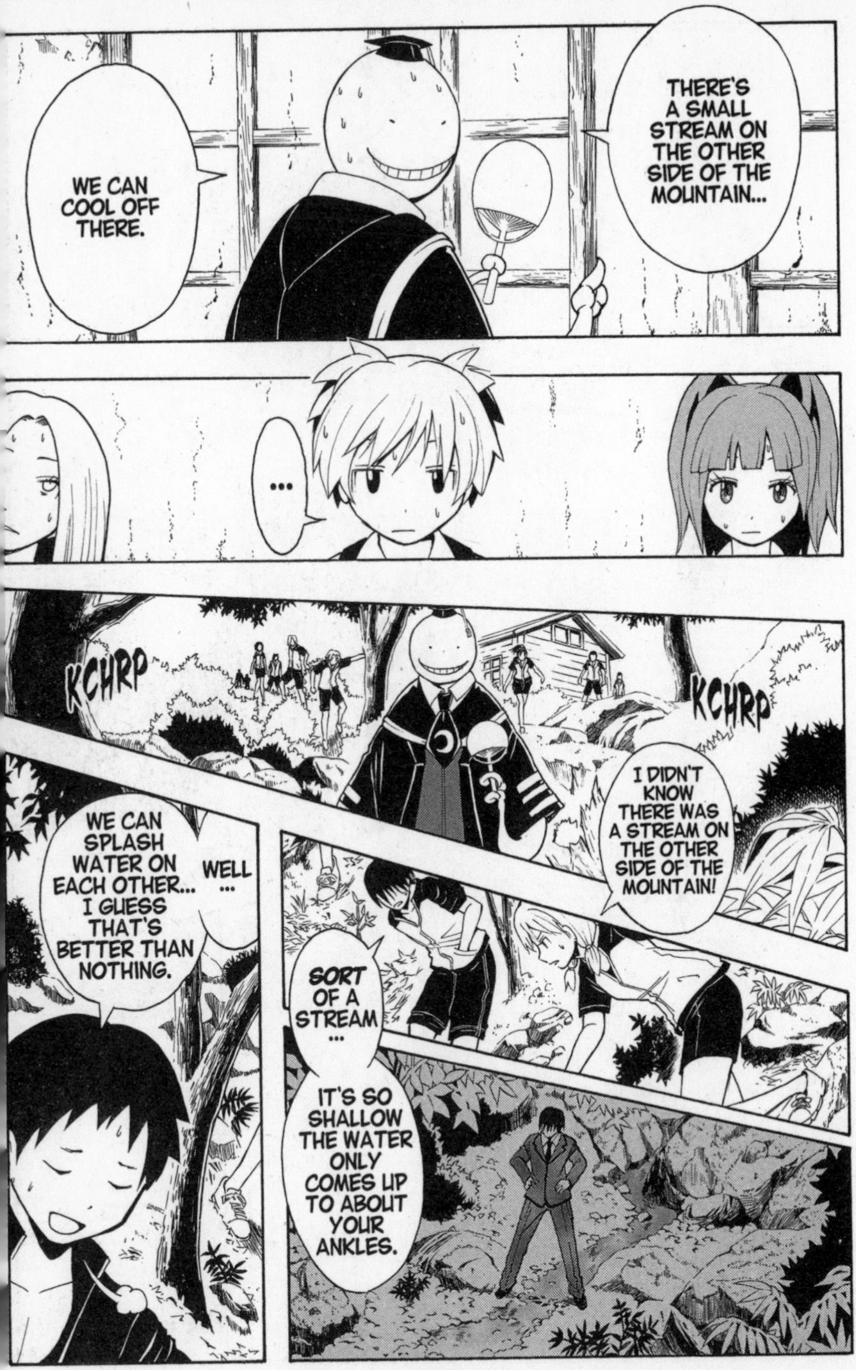
THERE'S A SMALL STREAM ON THE OTHER SIDE OF THE MOUNTAIN...
WE CAN COOL OFF THERE.
...
KCHRP
KCHRP
I DIDN'T KNOW THERE WAS A STREAM ON THE OTHER SIDE OF THE MOUNTAIN!
SORT OF A STREAM...
IT'S SO SHALLOW THE WATER ONLY COMES UP TO ABOUT YOUR ANKLES.
WELL...
WE CAN SPLASH WATER ON EACH OTHER... I GUESS THAT'S BETTER THAN NOTHING.

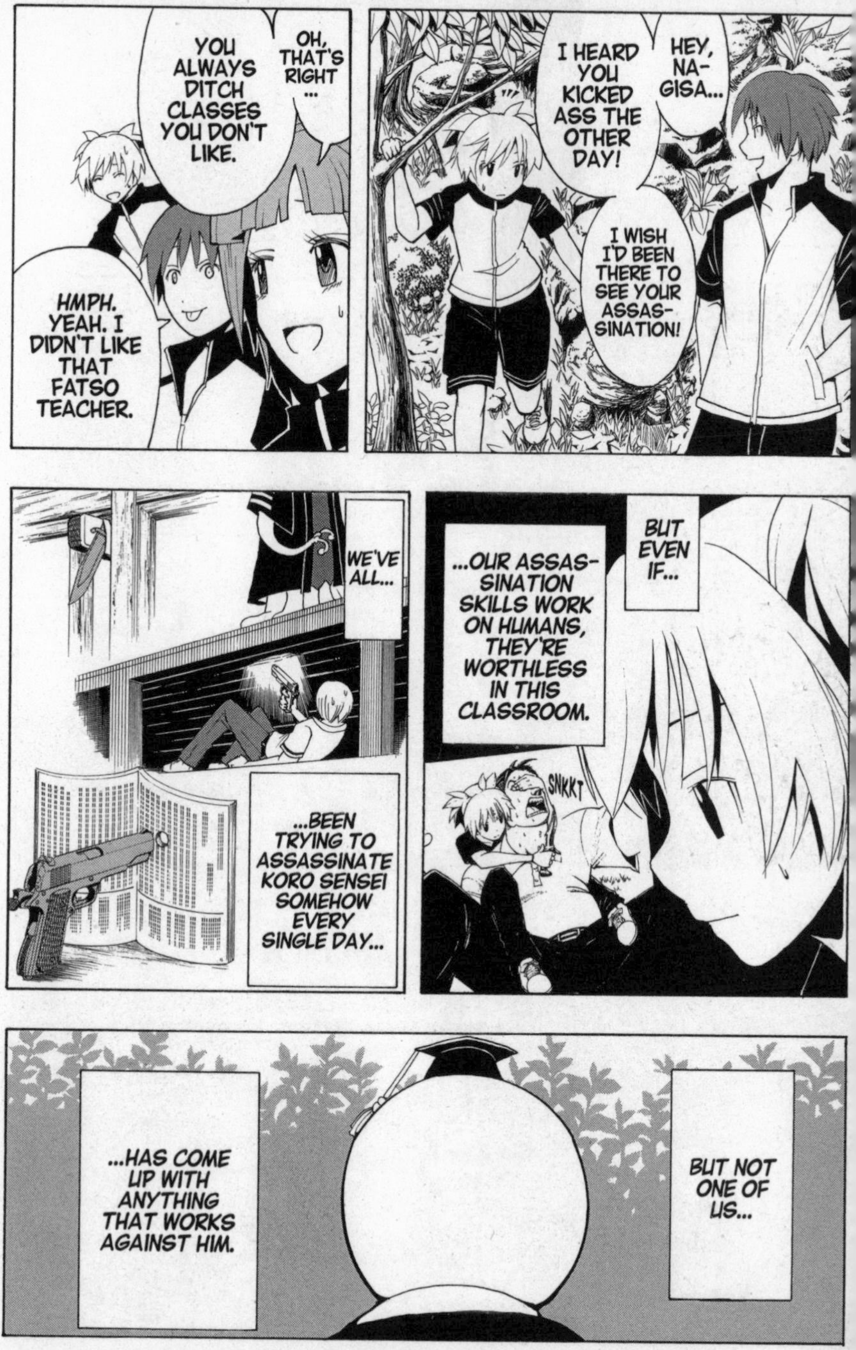
HEY, NAGISA...
I HEARD YOU KICKED ASS THE OTHER DAY!
I WISH I'D BEEN THERE TO SEE YOUR ASSASSINATION!
OH, THAT'S RIGHT...
YOU ALWAYS DITCH CLASSES YOU DON'T LIKE.
HMPH. YEAH. I DIDN'T LIKE THAT FATSO TEACHER.
BUT EVEN IF...
...OUR ASSASSINATION SKILLS WORK ON HUMANS, THEY'RE WORTHLESS IN THIS CLASSROOM.
SNKKT
WE'VE ALL...
...BEEN TRYING TO ASSASSINATE KORO SENSEI SOMEHOW EVERY SINGLE DAY...
BUT NOT ONE OF US...
...HAS COME UP WITH ANYTHING THAT WORKS AGAINST HIM.

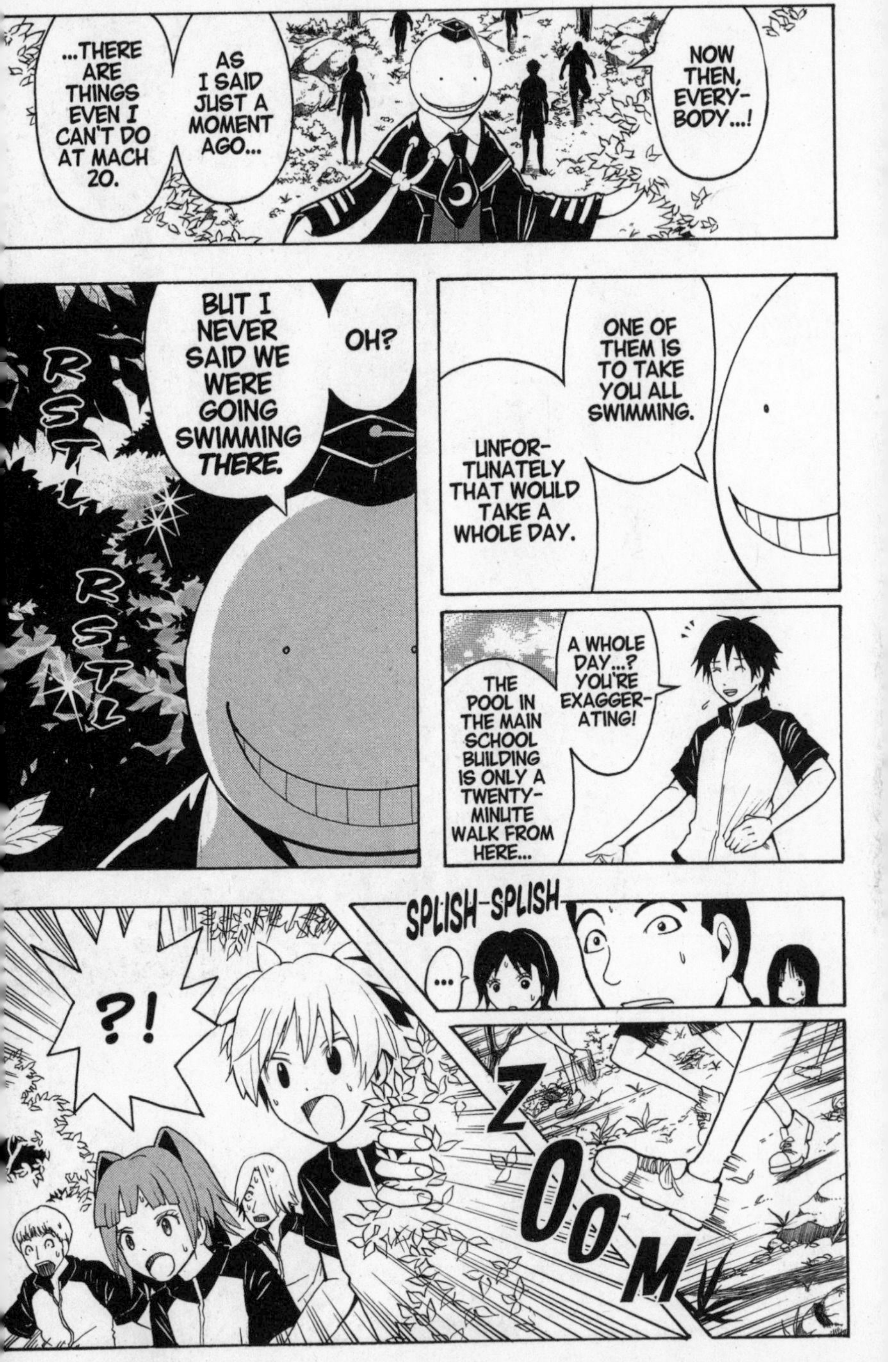
NOW THEN, EVERYBODY...!
AS I SAID JUST A MOMENT AGO...
...THERE ARE THINGS EVEN I CAN'T DO AT MACH 20.
ONE OF THEM IS TO TAKE YOU ALL SWIMMING.
UNFORTUNATELY THAT WOULD TAKE A WHOLE DAY.
A WHOLE DAY...? YOU'RE EXAGGERATING!
THE POOL IN THE MAIN SCHOOL BUILDING IS ONLY A TWENTY-MINUTE WALK FROM HERE...
OH?
BUT I NEVER SAID WE WERE GOING SWIMMING THERE.
RSTL
RSTL
RSTL
SPLISH-SPLISH
...
ZOOM
?!

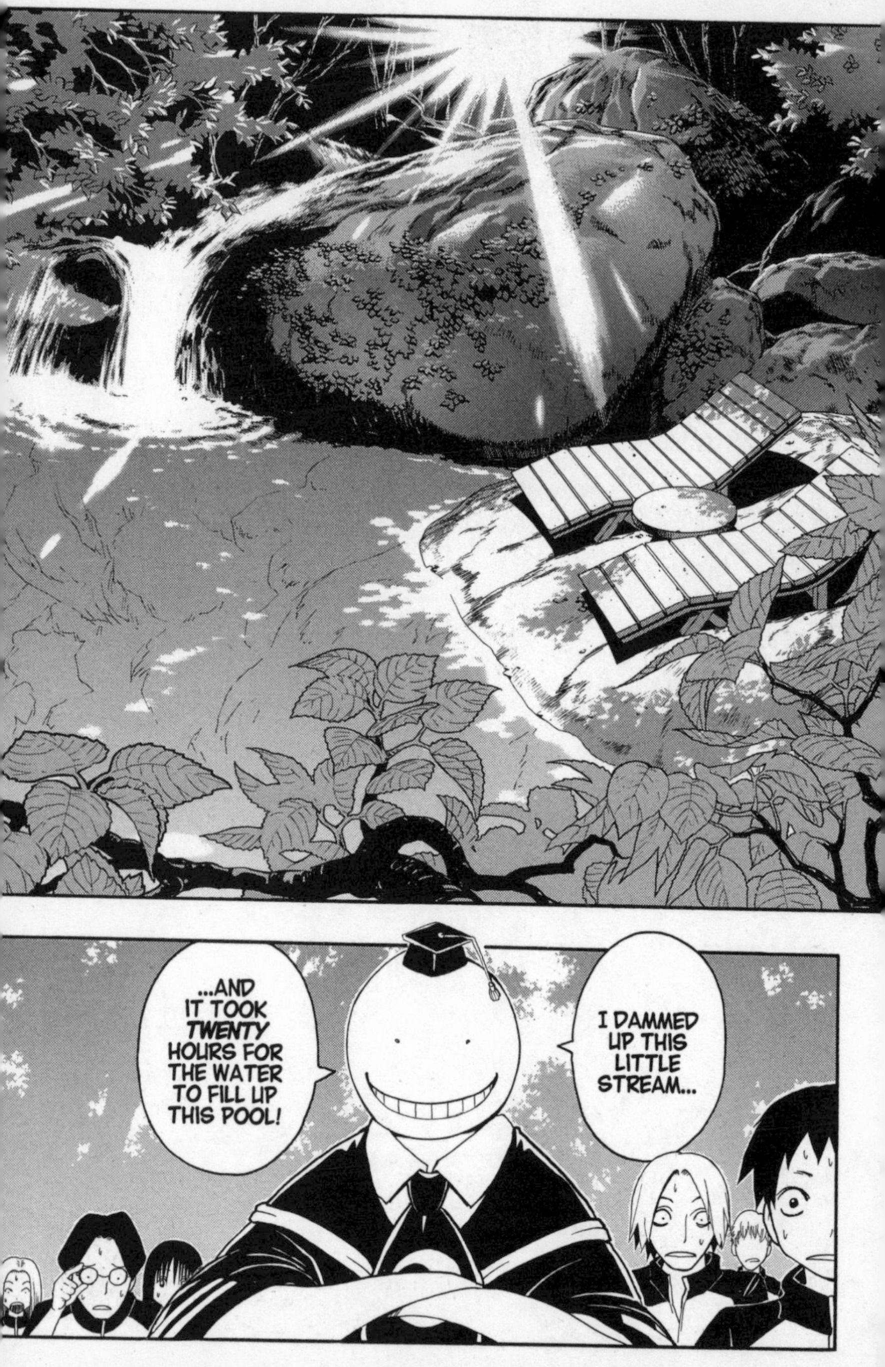
I DAMMED UP THIS LITTLE STREAM...
...AND IT TOOK *TWENTY* HOURS FOR THE WATER TO FILL UP THIS POOL!

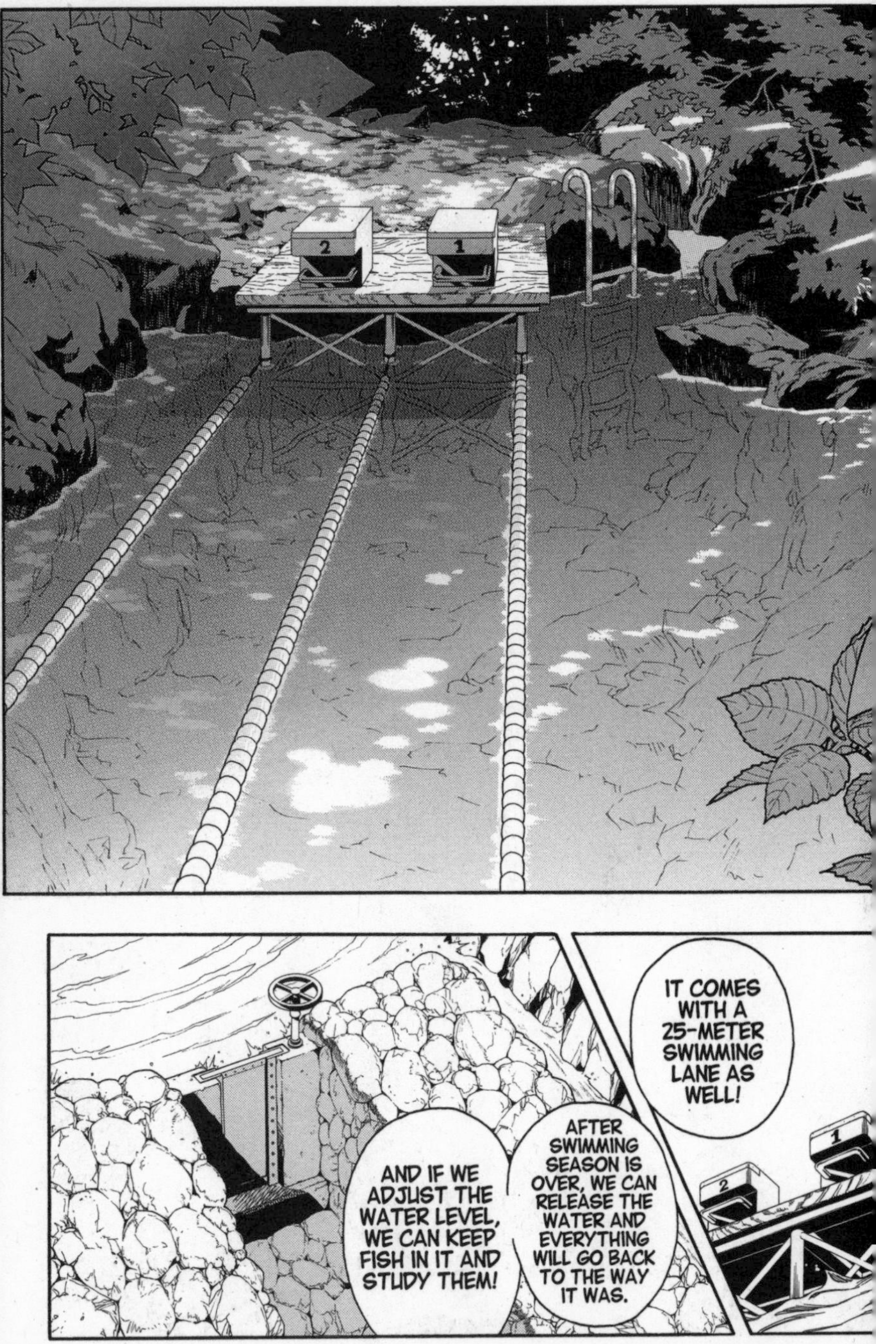
IT COMES WITH A 25-METER SWIMMING LANE AS WELL!
AFTER SWIMMING SEASON IS OVER, WE CAN RELEASE THE WATER AND EVERYTHING WILL GO BACK TO THE WAY IT WAS.
AND IF WE ADJUST THE WATER LEVEL, WE CAN KEEP FISH IN IT AND STUDY THEM!

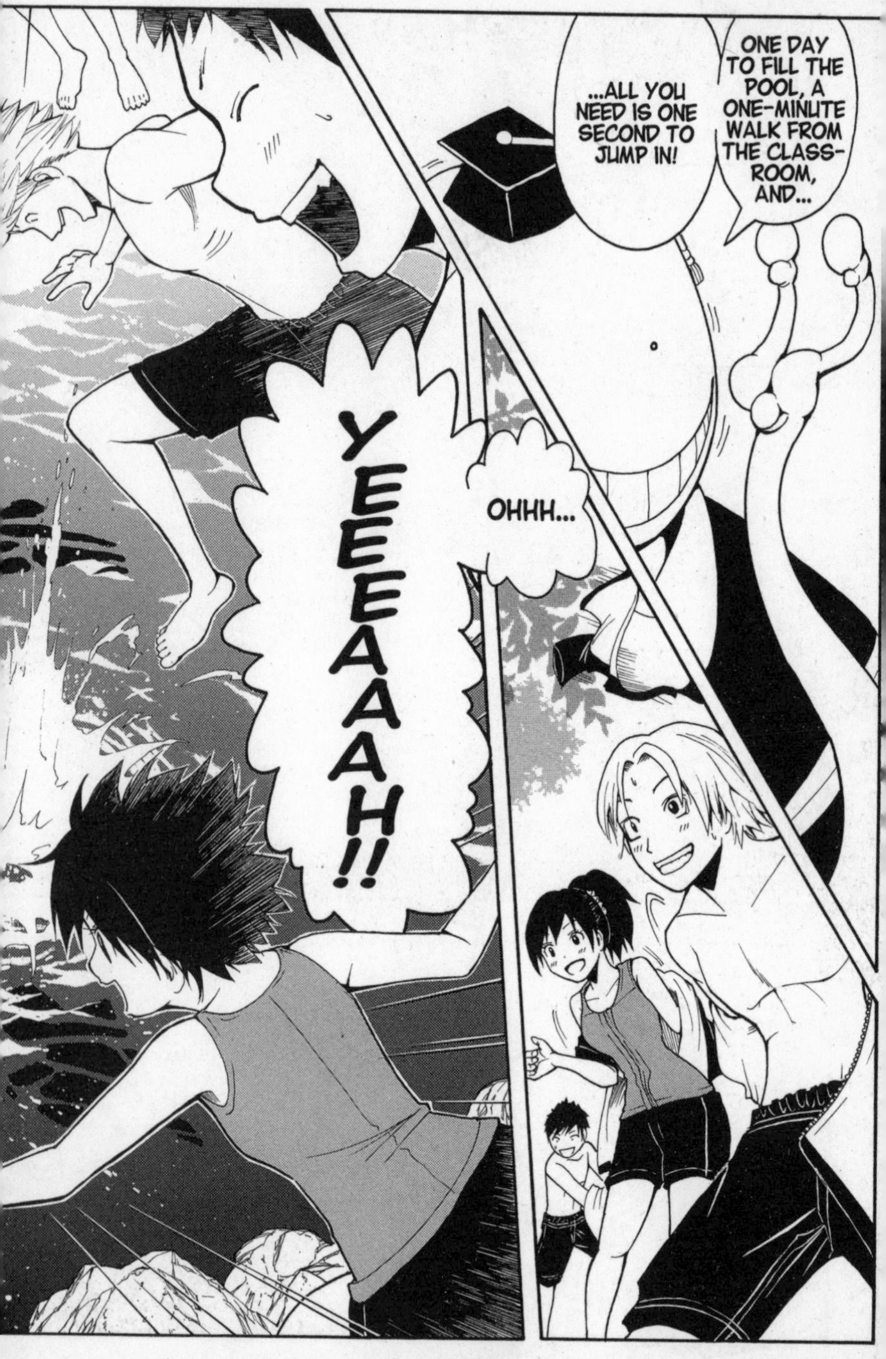
ONE DAY TO FILL THE POOL, A ONE-MINUTE WALK FROM THE CLASS-ROOM, AND...
...ALL YOU NEED IS ONE SECOND TO JUMP IN!
OHHH...
YEEEAAAH!!

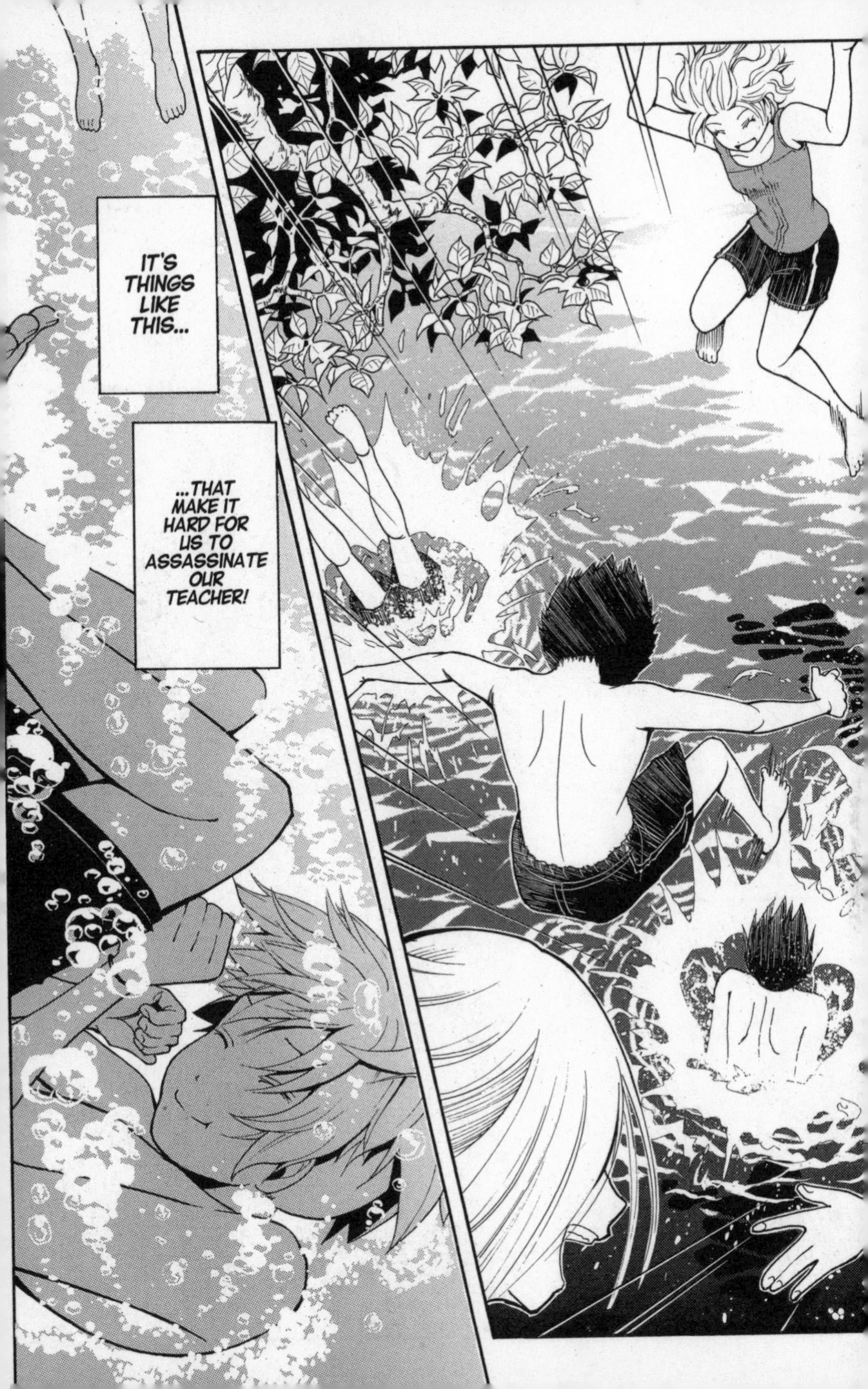
IT'S THINGS LIKE THIS...
...THAT MAKE IT HARD FOR US TO ASSASSINATE OUR TEACHER!

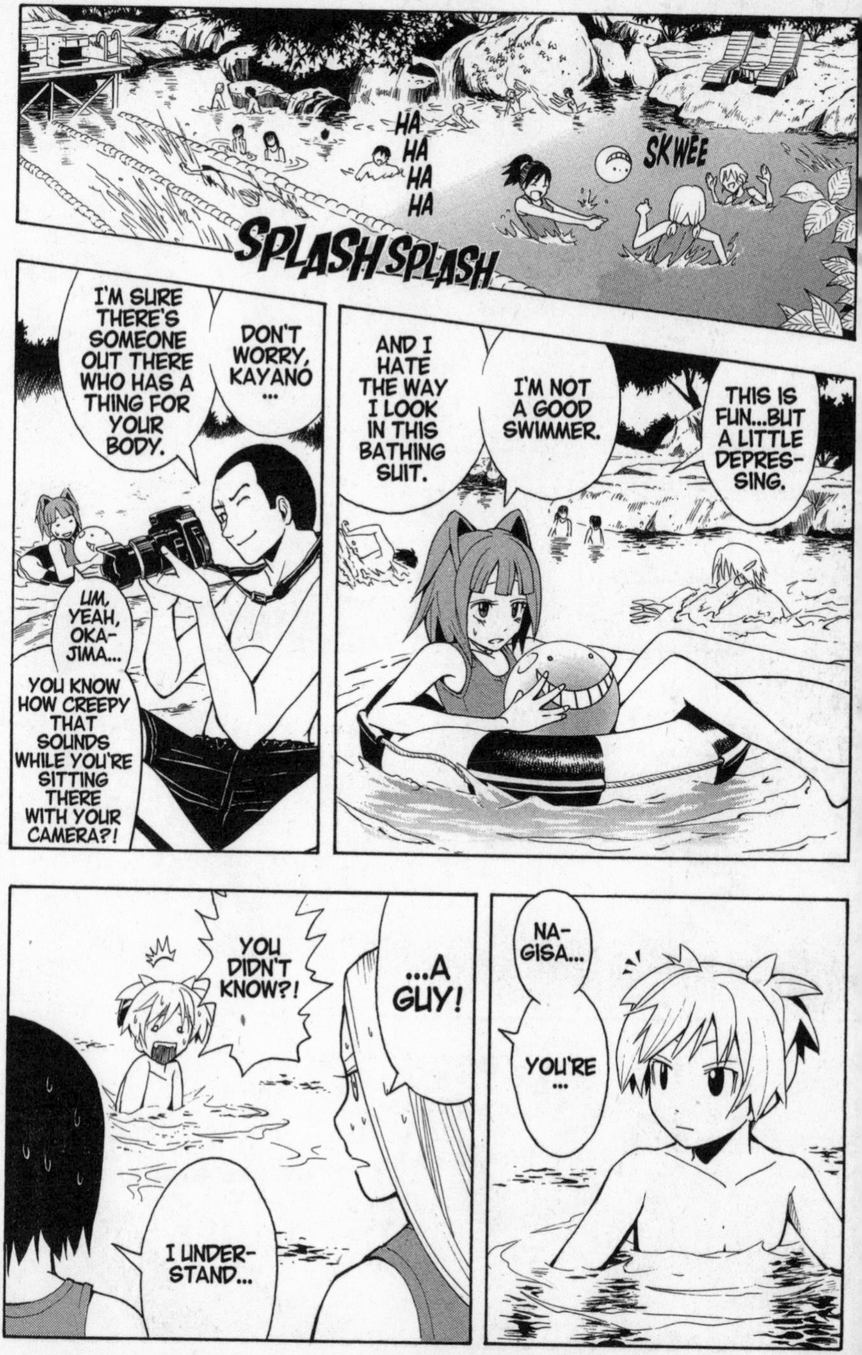
SKWEE
HA HA HA HA
SPLASH SPLASH
THIS IS FUN...BUT A LITTLE DEPRES-SING.
I'M NOT A GOOD SWIMMER.
AND I HATE THE WAY I LOOK IN THIS BATHING SUIT.
DON'T WORRY, KAYANO...
I'M SURE THERE'S SOMEONE OUT THERE WHO HAS A THING FOR YOUR BODY.
UM, YEAH, OKA-JIMA...
YOU KNOW HOW CREEPY THAT SOUNDS WHILE YOU'RE SITTING THERE WITH YOUR CAMERA?!
NA-GISA...
YOU'RE...
...A GUY!
YOU DIDN'T KNOW?!
I UNDER-STAND...

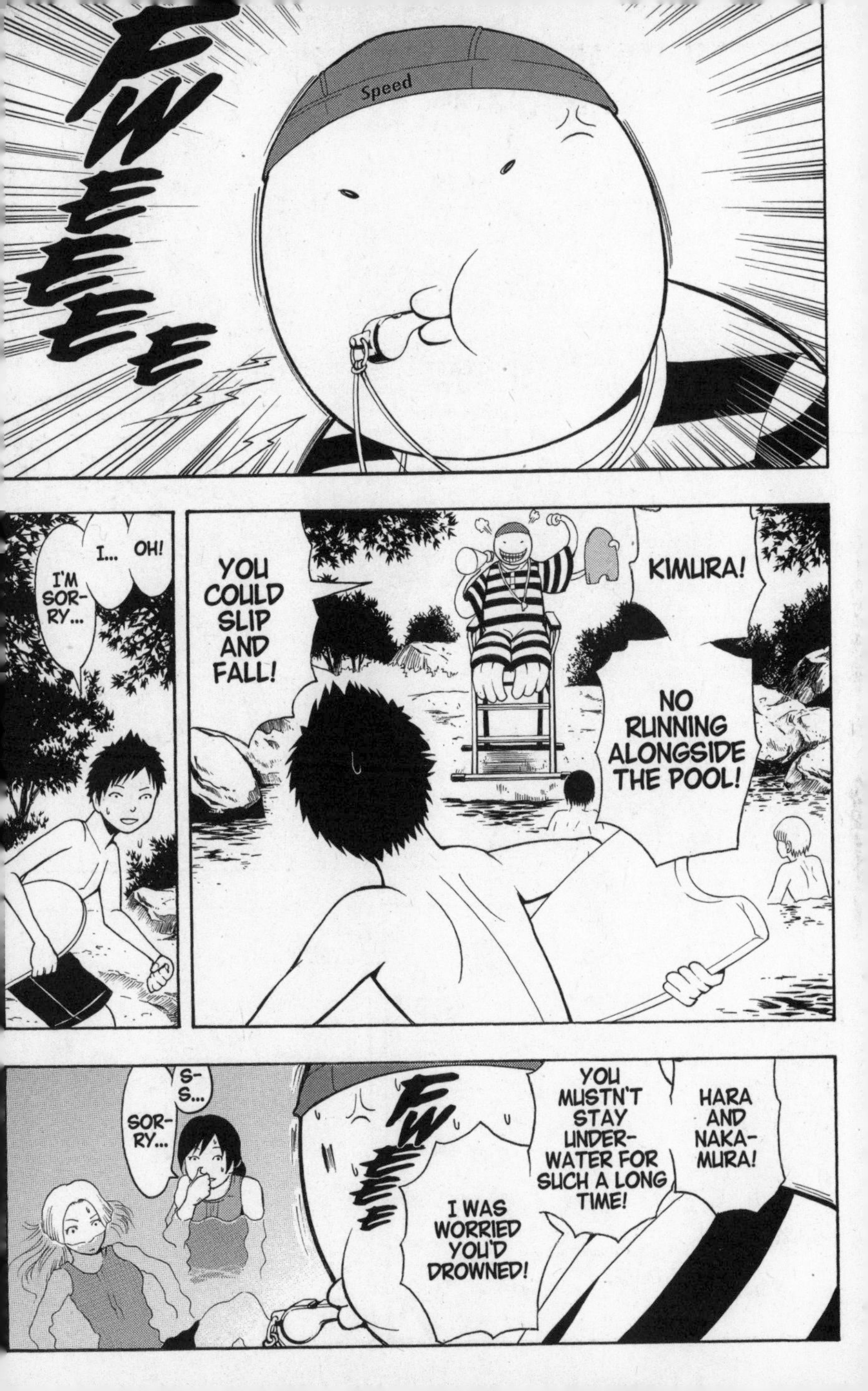
FWEEEEE
KIMURA!
NO RUNNING ALONGSIDE THE POOL!
YOU COULD SLIP AND FALL!
I... OH!
I'M SORRY...
HARA AND NAKAMURA!
YOU MUSTN'T STAY UNDERWATER FOR SUCH A LONG TIME!
I WAS WORRIED YOU'D DROWNED!
FWEEE
S-S...
SORRY...

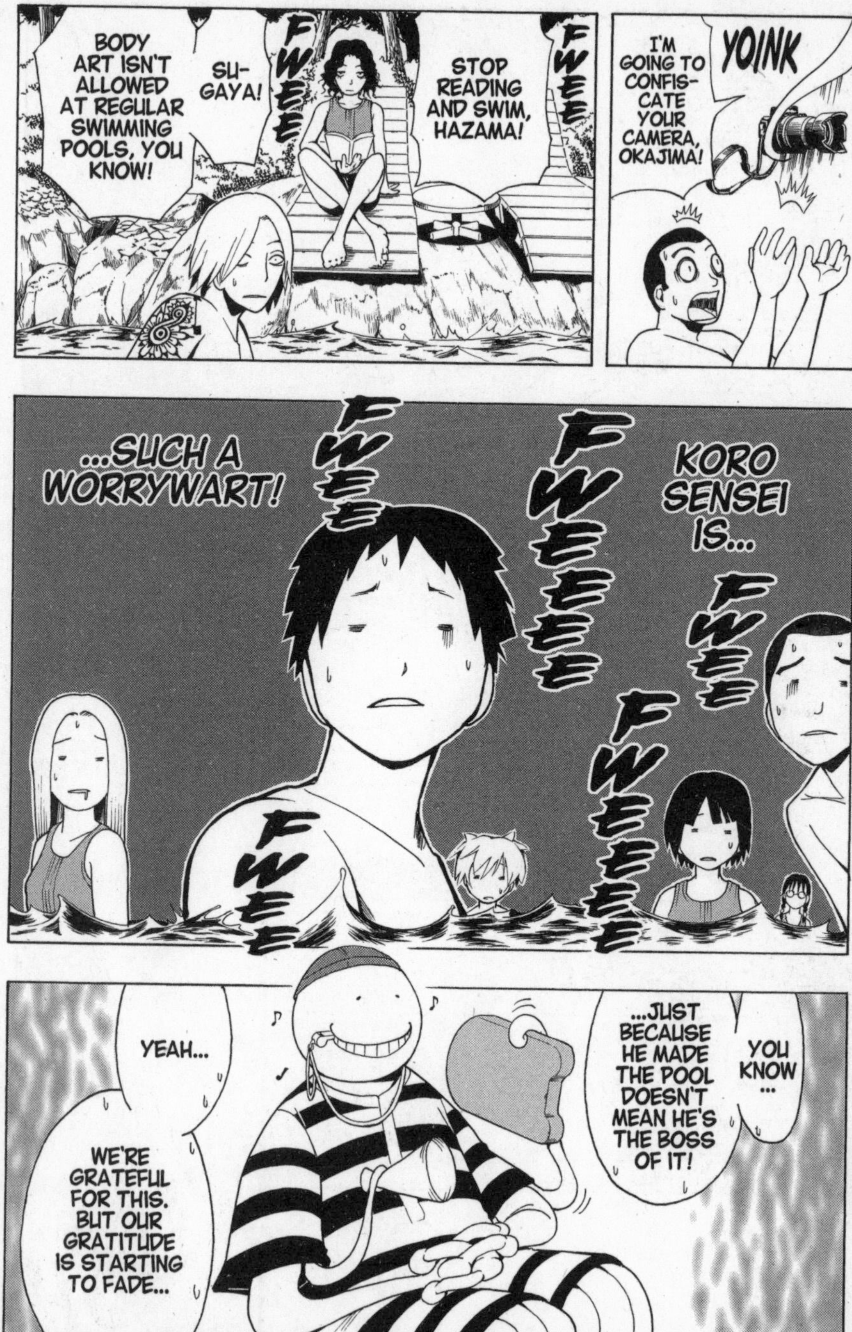
YOINK
I'M GOING TO CONFISCATE YOUR CAMERA, OKAJIMA!
FWEE
STOP READING AND SWIM, HAZAMA!
FWEE
SU-GAYA!
BODY ART ISN'T ALLOWED AT REGULAR SWIMMING POOLS, YOU KNOW!
KORO SENSEI IS...
FWEE
FWEEEEE
FWEEEEEE
FWEE
...SUCH A WORRYWART!
FWEE
YOU KNOW...
...JUST BECAUSE HE MADE THE POOL DOESN'T MEAN HE'S THE BOSS OF IT!
YEAH...
WE'RE GRATEFUL FOR THIS. BUT OUR GRATITUDE IS STARTING TO FADE...

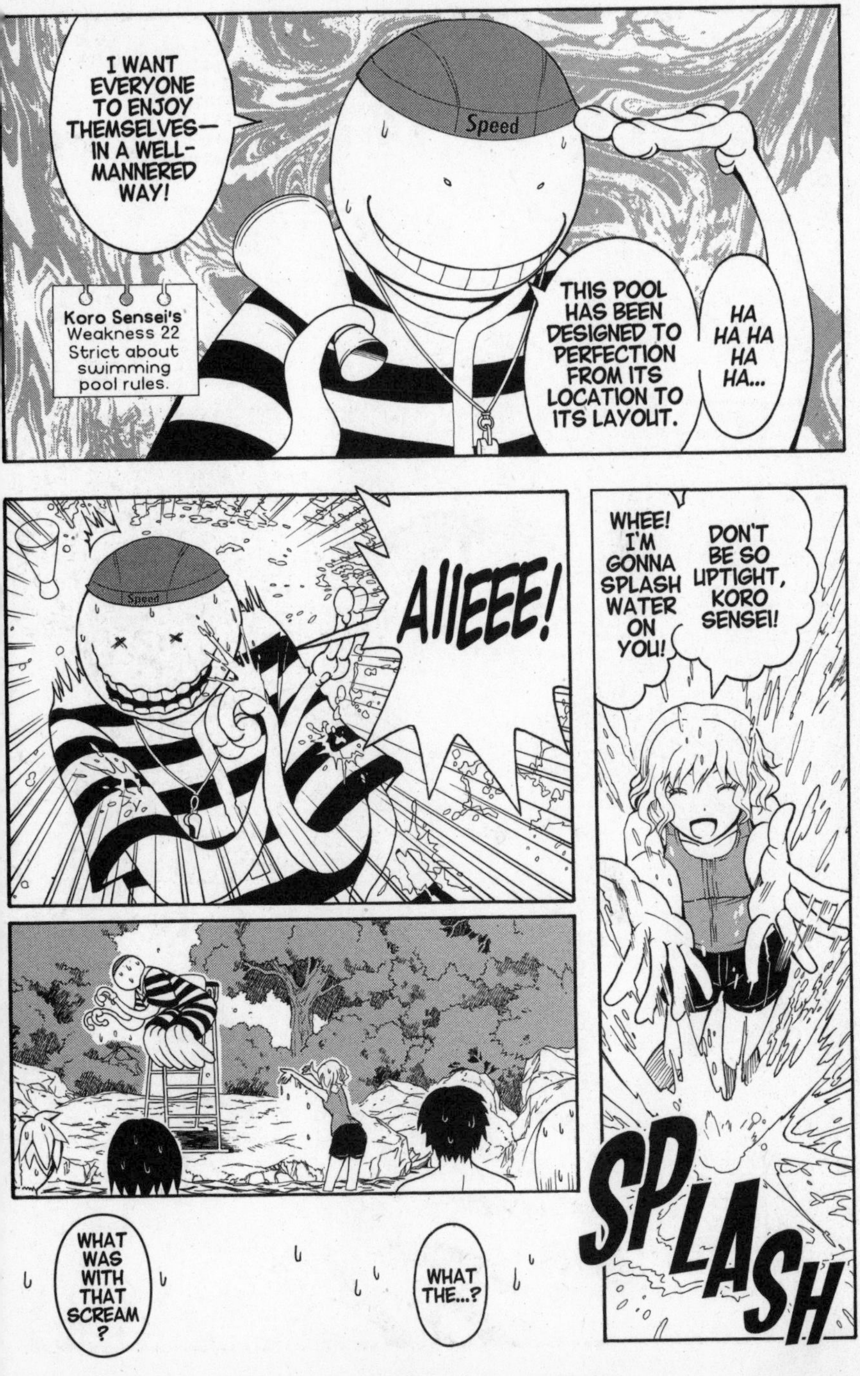
HA HA HA HA HA...
THIS POOL HAS BEEN DESIGNED TO PERFECTION FROM ITS LOCATION TO ITS LAYOUT.
I WANT EVERYONE TO ENJOY THEMSELVES—IN A WELL-MANNERED WAY!
Speed
Koro Sensei's Weakness 22 Strict about swimming pool rules.
DON'T BE SO UPTIGHT, KORO SENSEI!
WHEE! I'M GONNA SPLASH WATER ON YOU!
SPLASH
AIIEEE!
Speed
WHAT THE...?
WHAT WAS WITH THAT SCREAM?

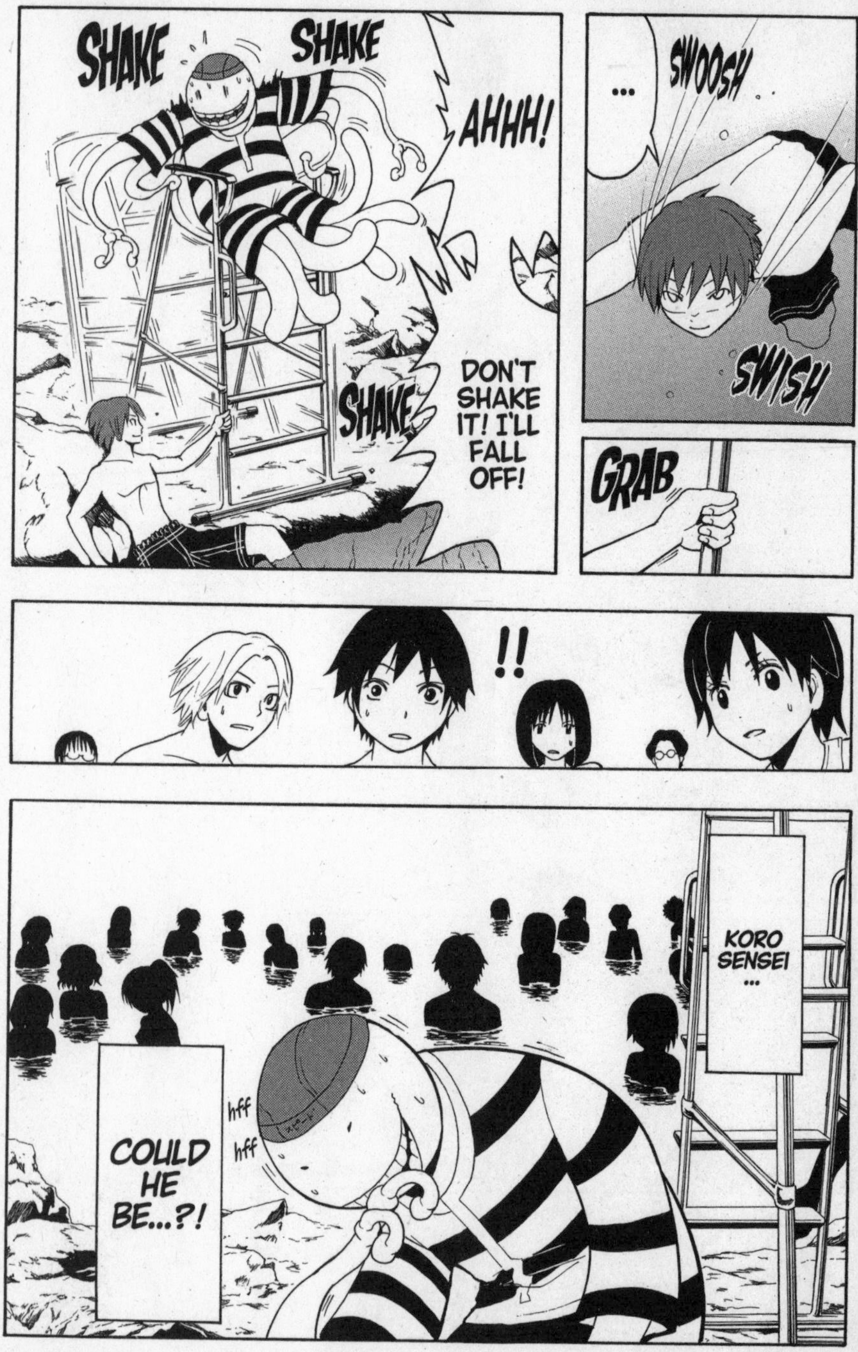
...
SWOOSH
SWISH
GRAB
SHAKE
SHAKE
AHHH!
SHAKE
DON'T SHAKE IT! I'LL FALL OFF!
!!
KORO SENSEI ...
hff
hff
COULD HE BE...?!

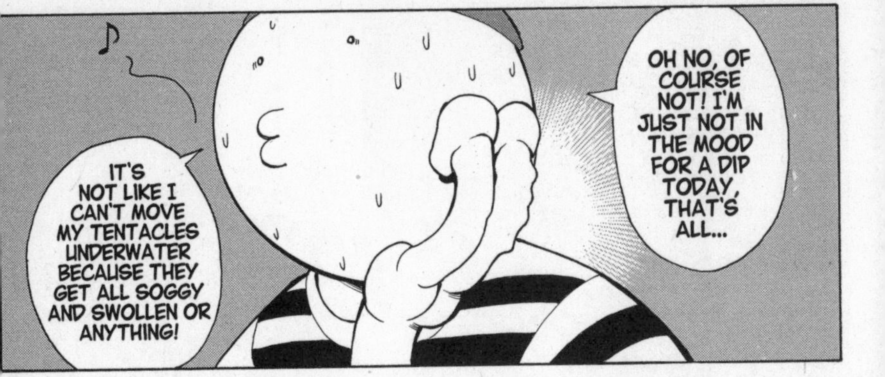
OH NO, OF COURSE NOT! I'M JUST NOT IN THE MOOD FOR A DIP TODAY, THAT'S ALL...
IT'S NOT LIKE I CAN'T MOVE MY TENTACLES UNDERWATER BECAUSE THEY GET ALL SOGGY AND SWOLLEN OR ANYTHING!

Koro Sensei's Weakness 23

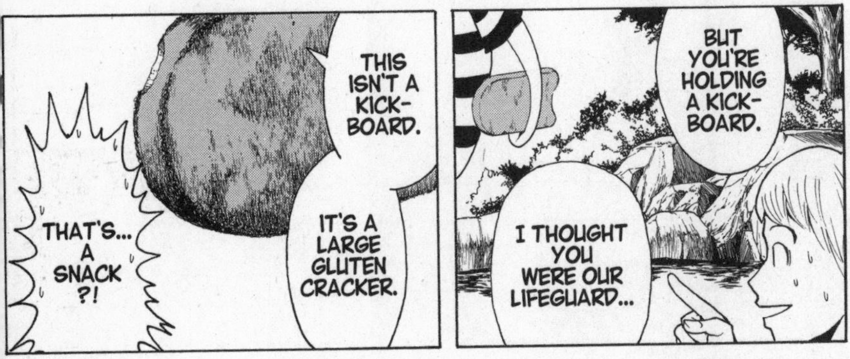
BUT YOU'RE HOLDING A KICK-BOARD.
I THOUGHT YOU WERE OUR LIFEGUARD...
THIS ISN'T A KICK-BOARD.
IT'S A LARGE GLUTEN CRACKER.
THAT'S... A SNACK?!

He can't swim.

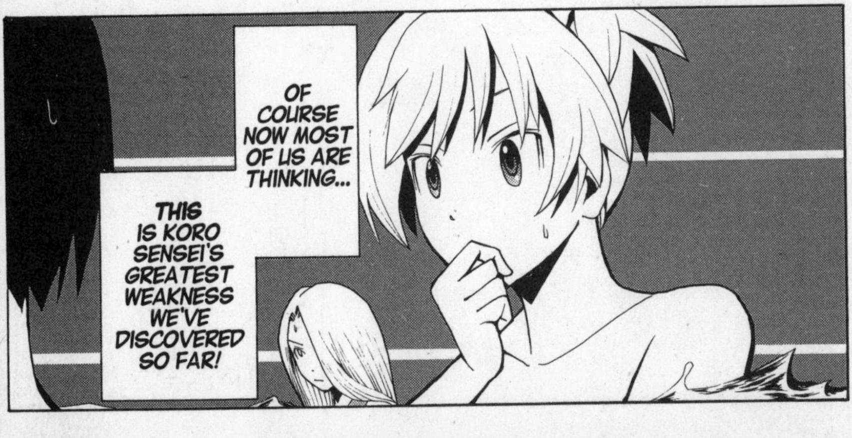
OF COURSE NOW MOST OF US ARE THINKING...
THIS IS KORO SENSEI'S GREATEST WEAKNESS WE'VE DISCOVERED SO FAR!

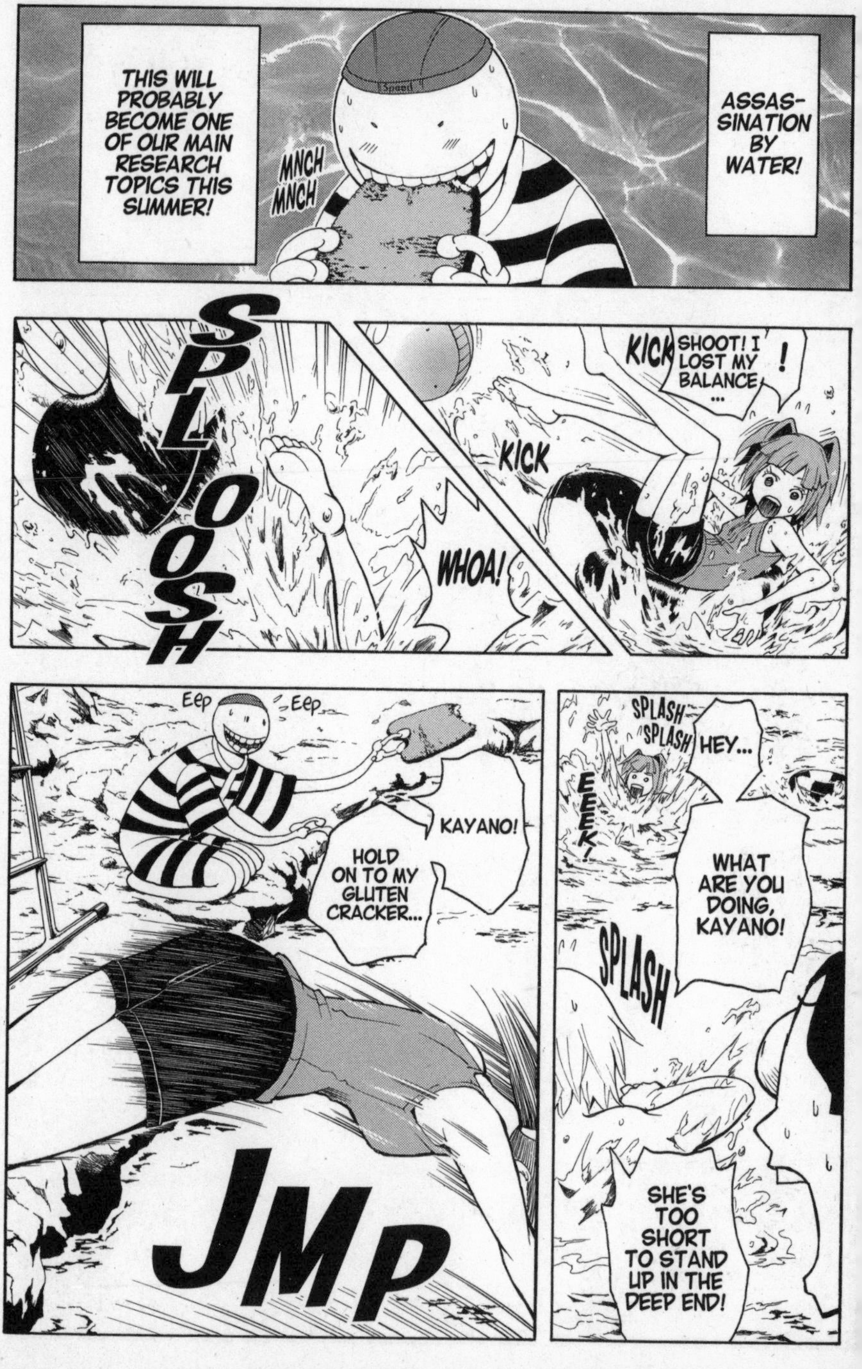
ASSAS-SINATION BY WATER!
MNCH MNCH
THIS WILL PROBABLY BECOME ONE OF OUR MAIN RESEARCH TOPICS THIS SUMMER!
KICK
SHOOT! I LOST MY BALANCE ...
!
KICK
WHOA!
SPLOOSH
SPLASH SPLASH
EEEK!
HEY...
WHAT ARE YOU DOING, KAYANO!
SPLASH
SHE'S TOO SHORT TO STAND UP IN THE DEEP END!
Eep Eep
KAYANO!
HOLD ON TO MY GLUTEN CRACKER...
JMP

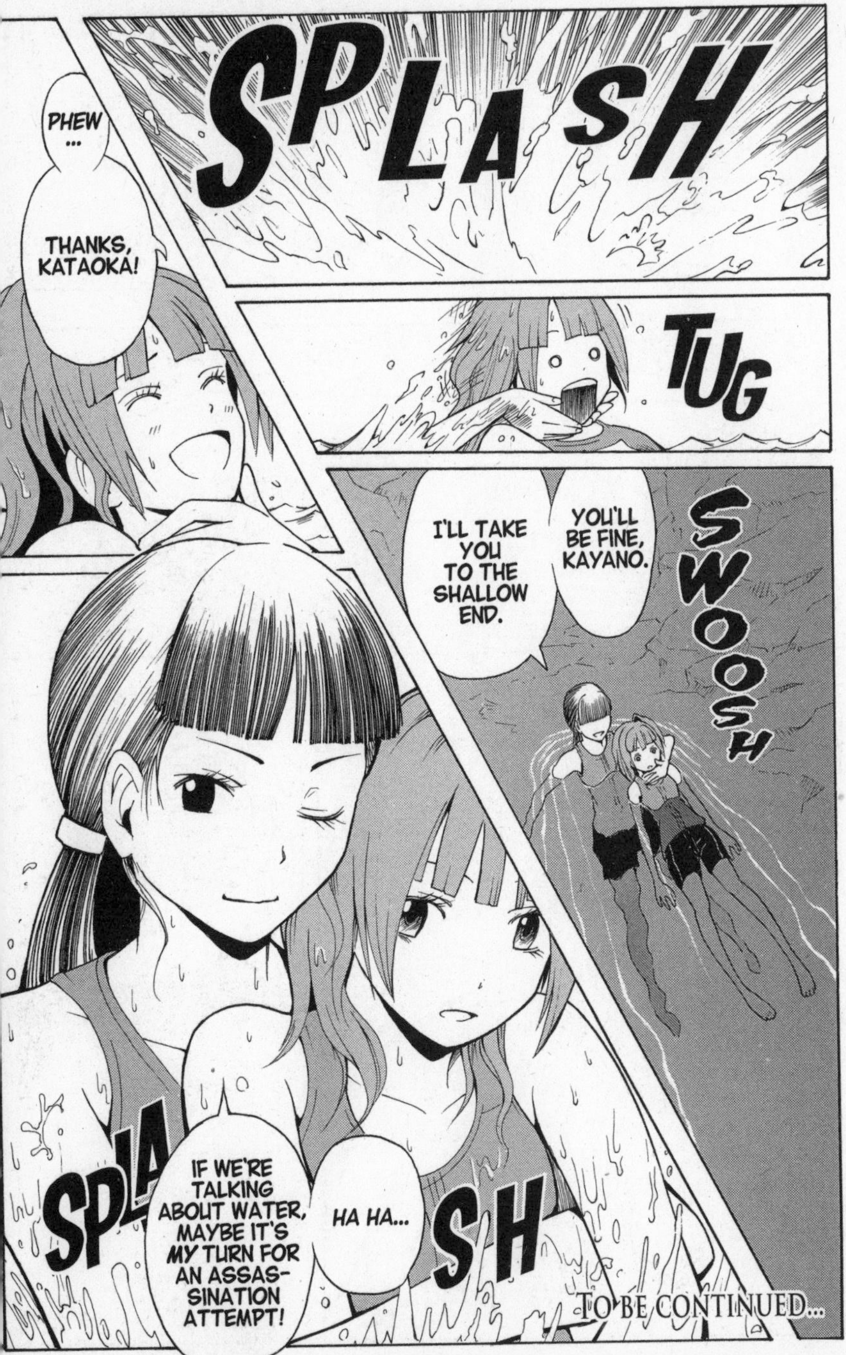
SPLASH
TUG
PHEW ...
THANKS, KATAOKA!
SWOOSH
YOU'LL BE FINE, KAYANO.
I'LL TAKE YOU TO THE SHALLOW END.
SPLASH
HA HA...
IF WE'RE TALKING ABOUT WATER, MAYBE IT'S MY TURN FOR AN ASSAS-SINATION ATTEMPT!
TO BE CONTINUED...

On Safari

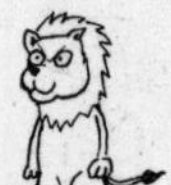

Packed

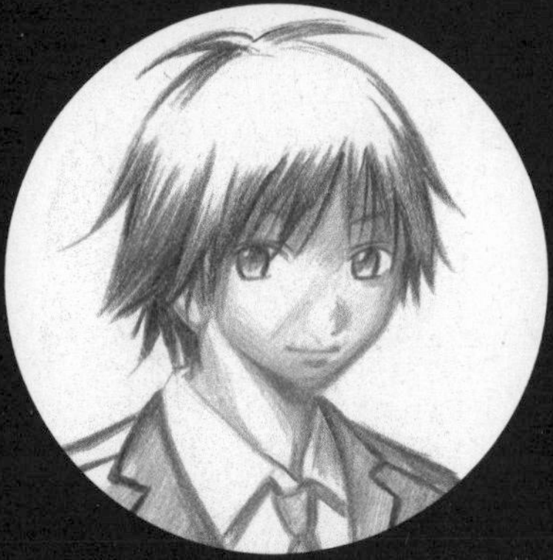

I know it's a simple-looking cover, but I'm not doing it to save time. (*Laugh*)

I meticulously adjusted the location of the mouth, looked at various different whites to find the right color, and created mock-up volumes to see what they would look like.

As a result, I've come to believe that white is a great color...

I usually see the color white on paper or the background of my computer, so it's refreshing to see it take on a more active role like this.

I want to become the kind of man who looks nice in a white shirt...

—Yusei Matsui

Yusei Matsui was born on the last day of January in Saitama Prefecture, Japan. He has been drawing manga since elementary school. Some of his favorite manga series are *Bobobo-bo Bo-bobo*, *JoJo's Bizarre Adventure* and *Ultimate Muscle*. Matsui learned his trade working as an assistant to manga artist Yoshio Sawai, creator of *Bobobo-bo Bo-bobo*. In 2005, Matsui debuted his original manga *Neuro: Supernatural Detective* in *Weekly Shonen Jump*. In 2007, *Neuro* was adapted into an anime. In 2012, *Assassination Classroom* began serialization in *Weekly Shonen Jump*.

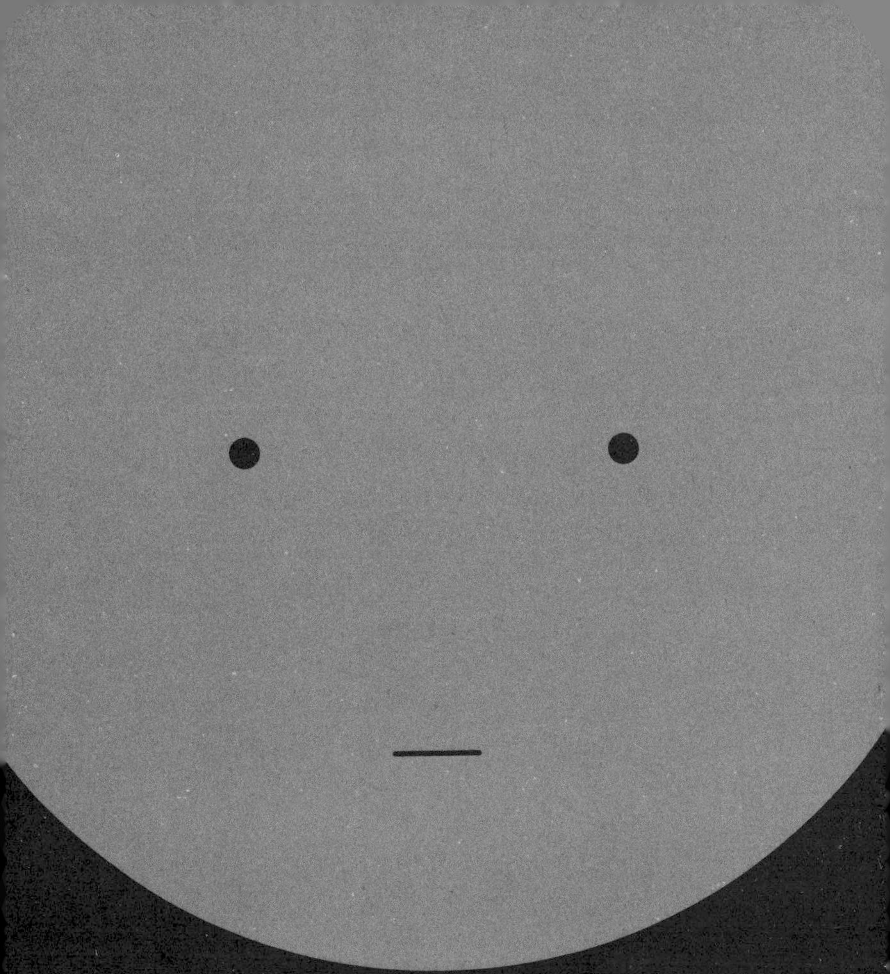

White is a straight face. Nothingness. It is nothingness...

ASSASSINATION CLASSROOM

YUSEI MATSUI

5

TIME TO SHOW OFF A HIDDEN TALENT

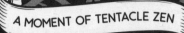
A MOMENT OF TENTACLE ZEN

He stole something quite
precious to you.
Your tentacles.

— Inspector Koro

ASSASSINATION CLASSROOM

Volume 5
SHONEN JUMP ADVANCED Manga Edition

Story and Art by YUSEI MATSUI

Translation/Tetsuichiro Miyaki
English Adaptation/Bryant Turnage
Touch-up Art & Lettering/Stephen Dutro
Cover & Interior Design/Sam Elzway
Editor/Annette Roman

ANSATSU KYOSHITSU © 2012 by Yusei Matsui
All rights reserved.
First published in Japan in 2012 by SHUEISHA Inc., Tokyo.
English translation rights arranged by SHUEISHA Inc.

The stories, characters and incidents mentioned in this publication are entirely fictional.

Printed in the U.S.A.

Published by VIZ Media, LLC
P.O. Box 77010
San Francisco, CA 94107

10 9 8 7 6 5 4
First printing, August 2015
Fourth printing, December 2017

www.viz.com
www.shonenjump.com

Syllabus for Assassination Classroom, Vol. 6

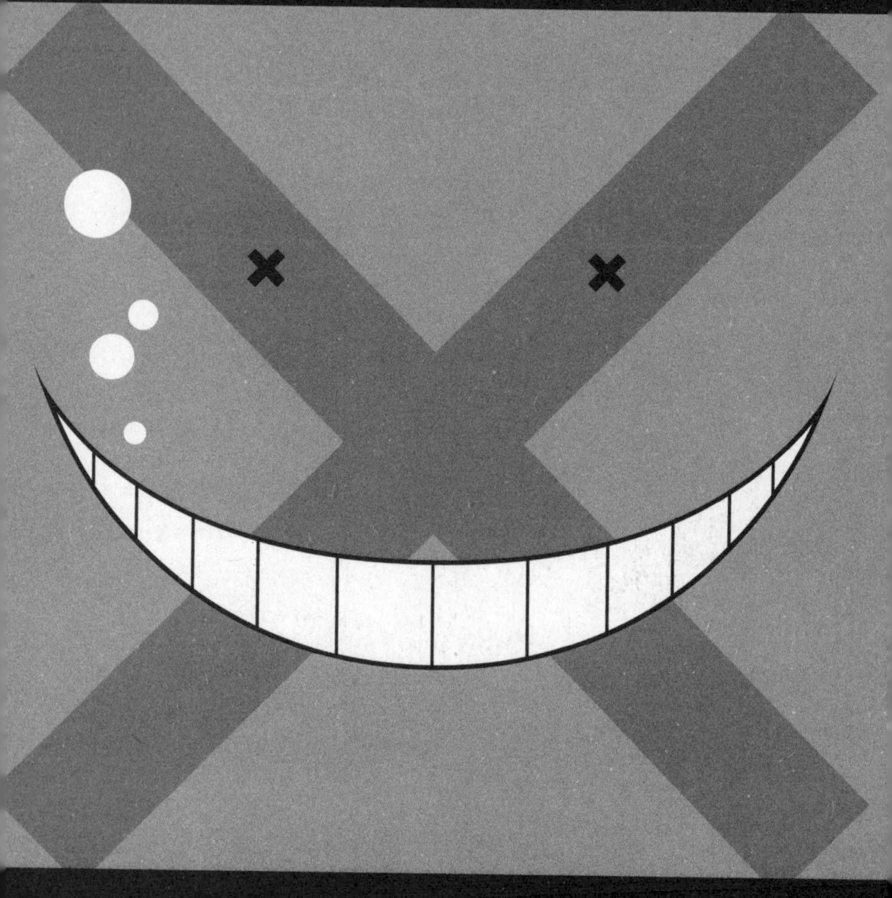

The 3-E students discover that Koro Sensei's greatest weakness might be a common substance. Will they be able to use it to assassinate him while he helps Meg, formerly of the varsity swim team, with *her* greatest weakness? The next assassination attempt, led by Terasaka, is more elaborate but endangers his fellow students. Can he save them without saving his target? Then, the top class at school, including Principal Asano's son, conspires to prevent 3-E from ever rising closer to the top!

Available NOW!

Love triangle!
Comedic antics!!
Gang warfare?!

A laugh-out-loud story that features a fake love relationship between two heirs of rival gangs!

Story and Art by
NAOSHI KOMI

NISEKOI
False Love

It's hate at first sight...rather, a knee to the head at first sight when **RAKU ICHIJO** meets **CHITOGE KIRISAKI**! Unfortunately, Raku's gangster father arranges a false love match with their rival's daughter, who just so happens to be Chitoge! Raku's searching for his childhood sweetheart from ten years ago, however, with a pendant around his neck as a memento, but he can't even remember her name or face!

AVAILABLE NOW!

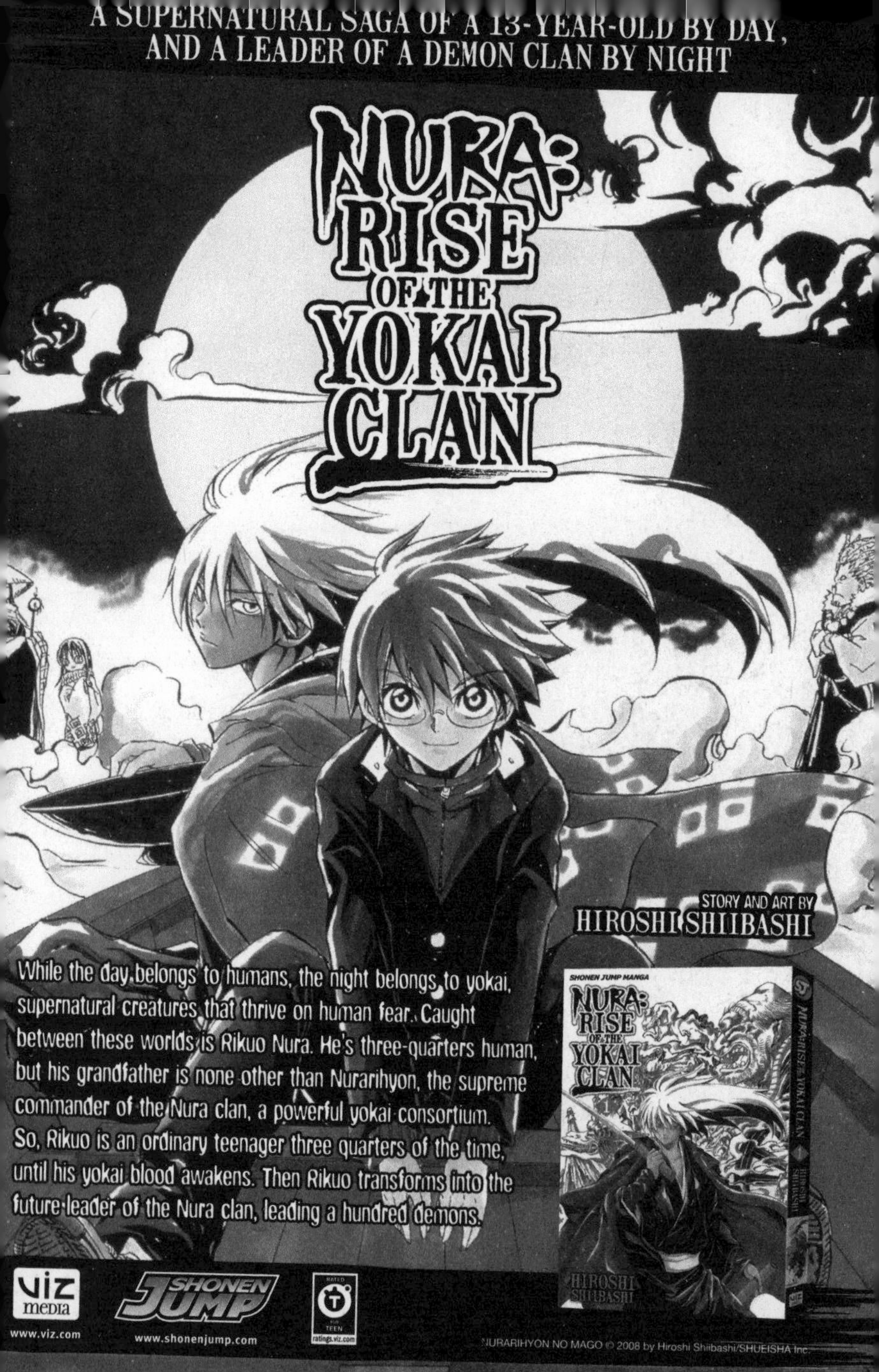
A SUPERNATURAL SAGA OF A 13-YEAR-OLD BY DAY, AND A LEADER OF A DEMON CLAN BY NIGHT
NURA: RISE OF THE YOKAI CLAN
STORY AND ART BY
HIROSHI SHIIBASHI
While the day belongs to humans, the night belongs to yokai, supernatural creatures that thrive on human fear. Caught between these worlds is Rikuo Nura. He's three-quarters human, but his grandfather is none other than Nurarihyon, the supreme commander of the Nura clan, a powerful yokai consortium. So, Rikuo is an ordinary teenager three quarters of the time, until his yokai blood awakens. Then Rikuo transforms into the future leader of the Nura clan, leading a hundred demons.
SHONEN JUMP MANGA
NURA: RISE OF THE YOKAI CLAN
1
HIROSHI SHIIBASHI
viz media
www.viz.com
SHONEN JUMP
www.shonenjump.com
RATED T FOR TEEN
ratings.viz.com
NURARIHYON NO MAGO © 2008 by Hiroshi Shiibashi/SHUEISHA Inc.

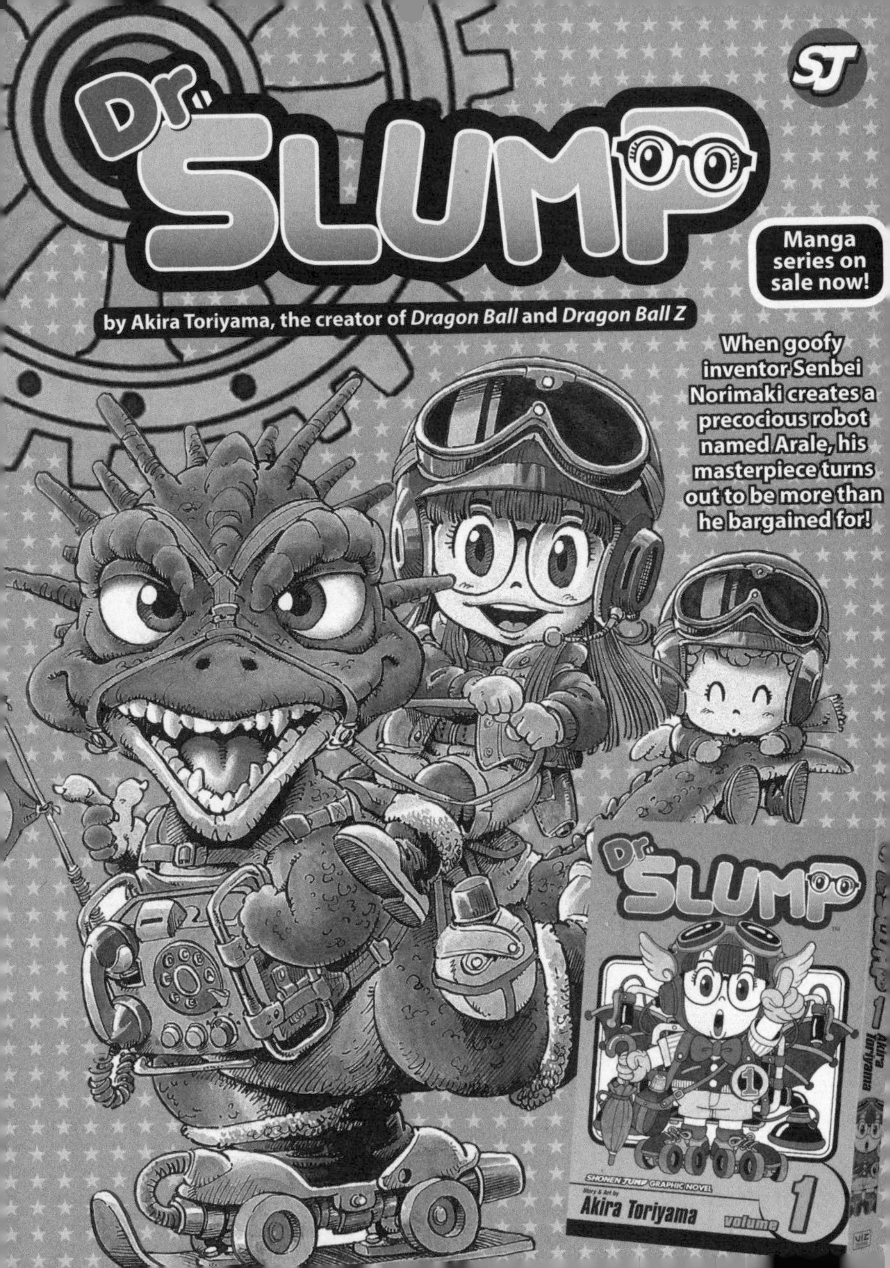
SJ
Dr. SLUMP
Manga series on sale now!
by Akira Toriyama, the creator of Dragon Ball and Dragon Ball Z
When goofy inventor Senbei Norimaki creates a precocious robot named Arale, his masterpiece turns out to be more than he bargained for!
Dr. SLUMP
SHONEN JUMP GRAPHIC NOVEL
Story & Art by
Akira Toriyama
volume 1

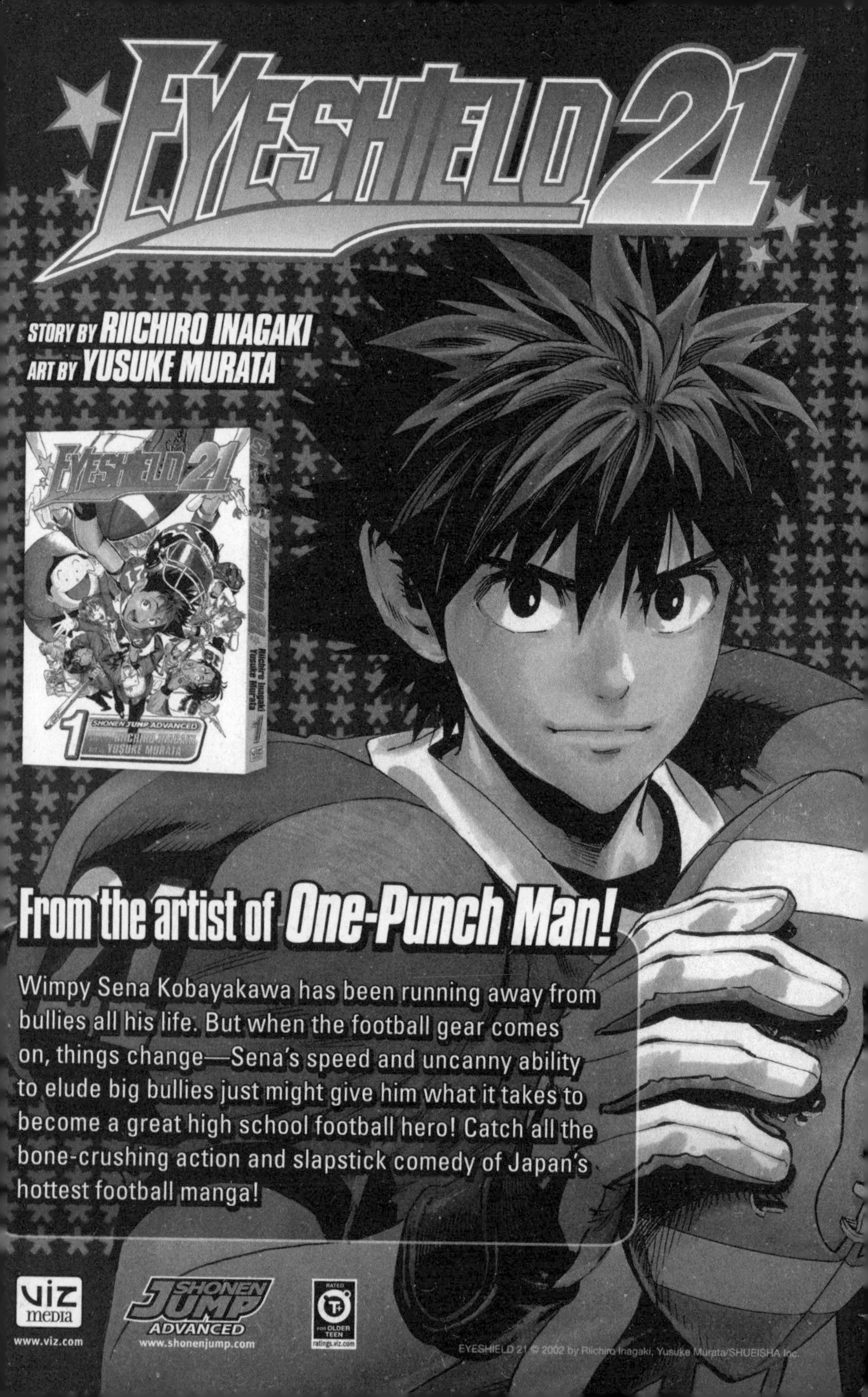
EYESHIELD 21
STORY BY RIICHIRO INAGAKI
ART BY YUSUKE MURATA
EYESHIELD 21
1
SHONEN JUMP ADVANCED
RIICHIRO INAGAKI
YUSUKE MURATA
From the artist of One-Punch Man!
Wimpy Sena Kobayakawa has been running away from bullies all his life. But when the football gear comes on, things change—Sena's speed and uncanny ability to elude big bullies just might give him what it takes to become a great high school football hero! Catch all the bone-crushing action and slapstick comedy of Japan's hottest football manga!
viz media
www.viz.com
SHONEN JUMP ADVANCED
www.shonenjump.com
RATED T+ FOR OLDER TEEN
ratings.viz.com
EYESHIELD 21 © 2002 by Riichiro Inagaki, Yusuke Murata/SHUEISHA Inc.

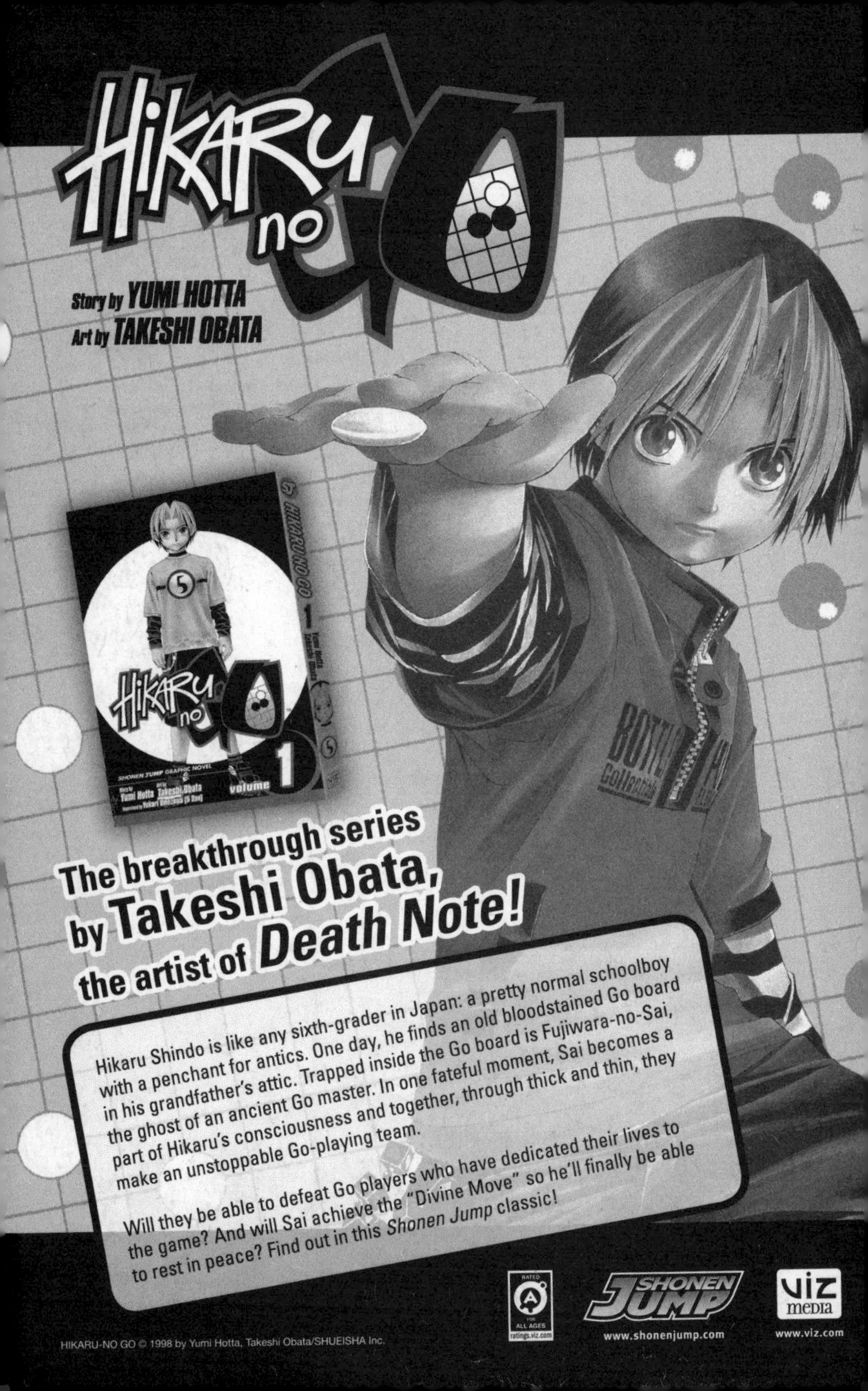
HIKARU no GO
Story by YUMI HOTTA
Art by TAKESHI OBATA
HIKARU no GO 1
Yumi Hotta Takeshi Obata
SHONEN JUMP GRAPHIC NOVEL
volume 1
The breakthrough series by Takeshi Obata, the artist of Death Note!
Hikaru Shindo is like any sixth-grader in Japan: a pretty normal schoolboy with a penchant for antics. One day, he finds an old bloodstained Go board in his grandfather's attic. Trapped inside the Go board is Fujiwara-no-Sai, the ghost of an ancient Go master. In one fateful moment, Sai becomes a part of Hikaru's consciousness and together, through thick and thin, they make an unstoppable Go-playing team.
Will they be able to defeat Go players who have dedicated their lives to the game? And will Sai achieve the "Divine Move" so he'll finally be able to rest in peace? Find out in this Shonen Jump classic!
RATED A FOR ALL AGES
ratings.viz.com
SHONEN JUMP
www.shonenjump.com
viz media
www.viz.com
HIKARU-NO GO © 1998 by Yumi Hotta, Takeshi Obata/SHUEISHA Inc.

You're Reading in the Wrong Direction!!

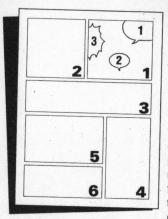

Whoops! Guess what? You're starting at the wrong end of the comic!

...It's true! In keeping with the original Japanese format, **Assassination Classroom** is meant to be read from right to left, starting in the upper-right corner.

Unlike English, which is read from left to right, Japanese is read from right to left, meaning that action, sound effects and word-balloon order are completely reversed... something which can make readers unfamiliar with Japanese feel pretty backwards themselves. For this reason, manga or Japanese comics published in the U.S. in English have sometimes been published "flopped"—that is, printed in exact reverse order, as though seen from the other side of a mirror.

By flopping pages, U.S. publishers can avoid confusing readers, but the compromise is not without its downside. For one thing, a character in a flopped manga series who once wore in the original Japanese version a T-shirt emblazoned with "M A Y" (as in "the merry month of") now wears one which reads "Y A M"! Additionally, many manga creators in Japan are themselves unhappy with the process, as some feel the mirror-imaging of their art skews their original intentions.

We are proud to bring you Yusei Matsui's **Assassination Classroom** in the original unflopped format.
For now, though, turn to the other side of the book and let the adventure begin...!

—Editor